MIMESIS
INTERNATIONAL

PHILOSOPHY
n. 47

PPPP

Pier Paolo Pasolini Philosopher

Edited by
Toni Hildebrandt and Giovanbattista Tusa

© 2022 – MIMESIS INTERNATIONAL
www.mimesisinternational.com
e-mail: info@mimesisinternational.com

Isbn: 9788869773921
Book series: *Philosophy*, n. 47

© MIM Edizioni Srl
P.I. C.F. 02419370305

CONTENTS

A Note by the Editors   7
Toni Hildebrandt and Giovanbattista Tusa

Pasolini, une pensée   9
Toni Hildebrandt

Sade–Pasolini   13
Roland Barthes

The Gray Mornings of Tolerance   17
Michel Foucault

Pasolini 'Provençal'?   21
Massimo Cacciari

'Volgar'eloquio': Pasolini and the Search for Language   29
Giorgio Agamben

Pasolini, an Improvisation (of a Saintliness)   43
Philippe Lacoue-Labarthe

The Southern Answer: Pasolini, Universalism, Decolonization   49
Cesare Casarino

Pasolini's Southward Quest(ion)   73
Luca Caminati

Pasolini: Love and Fear of the Pagan   93
Emmanuel Alloa

The Return of the Disappearance of the Fireflies   107
Evan Calder Williams

Residues of the Sacred   127
Ara H. Merjian in conversation with McKenzie Wark

EXPOSURE: PASOLINI IN THE FLESH 143
Michael Hardt

RESONANCES 153
Vega Tescari

BADIOU'S PASOLINI: A POETICAL EXERCISE IN *VICTORY* 167
Lia Turtas

PASOLINI'S SACRIFICIAL DEATH 187
Barbara Vinken

PASOLINI FOR THE FUTURE 211
Alessia Ricciardi

PASOLINI'S METABOLIC CRITICISM 233
Thomas Macho

PORNOGRAPHY AS PHILOSOPHY: REFLECTIONS ON PASOLINI'S 'PETROLIO' 245
Marcus Döller

PASOLINI AGAINST THE CINEMA OF POETRY: PASOLINI AND DELEUZE 257
Jun Fujita Hirose

PASOLINI AND STRATEGIES OF RE-ENCHANTMENT 269
Jay Hetrick

THE TESTAMENT (OPEN LETTER TO JEAN-MARIE STRAUB) 289
Pedro A.H. Paixão

DESTRUCTION, NEGATION, SUBTRACTION 297
Alain Badiou

COMMUNISM, CAPITALISM, FASCISM 305
Roberto Esposito

ON PASOLINI'S NOTES TOWARDS AN AFRICAN ORESTES 313
Harun Farocki

THE PASOLINIAN CENTURY 317
Giovanbattista Tusa

Toni Hildebrandt and Giovanbattista Tusa
A NOTE BY THE EDITORS

This book has been long in the making. It started with a finding in the Semiotext(e) Archive at Fales Library in New York in March 2015, which was followed by a series of seminars and lectures that we gave together at the *Maumaus Independent Study Programme* in Lisbon at the invitation of its director Jürgen Bock. Since then, many friends and colleagues have been helpful in the process of making those seminars finally become a reader. We would like to first of all thank the authors for their time and persistence. For their generous support in providing rights, translations and text manuscripts, we are grateful to Graziella Chiarcossi, Jay Hetrick, Joan Copjec, Karen Pinkus, Antje Ehmann, Volker Pantenburg and the Harun Farocki Institut in Berlin, Antonio Guerreiro and the journal *Electra*, as well as the publishers and institutions who granted us permission to reproduce previously published essays: *Critical Inquiry*, *The New Press*, the Department of Romance Literature at Stanford University, *Quodlibet*, *SubStance*, and *Umbr(a): The Dark God*. Philip Farah was an indispensable help in compiling the final manuscript. Valeria Dani translated, on last-minute notice, Roberto Esposito's essay and Ara H. Merjian was an excellent advisor towards the end.

Finally, we wish to dedicate this book to the memory of Sylvère Lotringer (15 October 1938 in Paris – 8 November 2021 in Ensenada, Mexico), the ever-inspiring literary critic and heretic cultural theorist, who conceived of editing and publishing as *une pensée* in his very own way. Sylvère left us in the final stages of editing this book, but he had given us his personal draft on Pasolini and Philosophy — an unfinished Semiotext(e) issue from the 1980s — which became the starting point of *PPPP*.

Toni Hildebrandt

PASOLINI, *UNE PENSÉE*

Film still from Jean-Luc Godard, *Histoire(s) du cinéma* (1988–1998).

In his 'Voyage en Italie', a short sequence of *Histoire(s) du cinéma* dedicated to Italian cinema, Jean-Luc Godard at one point suspends the chronology of his narration. The canonical historiography of Italian cinema, deriving its origin from its 'rebirth' in Rossellini's *Roma, città aperta* (1944), had — according to Godard — restituted to Italy the 'right of a nation' and led to 'the extraordinary gaze of Italian cinema'. For Pier Paolo Pasolini, however, this was neither a given nor, were it unambiguously true, sufficient. His 'cinema of poetry' marks a rupture in this narrative and suspends the ostensible temporality of splendor in an anachronic, insistent and exigent thought, brushing history against the grain. Godard characterizes this trait in Pasolini's oeuvre as 'une pensée', a meandering thought-provoking 'thinking that forms'. However, he superimposes this phrase over a portrait of Pasolini buried in thought to enmesh the thinking of this thinker in a chiasm of thought and form. Superimposed over a nameless portrait from Piero della Francesca's *Exaltation of the Cross* — the upper scene from his fresco on *The History of the True Cross* — Godard adds 'a form that thinks'. The chiasm thus reads fully as 'a thinking that forms / a form that thinks' [*une pensée qui forme / une forme qui pense*].

As a political artist, director, filmmaker, poet, editor, painter, writer, and self-styled ethnographer, Pasolini created works in all accessible mediums and forms of expression conceivable in the mid-20th century. He started as a poet after the second World War and Italian Fascism, edited popular poems in the Friulian dialect, joined and was expelled by the Italian Communist Party and wrote two long novels on the Roman suburbs — all before directing over twenty films. Pasolini created a body of visual works, too, studied art history and began a *tesi di laurea* with Roberto Longhi. Although Pasolini's *tesi di laurea* was interrupted by the war, its aesthetic questions lingered in his work for decades. It is less commonly known that he wrote several plays for the theater as well as a *Manifesto for a New Theatre*. In the 1960s, at the peak of structuralism, he developed his own theory of semiotics in direct confrontation with authors such as Umberto Eco, Alberto Asor Rosa and Roland Barthes.

Pasolini was a philosopher as much as a reader: he studied the complete works of Freud, Nietzsche and Gramsci in his childhood, and, since the 1960s, distinguished his style of thinking as 'Anti-Hegelian'. He knew the Greek classics from memory, engaged with mythology at several points during his life and translated Aeschylus into Italian before working on a cinematographic adaption. Only recently has it come to light that Pasolini was also familiar with the first translation of the writings of Walter Benjamin, with whom Pasolini, in many ways, bore an elective affinity. Through the work of the Czech philosopher Karel Kosik, whom he met in Prague and Rome, Pasolini became familiar with Heidegger's *Being and Time*, whose conception of *Dasein* he quoted in later writings. Also, Herbert Marcuse was a steady influence on Pasolini's conception of a universalist Marxism that did not flinch from an engagement with the afterlife and the profanation of religious or mythological issues. The later work of Giorgio Agamben, who famously acted as one of Christ's disciples in Pasolini's *Gospel According to Matthew*, sheds light on many of Pasolini's own intentions, while differing from his own thinking in several respects. As

Agamben has noted in an interview, Pasolini's last finished film, *Salò, or the 120 Days of Sodom*, marks just such a difference.[1] The same film's prologue sheds significant light on Pasolini's relationship to philosophy. He gives his spectators (or readers) an 'essential bibliography', listing Roland Barthes' *Sade, Fourier, Loyola*, Maurice Blanchot's *Lautréamont et Sade*, Simone de Beauvoir's *Faut-il brûler Sade*, Pierre Klossowski's *Sade mon prochain, le philosophe scélérat*, and Philippe Sollers's *L'écriture et l'experience des limites*, making *Salò* also in this sense an exception in the history of cinema.

The relation of Pasolini's work to philosophy is challenging precisely for this reason, for its chiasm of *a thinking that forms* and its resulting *form that thinks*. Different from other transgressive philosophers — and even from those writers such as Blanchot, who already sublated the difference between philosophy and poetry — we are confronted again and again in the case of Pasolini with a work that is at once an engagement with the explication of thought and its re-inscription in a form, where it is not poetically concealed, but exponentiated by the force of its figural potential to think beyond what is known and accepted.

---

1   Valeria Montebello, 'La nostalgia non basta, ma è un buon punto di inizio: Intervista con Giorgio Agamben', in *Lo Sguardo: Rivista di Filosofia*, 19, Pier Paolo Pasolini: resistenze, dissidenze, ibridazioni (2015), pp. 19–22 (p. 20).

Roland Barthes
SADE–PASOLINI[1]

Salo does not please fascists. On another side, since Sade has become for some of us a kind of precious patrimony, many cry out: Sade has nothing to do with fascism! Finally, the remainder, neither fascist nor Sadean, have an immutable and convenient doctrine that finds Sade boring. Pasolini's film therefore can win no one's adherence. However, quite obviously, it hits us somewhere. Where?

In *Salo*, what touches is the letter. Pasolini has shot his scenes *to the letter*, the way that they had been *décrites* [described] (I do not say *écrites* [written]) by Sade; hence these scenes have the sad, frozen, and rigorous beauty of large encyclopedic sheets. To make someone eat excrement? To enucleate an eye? To put needles in a dish? You see it all: the plate, the turd, the smearing, the package of needles (bought at the *Upim* of Salo), the grain of polenta; as the saying goes *you are spared nothing* (the motto itself of the letter). At such a degree of rigour, it is eventually not Pasolini's world that is bared, but our glance: our glance stripped naked, such is the effect of the letter. In Pasolini's film (this, I believe, was his very own thing) there is no symbolism: on the one hand a gross analogy (fascism, sadism) and on the other, the letter, scrupulous, insistent, displayed, over-polished like a primitive painting: allegory and letter, but never symbol, metaphor, interpretation (the same, but gracious, language in *Teorema*).

However, the letter has a curious, unexpected effect. One could believe that the letter does serve truth, reality. Not at all: the letter distorts the objects of conscience on which we are obliged to take a position. Remaining faithful to the letter of Sadean scenes, Pasolini comes to the point of distorting the object–Sade and the object–fascism: therefore it is with good reason that Sadeans and politicians are indignant and disapprove.

---

1   Previously published as 'Sade–Pasolini', trans. by Verena Conley, *Stanford Italian Review*, 2, 2, Pier Paolo Pasolini: The Poetics of Heresy, ed. by Beverly Allen (1982), pp. 100–02; originally published in French as 'Point de vue Sade–Pasolini', *Le Monde*, 16 June 1976.

The Sadeans (the readers delighted with Sade's text) will never recognize Sade in Pasolini's film. The reason for this is general: Sade can in no way be represented. Just as there is no portrait of Sade (except an imaginary one), there is no possible image of Sade's universe: the latter, because of an imperious decision made by the writer Sade, is entirely given over to the power of *écriture*. And if this is so, there exists undoubtedly a privileged agreement between *écriture* and phantasm: both are *perforated*; the phantasm is not the dream, it does not follow the continuity, whether contorted or not, of a story; and *écriture* is not painting, it does not follow the plenitude of the object: the phantasm can only be written in script, and not in description. That is why Sade will never be acceptable in the movies, and, from a Sadean point of view (from the point of view of the Sadean text), Pasolini could only commit an error — which he did stubbornly (to follow the letter is to be stubborn).

From a political point of view, Pasolini too was mistaken. Fascism is too serious and too insidious a danger to be treated by simple analogy, the fascist masters coming 'simply' to take the place of the libertines. Fascism is a coercive object: it forces us to think it accurately, analytically, philosophically. All that art can do with it, if it deals with it, is to make fascism believable, to show off [*démontrer*] how it happens not to show (*montrer*) what it resembles; in brief, I see no other way to treat it than *à la* Brecht. Or, better yet: it is a responsibility to present this fascism as a perversion; who will not be relieved to say in front of the libertines of Salo: '*I am really not like them, I am not fascist, since I do not like shit.*'

In short, Pasolini did twice what he was not supposed to do. From the point of view of its *worth*, his film loses on both sides, for all that which fantasizes [*irréalise*] fascism is bad; and all that which figures [*réalise*] Sade is bad.

And yet, all the same...? If, all the same, on the level of the affect, there were some Sade in fascism (a commonplace thing) and, even more, if there were some fascism in Sade? *Some fascism* does not mean: *fascism*. There is the 'fascism–system' and there is the 'fascism–substance'. For as much as the system requires a precise analysis, a reasoned discrimination which must forbid us to treat any kind of oppression as fascism, so much the substance can circulate everywhere; because the latter, in fact, is only one of the modes in which political 'reason' happens to color the death drive which, in Freud's words, can never be seen, unless tainted with some kind of fantasmagoria. *Salo* arouses this substance, starting from a political analogy which has here but a signatory effect.

A flop of figuration (both of Sade and of the fascist system), Pasolini's film has worth as obscure recognition, poorly mastered within each of us, but surely bothersome: it bothers everybody, for, on account of Pasolini's own *naïveté*, it prevents anybody from getting cleared through customs. That is why I wonder if, at the end of a long concatenation of errors, Pasolini's *Salo* is not, *all things considered*, a properly Sadean object: absolutely irredeemable: no one indeed, so it seems, can redeem it.

MICHEL FOUCAULT
THE GRAY MORNINGS OF TOLERANCE[1]

Where do children come from? From the stork, from a flower, from God, from the Calabrian uncle. But look rather at the faces of these kids: they do not do anything that gives the impression they believe what they are saying. Delivered with smiles, silences, a distant tone, looks that dart to the left and the right, the answers to these adult questions have a treacherous docility; they assert the right to keep for oneself those things that one likes to whisper. The stork is a way of making fun of grownups, of paying them back in their own false coin; it is the ironic, impatient sign that the question will go no further, that the adults are nosy, they will not get into the circle, and the child will continue to tell the 'rest' to himself.

So begins the film by Pier Paolo Pasolini.

Enquête sur la sexualité [*Inquiry into Sexuality*] is an odd translation for *Comizi d'amore*: love conference, meeting, or perhaps forum. This is the ancient game of the 'symposium', but out of doors on the beaches and the bridges, the street corner, with ball-playing children, boys hanging out, bored bathers, clusters of prostitutes on the boulevard, or workers after the factory job. Very far from the confessional, very far, too, from an inquiry where the most secret things are examined under an assurance of discretion, this is *Street Talk about Love*. After all, the street is the most spontaneous form of Mediterranean conviviality.

As if in passing, Pasolini offers the microphone to the strolling or sunbathing group: he asks an undirected question about 'love', about that vague area where sex, the couple, pleasure, the family, marital engagement with its customs, and prostitution with its rates all intersect. Someone makes up her mind, replies with a little hesitation, gains confidence, speaks

---

[1] Previously published as 'The Gray Mornings of Tolerance', trans. by Robert Hurley, in *Aesthetics, Methods, and Epistemology*, ed. by James D. Faubion, Essential Works of Michel Foucault, 2 vols. (New York: The New York Press, 1998), II, pp. 229–31; originally published in French as 'Point de vue sur un film de Pasolini *Les matins gris de la tolérance*', *Le Monde*, 23 March 1977.

for the others; they gather round, approve or grumble, arms on shoulders, face against face. Laughter, affection, a bit of fever quickly circulate among these bodies that bunch together or lightly touch one another. And that speak of themselves with all the more restraint and distance as their contact is livelier and warmer. The adults arrange themselves side by side and speechify; the young people speak briefly and intertwine. Pasolini the interviewer fades out: Pasolini the filmmaker watches, all ears.

The document is negligible when one is more interested in these things that are said than in the mystery that is not said. After the long reign of what is called (too hastily) 'Christian morality', one might expect, in this Italy of the early sixties, some sort of sexual effervescence. Not at all. Persistently, the replies are given in terms of right: for or against divorce, for or against the preeminence of the husband, for or against compulsory virginity for girls, for or against the condemnation of homosexuals. As if Italian society of that time, between the secrets of penance and the prescriptions of the law, had not yet found a voice for that public confiding of the sexual which our media currently propagate.

'You say they don't talk? It's because they are afraid', explains Musatti, the run-of-the-mill psychiatrist whom Pasolini questions from time to time, along with Moravia, regarding the inquiry that is underway. But Pasolini obviously does not believe a word of it. What pervades the entire film is not, in my opinion, the obsession with sex but a kind of historical apprehension, a kind of premonitory and confused hesitation with regard to a new system that was emerging in Italy — that of tolerance. And this is where the divisions are clearly visible, in that crowd that agrees to speak about rights when it is questioned about love. Divisions between men and women, country people and city dwellers, rich and poor? Yes, of course, but especially between young people and the others. The latter fear a regime that will upset all the painful and subtle adjustments that have ensured the ecosystem of sex (with the prohibition of divorce that binds the man and the woman unequally, with the brothel that figures as a complement to the family, with the price of virginity and the cost of marriage). The young people approach this change in a very different way — not with shouts of joy but with a mixture of gravity and mistrust, because they know that it is tied to economic transformations likely to renew the inequalities of age, fortune, and status. At bottom, the gray mornings of tolerance do not appeal to anyone, and no one feels that they promise a celebration of sex. With resignation or rage, the older people express their anxiety: What will happen to the law? And the 'young' stubbornly reply: What will happen to rights, to *our* rights?

This film, fifteen years old, can serve as a reference mark. One year after *Mamma Roma* Pasolini continues what will become, in his films, a great saga of young people. Of those young people in whom he did not at all see adolescents for psychologists but the current form of a 'youth' which our societies, since the Middle Ages, since Rome and Greece, have never been able to integrate, which they have feared or rejected, which they have never managed to subdue, except by getting it killed from time to time in war.

And then, 1963 was the period when Italy had just made a noisy entry into that movement of expansion-consumption-tolerance of which Pasolini was to give us the balance sheet, ten years later, in the *Scritti Corsari*. The book's vehemence corresponds to the film's anxiety.

1963 was also the period when there began almost everywhere in Europe and the United States that new questioning of the myriad forms of power which the wise men tell us is 'in fashion'. Very well, then! The 'fashion' risks being worn for awhile yet, as it is these days in Bologna.

MASSIMO CACCIARI
PASOLINI 'PROVENÇAL'?[1]

The first part of *La meglio gioventù* begins with words of Peire Vidal: 'Ab l'alen tir vas me l'aire | Qu'en sen venir de Proensa: | Tot quant es de lai m'agensa'. [The air which I feel from Provence comes towards me: | Everything which comes from there pleases me.] Is the twenty-year-old Friulan poet searching, then, for the *spiritus* of the troubadours' gay science? Does he wish to breathe and resound with it? Is he longing for the sharp pleasure bestowed by pure hope, absolutely 'free' from any conceivable fulfillment? Is no other joy greater than the enjoyment of 'amor de lonh'? (Jaufre Rudel: 'car nuhls autres jois tan plai / cum jauzimens d'amor de lonh' [Because no other joy pleases me | as much as the joys of amor de lonh].) These questions are, it seems to me, central to an understanding of the overall inspiration of the whole of Pasolini's early lyric verse in the Friulan tongue. If we were to answer affirmatively, a rift not easily mended nor easily understood would appear to divide this early production from Pasolini's subsequent production, and not only that in verse. If, on the contrary, we were to see nothing but a vague 'aura' in that 'dedication', we should perhaps lose the most precious quality of this lyric work and its specific difference with respect to that in the Italian tongue.

It must be said first of all that the image of Provence situates this poetry, from its first line, in a *mundus* metaphysically opposite to any immediacy, any denotative/representational intention. In this *mundus imaginalis*, far from realistically 'representing' the life of some world or its people, the use of Friulan distills that pathos of *distance* which nourishes the 'modesty' (the knowing how to withstand one's own meter, one's own measure, which Dante praised in the Angel) of all poetry; this not only because Pasolini's Friulan is a hybrid, a medley of the cadences and words of many places which is invented and discovered over and over again, but, and more to the

---

[1] Previously published as 'Pasolini "Provençal"?', trans. by Keala Jane Jewell, *SubStance*, 16, 2, 53, Contemporary Italian Thought (1987), 67–73; all subsequent notes by translator.

point, because its very use entails an *estrangement* from all immediacy. A sacred tongue before, and more than a maternal one, *this* Friulan each time has the resonance of a lost or forgotten word which we approach from afar, haltingly: an uprooted Subject's sacred tongue — a sacred and homeless tongue. The antithesis of belonging, of closeness, of the 'communal' spirit, Friulan is the language of memory and absence. Instead of defining an object, each of its words delimits a loss. Instead of naming persons, it recalls their farewell. The point is not simply what Pasolini taught us early on (with his anthology *Poesia dialettale del Novecento*, published by Guanda in 1952, almost as a coronation for his 'provençal' cycle); that is, that dialect poetry possesses a tradition no less learned and antipopular than that written in standard language, and that the dialect tradition asserts its dominance in the twentieth century (within the Veneto, we need only recall Noventa, Marin, and Zanzotto). The point is that dialect poetry (the most apparently 'maternal' kind of poetry), or poetry in languages such as Friulan, which obey the God Terminus and still entertain relationships with the *genius loci*, is the quintessence of what Goethe would have called singing a song in an unknown tongue. Friulan is *not* his and therefore it is the language of song, the language properly only of song — of song's detachment, its distance from the womb of words lived immediately.

Pasolini's poetry in Friulan preserves, then, not simply the Provençal lyric's 'aire | Qu'eu sen venir de Proensa', but its equation of love and song, along with the idea of song as word in loss, as Lacan put it, as a pure destining-sending which can never reach its destination or 'comprehend' the loved object. Song is the 'letter' which marks an insuperable distance — *the* distance. A gay *savoir*, song theorizes distance and 'leaves the lover his hunger' (as Mario Mancini has written in his excellent *La gaia scienza dei trovatori*, from which I have abundantly drawn). The 'letter' sanctions separation instead of closing in.

But one must be careful not to let this interpretive key work its seduction. The more intense Pasolini's recollection of Provence, the more recollection itself is caught in the dimension of distance. Pasolini's Friulan verses *reflect* the Provençal love song; they do not continue it or carry it on. That singing returns in the reflection, but *reversed*. Its spirit returns, with, at times, its music, but the *form* is another, the poetic *thought* is another. The lines patiently insist on this unfathomable difference, showing it everywhere and thereby rendering impossible a sentimental aura of nostalgia. It is as though Pasolini were boring through the unadorned music of Friulan, transforming it as he goes until origins can no longer be recognized, until the origin is *erased*. An *uprooted* 'aire de Proenza', sundered from any belief in the originary, sorrowfully traverses the material of these chants. The reversed image is a *delirious* image:[2] the Provençal lover wanders from his well-fixed meter's accomplished idealness. The expression of desire overflows beyond the perfect, narcissistic circle. 'Póros' and 'penía' are the true images of death: 'Jo ti recuardi, Narcìs, [...] quand li ciampanis | a sùnin di muàrt' [I recall you, Narcissus, [...] when the bells ring a death sound]. For Narcissus, 'Echo' is no longer the beautiful visage of his own desire, but the death knell of Casarsa's bells.

Jaufre Rudel finds 'joy' in the unappeasable nature of desire. No 'reality' can match his dream, his metaphysics of love. Jaufre Rudel loves the 'refusal' to be loved. Pasolini, instead, suffers in desperation. The Provençal *prays* that the perfect measure of distance may endure; the Friulan despairs it may not end. 'Amor de lonh' is no source of 'jauzimens' for him, but a 'meditatio mortis'. And the meditation does not direct itself to Woman, an inaccessible ideal, but to remembered 'frut, frutin, frututa, donzél, fì, zuvinùt, bambìn'[3]. (Asor Rosa, reading Pasolini, commented that no language was as 'rich in vocabulary for children and youth' as Friulan, noting that Pasolini's own translations into Italian made 'boy' into 'love'). He would like to be loved with the love of these favored figures, but they belong, out of iron necessity, to invisible or past dimensions.

There is one way in particular in which Pasolini's Friulan lyrics effect a reversal of the Provençal imagination or 'imaginary': for the latter, love is knowledge, *theoria*, the preeminence of contemplation over the 'different'. Love not only overcomes but abolishes the body, along with the mortality inextricably linked to it. Here, instead, the 'time' of love is confused, compounded; it is torn in violent chiaroscuro; it is blinded by shouts, mysteries, laments. Everywhere the *body* erupts into the filigree of its songs, cutting the weave, breaking the lines with tremors that no 'modestia' could tame. 'Amor del lonh' meditates and reflects, here, on the time of the body and of its death: 'far' is that *body* — already glimpsed 'sub specie mortis'. And song seems too weak to counter this necessity — that the boy's body should convert into a past, 'snows of the past', that its beauty should be transformed into the invisible. For Pasolini, too, love 'moves the sun and the other stars', but no longer according to the perfect 'construct' of Dante's cosmic mirror play, nor to correspondences which rigorously maintain all of the elements in the places destined for them; it

---

2   'Delirium' refers etymologically to 'de-lyra', to being outside a signed furrow; the author plays on the notion of Pasolini as an outsider.
3   The first three terms refer to children as fruits; the last four are 'damsel' (which could be masculine or feminine), 'son, youth, and boy'.

moves through painful, at times brutal, lightings of unappeasable desire, through impulse and rending. Pasolini's Friulan Narcìs, the 'fantassùt'[4], the 'donzél' of this lyric de lonh, is not the Other, the lord and master who functions as an orientation and a guide, as the *hermeneut* to knowledge of the Greatest Good. Rather, he is fixed in the same misery; he mingles in the very desperation of the poet who loves him and at-tends to him; he, too, is made of images and shadows which elapse, of words which are loss more than possession (Pasolini loved Noventa's line, 'each one who expresses himself, loses himself').

The *de-lirium* is twofold: on the part of the word, which seems to incarnate itself in the figures it evokes, toward the unreachable distance of the 'aire de Proensa'; on the part of the Provençal 'amor di lonh' toward the world of creatures. It is this 'dilemma' which creates the dissonance, the contrasting colors and sounds of Pasolini's Friulan poems. The death knell echoes the 'sera imbarlumida' [gleaming evening] (an extraordinary 'opening' which ought to title some of Van Gogh's starry nights); the color of smoke and dead summers echo 'il soreli' [the sun]; the evening shadows and the blinding light (Pasolini's 'translation' of 'imbarlumis'); the laughing little boy goes *sweetly* to *death*; the festive sound of bells is silence in the fields. The contrasts are neat, locked together in a single line or even in a single word; the dissonance brooks no mediation, no reconciliation. The quintessence of this dissonance is the *tie* between the word and silence: the birth itself of the word is a recognition of the necessity of silence. When a voice is born 'drenti al sen' 'a na fruta,' [in the bosom of a girl] then and only then does she become *mute*; she begins *mutely* to carry the poet's same cross: 'Sidina ta la ciasa | cu li peràulis strentis | tal còur romai perdùt | par un troi di silensi' [Silent in the house | with her words | held fast to her heart, already lost | along a path of silence]. The paths of our silence are the same as those of words — of words 'held fast to her heart', of the words most proper to us and, therefore, the most unpronounceable words which only at times flash forth in that language cut off from communication and comprehension, in that language which is used *not* to denominate, designate, make oneself understood, in that Friulan which has been transplanted in the 'aire de Proensa'.

Just as saying 'soreli' is saying shadow and smoke, to say words is to say silence, to speak of the body is the image of time lost. The body is always in Pasolini the figure of an *impossible* presence: not simple, immediate absence (which would still be a consolation related to the Provençal

---

4   The term derives from 'in-fans', without speech.

'amor de lonh'), but a concrete, real, index of something here, a *Dasein*, which does not, however, offer itself to our gaze or hand like any other phenomenon but resembles the consistency of the ungraspable 'reality' manifested in dreams, which is just as vital and 'external' as the waking one. The body's concreteness in these verses is as taut and sharp as the sensation we experience in dreams. Dream time has stretched, in all its paradox and antinomy, into waking time, invading the quotidian and thus transfiguring the bodies which inhabit it into the invisible.

The body is the name for absence and parting, for the most painful experiences, for the parting and abandoning whose necessity grows in proportion to its inexplicability. No discourse can ease its pain. Only in the presence of the body does one fully feel the grief of absence's necessity: 'I vuardi il me cuàrp | di quan'ch'i eri frut, | li tristis Domèniis, | il vivi pierdùt' [I look at my child's body, | at my sad Sundays, my lost life]. The elegy's meters and modes always express the vision (in all senses of the word) of the body; 'un plant d'infier' [an infernal cry] accompanies it like a deep basso continuo. Like the sound of the bells, the body loses its breath ['al si scunis'] in fields, along the 'troi di silensi', and over the ditches. It becomes a *spirit* of love, like the poet's, who 'al so païs al torna di lontàn' [returns from afar to his village], in order to meet, it seems, with the pain of that impossible presence, to initiate himself to it and with it. 'A ven scur in tal mond' [the world darkens], February freezes 'sgivìns, ledris, moràrs' [canals, flowers, mulberries] and the years pass 'par nuja' [uselessly]; yet the ghost of that presence incessantly returns in 'biondu, fruta, nini' — in an unreachable, incomprehensible beauty which lives, like words, only 'strentis tal còur'.

The body lives, but it lives in the way it lives time lost in the suffering which its parting produces. The body lives, but because living itself is a past. Life itself is past: 'Dut il me vivi | al è passàt' [My whole life is in the past]; if it returns, it returns in the way the perception of a forgotten sorrow or joy returns in a dream: 'Ah parsé tòrnitu | adès tal sun | da tanciu ains / dismintiàt?' [Ah, why do you now return in sleep, you, forgotten for so many years?]. The lights of the 'sera imbarlumida' illumine for brief instants 'il recuàrt de la me vita viva | come erba ta na nera riva' [the memory of my living life, | as grass on a dark river bank]. And if 'living life' is in its essence past, then the 'suspièt di no vej mai vivùt' is continually reborn. 'Living life' does not exist here and now, it only *was*. But what, here and now, might be the witness of that time? Did the poet's

Friuli ever exist, or might it not be 'vagu disperàt'[5], a void, an absence never truly inhabited by a peasant Narcissus?

No dream of an 'origin' or of 'innocence' can stand up to the interrogations typically constitutive of this poetry. What in appearance sounds like 'regression' to a rustic 'kingdom of mothers' turns out, in the end, to be the discovery of an unfathomable place, of a resonance, an inexhaustible play of echoes: running waters, fountains, bells, faded colors. The remembrance of living life endures only as remembrance. Living life would be really to meet the Mother again, to be able to imagine her as a 'fruta' against the festive backdrop of one 'séil nut', 'tra i figárs e i roj frescs di rasa' [naked sky, among the fig trees and oaks fresh with resin]. But this nostalgia quickly loses its breath in the brief 'suspìr' [sigh] of the verses themselves; it *is* this 'suspìr' and nothing else. Pasolini's Narcissus yearns to contemplate the visage of Mother as a girl — a Mother who is not his twin — in the 'fontana di aga' [fountain] of his town; but the reflection's eyes are 'neris coma il fons dal stali' [as black as the bottom of a stall]. A dark gaze and a form which is reduced to a mere glimmer echo the 'frut' who looks in the mirror, 'il so vuli al ghi rit neri' [his eyes darkly smiling at him]. The Mother 'lives' in this 'vagu disperàt'; indeed, her figure is identified with it, with the absence of a definite form, oblivion: 'Dutis dos dismintiadis, la mari e la rosa! | Zint cui sa dulà | al ni à dismintiadis' [Both forgotten, mother and rose! Going who knows where | he has forgotten us].

The Son holds in his bosom a Joker without a Mother ['un Mat sansa Marital sen']. The Son is, in his belonging, pure *de-lirium*: he is cast from the furrow of generations which elapse in the chain of Fathers and Mothers (Rilke's river god of the blood). *This* Son has broken the chain, and his guilt cannot be redeemed. He can return home only as a thief, climb 's-cialis di glas' [steps of glass] and 'al pissa | sot li stelis da la not lissa' [he pisses beneath the serene stars]. He did not know how to perpetuate living life; he transformed/condemned it to the mere past; he rendered it invisible in poetry's obsessive metaphor.

Like a thief, he now attempts to enter the Mother's room; like a thief, he is dismayed by light. Finally, now, a perfect Narcissus, he discovers his own authentic 'belonging' in the face without traces of that light: his already having lived, his *dead* survival. And that splendor dictates to him his two most beautiful lines: 'la so muàrt a è adés chistu clar | Ch'al impla la ciambra di zal' [his death now has this glimmer | which fills the room with yellow]: it is the yellow of the manifest, of existence, its sharp dissonance

---

5   This void refers to Pasolini's 'native' village, Casarsa.

as piercing as night, death, and the Joker's black gaze — like Van Gogh's *Cafe in the Evening*.

It seems to me that the *Seconda forma de 'La meglio gioventù'* adds nothing to the lyric season of the forties, if not a pedantic will to clarify, to achieve transparency. Take the 'Dedication': 'me paìs' [my village] becomes a 'paìs no me' [a village not mine]; 'l'aga pì fres-cia' [the freshest water] becomes 'aga pì vecia' [the oldest water]; 'rustic amòur' [rustic love] becomes 'amòur par nissùn' [love for no one]. The entire revisitation has the tone of a heavy and not at all 'spectral' pessimism deprived of an 'aire de Proensa'.

How desperately far this dedication from that of the youthful poet! Then all was said with the 'right' lightness of accent, with the modesty of the contained image. Now everything means something, said hurriedly, with explanatory anxiety and the 'indecence' of the naked heart.

And yet, beyond the tired, facile 'overturnings', the felicity of those early verses glimmers in these late ones, along with the desperate consciousness of the end of every 'return', of already having lived: 'i no plans parsé che chel mond a no'l torna pì | ma plans parse che il so tornà al è finit' [I do not cry because that world will never return | but because its returning is over]. The twenty-year-old poet, chasing his own image in Casarsa's 'vagu disperàt', had already said that the body was 'il siun di un cuàrp' [the dream of a body], but without a trace of resentment, without the apodictical weight of accusatory acts. Pasolini's Friulan *lied* retains only the elegy and the lament of the *Klagelied*. In *Seconda forma*, Pasolini weights it with an invective denunciation. But at times language once again leads him, the language so rich in names for Narcissus and young Mothers; and then the rhythm once more stretches into ample shadows. Bodies become the sounds of longing and the world's patterns, pure colors.

Giorgio Agamben
'VOLGAR'ELOQUIO'
Pasolini and the Search for Language[1]

1.

In February 1945, a young man of twenty-three years — who had already published a small book of poems in the Friulian dialect two years before — founded the *Academiuta di lenga furlana* with a small group of friends in the town of Casarsa, and published the journal *Stroliguts* (a 'little almanac', two of which had already been issued in 1944 under the title *Stroligùt di cà da l'aga*), again in dialect.[2] The cover of the *Stroliguts* bore the symbol of an *ardilut*: the flower of the wild or 'sweet' valerian.[3] (One notes the constant use of the diminutive '*–ut*', to describe a little almanac, a little academy, a little valerian flower which, while certainly characteristic of the Friulian dialect, is nevertheless quite intentional, referring to the Friulian Philological Society's own journal, *Strolic*). If, as has been suggested, the center of gravity of Pasolini's work has decidedly shifted since his Friulian years,[4] the hypothesis we intend to defend here is that only a careful reading of his thoughts on dialect and language can provide a thread to pull on when attempting to untangle a body of work that appears so intertwined and contradictory. The question — the *quête* — of language is, in our opinion, the original, brilliant nucleus from which

---

[1] Translated by Richard Braude. Originally published as '"Volgar' eloquio": Pasolini e la ricerca della lingua', in *Categorie Italiane: Studi di poetica e di letteratura* (Macerata: Quodlibet, 2021), pp. 167–180.

[2] The name of the academy and its journal are in Friulian: the *Academiuta di lenga furlana* ('Little Academy of the Friulian Language'); *Stroligut* is the diminutive of *strolic*, which has the same etymological derivation as 'astrologer'. As the author partially clarifies, this was the name given by the Friulian poet Pietro Zorutti to his poetical almanacs. The proverb '*di cà da l'aga*' means 'From here, from the water'. [*Trans.*]

[3] *Valerienella locusta*, i.e. the lamb's lettuce. [*Trans.*]

[4] Franco Brevini, 'Una vita trascorsa ricordando il Friuli', *Corriere della sera*, 24 December 1994.

all of Pasolini's other inquiries erupt. In what is almost a confirmation of Contini's theory according to which bilingualism in 'illustrious poetry' and in 'dialect poetry' is the 'original and constitutive' moment of Italian literature,[5] we propose that Pasolini's inquiry into language was marked, right from the start, by the sign of a certain duality and diglossia.

It was Dante who first marked out Italian poetry under the sign of bilingualism. In *De vulgari eloquentia* (I, I, 2), Dante makes a distinction between two languages: a first language, which he calls 'vernacular' (*volgare*), which 'children gather from those around when they first begin to articulate words' [*vulgarem locutionem appellamus eam qua infantes assuefiunt ab assistentibus cum primitus distinguiere voces incipiunt*], that is, 'that which we learn without any rules at all by imitating our nurses' [*quam sine omni regula nutricem imitantes accipimus*]. Then there is another 'secondary language which the Romans call grammar', which the Greeks have but which not all peoples possess [*hanc quidem secundariam Greci habent et alii, sed non omnes*], and it is 'only in the course of time and by assiduous study that we become schooled in its rules and art' [*non nisi per spatium temporis et studii assiduitatem regulamur et doctrinamur in illa*].[6] He further adds that 'they invented grammar because of the variation of speech that fluctuates' [*propter variationem sermonis arbitrio singularium fluitantis*] and to obtain 'a certain unalterable identity of speech unchanged by time and place' [*quedam inalterabilis locutionis ydemptitas diversis temporibus atque locis*] (I, IX, II).[7]

> Of the two, the nobler is the vernacular: first because it is the first language ever spoken by mankind; second because the whole world uses it though in diverse pronunciations and forms; finally because it is natural to us while the other is more the product of art. (I, I, 5)

In the same way, Dante wrote in the *Convivio* — where Latin is, nevertheless, defined as more noble than the vernacular because it is 'stable and not corruptible' (I, V) — that 'it is single and alone in [a man's] mind before any other' and for this reason 'most nearest to him' (I, XII, 4).[8] Having already described the bilingualism of vernacular and grammatical

---

5   Gianfranco Contini, 'Introduzione alla *Cognizione del dolore* (1963)', in *Varianti e altra linguistica* (Turin: Einaudi, 1970), p. 614.

6   Dante, *De vulgari eloquentia: Dante's Book of Exile*, trans. by Marianna Shapiro (Lincoln and London: University of Nebraska Press, 1990), p. 47.

7   Ibid., p. 57.

8   Dante, *The Convivio*, trans. by Philip H. Wicksteed (London: Dent, 1903), pp. 23, 54–55.

language, Dante then immediately adds a second kind of bilingualism, namely municipal vernacular and the illustrious vernacular. Employing an image taken from bestiaries, he compares the latter to the panther, who does not live in any one city but sprays his scent across all of them. Following this reasoning, Dante also compares the illustrious vernacular to a form of royalty in which the person of the sovereign themselves is missing but the members of the court are present, a sovereignty that exists 'albeit dispersed in body' [*licet corporaliter sit dispersa*]' (I, XVIII, 5).⁹ One would do well to reflect upon the peculiar non-identity and insubstantiality of this perfumed panther — as indeed Pasolini did not cease to do — in relation to an exegetic tradition that is otherwise regarded as illegitimate, i.e. that the illustrious vernacular is not a language in the way that we moderns are used to attributing to this term.

Let us try and put some of the young Pasolini's thoughts within this problematic context. The first *Stroligùt di cà l'aga* (April 1944) opens with a text entitled *Dialet, lenga e stil* — which, despite the decidedly resigned tone with which he addresses his *paisàns*, has all the air of a programmatic statement. Dialect is proudly claimed and opposed to a national language in terms not dissimilar from those with which Dante defended the vernacular:

'[...] that dialect that you learned from your mother, your father, your elders. The children of these places have passed centuries suckling on that dialect from their mothers' breast [...]. And in order to learn it, no syllabaries, books or grammars were needed; one learns it just like that, as one eats and drinks.¹⁰

For the author of the *Stroligùt*, this means no less than removing dialect from its subordinate position in relation to language, i.e. to use it 'not to write a few stupid lines to make someone laugh or to tell a few stories from your village (because in this way dialect remains dialect, and stops there) but instead to aim at maybe saying something more difficult, more elevated', convinced of being able to express oneself in a 'newer, fresher, stronger' way than allowed by a 'national language learned from books'. If someone writes in dialect in this way, and others follow their example, then 'that dialect becomes 'language''. The text continues that Italian was not in itself originally anything other than

---

9   Dante, *De vulgari eloquentia*, p. 67.
10 Pier Paolo Pasolini, *Stroligùt di cà da l'aga* (April 1944), p. 5. We cite the anastatic edition edited by Nico Naldini, *L'academiuta friulana e le sue riviste* (Vicenza: Neri Pozza, 1994).

a dialect spoken by the poor folk, by peasants, families, servants, while lords and scholars spoke and wrote in Latin. In other words, Latin then was as Italian is for us today; Italian (along with French, Spanish and Portuguese) was a dialect of Latin, just as now Emilian, Sicilian and Lombard [...] are dialects of Italian for us. But then suddenly there were writers and poets in Tuscany who wanted to express their feelings with greater sincerity and liveliness, in a way that everyone would understand: and thus they put themselves to work, writing in their Tuscan dialect. Dante wrote his *Divine Comedy* in Tuscan, Petrarch wrote his poetry in Tuscan, and thus that dialect little by little became a language, and came to replace Latin.[11]

And when a dialect becomes a language, every writer uses it according to their own ideas and character, i.e. according to their own style; and 'a style is neither Italian nor German nor Friulian: it is simply the poet's own'.[12]

The opening text — curiously written in Italian — of the first issue of the Academiuta's *Stroligùt* (August 1945) inscribes the young academy's project not in the Friulian tradition as such, which 'if it has anything specifically poetic, is entirely vernacular', but in the tradition of its romance origins, 'from which Friulia ought to have been born, which has instead remained barren'.[13] Pasolini shared with Isaia Ascoli the theory that the Friulian language derived directly from Latin and not from Italian, a pre-Alpine dialect, situating it alongside Italian, French and Provençal (Pasolini maintained a constant engagement with the troubadours in those years, beginning with the citation of Peire Vidal in the epitaph to his *Poesie a Casarsa*) but as a branch that bore no fruit in its romantic origins. For this reason, if 'the tradition that we naturally follow is to be found in today's Italian and French literature' even though these languages seem to have reached 'a moment of extreme consummation [...] then our own language can depend on all its rustic, Christian purity'.[14] This project of locating Friulian poetry not in a tradition of dialect but in a linguistic one was to be reiterated many times over in the texts that were to follow.

Pasolini's university thesis on Pascoli, examined by Carlo Calcaterra in November 1945, begins with a diagnosis of a particular antinomy in Pascoli's poetic language 'between a romantic taste for spoken language, i.e. romance language, and nostalgia for the discourse, syntax, detachment

---

11 Ibid., p. 6.
12 Ibid., p. 7.
13 *Stroligùt*, 1 (August 1945), p. 2.
14 Ibid.

and elegance of classical language.'[15] In truth, this represents the coexistence of 'two languages that are, by their very nature, extremely different',[16] even if they converge in 'Pascoli's unique attempt to depart from convention and instead invent a language that could be *other*, a language as close as possible to that of Adam'.[17] The *Myricae* and the *Canti di Castelvecchio* are clear examples of this 'spoken Pascoli' (for instance, in the glossary of 'little words that are easily confused', or the demands for a 'vernacular' and a 'maternal language' that conclude the *Canti*), which Pasolini describes, in an essay published two years later, as a living 'node of exchange between language and dialect'.[18]

> Aside from his dictionary of technical terms or strict dialect, and aside too from his syntax and vocabulary — sometimes taken entirely from the *koiné diàlektos* — all of Pascoli's language moves within the atmosphere of a minor language (dialect, in other words, again in the presence of traditional language).[19]

It is little surprise that the presence of Pascoli (already indicated by Contini in his own timely review) accompanies Pasolini's Friulian experiments in a discrete but constant manner: in the appendices to this thesis, Pasolini had already translated three poems from the *Myricae* and the *Canti*. With his 'two languages' — one 'romantic' and 'spoken', the other 'classical' and 'traditional' — Pascoli perfectly embodies the paradigm of bilingualism that was to define the young Pasolini's poetic project.

2

A year later, in a text titled *Volontà poetica ed evoluzione della lingua* [*Poetic Will and the Development of Language*] — published in the second *Stroligùt* and collocated immediately after Contini's review of *Poesie a Casarsa* — the Friulian dialect, once 'every habit of writing as dialect,

---

15 Pier Paolo Pasolini, *Antologia della lirica pascoliana* (Turin: Einaudi, 1993), p. 32.
16 Ibid., p. 108.
17 Ibid.
18 Pier Paolo Pasolini, *Sulla poesia dialettale*, reprinted in Pier Paolo Pasolini, *Saggi sulla letteratura e sull'arte* (Milan: Mondadori, 1998), p. 249.
19 Ibid.

every glottological and folkloristic interest has been cast off',[20] is viewed as decidedly the language of poetry.

> For me it appears as a very ancient language, yet at the same time completely virgin, in which even the most common of words — such as *còur*, *fueja, blanc* — managed to suggest original images. A kind of Greek dialect or vernacular that had only just broken off from a pre-romance language, with all the innocence of a language's first texts [...]. It was thus that the language itself, the purely spoken language of the people of Casarsa, could become a poetic language without time or place, could morph into a vocabulary without prejudices, full of sweet aesthetic violences [...]. Friulian — uncorrupted by a poetic conscience that, as happens in phonetics through use, consumes the hidden sense of a language by making it develop all the way into extreme crises ('*Je ne sais plus parler*', Rimbaud) — conserves the old health of the vernacular as when it first came to light.[21]

An article published in the same year on 'The Literary Fair' makes an even stronger claim about the poetic linguistic character of Friulian:

> Poetically speaking, this language is not the dialect of the Zoruttiani [Zorutti, the canonical poet of nineteenth-century Friulian, was the privileged target of the young Pasolini's sarcasm], nor is it the spoken dialect of the people, however suggestive it might be, but is instead an invented tale, to be inserted in the trunk of the Italian tradition, and not only in the Friulian one; to be used with all the delicacy of an uninterrupted, absolute metaphor.[22]

In the essay *Sulla poesia dialettale* published in *Poesia* in 1947, Pasolini asks 'how a dialect poet can situate themselves today in the Italian tradition', reprising the idea of dialect as an 'ideal translation' or 'metaphor' of Italian.[23] That 'internal translatability of a language', discussed by Contini in his review of *Poesie a Casarsa*, does not move here from dialect into Italian, but from Italian into dialect.

In this strong claim of a 'poetic will' (the title of the article in the *Stroligùt* prefigures the title of another essay twenty years later, *La volontà di Dante a essere poeta* [*The Will of Dante to Be a Poet*],[24] we note the important appearance of a theme to which Pasolini will frequently return:

---

20 *Stroligùt*, 2 (April 1946), p. 14.
21 Ibid., p. 15.
22 Pier Paolo Pasolini, 'Lettera dal Friuli', *La fiera letteraria*, 29 August 1946.
23 Pasolini, *Sulla poesia dialettale*, p. 257.
24 Pier Paolo Pasolini, 'La volontà di Dante a essere poeta', in *Emperismo eretico* (Milan: Garzanti, 1971) ['Dante's Will to Be a Poet', in *Heretical Empiricism*,

the relation between poetic language and spoken language, and between the individual use of a language and institutional language. 'I am referring to a poetic will', he writes, 'rather than learning more broadly, inasmuch as it is first necessary to identify the bonds between the poet and those who speak the language, bonds that are so mobile as to evade every form of experience.' The following emphasis on the 'Bertonian distinction between '*lingua*' and '*linguaggio*'' refers to the opposition developed by the romance philologist Giulio Bertoni between '*lingua*' as a collective institution defined by a grammar, and '*linguaggio*' as an act of individual expression by a single person. The bilingualism of dialect and language is thus now joined by the bilingualism of individual spoken language and language as a collective institution. The young Pasolini's poetic work in Friulian is thus to be located, according to all the evidence, on the side of *linguaggio*, i.e. the individual act of expression; and yet, precisely for this reason, it necessarily implicates a reference to institutional *lingua*. The far from obvious dialectical relationship between spoken language and institutional language (along with that other relationship, which does not perfectly align with the first, between the individual poetic act and collective language) will remain at the centre of Pasolini's thought up till the *Nuove questioni linguistiche* [*New Linguistic Questions*] of 1964, and even up till his final public speech given in Lecce shortly before his death.

In an article from 1948, this relationship took the form of an opposition (within the same dialect) between Friulian as an institution and Friulian as a poetic act.

> Aside from the now strikingly obvious distinction between 'spoken language' and 'written language', there also exists a still more basic distinction between literary language as *interventum* and language as *inventio*. The first is institutional language, that which is not only a communal necessity among speakers [...], but especially for common writers, i.e. not poets; the second is anti-constitutional language, which is employed, as we have seen, both by the speakers of that language within a colourful, dynamic contamination with institutions (from which language develops) as well as by writer-poets.

The salvaging of Friulian as an institution and as a poetic act are thus 'two different problems, the confusion of which simply damages the earnestness' of the discussion: on the one hand, there are linguistic institutions as 'a historical fact that have a certain social, political and economic necessity',

---

trans. by Ben Lawton and Louise K. Barnett (Washington, DC: New Academia Publishing, 2005), pp. 102–12].

on the other there is love for Friuli, which is not a practical sentiment but a 'pure sentimentality' or, better still, 'pure emotion'.[25]

In the final issue of the *Academiuta* (no longer under the name *Stroligùt* but instead *Quaderno romanzo*), Pasolini signed a long article with the meaningful title *Il Friuli autonomo* [*Independent Friuli*]. The demand for regional independence for Friuli (in January of the same year, Pasolini was among the founders of the Friulian Popular Movement for Regional Autonomy) went hand in hand with the claim of a 'poetics of poetry in dialect as anti-dialect, i.e. as language'.[26]

The reason for this is not only because of the existence of a 'Ladine language [...] rather than an Alpine dialect', but because every dialect contains 'the possibility of a language'.[27] And while 'the principal languages are momentarily blocked in the overly conscious effort to reach that poetic extreme that pre-exists the poet', the poet of dialect is in the condition to be able to experience that truth which Pasolini finds in the quote from a Catalan poet, according to whom '*la poésie n'est que création de langue*'[28] (even if already in the first *Stroligùt di cà da l'aga*, the citation from Shelley as the epitaph to the essay *Dialet, lenga e stil* had recalled that 'in the infancy of society every author is necessarily a poet, because language itself is poetry').[29] Poetry is thus constitutively the researching and experiencing of language but, in Pasolini's case, just as with the origins of Italian poetry, the poet is constitutively bilingual; they must come to terms with a diglossia, the poles of which are simultaneously distinct and dialectically connected.

3

Contini's precocious interpretative essay *Prolegomeni sulla lingua del Petrarca* [*Prolegomenon on Petrarch's Language*], published in *Paragone* in April 1951, provided Pasolini with the opportunity to lay out the question of bilingualism in a broader historical perspective. In his essay, Contini had opposed his study of a Petrarchian 'uni-lingualism', that dominates

---

25 Pier Paolo Pasolini, 'Ragioni del friulano', in *Saggi sulla letteratura e sull'arte*, pp. 298–99.
26 *Quaderno romanzo*, 3 (June 1947), p. 3.
27 'Ladine', in reference to the language group spoken across North-Eastern Italy and the Dolomites, and to Isaia Ascoli's *Saggi Ladini* of 1873. [*Trans.*]
28 *Quaderno romanzo*, 3 (June 1947), p. 5.
29 Percy Bysshe Shelley, 'A Defence of Poetry'. [*Trans.*]

our literary tradition and characterizes the unity of tone and vocabulary, to Dante's 'pluri-lingualism', defined by a 'polyglottism of styles and literary genres', a 'plurality of tones and lexical layers', but also a heavy theoretical engagement that establishes a 'linguistic philosophy' as well as by an 'incessant experimentation'.[30] Pasolini's essay on *Poesia dialettale del Novecento*, published by Guanda in 1952, opens with a reference to 'Gianfranco Contini's beautiful study' in which — with an implicit allusion not only to Pascoli and Verga's realism but also to dialect poetry — Dante's 'bilingualism' (and no longer 'pluri-lingualism', as in Contini) becomes an 'immediate stylistic form, rising up from the lower layers of language'.[31]

The clear analogy between Dante's position between municipal vernacular, illustrious vernacular, and grammatical language, and the young Pasolini's position between Friulian, poetic language and the Italian language has been often noted. Furthermore, in both cases there is an oscillation (not without contradictions) between a general reflection on language (which for Dante is also theological) and an individual manifesto of poetics. It is important to note here, however, the apparent divergences as well. If Dante's poetic research — the hunt for the perfumed panther — draws him into the forests of the vernacular (or dialects) without resting long in any of them, then Pasolini's own journey takes the form of a complex dialectic between Friulian and the national language; for Dante, the distinction was unthinkable in these terms. It is significant that Pasolini never mentions the illustrious vernacular, which Contini even evoked in his review of *Poesie a Casarsa*, in order to define the young poet's project. Despite the undeniable differences of context, the substantial proximity of intentions is nevertheless striking. If the choice to insert Friulian not into a tradition of dialect, but into that of Italian, would not have made any sense in relation to Dante's grammatical language, it nevertheless appears to respond to an analogous requirement. From this standpoint one understands better what Pasolini means in the aforementioned essay from 1947, *Sulla poesia dialettale*, when he writes that by locating Friulian in the tradition of language, he does so 'by using real dialect as an ideal translation of Italian; but more than as translation [...] as metaphor'.[32] As suggested in the passage immediately following this, in which Giotti's Triestian dialect appears as the purification of Saba's language, and Luciani's Abbruzzese as a return to the language of Jacopone, the task at hand is to lead Italian

---

30 Now in Gianfranco Contini, *Varianti e altra linguistica* (Turin: Einaudi, 1970), p. 172.
31 Now in Pier Paolo Pasolini, *Passione e ideologia* (Milan: Garzanti, 1960), p. 8.
32 Pasolini, *Sulla poesia dialettale*, p. 257.

— by now, like French and Spanish, 'blocked in the overly conscious effort to reach that poetic extreme that pre-exists the poet'[33] — back to a pre-archaic, flourishing condition.[34] At this stage, which is that of both Pasolini's Friulian works and Dante's vernacular, the Bertonian difference between *lingua* and *linguaggio* — and, we might add, also that between the Saussurian *langue* and *parole* — disappears, it 'burns away in an instant', and dialect is immediately 'poetry-language'.[35] In the terms of the *De vulgari*, where secondary language is not only Latin but any language established by a grammar, dialect leads Italian back to a pre-grammatical condition.[36]

It is in this sense that one must understand the question of the 'regression to the speaker' about which much has been said — and not always in a positive tone — in relation to the early Pasolini.[37] As specified in the essay on *Poesia dialettale del Novecento*, regression does not occur 'within dialect', and does not move 'from one speaker (the poet) to another presumably purer one';[38] it is instead a regression that moves from one language (Italian) to another (Friulian) that is 'precedent and infinitely purer'.[39] Dialect is thus for the young Pasolini the vehicle of a happy regression — in the words used by the *Stroligùt* — towards a 'language that is very ancient and yet at the same time completely virgin [...] a kind of Greek dialect or vernacular that has only just broken off from a pre-romance language',[40] which was exactly what the vernacular meant for Dante. When evoking his poetic experience in Casarsa, Pasolini writes (in his pages on Friuli in his book from 1952) that this language was for him 'closer to the world', 'its regression from one language to another [...] was a regression along the levels of being.'[41]

---

33 Ibid., p. 258.
34 Virgilio Giotti; Umberto Saba; Alfredo Luciani; the medieval poet-friar Jacopone da Todi. [*Trans*.]
35 Ibid.
36 On this springing forth of dialect, Zanzotto would write that it 'is felt as if it derives from there where there is neither writing [...] nor grammar: the site of a *logos* that remains forever "erchomenos", that never freezes into the design of a particular event, but remains "quasi" infantile in its mode of expression'. Andrea Zanzotto, *Filò* (Venice: Edizioni del Ruzante, 1976), p. 91.
37 Paolo Desogus, 'La nozione di regresso nel primo Pasolini', *La rivista*, 4 (2015), pp. 107–19.
38 Now in Pasolini, *Passione e ideologia*, p. 132.
39 Ibid., pp. 132–33.
40 *Stroligùt*, 2, p. 15.
41 Pasolini, *Passione e ideologia*, p. 133.

4

Pasolini's mature reflections on language, gathered together in the volume *Empiricismo eretico* in the essay from 1964 on *Nuove questione linguistiche*, signal a certain detachment from the thesis of his younger self; even here, however, an attentive reading shows that the *quête* of poetic language from the Friulian years is still present, even if in a different form. The new element, that functions as a watershed between the two moments, is the birth of Italian as a national language. The essay from 1964 opens with the claim that till that point, there had never existed a 'truly national language' in Italy, but only a spoken *koiné* and a literary language, that covered over a fragmented reality both in the sense of a vertical stratification and in the sense of the regional diversity of dialects, a claim that then cedes its place to a bitter but firm diagnosis — through a celebrated analysis of a speech given by Aldo Moro — of the birth of the Italian national language as a 'technological language typical to and necessary for technocratic capitalism'[42] ('I reached the apodictic, unbiased conclusion that 'Italian was born as a national language' in the same way that a diagnosis is unbiased in declaring the presence of something wrong').[43] Faced with this new situation, the way of looking at dialect and its relation to language also necessarily had to change. 'Dialects' wrote Pasolini, taking a position against Calvino, 'have expired just as the problem of the relationship between dialect and language has, because the cultural period in which one once believed that the Italianization of Italy might take place in a balanced way, with parity for the different common sub-languages, has expired — it has been overtaken by reality.'[44] In his last public intervention, given in Lecce a few days before his death, significantly titled *Volgar'eloquio* ('vernacular speech'), Pasolini seems to distance himself from his poetic work in dialect, in his Friulian years, which now becomes a decisively political, revolutionary question, right up to the point of becoming confused with separatism.

> In these last ten years, the Italian anthropological and cultural situation — or rather, Italian anthropological culture — has been completely overturned [...]. The teaching and protecting of dialect has either become part of traditionalism, conservativism (which I consider entirely healthy, inasmuch as there exists a 'sublime right-wing'), or must become deeply revolutionary (in a way that

---

42   Pasolini, *Empirismo eretico*, p. 37.
43   Ibid., p. 40.
44   Ibid.

the defence of language is in the Basque Country, or for the Irish), up to the point of separatism, which would be an extremely healthy struggle, because the struggle for separatism is none other than the defence of cultural pluralism, which is the reality of culture itself. This means either being conservatives, but illuminated ones, in a completely new way, which has nothing to do with the classically right-wing sense of conservativism; or being actual revolutionaries. Until ten years ago, the situation was entirely reasonable, correct even: Italians spoke Sicilian or Roman or Friulian, and so we defended these languages, they got used to speaking a dialectized Italian, to love their dialect, to fill their Italian with an extreme lexical abundance [of dialects…], today instead this all has to take on completely new connotations […]; today we must find a new way of being free.[45]

It is common knowledge — by now repeated thoughtlessly, even — that in the face of the 'consumerist genocide', the tone of Pasolini's writings from the end of the 1960s became increasingly dark and pessimistic. The most basic philological caution suggests, however, that one ought to not confuse the author's own psychological states — as dark as they may be — with the careful dictation of his thought. An unprejudiced reading of the text entitled *Dal laboratorio*, which closes the section on language in *Empirismo eretico*, shows how Pasolini constantly returned to confronting the problem of the poetic experience of a purely spoken language, which he locates outside of the Saussurian opposition of *langue* and *parole*. Pasolini does not seem to have known the writings of Émile Benveniste, who had radicalized the Saussurian distinction into an insuperable division, whose terms have no transition between each other. Reflecting on the *aporia* of the dichotomy between language as a collective system of signs and as the individual act of a word, Pasolini attempts to overcome them by introducing a third term, which he calls 'the purely oral moment of language'.[46] This moment, which forces him to excavate beyond the limits of linguistics in the direction of 'psychoanalysis, ethnology and anthropology', 'corresponds to a philosophical moment of man: it is both historical (prehistoric human communities) and absolute (the category of the prehistoric which permeates our unconscious)'.[47] This is, he specifies, a 'poetic hypothesis', which he intends to 'offer timidly to linguistics' but the importance of which he stresses by writing in italics: '*The third term*

---

[45] Transcription of the intervention of 21 October 1975 in Lecce, available online. [Also published as Pier Paolo Pasolini, *Volgar'eloquio*, ed. by Gian Carlo Ferretti (Rome: Editori Riuniti, 1987), pp. 50–51; *Trans*.]
[46] Pasolini, *Empirismo eretico*, p. 70.
[47] Ibid.

between langue *and* parole (whose radical dichotomy seems untenable) *is perhaps the purely oral moment of language.*⁴⁸ Without doubt, this purely vocal language, where language and word coincide, is almost a 'phantasm', that exists only 'at the very limit' in wild peoples and, as such, 'belongs to a different human moment in civilization, to *another culture*'.⁴⁹

In this prehistoric, purely vocal, phantasmatic language, which is no longer either language as collective institution nor its simple individual realization, one can, nevertheless, perceive more than an echo of that language-poetry in which 'the movement from *lingua* to *linguaggio* [...] is a moment that burns away in an instant', and which twenty years earlier in Casarsa a young poet had thought to have discovered in the 'factious and naive' but nevertheless 'intoxicating'⁵⁰ practice of the Friulian illustrious vernacular. The final book published in Pasolini's lifetime was *La nuova gioventù* [*The New Youth*], a new and amplified edition of his Friulian poetry collected together originally in 1954 in *La meglio gioventù* [*The Best Youth*].

---

48   Ibid. It is probable that Zanzotto was recalling these words when he wrote that 'dialect proposes itself as the general grounds in which *langue* and *parole* tend to identify with each other'; Zanzotto, *Filò*, p. 92.
49   Pasolini, *Empirismo eretico*, p. 60.
50   Pier Paolo Pasolini, 'La libertà stilistica', in *Passione e ideologia*, pp. 483–84. In this text from 1957, Pasolini tries to clarify the reasons behind his renouncing of that Friulian poetic work where it was possible 'to invent an entire linguistic system, a private language [...] finding everything perhaps already there, and with such splendour, in dialect'. The renunciation coincides with his decision to substitute prose for poetry, to lower a language 'that had been given over entirely to the level of poetry' to the level of prose. It is meaningful, however, that even here Pasolini notes the presence of a 'contradictory, undecided, problematic moment', that translates into a 'stylistic experimentalism' that cannot find satisfaction in any pre-constituted ideological form, in the name of 'a physical, experimental love for the phenomena of the world'. It is little surprise, then, that the article concludes with an unlabelled poetic citation from *Le ceneri di Gramsci*, only slightly changed from the original line: '*to be* with sentiment, at the point in which the world is renewed.'

PHILIPPE LACOUE-LABARTHE

PASOLINI, AN IMPROVISATION (OF A SAINTLINESS)[1]

Of him I know only his act and only his death
The other to the one gives no authority
nor is it nevertheless inscribed in advance nor
the other the first (or perhaps the second)
where no epitaph to read no index
that he knew the storm of sanction near.
Isn't this also what he had always said?

Hypothesis I

'*Perhaps saintliness, since the advent of the modern, has found refuge (asylum) in art: in the* act *of art.*'

Saintliness: the signification of this word must be extracted from Christianity, even still latent. And from religion — it, probably, indelible.

Modern is devastation, desolation: the one who enters into it and stays there, thereby in solitude, but not in mourning, is atheistic, 'deprived of god' (Sophocles, *Oedipus the King*, 661). His melancholy is heroic; it is a furor, wrath ('*Menin aeide, Thea*').

The act, which is older than the work, is the enigma of its cessation: grace without mercy. 'I did say act. In any case, no question of creation. You know?'

Solitude — desolation — is indeed the desert: *ego vox clamantis in deserto*, 'the desert grows'. In ancient tragedy, where the god is 'present in the figure of death', this can be said thus:

---

[1] Previously published as 'Pasolini, an Improvisation (of a Saintliness)', trans. by Steven Miller, *UMBR(a)*, 1, The Dark God (2005), 87–92; originally published in French as *Pasolini, une improvisation (D'une sainteté)* (Bordeaux: William Blake and Co., 1995).

> *It is a great resource of the secretly working soul that at the highest state of consciousness it evades consciousness [...]. Consciousness at its highest, then, always compares itself to objects that do not have any consciousness, yet which in their destiny assume the form of consciousness. One such object is the land that has become a desert, which in originally abundant fertility increases the effects of sunlight too much and therefore dries out.*
>
> (Hölderlin, *Remarks on 'Antigone'*, §2)[2]

*

He follows the ancient to its traces: he tracks vestiges. He wanders 'under the unthinkable' (Hölderlin, but this time on Oedipus).

*

Left behind, abandoned — he has simply been *dropped*. If he strays, it is, consequently, governed by what he lacks: the very one.
'What do you mean, exactly?'

*

Religion is peasant: here to stay. But it is unchained, now that the dissociation has taken place, now that they have all been deported. It is even the 'disappearance of the fireflies':[3] *Mors stupebit et natura...*

*

The mother and child in the immemorial prairie (*vaffanculo*) and the anterior noise of the wind: presentation by breath, the most acrid. The mother, a slowness; and child, the overturned gesture of desire, with an absolute precision, more powerful than the innocence that troubles him.

---

[2] Friedrich Hölderlin, 'Remarks on "Antigone"', in *Essays and Letters on Theory*, ed. and trans. by Thomas Pfau (Albany: State University at New York Press, 1988), pp. 111–12. [*Translation modified*]

[3] Pier Paolo Pasolini, '1 febbraio 1975. L'articolo delle lucciole', in *Scritti Cosari* (Milan: Garzanti, 1975), pp. 160–68.

> Madame stands up too straight in the prairie
> Nearby, where threads of work snow down...
> (Rimbaud, *Memory*)[4]

*

A music, sacral and choral, common passion at a distance, there, unbreathable aura of the dry *banlieue*. The faces are primitive, the smiles are those of bad violence and obscenity — of pure goodness.

Filth. The gazes are fleeting, also, and sly, daring. Vain courage, but courage still, furtive, halting: a frankness.

*

Religion is familial: the unchecked fall (of everyone: father and mother, brother and sister, or son and daughter), and the improbable elevation of the peasant woman, the servant (*au grand cœur?*).[5]

> *Blank is the instant.*
> (Hölderlin, *Bread and Wine*)

*

Behind the ones whom one could say were in a state of resemblance to the saints, the homeless of Assisi and Siena, speechless but in dialogue with the beasts, the birds most of all, there are the Greeks and their native oriental savagery: these are brutal and ferocious, not truly superstitious but restless, without respite, opening their ears (organs of fear: night and music), to listen for another noise. They shiver at the murmur of what is, indiscernible, and they avow as much (Hegel).

Other times, in terror, they are mute.

The heaven of the saints under their feet is the earth itself.

They, the Greeks, they fall and raise themselves up, they never stop crossing the distance that never separates the highest from the lowest.

---

4   Arthur Rimbaud, 'Memory', in *Rimbaud Complete*, ed. and trans. by Wyatt Mason (New York: Modern Library, 2002), p. 351. [*Translation modified*]

5   See Charles Baudelaire, 'La servante au grand cœur dont vous étiez jalouse', rendered as 'That kind-heart you were jealous of...', in *Flowers of Evil*, trans. by James McGowan (Oxford: Oxford University Press, 1993), p. 203.

*

Depopulated peasantry:

> Where do they presage, the wise peasant sentences?
> (Hölderlin, *Bread and Wine*)

*

He has — they have — no age.

Hypothesis II

'*Saintliness is a discipline of the thing. It engages the experience of the abject.*'

The saint experiences the inhuman in man: the fact of man, that outstrips him inside, his most intimate outside.
Interior intimo meo.
It is his ferocity.

*

He says:

> *It is obvious that I have always been of an inferior race. I cannot understand revolt. My race never rises up except to pillage: like wolves who go after the beast they did not kill.*

Before that, he claimed the right to 'idolatry and love of sacrilege; — oh! all the vices, wrath, luxury — it's magnificent, luxury; — but, most of all, deceit and sloth' (Rimbaud, *A Season in Hell*).[6]
This is not false, he responds, but it is revolt: to consider this step already taken, all revolt is logical, etc. Not the least effusion. Already said.

*

---

6   See Rimbaud, *A Season in Hell*, p. 196. [*Translation modified*]

Religion: always archaic: the thing consumes us. Do not encircle it with precautions, nor single it out. No luster. The most consequential among them dispense with objects.

*

He has nothing *to do* except with materialities: sounds, pigments; languages, light. Or with bodies whose soul is their indecency.
A nothing will attract him.

*

No murder: one must elude figuration.

*

Saintliness, because it demands and responds, is rigorous, as exact as a calculation. It derives from a theorem, that is, from pain. Such is the act.

*

This can be repeated thus:

> *It is a great resource of the secretly working soul that at the highest state of consciousness it evades consciousness and that, before the present god actually seizes it, the soul confronts him in a bold and frequently even blasphematory manner, and thus keeps alive the holy possibility of the spirit.*
> (Hölderlin, *Remarks on 'Antigone'*, §2)[7]

*

He experiences debasement; it is required by being defiled. The pigpen is not the world, but reality: the dull blooming of things, barely lit: natural evil.

*

---

7   Hölderlin, 'Remarks on "Antigone"', p. 111. [*Translation modified*]

(While he dies, falsely crucified, it is for real. Welles, if I remember correctly, missed the whole thing.)

*

It is the animal that palpitates in him and strives, the ancient ferocious god, bristling. That's why his very history is natural, blue as a myth.
... *I have been handed over to the ground, with a duty to seek, and coarse reality to embrace! Peasant!* — It has been said once and for all.

*

Whence his rage, his joy, his perfectly intransigent 'one must'. *Cazzo.* He neither prays nor supplicates, he sings torment. Superb atonal voice.

*

Three remarks (for Armando Battiston).
No effusion: Monk and Dolphy — not Coltrane; Morandi, Bram van Velde — not Kandinsky. No 'spiritual in art'.
There are three of them, one for each of Western (hesperian) Europe's three religions: Kafka, Beckett, and him, Pasolini.
Practically, he was just.

Cesare Casarino

THE SOUTHERN ANSWER
Pasolini, Universalism, Decolonization[1]

> *Minorities do not receive a better solution of their problem by integration, even with axioms, statutes, autonomies, independences. Their tactics necessarily go that route. But if they are revolutionary, it is because they carry within them a deeper movement that challenges the worldwide axiomatic. The power of minority, of particularity, finds its figure or universal consciousness in the proletariat.*
>
> Gilles Deleuze and Félix Guattari

> *There is no revolution without universalism.*
>
> Jean-Luc Godard

Having ushered us unaware into the English cemetery in Rome — where Antonio Gramsci lies buried among 'billionaires', 'princes', and 'pederasts', while the proletarian sounds of the adjacent working-class district occasionally reach into and disturb the 'Patrician ennui' of this northern enclave ensconced in the throbbing midst of the southern city — the painfully ambivalent first-person narrator of Pier Paolo Pasolini's 1954 poem 'The Ashes of Gramsci' addresses Gramsci's remains thus:

> There you lie, banished, listed with severe | non-Catholic elegance, among the foreign

---

[1] Previously published as 'The Southern Answer: Pasolini, Universalism, Decolonization', *Critical Inquiry*, 36 (Summer 2010), 673–96.
  To the African immigrants who had the courage to revolt in the face of savage racism and brutal exploitation in January 2010 in Rosarno (Calabria), Italy.
  I am very grateful to Jason Christenson, Bishnupriya Ghosh, Qadri Ismail, Eleanor Kaufman, Kiarina Kordela, Saree Makdisi, John Mowitt, and Bhaskar Sarkar, who, in various ways, helped and encouraged me in writing and rewriting this essay.
  All translations, unless otherwise noted, are my own.

dead: The ashes of Gramsci [...] Between hope | and old, discouraged, mistrust, I accost you, | having chanced upon this drab greenhouse, before
your tomb, before your spirit, still alive | down here among the free. (Or, perhaps, it's | something else, different, more ecstatic
and even humbler: an intoxicated, adolescent | symbiosis of sex and death [...]) | And in this country where your passion never
rested, I feel at once how wrong | — here, in the quiet of these graves — and | how right — in our disquieting
fate — you were, as you drafted your supreme | pages in the days of your murder. | Here, attesting to the still persistent seed
of their ancient domination, lie these | dead men possessed by a greed | whose grandeur and abomination
run deep down the centuries; and at the same time, | attesting to its end: obsessed | striking of anvils, stifled and heart-rending,
comes muffled from the modest neighborhood.[2]

These verses constitute as good a point of departure as any for an interpretation of Pasolini as the most important and most original inheritor of the Gramscian project. Such importance and originality consist primarily of the fact that Pasolini catapulted Gramsci's engagement with the southern question at once in the planetary as well as in the sexual arenas — thereby tying together these different realms of power and resistance in ways that I believe make him an inescapable figure for the current and ongoing dialogues between the disciplinary fields of queer theory and postcolonial studies, as well as an inescapable figure for the related and emergent network of critical discourses that is coalescing nowadays around the Janus-headed question of biopolitics and globalization. In this sense, these verses — and, indeed, the whole poem — are eminently programmatic, as here Pasolini presents in a highly condensed form that problematic which will trouble and occupy him for the next two decades: the volatile and perilous crossroads between politics and sexuality and, in particular, between, on the one hand, North-South relations and, on the other hand, that technology of power which Michel Foucault will call the deployment of sexuality. In a complementary, companion piece — 'Can the Subaltern Confess?' — I have explored this crossroads by articulating the nexus of relations binding subalternity, confession, sexuality, and North-South relations in Pasolini's cinema, as well as in Gramsci's and Foucault's writings.[3] Here, I focus on

---

[2] Pier Paolo Pasolini, 'The Ashes of Gramsci', in *Poems*, trans. and ed. by Norman MacAfee and Luciano Martinengo (New York: Random House, 1982), pp. 5, 3, 7, 9. [*Translation modified*]

[3] See Cesare Casarino, 'Can the Subaltern Confess? Pasolini, Gramsci, Foucault, and the Deployment of Sexuality', in *The Rhetoric of Sincerity*, ed. by Ernst van

Pasolini's poetry of the 1950s and 1960s, which (earlier than his cinema) constituted the springboard for his leap from the Italian South to the global South and for his engagement with the question of decolonization, as he attempted to articulate something that for lack of a better term I will call a *transnational universalism*.

The narrator of 'The Ashes of Gramsci' may well have gone to the English cemetery in search of sex — for, after all, this used to be and still is a notorious cruising ground. Rather than cruising the living among the dead, however, he finds himself cruising the one dead man whose 'spirit' is 'still alive | down here among the free'.[4] At first, the narrator makes it seem as if he has stumbled upon Gramsci by chance — 'having chanced upon this drab greenhouse, before | your tomb, before your spirit' — even as he describes himself approaching the tomb with words that resonate with all the longing and trepidation of a sexual advance to a stranger: 'Between hope | and old, discouraged, mistrust, I accost you'.[5] On second thought, in fact, chance seems to have played a negligible role here, as the narrator admits in the immediately following verses that what brought him there, before Gramsci's tomb, is 'perhaps [...] | something else, different, more ecstatic | and even humbler: an intoxicated, adolescent | symbiosis of sex and death [...]'.[6] Whatever else it may be, the encounter with Gramsci here is also a sexual encounter — an encounter demanded and overdetermined by a desire that periodically punctuates this poem with intense sexual fantasies, as when, for example, the narrator, entranced before Percy Shelley's tomb, gives voice once again to that ecstatic 'adolescent | symbiosis of sex and death' by dreaming the scene of his fellow poet's death by drowning 'in the blinding turquoise of the Tyrrhenian Sea' while ashore, amidst 'swarms of baroque pines and delicate | yellowing glades of rucola', 'a young | Roman peasant sleeps, penis swollen | among his rags, a Goethean dream [...]'.[7] It is unclear who is dreaming whom in this oneiric hall of mirrors, as Pasolini

---

Alphen, Mieke Bal, and Carel Smith (Stanford, CA: Stanford University Press, 2009), pp. 121–43. Both 'Can the Subaltern Confess?' and the present essay are part of a larger, ongoing project on Pasolini's reelaboration of the Gramscian legacy and, in particular, on the ways in which such a reelaboration manifests itself in Pasolini's work as an attempt to conjoin inextricably, on the one hand, a sustained (though problematic) political engagement with the global South and, on the other hand, a sustained (though ambivalent) critique of the deployment of sexuality.

4 Pasolini, 'The Ashes of Gramsci', p. 9.
5 Ibid.
6 Ibid.
7 Ibid., pp. 15, 17.

summons no fewer than two contemporaneous northern European poets (Shelley and Goethe, both obsessed with the southern Mediterranean), so as to dream through them, in their company and with their license, of a southern peasant caught in the act of dreaming his own amply arousing dreams. What is clear, though, is that for Pasolini the South haunts the dreams of the North as asleep yet dreaming, dormant yet aroused, unconscious yet full of life. This is a life that must appear all the more urgent and vital in this funereal setting, if one is to judge from the fact that this word — 'life' — constitutes a veritable mantra here, as the narrator repeats it more than twenty times during the course of the poem, especially when imaging the Roman proletariat bustling around and bursting with it just beyond the cemetery walls.

What is also clear is that cruising Gramsci proves to be a difficult, complex task. For what exactly does it mean to try and seduce the founding father of the Italian Communist Party? Above all, perhaps, it means to accost him — that is, to address, hail, and hence interpellate him — precisely not as a paternal figure but as a fraternal one. This is, in fact, how the narrator first refers to Gramsci in the poem: 'not father: rather, humble | brother'.[8] And this line at the time must have proven more irksome even than all the explicit homosexual reveries to the largely bigoted and petty-bourgeois ideologues of the Communist Party, invested as they were in a hagiographical and didactic interpretation of Gramsci as the infallible patriarch and guiding light of the Italian way to communism — an interpretation that, sadly, made Gramsci insufferable and unreadable for many Italian leftists of the postwar generations.[9] (It should be noted, furthermore, that the narrator's invocation of Gramsci as 'humble | brother' has the effect not only of defamiliarizing and critiquing the official beatification of Gramsci as communist patriarch but also of linking Gramsci all the more directly and intimately to the narrator's own 'adolescent | symbiosis of sex and death', since the latter is referred to by the narrator precisely as 'humble'). But once Gramsci has been disengaged from the patriarchal-nationalist iconography of founding father of the Italian Communist Party — an iconography that was at once provincially local, in the sense that it was myopically restricted to the Italian context, as well as already partially global, in the sense that it

---

8   Ibid., p. 3.
9   On the ways in which Gramsci was used, abused, or altogether avoided in the postwar period in Italy, see Cesare Casarino and Antonio Negri, *In Praise of the Common: A Conversation on Philosophy and Politics* (Minneapolis: University of Minnesota Press, 2008), pp. 160–65.

was also dictated by cold war exigencies — the ground has been prepared for a further political leap.

In the verses quoted above, in fact, we witness Gramsci in the middle of two concentric circles, which correspond to two opposing historical blocs and political force fields. First of all, there is the inner circle of the dead souls of the founding fathers of the British Empire — 'Here, attesting to the still persistent seed | of their ancient domination, lie these | dead men possessed by a greed | whose grandeur and abomination | run deep down the centuries'[10] — and, importantly, these are verses that echo the narrator's famous exclamation in Joseph Conrad's *Heart of Darkness*: 'The dreams of men, the seed of commonwealths, the germs of empires'.[11] Secondly, there is the outer circle of the surrounding working-class district, whose laboring clangs threaten and, indeed, promise to bring that domination down: 'and at the same time, | attesting to its end: obsessed | striking of anvils, stifled and heart-rending, | comes muffled from the modest neighborhood'. In thus encircling and framing Gramsci, Pasolini achieves two remarkable and discordant feats in one single stroke. On the one hand, he extricates Gramsci from the reductive role of ideological pawn in the Italian version of the tug of war between First World and Second World — which in Italy was being played out in the contest for hegemony between the Christian Democratic Party and the Communist Party — and situates him instead squarely in the midst of another and related tug of war, namely, the expanding global spiral of First World–Third World conflicts over the fate of colonialism. While the dominant interpretation of Gramsci at the time suffered from being largely monopolized by and limited to cold war concerns, in other words, Pasolini understood with rare foresight that the question of decolonization would provide the most appropriate and fertile ground for further elaborations of the Gramscian project. On the other hand, he elaborated such a reconceptualization of the Gramscian project also by subsuming the Third World into the world of the Roman proletariat in ways that are at once highly productive and highly problematic.

In a sense, the narrator here is prey to a historical hallucination because the political forces that at the time were bringing about the end of the British Empire had little to do with the Roman proletariat. Such a hallucination is undoubtedly triggered by conflicted allegiances and troubling identifications. We have already seen, for example, how the narrator enlists both Shelley and Goethe in the service of his own voyeuristic fantasy,

---

10   Pasolini, 'Ashes of Gramsci', p. 9.
11   Joseph Conrad, *Heart of Darkness* (New York: Penguin Books, 1990), p. 2.

whose unaware object is an asleep and aroused young Roman peasant. Moreover, immediately prior to that fantasy, the narrator had addressed Gramsci thus:

> [...] Ah, how well | I understand, silent in the wind's wet
> humming, here where Rome is silent, | among wearily agitated cypresses, | next to you, that soul whose inscription calls out
> Shelley [...] How well I understand the vortex | of feelings, the capricious whim (Greek | in the aristocratic, Nordic vacationer's
> heart) which swallowed him in the blinding | turquoise of the Tyrrhenian Sea; the carnal | joy of adventure, aesthetic
> and childish.[12]

The narrator understands Shelley so well that he too seems to be drowning here — in the overemphatic bathos of his own lyricism. It would be a mistake to excuse such heavy-handed identification merely as a momentary and aberrant lapse of both political judgment and poetic diction attributable to sexual persecution and ostracism. It is certainly the case that one always makes do with what one has and hence that often one elects one's own affinities on the basis of unlikely projections, thereby ending up in the company of just as unlikely bedfellows. In particular, it has often been the case in the twentieth century that the imagined community of a homosexual (dis)continuum with nineteenth-century figures has constituted a necessary and enabling fiction for the expression — poetic and otherwise — of an oppressed sexual desire at the expense of historical-political precision (think, for example, of Federico García Lorca's identifications with Walt Whitman or of David Wojnarowicz's identifications with Arthur Rimbaud). It is also the case, however, that in the context of a critical engagement with the thinker of the southern question — an engagement that, among other things, draws attention to the historical irony of this thinker's interment in such distinguished and imperialist company — the narrator's identification with the 'aristocratic' and 'Nordic' 'vacationer' cannot be explained solely in sexual terms and cannot be understood on identitarian grounds, sexual or otherwise.

What we are confronted with here, rather, is the mutual overdeterminations of politics and sexuality and, in particular, the spellbound crossroads where sexual orientation and sexual Orientalism are at once distinct yet indiscernible from one other. What we are confronted with here, in other words, is a sexually driven identification with that Orientalist political

---

12   Pasolini, 'Ashes of Gramsci', p. 15.

imaginary that blinded the likes of Shelley and of his spiritual progeny to any significant qualitative difference. This is not only the difference between a Roman peasant and, say, the peasant subjects of the Ottoman Empire, who were being pictured as similarly unconscious and dreaming just a few hundred kilometers down the road but also the difference between themselves (that is, Shelley and company) and carefully selected southerners (see, for example, the famous line in the preface to 'Hellas' in which Shelley, writing in defense of the Greeks' struggle against their Ottoman rulers, triumphantly declares: 'We are all Greeks!' — a line echoed here in the narrator's assertion that the 'capricious whim' that led to Shelley's drowning was, somehow, 'Greek').[13] It should come as no surprise, thus, that someone who can so empathetically borrow and adopt such an imaginary could then freely substitute the 'obsessed striking of anvils' of a Roman worker for the gunshots that at the time were being fired throughout the Third World in the attempt to send northerners of all sorts packing. In short, Pasolini produces here nothing less than a Shelleyan, Goethean, Orientalist reading of Gramsci — a reading that leads him to declare just as triumphantly that there is simply no difference between Roman proletariat and Third World, between the Italian South and the global South.

It is not the aim of this essay, however, merely to critique or altogether to dismiss Pasolini on grounds of sexual Orientalism — which, for better and for worse, would only grow more excessive, luxuriant, and efflorescent in his work throughout the rest of the 1950s, 1960s, and 1970s so as to reach its literally orgiastic apotheosis in 1974 with a cinematic phantasmagoria such as *The Flower of the Thousand and One Nights*. To dismiss Pasolini on these grounds would be much like saying that C. L. R. James — to mention another heretical Marxist intellectual of his time — no longer has any value for us today because on occasion he could be tritely and predictably homophobic.[14] To critique Pasolini's Orientalism is indeed necessary; and, yet, not only is his Orientalism too easy and too predictable

---

13 Percy Bysshe Shelley, 'Preface to *Hellas*', in *Shelley's Poetry and Prose*, ed. by Donald H. Reiman and Sharon B. Powers (New York: Norton & Company, 1977), p. 409.

14 I am referring here to regrettable moments in James's otherwise illuminating readings of Herman Melville's work in his superb study of this author. See, for example, C. L. R. James, *Mariners, Renegades, and Castaways: The Story of Herman Melville and the World We Live In* (London: Allison and Busby, 1985), pp. 48–49, 98. On the presence of both homoeroticism and homophobia in James's study of Melville, see my *Modernity at Sea: Melville, Marx, Conrad in Crisis* (Minneapolis: University of Minnesota Press, 2002), pp. 118–21.

of a target but also merely critiquing it constitutes an insufficient and inadequate hermeneutical gesture in and of itself.[15] (After all, if there is something I hope to have learned from Pasolini himself, among others, it is precisely that the critique of ideology, when left to its own devices, is at best a necessary evil and at worst a conceptual as well as a political dead end). To critique Pasolini's Orientalism along the lines that I have briefly sketched above would mean to understand the sweeping gesture by which he subsumes the Third World into the Roman proletariat — and the global South into the Italian South — as the epiphenomenon of that universalism which goes by the name of Eurocentrism. In particular, Pasolini's is a specifically Hegelian type of Eurocentrism. This is a Eurocentrism that functions according to soluble contradictions and that determines the identity of that totality and center that is Europe by means of a relative and recuperative negation of all that is perceived as not European — that is, by selectively sublating the different into the identical.[16] Such a Hegelian Eurocentrism finds its opposite complement in that Kantian Eurocentrism that functions not according to soluble contradictions but according to dynamic antinomies and that determines the identity of that totality and center that is Europe by means of a relative yet nonrecuperative negation of all that is perceived as not European — that is, by selectively excising the different from the identical. If the most dangerous political manifestations of the former amount to total assimilation and domestication, the most dangerous political manifestations of the latter amount to complete ostracism and extermination tout court. Both, in any case, ultimately lead to the same end, that is, the obliteration of difference.

If Pasolini is not guilty of the latter, he is at times guilty of the former.[17] But in order to go beyond the limits of such a critique of Pasolini as part

---

15 On the insufficiency and inadequacy of this type of critique, I concur with Luca Caminati in his valuable study of the Orientalism of Pasolini's cinema. See Luca Caminati, *Orientalismo eretico: Pier Paolo Pasolini e il cinema del terzo mondo* (Milan: Bruno Mondadori, 2007), pp. ix–x.

16 It is on the basis of such a Eurocentric sublation of difference that Michael Hardt and Antonio Negri criticize Pasolini's encounter with India (and — they seem to imply — with the rest of the Third World). See Michael Hardt and Antonio Negri, *Multitude: War and Democracy in the Age of Empire* (New York: The Penguin Press, 2004), pp. 127–29. As it will become clear shortly, I find such an assessment of Pasolini's engagement with the Third World partly accurate as well as ultimately unfruitful. On such an assessment of Pasolini, see also Casarino and Negri, *In Praise of the Common*, pp. 162–67.

17 It is important to emphasize, however, that, even though residual Hegelian tendencies are indeed present in his work, Pasolini was nonetheless explicit and

and parcel of a Hegelian tendency within Eurocentrism and in order to posit such a critique as the beginning rather than as the endpoint of a critical investigation it is also necessary to insist that it is precisely in his Orientalism and Eurocentrism that Pasolini's most productive political gestures lie. Furthermore, I believe that it is paradoxically *because of* rather than *despite* such Orientalism and Eurocentrism that we ought to say of Pasolini's works what another fellow Gramscian intellectual — Edward Said — has said of Jean Genet's works in his *Culture and Imperialism*, namely, that they ought to be considered an integral part of the literatures of decolonization, alongside the works of James, Aimé Césaire, and Frantz Fanon, among others.[18] I would argue, in other words, that Pasolini is most usefully understood within that constellation of intellectuals — spanning across the First World and the Third World — who, throughout the 1950s and 1960s, were in the process of articulating a transnational universalism in the revolutionary tradition of the likes of Toussaint L'Ouverture, Karl Marx, and Leon Trotsky. (In this sense, the rapid ascent and increasing ascendance of the evil twins of biopolitics and globalization from the 1980s onwards in retrospect looks very much like a virulent reaction against the emergent transnational universalism of that earlier moment and like a last-ditch effort either to suppress by naked force or to exploit by fancily dressed cooptation the revolutionary impetus of that earlier historical conjuncture. This is also to say that one could do worse than returning to that ebullient historical moment in search of whatever unspent political energies and unfulfilled promises it might still have in store for us today.) If Pasolini's sexual-Orientalist reading of Gramsci — with its attendant, sublative, and strategic misrecognitions of the global South as the Italian South — smacks of the worst type of Hegelian Eurocentrism, such a reading has nonetheless the invaluable merit of asserting that now, in 1954, Gramsci's engagement with the Italian South needed to be linked to the political struggles of the global South and that the southern question could make sense only if posed in transnational terms and could be adequately addressed only on a fully

---

vocal in denouncing the limitations of Hegelian thought (well before the emergence of a full-fledged anti-Hegelian Left in Italy). Such polemical denunciations constituted a crucial element of his reelaboration of the Gramscian legacy and of his attempt to wrest Gramsci away from the dialectical interpretations and proprietary deployments of the Communist Party. On this matter, see Maurizio Viano, 'The Left According to the Ashes of Gramsci', *Social Text*, 18 (Winter 1987–88), 51–60 (esp. pp. 55–56).

18 See Edward Said, *Culture and Imperialism* (New York: Vintage Books, 1994), pp. 185, 317.

planetary scale — which is precisely how it was posed and addressed one year later in Bandung. In short, Pasolini's admittedly problematic disregard for national and cultural specificities, geopolitical particularities, as well as historical accuracy — namely, his indifference with respect to both diachronic temporality and identitarian deployments of difference — ought to be understood as an attempt to produce a genuinely transnational universalism based on common potentials and common projects as opposed to those (either Kantian or Hegelian) universalisms that find their stable ground in shared and essential identities.[19]

---

[19] In this sense, Pasolini is highly relevant to the recent resurgence of interest in universalism as a political and philosophical question. I am thinking in particular of contemporary thinkers who at one and the same time critique (and rightly so) the current relativist and particularist orthodoxies — for example, the discourse of multiculturalism — as specifically capitalist ideologies that function as barely disguised universalisms of the aforementioned Hegelian or Kantian varieties, as well as assert explicitly the urgent need to reconceptualize and endorse universalism on nonessentialist and nonidentitarian grounds. See, for example, Alain Badiou, who in his book on Saint Paul denounces particularist solutions to the problem of difference and attempts to recuperate Saint Paul as a thinker of 'universal singularity' who articulated universalism in effect as an egalitarianism that is respectful of difference (Alain Badiou, *Saint Paul: The Foundation of Universalism*, trans. by Ray Brassier [Stanford, CA: Stanford University Press, 2003], p. 104; see also pp. 105–6, 6–7, and 14). Incidentally, it is not a coincidence that Pasolini was particularly interested in Saint Paul, whose life and writings were the topic of a screenplay that Pasolini wrote but ultimately never turned into a film; we need to thank Armando Maggi for having resurrected this important screenplay from near oblivion and for having devoted to it the critical attention it deserves. See Armando Maggi, *The Resurrection of the Body: Pier Paolo Pasolini from Saint Paul to Sade* (Chicago: University of Chicago Press, 2009), pp. 21–106. Similarly universalist positions can be found in Slavoj Žižek; see, for example, his exchanges with Judith Butler and Ernesto Laclau in Judith Butler, Ernesto Laclau, and Slavoj Žižek, *Contingency, Hegemony, Universality: Contemporary Dialogues on the Left* (London: Verso, 2000). I am not sure that either Badiou's or Žižek's attempts to produce nonessentialist and nonidentitarian concepts of universalism are fully successful in the end. In a different — and, as far as I am concerned, more effective — way, Gilles Deleuze and Félix Guattari had made analogous arguments already two decades earlier when discussing the question of minorities in *A Thousand Plateaus* (it being understood that 'minority' for Deleuze and Guattari is a strictly qualitative rather than quantitative category). See Gilles Deleuze and Félix Guattari, *A Thousand Plateaus: Capitalism and Schizophrenia II*, trans. by Brian Massumi (Minneapolis: University of Minnesota Press, 1987), pp. 469–73. The first epigraph of this essay stands as an implicit endorsement of Deleuze and Guattari's universalist position on this question — a position that I find also more consonant with Pasolini's universalism, especially as articulated in his 1962 poem 'Prophecy', with which I engage below.

And yet — one might protest — exactly what is so transnational about the universalism of the historical moment of decolonization, when the questions of national consciousness, national culture, and national independence were posed as the *conditio sine qua non* of revolutionary struggles across the Third World? How is, for example, a quintessential manifesto of that revolutionary moment such as Fanon's *The Wretched of the Earth* (1961) to be read as a transnationalist work? Others have already given admirable answers to such questions, and hence I refer the skeptics among us to those passionately antiidentitarian readings of Fanon's work such as the ones Said articulates in *Culture and Imperialism*, where Said shows — among other things — how in Fanon the anticolonial struggle for national independence was inseparable from a distinctly transnational struggle for liberation from imperialism on a global scale. Said's definitive readings notwithstanding, I would like nonetheless to make my own contribution to such an exegesis of Fanon by addressing a particularly suggestive moment in *The Wretched of the Earth* in order to return then to Pasolini via a different angle.

At one point in this work, Fanon cites Sékou Touré, the Guinean poet and intellectual who led his country to independence from France in 1958 and who then became its first president:

> In the realm of thought, man may claim to be the brain of the world; but in real life where every action affects spiritual and physical existence, the world is always the brain of mankind; for it is at this level that you will find the sum total of the powers and units of thought, and the dynamic forces of development and improvement; and it is there that energies are merged and the sum of man's intellectual values is finally added together.[20]

Before commenting on Fanon, let me first address Touré's remarks. Irredeemable humanist rhetoric notwithstanding, I believe Touré is making an important intervention in the theory of revolutionary praxis. On the one hand, he begins by positing a distinction between 'the realm of thought' and the realm of action (the latter being the domain of 'real life where action' takes place) — thereby implying at once that thought is not part of 'real life' as well as that there can be such a thing as 'thought' separate from 'action'. On the other hand, what he says about 'real life' immediately problematizes the distinction he has just posited between 'thought' and 'action'. If in 'real life [...] every action affects spiritual and physical

---

20 Frantz Fanon, *The Wretched of the Earth*, trans. by Constance Farrington (New York: Grove Press, 1968), p. 200.

existence,' and if 'spiritual' here includes or overlaps to some extent with 'thought,' it follows then that 'action' always leaves its mark on 'thought' and hence that 'action' is present in 'the realm of thought' — at the very least as an absent cause immanent in its own effects. Furthermore, if in the realm of action 'the world is always the brain of mankind', then it also follows that 'thought' too is present in the realm of action, if indeed the 'brain' is construed here as the thinking organ. It turns out, in other words, that the real difference between these two realms is not at all that in one we find only thought while in the other we find only action. Rather, what is different in each is the one who thinks as well as the very definition of thought. In 'the realm of thought, man may claim he is the brain of the world', that is, may act as if he is the Cartesian ego who thinks in the world and for the world and who can construe thought as a private, individual matter. In the realm of action, however, 'the world is always the brain of mankind' — namely, whenever one acts, it is the world that thinks in one. Why? Because it is only when one's brain is the world that one does not think alone and that thought is not private and individual: 'for it is at this level that you will find the sum total of the powers and units of thought, and the dynamic forces of development and improvement; and it is there that energies are merged and the sum of man's intellectual values is finally added together'. Put differently, the condition of possibility for revolutionary praxis is the world defined at once as the powers of thought and the realm of force relations, namely, thought intended as an irreducibly collective force, as the experience of a universal common power; whenever one acts, there the many think in common.[21] I believe Touré is not far here from what Marx refers to as 'the general intellect' in the *Grundrisse* — a concept that, around the time when Touré was writing this passage, was just beginning to find its fortune within that heretical tendency within Italian Marxism known as *operaismo* (workerism), which saw in this concept the precondition of revolutionary praxis.[22]

---

21   On the power of thought as a definitionally common power, see — among others — Giorgio Agamben, 'Form-of-Life', in *Means without End: Notes on Politics*, trans. by Vincenzo Binetti and Cesare Casarino (Minneapolis: Minnesota University Press, 2000), pp. 9–12. On these and related matters, see also my essay 'Surplus Common: A Preface', in Casarino and Negri, *In Praise of the Common*, pp. 8–13 and 37–38.
22   Karl Marx, *Grundrisse: Foundations of the Critique of Political Economy (Rough Draft)*, trans. by Martin Nicolaus (Harmondsworth: Penguin Books, 1974), p. 706. For a concise outline of the significance of this concept for late-twentieth-century Italian Marxism, see Paolo Virno, 'Notes on the "General Intellect"', trans. by Cesare Casarino, in *Marxism beyond Marxism*, ed. by Saree Makdisi,

The point is, in any case, that Touré puts forth here two powerful theses regarding the relation between universalism and revolution. First of all, Touré posits the level of the universal as the presupposition of revolutionary praxis rather than positing it as the telos that revolutionary praxis ought to realize. Revolution does not find its raison d'être in a universal to come — such as the people, the nation, or the state. Revolution starts from a universal that already is in the world — and that, indeed, *is* the world — rather than working its way towards a universal, which, once instituted, will inevitably decree the end of the revolution itself. Secondly, unlike those universals that are posited as telos and endpoint of revolutionary praxis — namely, the people, the nation, and so on — that universal which Touré understands as the condition of possibility for revolutionary praxis is not predicated on an essence or identity: 'the world' as 'the brain of mankind' is a collective force, a common power, a general intellect. In short, what we find in Touré is precisely a transnational universalism, namely, a universalism that already exists here and now across nations and peoples as the general faculty to transform that which is, as the common potential to produce the world anew.

Commenting on Touré's passage, Fanon writes: 'Individual experience, because it is national and because it is a link in the chain of national existence, ceases to be individual, limited, shrunken and is enabled to open out into the truth of the nation and of the world'.[23] Compared to Touré's dizzying image of 'the world' as 'the brain of mankind', Fanon's commentary is, admittedly, somewhat prosaic. And, yet, Fanon's decidedly Hegelian and reductive interpretation of Touré — which posits the nation as the mediation between the individual and the universal — does nonetheless articulate an intriguing synchronicity. If it is the case that here 'the nation' and 'the world' are posited as the *telos* of 'individual experience', it is also the case that 'individual experience' does not become 'national' at some later moment of development as it is already 'national' to begin with. And it is precisely the fact that 'experience' is at one and the same time 'individual' and 'national' that enables it to be transformed even further, namely, that constitutes the condition of possibility for a revolutionary becoming. It should come as no surprise, thus, that later in the text Fanon can write, 'it is at the heart of national consciousness that international consciousness

---

Rebecca Karl, and Cesare Casarino (New York: Routledge, 1996), pp. 265–72. But see also Hardt and Negri's discussion of this concept in *Empire* (Cambridge, MA: Harvard University Press, 2000), pp. 28–30 and 364–67.

23 Fanon, *The Wretched of the Earth*, p. 200.

lives and grows'.²⁴ If in the earlier passage 'individual experience' was already 'national', here 'national consciousness' is already 'international' or at the very least contains a live international element pulsating at its very heart. Granted, in Fanon 'experience' and 'consciousness' are not exactly one and the same. And, yet, I do not think it is far-fetched to say that for Fanon, if the level of the international lives within the level of the national, and if the latter is coextensive with the level of the individual, then — according to a logic of transitivity — the level of the international is not only present at the level of the individual but also constitutes the life of both these levels, namely, that driving force which makes them grow, expand, change. In short, here, too — much as in Touré — a universal is posited as the enabling presupposition rather than as the telos and endpoint of a revolutionary becoming.

But exactly what type of universal is this 'international consciousness' that constitutes the heart of the microcosms of the national and of the individual? It is here that I find Said's reading of Fanon to be most inspiring. At a crucial moment in his engagement with Fanon, Said puts forth a philologically dubious and yet conceptually powerful hypothesis, namely, that while writing *The Wretched of the Earth* Fanon was reading Georg Lukács's *History and Class Consciousness*, which had just appeared in French in 1960. Heedless of the fact that such a hypothesis may well turn out to be unfounded, Said nevertheless proceeds to identify two important Lukácsian echoes in Fanon's discussion of the historical situation of the colonized. First of all, Said points out that Fanon describes the condition of the colonized in ways that resonate with Lukács's articulation of the condition of the worker under capitalist exchange relations — both, in other words, are conditions of reification and fragmentation. Second, Said writes that for Lukács such a condition 'could be overcome by an act of mental will, by which one lonely mind could join another by imagining the common bond between them, breaking the enforced rigidity that kept human beings as slaves to tyrannical outside forces' and suggests that — likewise — Fanon posits such a feat of the imagination as part and parcel of that practice of violence which is necessary for the overthrow of colonialism. 'It so happens' — Fanon writes, as quoted by Said — 'that for the colonized people this violence, because it constitutes their only work, invests their character with positive and creative qualities. The practice of violence binds them together'. Said comments thus: 'Fanon is not only reshaping colonial experience in terms suggested by Lukács,

---

24   Ibid., p. 247–48.

but also characterizing the emergent cultural and political antagonism to imperialism'.[25]

Regardless of whether or not this constitutes an accurate reading of Lukács — and I would argue that it is at least partially accurate — the point is that Said here puts his finger on the kernel of Fanon's profoundly antiidentitarian universalism. For Fanon, the wretched of the earth are bound together not only negatively — that is, by virtue of the fact that they share a common condition of oppression that manifests itself as fragmentation and reification. More importantly, the wretched of the earth are bound together also positively in the sense that they share in a common capacity for violence intended as a destructive and as a productive, as a dissolving and as a constitutive force — namely, a common power at once to destroy and to create. The wretched of the earth do not derive their revolutionary impetus from the fact that they might share an identity that is determined by negation, such as, for example, an identity determined by having the same oppressor; rather, they derive such an impetus from the fact that they share in a positive transformative potential. In this sense, it is of fundamental importance that Said quotes Fanon precisely at the point in which Fanon defines the violence of 'the colonized people' as 'their only work'. If Lukács is relevant here, in fact, he is so ultimately because his analysis starts from the Marxian concept of labor power, which, as Marx writes in *Capital*, is 'the aggregate of those mental and physical capabilities existing in the physical form, the living personality, of a human being'.[26] For Marx, what human beings have in common is a generic and undetermined potential for production, which includes all mental and physical capacities. But isn't such a potential precisely what is at stake in Fanon's definition of violence? It is because Fanon understands violence as a common, transformative, productive power that he sees 'the practice of violence' as that which binds people together, 'invests their character with positive and creative qualities', and, indeed, 'constitutes their work'. The universal that Fanon posits as the condition of possibility for revolution and that cuts across international, national, and individual forms is a common potential for production, a common power to produce ourselves and the world anew. The wretched of the earth are not identical to one another and have nothing essentially in common, for what they have in common is neither an essence nor an identity but a potential; for what

---

25 Said, *Culture and Imperialism*, pp. 270, 271.
26 Karl Marx, *Capital: A Critique of Political Economy*, trans. by Ben Fowkes, 2 vols. (Harmondsworth: Penguin Books and New Left Review, 1990), I, p. 270.

they have in common is not what they are but the power to become other than what they are.

If Fanon can be read in a nonidentitarian manner — as Said has shown — I believe Pasolini too can and ought to be read in a similar manner. As I claimed earlier, Pasolini's problematic misrecognition of the Third World as Roman proletariat and of the global South as Italian South nonetheless recasts Gramsci's engagement with the southern question in global terms and hence points towards a universalism of the type we just witnessed in Touré and Fanon — namely, a transnational universalism based on common potentials and common projects — rather than pointing towards the various essentialist and identitarian types of universalism. Now this claim can be corroborated further by drawing attention to the fact that Pasolini's strategic misrecognition is articulated on the basis of a common potential for production and indeed constitutes a recognition of labor power. The narrator of 'The Ashes of Gramsci' tells us that 'the obsessed striking of anvils' — which can be heard in the English cemetery and which comes from the nearby working-class neighborhood — attests to the end of 'that ancient domination' that is the British Empire. While in the presence of Gramsci's remains, and surrounded by the tombs of the leaders of the British Empire, the narrator at once perceives a metallic clang, recognizes it as the familiar sound of a hammer beating on an anvil, and hears the Third World striking against colonialism in it, as if, perhaps, laboring to bend and break its shackles. A series of arbitrary juxtapositions and contingent encounters (between Gramsci and his illustrious and imperialist company as well as between all these dead men inside the cemetery and the alive and laboring ones just outside the cemetery) is turned here into a series of necessary associations and urgent political relations; the sound of the invisible and obsessed hammer is the *clinamen* that makes these disparate elements collide with one another and crystallize into a coherent and necessary constellation — the *clinamen* that turns contingency into necessity. When discussing the concept of the *clinamen* in Democritean and Epicurean atomistic materialism, Louis Althusser writes, 'rather than thinking of contingency as a modality of necessity or as an exception to necessity, one ought to think of necessity as the becoming-necessary of the encounter of contingencies'.[27] The *clinamen* — as you will recall — is that inclination or curve in the free fall of atoms that ultimately causes them to collide with one another, thereby begetting the world; the clinamen marks

---

27 Louis Althusser, 'Une Philosophie pour le marxisme: "La Ligne de Démocrite"', *Sur la philosophie* (Paris: Gallimard, 1994), p. 42.

that bending force which produces contingency and necessity as immanent to one another rather than producing one as transcendent with respect to the other, that force which produces the world of necessity as the becoming-necessary of the contingent encounters of the atoms. Similarly, the sound of the hammer marks that force which is labor power and which produces the world of the narrator as a world in which contingent juxtapositions become necessary political relations, as a world in which the sound of the Roman proletariat at work necessarily resonates with the sounds of the Third World proletariat in revolt. The syntagmatic and metonymic logic of these verses — which is the very logic of the political unconscious — is driven by labor power; it is the sound of labor power in its process of actualization that produces the Roman proletariat as the metonymic displacement of the Third World and its struggle for decolonization. It is a forceful, powerful potential rather than an essential identity that makes one resonate in the other. In Pasolini, the political relation between the Italian South and the global South is articulated on the basis of a universal power of production — a common potential for producing the world as always already transnational.

Such a revolutionary potential is nowhere more evident perhaps than in Pasolini's idiosyncratic engagement with the Algerian War of independence from France. If in 'The Ashes of Gramsci' (which was written at the beginning of this crucial chapter in the history of decolonization) the Roman proletariat is posited as metonymic displacement of Third World struggles against colonialism, in a poem entitled 'Profezia' [Prophecy] and written in 1962 (hence at the very end of the Algerian War), Pasolini articulates a far more complex set of relations between the Italian South and the global South.[28] 'Prophecy' bears a dedication: 'To Jean-Paul Sartre, who told me the story of Blue-Eyed Alí'.[29] It is only towards the end of this long poem that we shall hear about Alí. 'Prophecy', in fact, begins elsewhere: 'A son was in the world | and one day he went to Calabria' — Calabria being the southernmost region of mainland Italy — and what follows is a series of

---

28   In the early 1960s, Pasolini wrote several other poems articulating complex resonances and correspondences between the Italian South and the global South. A more complete investigation would have to engage at the very least with poems such as 'La Guinea' [Guinea], 'Poema per un verso di Shakespeare' [Poem for a Verse by Shakespeare], as well as 'L'alba meridionale' [Southern Dawn] — all included in the same collection as 'Profezia', namely, *Poesia in forma di rosa* [*Poetry in the Shape of a Rose*] (Milan: Garzanti, 1976).

29   Pasolini, 'Profezia', in *Poesia in forma di rosa*, p. 93.

devastating descriptions of the impoverished rural South of Italy.[30] These descriptions are in turn followed by a series of scathing remarks addressed to the northern Italian organized industrial working class, denouncing their petty-bourgeois aspirations as well as their patronizing posture of enlightened and progressive political force with respect to the culturally traditional, economically underdeveloped, and politically backward rural South. Because of their membership in Communist Party unions, factory counsels, and Interior Committees — Pasolini reasons — Milanese workers feel and behave like gods, whom the southern peasant ought to worship.[31]

These polemical verses express a profound disillusionment with Marxist projects of development and modernization and, more specifically, with the Italian Communist Party's postwar implementation of the Gramscian answer to the southern question. In 1927, Gramsci could write that 'the revolutionary workers of Turin and Milan have become the protagonists of the southern question' and could still endorse the 1920 resolutions of the Turin communists as expressed in their newspaper *L'ordine nuovo*, from which Gramsci quotes:

> The bourgeoisie of the North has subjected southern Italy and the Islands [Sardinia and Sicily] and reduced them to the status of exploited colonies; the proletariat of the North, in emancipating itself from capitalist enslavement, will emancipate the peasant masses of the South who are chained to the banks and the parasitic industrialism of the North [...]. In imposing workers' control over industry, the proletariat will direct industry towards the production of agricultural machinery for the peasants, of textiles and shoes for the peasants,

---

30   Ibid.
31   Ibid., pp. 94–95 : 'Ah, how much longer will you, factory worker in Milan, struggle just for | your wages? Can't you see how these people [Calabrians] venerate you? | Almost like a boss, like an owner. | They would bring you | animals and fruits, | and obscure fetishes, | from their ancient region, | and they would lay them down | with proud rites | in your perfect little rooms | decorated in early-nineteen-hundred style | between the refrigerator and the television, | attracted by your divinity | You, of the Internal Committees, | you of the CGIL [Communist Party union], | you, Divine ally | in the marvelous Northern sun'.
    Much ought to be said about the peculiar typographical and prosodical specificities of this poem. Here, let me simply note that this poem is divided into seven long stanzas, each of which occupies a full page and is set on the page in the shape of a cross (a shape that I have attempted to retain as much as possible in my translation); this is, in fact, one of the two poems comprising the fourth section of the collection *Poesia in forma di rosa* — a section titled 'Il libro delle croci' ['The Book of Crosses'].

and of electrical energy for the peasants [...]. [In doing so] the workers will break all the chains which bind the peasant to poverty and despair.[32]

In 1962, Pasolini's verses constitute a direct reply to this political project and to its failures. Lamenting the disastrous effects of modernization on southern peasantry — and especially the continued waves of emigration to the industrial North of Italy and of Europe, the consequent depopulation of entire regions and deterioration of arable land, and, in short, the violent, wholesale destruction of a world, a people, and a culture — Pasolini addresses the Milanese factory worker thus:

> In their Land of multifarious | races, only the moon is left to | cultivate a countryside that you | procured for them pointlessly. | In their Land of Familial | Beasts, only the moon is left | to teach souls that you | have modernized pointlessly.[33]

One could reasonably protest that it is historically unfair and politically irresponsible to blame the northern Italian organized working class for the fact that industrial modernization, far from fulfilling its promises of emancipation, had actually exacerbated all that Gramsci had summarized succinctly and accurately when writing, 'the South can be described as an area of extreme social disintegration'.[34] And, yet, the point is that the target of Pasolini's attack here is the fact that the bourgeois ideologies of modernization, of progress, and of work understood as the key to emancipation and liberation — and, indeed, as that which ennobles and dignifies human life — had crept into and had been uncritically adopted by the official Marxist Left and, in fact, had been present already in Gramsci's own version of the Enlightenment project. One of the most bitter refrains of this poem is the following verse, which is repeated several times in slightly different versions: 'Ah, how much longer will you, Milanese factory worker, go on struggling just for your wages?'.[35] Pasolini is painfully aware of the fact that the unionist struggle to improve workers' conditions, precisely because of its inability and unwillingness to distance itself from those ideological constructs, in the end had backfired by dovetailing with the Keynesian project of cooptation of the industrial working class through

---

32   Antonio Gramsci, 'The Southern Question', in *'The Modern Prince' and Other Writings*, trans. by Louis Marks (New York: International Publishers, 1957), pp. 30, 28–29.
33   Pasolini, 'Profezia', p. 96.
34   Gramsci, 'The Southern Question', p. 42.
35   Pasolini, 'Profezia', p. 93.

higher wages and substantial social services — namely, that welfare state which many of us never dreamt we would one day so sorely miss — and hence had left the concept of work unsullied by any type of sustained critical examination, thereby positing it by default as its operative guiding principle.

In this sense, Pasolini's verses uncannily resonate with the rallying cry of *operaismo*, which at the time had just begun to critique the concept of work by refusing to consider it as the defining element of human life. If the official Marxist Left had long assumed that what makes work alienating is capitalist exploitation, *operaismo* asserted that the prime cause of alienation is, rather, the reduction of life to work tout court. Both Pasolini and the exponents of the movements of *operaismo* asserted — each in their different ways — that the fatal mistake of the official Marxist Left had been to misrecognize the actualization of labor power as work or, more precisely, to mistake what was a specifically capitalist actualization of the universal potential for production as its only possible and necessary actualization. While work can constitute only the capitalist exploitation of labor power — regardless of whoever happens to own the means of production, workers included — labor power not only does not find its necessary telos and does not fulfill its inevitable destiny in and as work but also harbors within itself a revolutionary force that does not necessarily pass through and finds expression through its actualization as work. It is also in this sense that one ought to understand Pasolini's ambivalence in 'The Ashes of Gramsci', in which, as you will recall, the narrator had spoken to Gramsci thus:

> And in this country where your passion never
>   rested, I feel at once how wrong | —here, in the quiet of these graves—and | how right—in our disquieting
>   fate—you were, as you drafted your supreme | pages in the days of your murder.

At once 'right' in his insistence on the centrality of the Southern Question for any revolutionary project and 'wrong' in his idealist faith in the emancipating power of modernization, Gramsci constitutes for Pasolini that inescapable and irresistible 'humble brother' who at one and the same time must be mourned — that is, worked through — and yet never fully left behind, given that his passion continues to fuel what Pasolini, in his melancholy lyricism, identifies as his own 'desperate | passion of being in the world'.[36]

But where is Algeria in all this? Immediately after those verses in which Pasolini voices his skepticism with respect to modernization and his critique of the coopted unionist projects of the industrial working class, the son of the first line of the poem suddenly returns, and a radically different political development begins to be envisioned. These verses are written, once again, in the form of a direct address to the Milanese worker:

> Ah, but the son knows: the grace of knowledge is a wind that changes | direction in the middle of the sky. Now it blows perhaps from Africa and | you, listen to what the son knows by grace. (If he doesn't smile | that's because hope for him | wasn't light but rationality. | And may the light of Africa's | sentiment, that suddenly sweeps | across Calabria, be a sign | without meaning, | valid for future times!) That's it: | you shall stop struggling | for your wages | and you shall put weapons | in the hands of Calabrians.[37]

A wind of change blows from Africa and sweeps across Calabria. The ongoing Third World struggles for decolonization are posited here as an exemplary political lesson: emancipation and liberation — Pasolini seems to be saying — can only be achieved through armed revolutionary struggle rather than through easily cooptable unionist bargaining over wages. Whereas the Calabrian son already knows this lesson 'by grace', the Milanese factory worker needs to learn such a lesson from scratch by listening with humility to the voice of the African wind — the voice of grace. But what does it mean to know 'by grace'? It means to know always already. It means immediately to recognize something as resonating with your own history. As it is so often the case in Pasolini, transcendent diction and religious iconography are turned into vehicles for profoundly materialist historical insights (think, for example, of the Leninist Christ of *The Gospel According to St. Matthew*, which Pasolini filmed only two years after writing these verses). Knowledge "by grace" constitutes here a resonance — or, perhaps, what Charles Baudelaire might have called a *correspondence* — in the sense that the Third World struggles for decolonization cannot but resonate here with the long and bloody history of southern Italian peasant uprisings in the face of premodern feudal oppression and of modern capitalist colonial exploitation alike. The

---

36 Pasolini, 'Ashes of Gramsci', p. 17.
37 Pasolini, 'Profezia', p. 96.

African wind — Pasolini seems to be saying — will resuscitate an ancient history of resistance and insurrection.

In the wake of the wind of grace that blows from Africa, however, something else also sweeps through the Italian South. Towards the end of Pasolini's 'Prophecy', we read:

> Blue-Eyed Alí | one of the many sons of sons | shall come down from Algiers, on sailships | and oared ships. Thousands of men | with emaciated bodies | and with poor dog eyes like their fathers | shall be with him on boats launched from the Kingdoms of Hunger. | They shall take along with them their children, and bread and cheese, in yellow Easter Monday paper. They shall take along with them their | grandmothers and their donkeys, on the triremes stolen from the colonial ports. | They shall land in Crotone or in Palmi [towns on the Calabrian coast], | by the millions, dressed in Asiatic | rags, and in American shirts. | Calabrians immediately shall say, | as rascals to rascals: | 'Here they are, the old brothers, | with their sons, and bread and cheese!'
>
> From Crotone or Palmi they shall go up | to Naples, and from there to Barcelona | to Salonika and to Marseille, | into the Cities of Crime. | Souls and angels, mice and lice, | with the germ of Ancient History | they shall fly before the wilayat.
>
> [...] renouncing the honesty | of peasant religions, | forgetting the honor | of the underworld, | betraying the purity | of barbarian peoples, | marching behind their Blue-Eyed | Alís, they shall come out from underneath the earth to loot — they | shall come up from the bottom of the sea to kill, — they shall come | down from the heights of the sky to expropriate, — and to teach the | joy of life to their comrades the factory workers | and to teach the joy of freedom | to the bourgeoisie | and to teach the joy of death to all Christians | — they shall destroy Rome | and they shall lay the germ | of Ancient History | on its ruins. | And then — with the Pope and | with every sacrament — | they shall go like gypsies | up to the West and to the North | with Trotsky's red flags | waving in the wind [...].[38]

Much could be said about these delirious verses (which, incidentally, anticipated by three decades as well as inspired Kathy Acker's just as delirious vision of a postrevolutionary Paris destroyed, invaded, and run by Algerian cyborgs in her novel *Empire of the Senseless*). Rather than embarking on a detailed exegesis, I would like simply to draw attention to the way in which Calabrians here greet such an apocalyptic invasion: "'Here they are, the old brothers'". Speaking 'as rascals to rascals', Calabrians seem to be saying not only that the arrival of this ragtag Trotskyite army from the Algerian shores had been long awaited but also that such an arrival

---

38   Ibid., pp. 97, 99.

constitutes nothing short of a family reunion. If in 'The Ashes of Gramsci' the global South in revolt could be heard in the sounds of the Italian South at work, here the Italian South has been turned into the gateway for a global southern invasion of the North, into the springboard for a revolutionary leap into the North. In both cases, these old southern brothers all share in what Pasolini twice here refers to as an 'Ancient History' — which is posited here as the condition of possibility for such revolutionary leaps and invasions. In 'Prophecy', Pasolini imagines and articulates the southern answer to the southern question: Southerners of the World — Unite!

Orientalist? Eurocentric? Utopian? Naïve? Yes, sure. And, yet, the fact that this prophecy did not come to pass does not take anything away from its power. In resituating and rereading Pasolini in the context of the revolutionary historical conjuncture of the 1950s and 1960s — when a transnational universalism was being articulated across both the First World and the Third World — I have attempted to suggest that if we stand to learn anything at all from past history, we stand to learn not from what actually happened but from what could have happened and never did, from what could have been and never was. Pasolini delivers us to a delirium of history. His 'passion of being in the world' expresses the unspent energies and potentials of that impossible history that makes anything at all possible once again.

Luca Caminati
PASOLINI'S SOUTHWARD QUEST(ION)[1]

The revolutionary fervor that animated many Third-Worldist European intellectuals during the years of decolonization is well captured by Pier Paolo Pasolini in one of his poems, *Profezia* (Prophecy), dedicated to Jean-Paul Sartre:

> [...] *Alì dagli occhi Azzurri | uno dei tanti figli di figli, | scenderà da Algeri, su navi | a vela e a remi. Saranno | con lui migliaia di uomini | coi corpicini e gli occhi | di poveri cani dei padri | sulle barche varate nei Regni della Fame. Porteranno con sé i bambini, | e il pane e il formaggio, nelle carte gialle del Lunedì di Pasqua. | Porteranno le nonne e gli asini, sulle triremi rubate ai porti coloniali. | Sbarcheranno a Crotone o a Palmi, | a milioni, vestiti di stracci, | asiatici, e di camice americane. | Subito i Calabresi diranno, | come malandrini a malandrini: | 'Ecco i vecchi fratelli, | coi figli e il pane e formaggio!' | Da Crotone o Palmi saliranno | a Napoli, e da lì a Barcellona, | a Salonicco e a Marsiglia, | nelle Città della Malavita. [...] | Poi col Papa e ogni sacramento | andranno su come zingari | verso nord-ovest | con le bandiere rosse | di Trotzky al vento* [...].

> [...] Alì Blue Eyes | one of the many sons of the sons, | will make his way from Algiers, on ships | with sails and with oars. With him | thousands of men | with the bodies and eyes | of the lowly dogs of the fathers | on boats launched in the Kingdom of Famine. With them they will bring the children | and bread and cheese, wrapped in yellow Easter Monday sheets. | They will bring with them grandmas and donkeys, on triremes stolen from colonial ports. | They will land at Crotone or Palmi | in millions, dressed in Asian / rags, and American shirts. | The people of Calabria will say, | scoundrels to those scoundrels: | 'Here are our elderly brothers, | with their children and bread and cheese!' | From Crotone or Palmi they will travel up | to Naples, and from there to Barcelona, | to Thessaloniki and to Marseille, | in the Cities of the Underworld

---

1 An earlier shorter version of this article was published as 'Pasolini's Southward Quest(ion)', *Estetica: Studi e ricerche*, 2 (2017), 273–92.

[...] | Then with the Pope and the sacraments | they will travel like gypsies | to the Northwest | with the red flags | of Trotsky in the wind [...][2]

Several years later, that same sentiment was concisely articulated by Pasolini in an interview, even though Lenin had now taken Trotsky's spot on the flag, as he fine-tuned his pitch towards Third-World issues: 'Years ago I dreamt of the peasants coming up from Africa with a Lenin flag, taking up the Calabrians and marching West together.'[3] While from today's historical distance this statement sounds naïve — perhaps at best charming, but certainly historically short-sighted — it helps capture the structure of feeling of this specific ideological configuration. It shows, first and foremost, the persistently profound Hegelian logic at play in discourses surrounding liberation movements and international solidarity as read through a Marxist lens, and a belief in dialectics — or at least, a dialectical movement which, in the case of Pasolini, involved a geographical border-crossing. But, *Zeit* moved differently, as we know, and the red of the Lenin flag was replaced by orange, the color of the migrants' life vests, crossing the Mediterranean at great personal peril, welcomed not by friendly Calabrian peasants but by soldiers, cops, camps, and general hostility. This new 'postcolonial condition', as defined by Sandro Mezzadra,[4] has placed not the capital, the worker, or the peasant (as envisioned by Marxist thought), but the sea, the border, the body, and the crossing at the center of twenty-first century struggles, as paradoxically foreshadowed by Pasolini. These are the new 'permanently temporary zones' of mass migrations, as defined by Federico Rahola in his eponymous volume, where the camp has become a structuring model for control.[5] These new areas of international lawlessness can be read as iconic mirror images of the failure of the political vision of Pasolini, who, along with so many others, believed in a non-bipolar world order and the revolutionary potential of liberation struggles. If his dream has now been turned into a nightmare, reconstructing Pasolini's geopolitical stance from a contemporary vantage point can help us capture that multifaceted constellation clustered around Southern Italian thought,

---

2   Pier Paolo Pasolini, 'Profezia', in *Parallel Texts: Words Reflected*, trans. by Matilda Colarossi <https://paralleltexts.blog/2015/09/26/profeziaprophecy-by-pier-paolo-pasolini/> [accessed 28 September 2021].
3   Pier Paolo Pasolini, *Saggi sulla politica e sulla società* (Milan: Mondadori, 1999), p. 1638. [*Translation mine*]
4   Sandro Mezzadra, *La condizione postcoloniale* (Verona: Ombre Corte, 2008).
5   Federico Rahola, *Zone definitivamente temporanee: I luoghi dell'umanità in eccesso* (Verona: Ombre Corte, 2003).

international Marxist solidarity, and what we might call transnational revolutionary universalism, or, using the apt definition coined by Sohail Daulatzai, 'Bandung Humanism'.[6] In doing so, we might come to terms with both the lost potentialities of Pasolini's thought and its overdetermined historical limitations.

Notes from a Fanonian

It has become a sort of ideological pastime in leftist groups to imagine in a future-anterior mode what Pasolini would have said about some contemporary event or other, in order to enlist him as a comrade in contemporary quarrels. In turn, Pasolini has been dressed as a non-global protester, an environmental activist, a gay rights icon, and so on. This desire to taxonomize Pasolini testifies to the great impact that his work and thought had, and still has, on Italian — and more generally, left-wing — global culture. And yet, once we drop the activist zeal that might blind our judgement and attempt to look at Pasolini's theory and practice vis-à-vis politics and society, what emerges is a fascinatingly non-conformist approach. This is particularly the case with Pasolini's own version of *terzomondismo* (Third-Worldism) and geopolitics, which I elsewhere define as 'heretical orientalism'.[7] The transnational message of *Profezia*, quoted earlier, may smell of pinky kumbaya to a contemporary reader, but in 1964 it was seen as true ideological and political heresy and a decisive departure from the ambivalent position of the PCI (The Italian Communist Party) on issues that threatened to disrupt the bipolar world order that resulted from the Cold War. The PCI in the '60s was largely in line with USSR directives on geopolitics and issues of decolonization, such that post-colonial self-determination and the Non-Aligned Movement became particularly disruptive for the Party.[8] However, despite their lukewarm reception by the hegemony of the Communist establishment, Third-Worldist thinkers like Frantz Fanon were being translated and disseminated in the Italian context, and their works were translated so as to promote the idea that it is the anti-colonial struggle that should constitute the model of political action for Italian intellectuals. As Neelam Srivastava underscores, Fanon

---

6   Sohail Daulatzai, *Fifty Years of* The Battle of Algiers (Minneapolis: Minnesota University Press, 2016).
7   Luca Caminati, *Orientalismo eretico* (Milan: Bruno Mondadori, 2007).
8   Marco Galeazzi, *Il PCI e il movimento dei paesi non allineati (1955–1975)* (Milan: Franco Angeli, 2011).

was speedily introduced into the Italian cultural scene: the first translation appeared as early as 1959, and each of his subsequent volumes were released soon thereafter by the publishing company Feltrinelli, thanks to the curatorial work of Giovanni Pirelli.[9] Poet and Marxist activist Giovanni Giudici published a much-discussed essay on Fanon in 1963 through *Quaderni piacentini*, the countercultural magazine whose editorial board aligned itself with anti-imperialist struggle. Giudici's reading of Fanon, is, I believe, essential to understanding the vicissitudes of Italian Fanonism in general, and Pasolini's engagement with the Martinique-born Algerian revolutionary in particular. For example, Giudici was eager to normalize Fanon as part of the 'global battle always already in place to bring about the discovery and liberation of man'. Giudici disavowed the so-called 'myth of *négritude*', only to proclaim that the specificity of African violence was due to the 'tribal condition of living',[10] a phrase that betrays its own racial politics. Following the analysis in *Culture and Imperialism* by Edward Said of Jean Genet's role in the nascent postcolonial movement,[11] I would suggest that Pasolini needs to be reconsidered as an integral part of the literature of decolonization, inspired by Aimé Césaire, Edouard Glissant, and Frantz Fanon, alongside Jean Genet, Jean-Paul Sartre, and the other European Marxists working throughout the 1950s–1960s to articulate a form of transnational revolutionary universalism. This move would help solidify an early link between the anticolonial struggle and European leftists' intellectual movements. What is revealing in both Giudici's and Pasolini's readings of Fanon, is this understanding of the Third-World struggle beyond the notion of identity, detached from local specificities of, above all, race. This rereading was in part inspired by Fanon himself, who, in his attempt to move beyond the strict notion of *négritude* as conceived by Aimé Césaire, promoted a different notion of the role of the black man in the liberation struggle.[12] Such a position — dialectically subverting

---

9 Neelam Srivastava, 'Frantz Fanon in Italy', *Interventions*, 17, 3 (2015), 309–28 (p. 310), and Rachel E. Love, 'Anti-fascism, Anticolonialism and Anti-self: The Life of Giovanni Pirelli and the Work of the Centro Frantz Fanon', *Interventions*, 17, 3 (2015), 343–59.

10 Giovanni Giudici, 'L'uomo dalla rucola', in *Prima e dopo il '68: Antologia dei Quaderni piacentini*, ed. by Goffredo Fofi and Vittorio Giacopini (Rome: Minimum Fax, 1998), pp. 147–52 (p. 149).

11 Edward Said, *Culture and Imperialism* (New York: Vintage Publishing, 1994), pp. 185, 317.

12 The *négritude* movement sought to define itself in terms of cultural, racial, and historical ties to the African continent as a rejection of French colonial political hegemony and of French cultural, intellectual, racial, and moral domination. Aimé

the role of race and national culture as constitutive of the post-colonial struggle — allowed for Italian intellectuals to re-inscribe themselves into this process. It does not come as a surprise, then, that in 1968, in the 'Apologia' of his poem *Il PCI ai giovani* (*Poem to Young Communist Students*), Pasolini provocatively defined himself as a Fanonian Marcusian intellectual ('intelletualli marcusiani e fanoniani, me compreso').[13] To call oneself *fanoniano* was a political and rhetorical gesture of rebellion and amounted to joining the ranks of many other young Turks of the *sinistra extraparlamentare* (extra-parliamentary left), the radical leftist groups opposed to the Communist Party who coalesced around the 1968 student movement during that time.[14]

Southward

Pasolini's commitment to Fanon, however, needs to be explored not entirely on its own terms but in relation to his engagement with the ideas of Antonio Gramsci, and — equally importantly, although less widely known — with those of Ernesto De Martino. I will argue here that it was Gramsci and De Martino who acted as mediators in Pasolini's appropriation of Fanon's theoretical corpus. Pasolini's relationship with Gramsci's life and works has been investigated at length in prior scholarship,[15] and Pasolini's own debt to him was made public in his poetry collection entitled *Gramsci's Ashes* (1957). It is as a result of Gramsci that Pasolini understood the revolutionary value of the sub-proletarians and the role of counterhegemonic cultural interventions, both of which form the true

---

Césaire and his contemporaries considered the shared black heritage of members of the African diaspora as a source of power and self-worth for those oppressed by the physical and psychological violence of the colonial project. In arguing for Pasolini's role in the movement of decolonization, I am following a reading of Fanon already put forth by Said in *Culture and Imperialism*, where he detects the influence of György Lukács's *History and Class Consciousness* on Fanon's thinking, therefore justifying the contemporary reading of a 'postcolonial Fanon' as already present in Fanon's own writings (Said, p. 12).

13 Pier Paolo Pasolini, *Saggi sulla letteratura e sull'arte* (Milan: Mondadori, 1999), p. 1450.
14 Srivastava, pp. 309–28.
15 Zygmunt Baranski, 'Pier Paolo Pasolini: Culture, Croce, Gramsci', in *Culture and Conflict in Postwar Italy*, ed. by Zygmunt Baranski and Robert Lumley (Basingstoke: Macmillan, 1990), pp. 139–59; and Wallace P. Sillanpoa, 'Pasolini's Gramsci', *MLN*, 96, 1 (1981), 120–21.

backbone of his political activism. Moreover, it is Gramsci's meditation on the organic intellectual that informed Pasolini's own role as an *engagé* artist. But Pasolini's profound intellectual debt to Ernesto De Martino is probably less well known. De Martino had been working since the 1930s on different ethnographies of Southern Italian peasants. With a keen interest in ancient religious practices, De Martino was among the first to make active use of so-called new media (photography, phonography, film) to document his fieldwork. The recent translation into English of his canonical *Sud e Magia* (1959) as *Magic: A Theory from the South*, which focuses on the southern region of Basilicata, allows us to fully understand the profoundly modern conceptualizations offered by De Martino, who was moving away from the evolutionist framework that was in vogue at the time as well as from racially based readings of marginal cultures.[16] While there is only one recorded instance of the two men meeting (in Crotone in 1959), it is clear that Pasolini knew and read De Martino's work. Pasolini's encounter with De Martino's very peculiar and innovative form of anthropology took place during his early work as a gun-for-hire in the Roman film industry, where he contributed to anthropological films by Cecilia Mangini, a young and fearless documentary ethnographer influenced by De Martino. Pasolini worked on three of her first films: *Ignoti alla città* (1958), *Stendalì* (1960), and *La canta delle marane* (1952). *Stendalì* stands out because Pasolini helped solve a problem typical of early ethnographic cinema: sound. Mangini did not film with a proper sound camera (unthinkable in our digital age), a decision which left her with beautiful but silent images of funerary rites from Puglia (inspired by De Martino's *Morte e pianto rituale nel mondo antico* (1958)). Pasolini composed a litany for her footage, sampling lines based on Greek tragedies, to be later performed on the soundtrack. This sonoric approach was a particularly apt encapsulation of Mangini's own artistic method. Her films, rather than attempting to serve as an objective record, were closer to Jean Rouch's cine-ethnographies: highly mediated reconstructions of actual events, more like docu-dramas or docu-fictions than the earlier scientific models of ethnographic visual accounts. As Maraschin details, this schooling in anthropological work has been systematically neglected in scholarship on Pasolini, in an attempt to highlight how his work resonates directly with the European New Wave modernism rather than the kind of ethno-documentary strand represented

---

16 Ernesto De Martino, *Magic: A Theory from the South* (Chicago: Hau Books, 2015).

by the likes of Rouch.[17] Rather than being a sign of his adherence to the aesthetic experimentations of the New Cinemas, it was probably the Roman anthropological circles that inspired Pasolini to mix genres and modes of filmmaking.[18] As Cesare Casarino comments, 'for Pasolini, it is precisely as an anachronistic narrative straight out of the archaic substrata of folklore and myth that the history of modernization becomes conceptualizable and representable'.[19] It is also through ethnographic images that this 'archaic substrata' renders itself visible and (re)acquires its revolutionary potential. The same principle is at play for Pasolini, whether the object of the ethnographic gaze is positioned in geographic proximity or at a great remove. It goes without saying that his early contributions to Italian visual ethnography had an impact on his experience of filming in Third-World, or 'Southern', countries (Palestine, Yemen, India, etc.), as cultural sites which pushed Pasolini in new and previously unexplored directions. The discovery of what in the twentieth century we called the Other, the mixing of narrative techniques between fiction and documentary, the investigation of modernity in the living bodies of colonized peoples, and the first phases of the postcolonial era, are all expressed in Pasolini's films through hybrid techniques learned during his field work and subsequent discussions with the filmmakers involved in De Martino's circle.

What we see, as we move chronologically through Pasolini's career, is a clear continuity between his ethnographic archaeology of the revolutionary potential of the *borgate romane*, the exploited southern Italian peasants, and the African liberation movements. This Mediterranean expansion, infused with revolutionary Fanonian ideology, bestows both a continuity with earlier works and a renewed political rigor to Pasolini's 'non-Western' productions. It was at this point, under the influence of both Fanonian and

---

17   Donatella Maraschin, 'Ricerche sul campo nel period 1950–60: Pasolini antropologo', *The Italianist*, 24, 2 (2004), 169–207.
18   Anne-Violaine Houcke, 'Ignoti, banditi, dimenticati: Le (hors-)champ de l'Italie (post-) fasciste', in *Eisenstein, leçons mexicaines: Cinéma, anthropologie, archéologie dans le mouvement des arts*, ed. by Laurence Schifano and Antonio Somaini (Nanterre, Presses Universitaires de Paris Ouest, 2016), pp. 263-278. Other recent in-depth studies by Anne-Violaine Houcke have also pointed out the impact of Mangini's first short, *Ignoti alla città*, which documents the life of *borgatari*, displaced by the gentrification of the Roman city centre. Mangini's style in *Ignoti* is closer to Soviet-style filmmaking, favouring dramatic close-ups and camera movements, which will be fully rejected by the iconoclastic film style of early Pasolini, devoted as it was to de-dramatizing the long shot and close-up.
19   Cesare Casarino, 'The Southern Answer: Pasolini, Universalism, Decolonization', *Critical Inquiry*, 36, 4 (2010), 673–96 (p. 676).

ethnographic theories, that he found an artistic method best suited to his political goals: the essay film.

The Essay Film as Political Form

Film, Pasolini believed, provided a unique and indispensable instrument in the pursuit of anti-capitalist Third-World struggles. Despite the centrality of the archaic for Pasolini's political quest, the battle that was waged while shouldering the faithful Arriflex camera was against that which Pasolini himself dubbed *irrealtà*; the 'unreality' of modernity. What did Pasolini mean by *irrealtà*? Not dissimilarly from what Guy Debord — in that same year, 1967 —called *'la société du spectacle'*, *l'irrealtà* is the neocapitalist world of audiovisual media which permeates every layer of society and culture, and which presents itself as being outside of politics and beyond ideology. It is this condition of *irrealtà* that evidently led the rural world toward an irreversible 'anthropological mutation' which further alienated people and rendered them incapable of meaningful political action. Pasolini's call in *Heretical Empiricism*, 'we must de-ontologize, we must ideologize', was an appeal to battle the unreality of the flattening representation of the (then) nascent 'society of the spectacle', which directly acted on the world of reality. The ideological disengagement from reality triggered by media, urbanization, loss of traditions: to this Pasolini opposed the existing 'reality' of the agricultural and sub-proletarian past, and primitive religious sentiment, which, for him — following Ernesto De Martino's teachings — contained revolutionary potentiality and possessed a particular force in the Third World.[20] Thus, this turn Southward was not an escape but rather a way to reconnect to the archaic past that was still present in a substratum of social and cultural reality, and therefore to give voice to a possible political alterity. Revealing this reality in its many forms (as well as exposing its origins in neocapitalist rhetoric) makes cinema a powerful weapon due to its indexical power, and the open form of the essay film is particularly suited to such a political challenge.

Pasolini's understanding of the essay film resonates with Adorno's notion of the essay as a form that actualizes the negative dialectic, and as such gives voice to the defeated. What Pasolini called a suspended dialectic, a form of permanent contradiction, is a fixed and yet productive dialectic

---

20 Pier Paolo Pasolini, *Heretical Empiricism*, trans. by Ben Lawton and Louise K. Barnett (Washington: New Academia Publishing, 2005), p. 226.

where the two parts live side by side, without sublimation into a synthesis. As Antonio Vázquez-Arroyo explains, Adorno in his 'The Essay as Form' seeks to grasp historical experience by breaking the silences that pervade hegemonic historical narratives and by lending voice to the sufferings of the defeated, in many cases the nameless others sacrificed by the principle of identity inscribed in the idea of progress.[21] This unearthing and restaging of voices is accomplished through constellation, or constellational method. In short, blind spots outside of dialectics become a third space where the permanent contradiction allows for the emergence of unaccounted voices.[22] The essay film became, for Pasolini, a form of suspended dialectic, and his constellational method had the potential to reveal the true reality of our historical condition beneath the placating vision of progress imposed by the mainstream majority of audiovisual media. It is not surprising, then, that Pasolini's engagement with the essay form included quite an extensive list of films, shot throughout his long career. Some are direct responses to the Italian political context, such as the found-footage medium-length *La rabbia* [*Rage*] made in 1963, and *12 dicembre* [*December 12*] from 1972; or the *cinéma vérité*-inflected *Comizi d'amore* [*Love Meetings*] in 1964 (not dissimilar from Jean Rouch and Edgar Morin's *Chronique d'un été* (1960)), a travelogue on love, gender, and sexuality; and the architectural *Pasolini e la forma della città* (*Pasolini and the Form of the City*) from 1975. But it is in Pasolini's 'Third World' essay films that his political commitments to the southward quest(ion) come to the fore.

The Third World

A quick survey of Pasolini's oeuvre demonstrates the crucial role played by Third-World locations. While abroad, Pasolini was inspired to make a variety of works, including two feature films, *Edipo re* [*Oedipus Rex*, 1967] and *Il fiore delle mille e una notte* [*Arabian Nights*, 1974]; as well as the documentaries and medium/short films, *Sopralluoghi in Palestina per il vangelo secondo Matteo* [*Location Scouting in Palestine*, 1963–64], *Appunti per un film sull'India* [*Notes for a Film on India*, 1968], *Appunti per un'Orestiade Africana* [*Notes for an African Oresteia*, 1970], and *Le mura di Sana'a* [*The Walls of Sana'a*, 1971]; and a screenplay for an unrealized

---

21 Antonio Vázquez-Arroyo, 'Universal History Disavowed: On Critical Theory and Postcolonialism', *Postcolonial Studies*, 11, 4 (2008), 451–73 (p. 452).
22 Theodor Adorno, 'The Essay as Form', *New German Critique*, 32 (1984), 151–71 (p. 171).

film, *Il padre selvaggio* [*The Savage Father*, released posthumously in 1975]. In addition to these works, he undertook a large and ambitious unrealized project entitled *Appunti per un poema sul Terzo Mondo* [*Notes for a Poem on the Third World*, 1968], of which the Palestinian, Indian, and African films were to comprise parts.

When Pasolini moved to Rome in 1950 from Friuli, he claimed that it was the 'discovery of the elsewhere' that drove him towards writing his early realist novels, *Ragazzi di vita* [*The Ragazzi*, 1955] and *Una vita violenta* [*A Violent Life*, 1959].[23] This desire for 'elsewhere' became a desire for alterity, in opposition to the 'anthropologically mutated' West. Pasolini attempted to find its antithesis both in hidden pockets within the West itself — which still retain traces of authenticity amidst the ruins of modernity — and in countries beyond Europe that were struggling to free themselves from colonial bonds. Like few others, Pasolini saw the need for a radical alternative to the neocapitalist Western model, a need which required an acceptance of a profound alterity, of which he felt himself to be, in many ways, the actualization.[24] Pasolini was a communist expelled from the party, a homosexual unaffiliated with the gay movement, and a polemicist against both the mainstream and the alternative niches of Italian culture. This engagement with the Third World moves beyond both a naïve orientalist vision of the East and the classical Marxist position on the revolutionary potential of the 'underdeveloped peoples'. Rather, I suggest, Pasolini promotes a radical *terzomondista* attitude rather new for the Italian intellectual circles of the time, and his essay films dealing with this subject are perhaps the clearest manifestation of his unique political vision.

The Appunti *Experiment*

Pasolini's first experiment with what would become a new way of making films — a combination of voiceover narration, non-fictional documentation, choreographed re-enactments, impromptu musical adaptation, and everything else that went under the hodgepodge heading of *Appunti* (*Notes*) — was carried out during his first trip to Palestine in 1964. Pasolini was in Palestine location scouting for *Il Vangelo secondo Matteo* [*The Gospel According to Matthew*, 1964] from June 27 to July 11, 1963, and was accompanied by a cameraman, a small crew, and two

---

23 Tommaso Anzoino, *Pier Paolo Pasolini* (Florence: La Nuova Italia, 1974), p. 2.
24 Casarino, p. 680.

priests from *Pro Civitate Christiana*, a post-Vatican II religious association based in Assisi.²⁵ The trip was undertaken as an excuse to travel through the Middle East rather than to secure locations, given that at this point Pasolini had already decided to shoot his film in Matera in Southern Italy. After returning to Rome, Pasolini edited the material, adding his own off-screen voice and creating a travel diary that included conversations recorded during the trip. *Sopralluoghi in Palestina per il Vangelo secondo Matteo* focuses centrally upon Pasolini's ruminations that the modernity of the Palestinian landscape did not end up lending itself to the film. The political and intellectual import of the progressive Christian group to this project should also not be underestimated: Third-Worldist agendas deeply implicated certain fringe groups of European Catholics in the liberation movement.²⁶ In fact, we could say that it was precisely in these small circles, which were emerging all over Latin America, that a dialogue was created between liberation theology and other radical political movements within Catholicism. The ideological openness brought about by Vatican II created an ideological gap where the bipolar Cold War order could truly be challenged.

Several years later, Pasolini developed a project for a full-length film that would have been entitled *Appunti per un Poema sul Terzo Mondo* [*Notes for a Poem on the Third World*, 1968] — made up of five episodes from the 'Notes' series — which was to be filmed in India, Africa, several Arab countries, Latin America, and the black ghettoes of the United States. In this unrealized project, we can finally see the large sweep of solidarity that this film would entail:

> The feeling of the film will be violently and even foolhardily revolutionary: as though to make the film itself a revolutionary action (not related to any political party, of course, and absolutely independent) [...] The immense quantity of practical, ideological, sociological, and political material that goes into constructing such a film objectively prevents the manufacture of a normal film. This film will thus follow the formula: 'A film on a film to be made' [...]. Each episode will be composed of a story, narrated with a summary and told through the most salient and dramatic scenes and the preparatory sequences for the story itself (interviews, investigations, documentaries, etc.) [...]. Stylistically, the film will be composite, complex, and spurious, but the

---

25 Tomaso Subini, 'Pasolini e la Pro Civitate Christiana: Un carteggio inedito', *Bianco & Nero*, 1–3 (2003), 253–62.
26 Ibid.

stark clarity of the problems treated and its function as a direct revolutionary intervention will simplify it.[27]

Resonating with experimental literary forms such as Umberto Eco's *Opera aperta*, Pasolini developed a notion of *da farsi* [to be done, or, to be completed] which was related to the necessity of creating a work with a fluid and open-ended structure that reflected the Marxist socio-political vision of the *da farsi* society: the political work of art must be completed by the audience, in the same way as citizens must fill the void of formal democracies. This notion of Marxist praxis resonated with the situation in many African countries in the 1960s that were transitioning to forms of democratic-socialist governance. The self-reflexivity of the 'Notes' genre, with its embrace of the unfinished form, is exemplary of an aesthetic in which the artist's tyrannical authority is renounced, opening spaces for new configurations, to use Rancière's terminology, and in so doing, challenging the traditional hierarchies and stable assumptions regarding the relationship between the filmmaker and his subjects, and his viewers.[28] Thus, we do not have a series of documentaries *on* a place (Africa, India, Palestine, Sana'a), but a film on a film *for* a place (Africa, etc.), where the film intervenes within a larger debate and calls for immediate action by gesturing toward a potential international solidarity. Thus, only through such an aesthetic approach could we make sense of the 'direct revolutionary intervention' that Pasolini suggests is the basis for his *Notes for a Poem on the Third World* project—transforming his own works from orientalist narratives into open artistic and political experiences, both cinematically and philosophically.

Can the Gramscian Speak?

Although *Notes for a Poem on the Third World* never reached its final realization, from its fragments we can come to understand Pasolini's idea of what postcolonial essay filmmaking would and could be. In clarifying this term, I distance myself from Rascaroli, who claims that the inherent postmodern nature of the essay film is a product of the phenomenon of the

---

27   Michelle Mancini and Giuseppe Perrella, *Pier Paolo Pasolini, corpi e luoghi* (Rome: Theorema, 1981), p. 7. [*Translation mine*]
28   Jacques Rancière, *The Emancipated Spectator* (New York: Verso Books, 2009), p. 18.

diminishing of authority found in and promoted by postmodern discourse,[29] as well as being a product of the 'waning of objectivity as a compelling social narrative' that postmodernity generated.[30] While this may be true for a certain kind of 'personal cinema' privileged by Rascaroli (embodied through the works of Agnès Varda, Jonas Mekas, etc.), the political brand of Pasolini's experimentations was forged in the ideological battles of the literary circles of post-war Italian Marxist culture. This culture was in turn moulded through the dialectical relationship between the powerful influence of the Lukacsian imperatives that provided the Italian Communist Party with its blueprint for a non-Stalinist aesthetic, and the alternative Brechtian framework that was drawn upon by the artistic and literary avant-garde of the late '50s (including both the literary experimentalism of *Gruppo 63* and *arte povera* political modernism), and, more importantly, the new decolonial and postcolonial theories of non-Western theorists. For all of them, the objective reality of political and economic oppression and the resulting emancipatory struggles were never in question. What was debated, instead, was the position and political responsibility of the artist and the intellectual in these struggles; the destabilization of authorial power in the essay film reflected for figures like Pasolini the moral dilemmas involved in filming the Other. In line with works of contemporary television *vérité*, such as the French activist René Vautier[31] or the Swiss Gilberto Bovay,[32] I find the 'Notes' films exciting in the way that their status as both films and political interventions is never fully fixed in place by the participation of the people whose subjectivity is, quite literally, at stake. While a desire to reach out and understand the social issues at play is evident, the style and construction of these *Appunti* obscure and complicate our experience of encountering their subjects. Thus, it is not a surprise if many perceive this speaking through as a 'speaking for' — to evoke Gayatri Spivak's political essay 'Can the Subaltern Speak?' — and therefore as a loss of agency on the part of the subjects Pasolini sought to bring to the screen.[33] However,

---

29 Laura Rascaroli, *The Personal Camera: Subjective Camera and the Essay Film* (London and New York: Wallflower, 2009), p. 14.
30 Michael Renov, *The Subject of Documentary* (Minneapolis: University of Minnesota Press, 2004), p. xvii.
31 Matthew Croombs, 'Questions of Militant Cinema: René Vautier and the Anti-Colonial Combat Film', *Institute of African Studies, Toronto* (2014).
32 Giulio Latini, *L'energia e lo sguardo: Il cinema dell'Eni e i documentari di Gilbert Bovay* (Rome: Donzelli, 2011).
33 Gayatri Spivak, 'Can the Subaltern Speak?', in *Marxism and the Interpretation of Culture*, ed. by Cary Nelson (Champaign: University of Illinois Press, 1998), pp. 271–316.

what I would like to suggest here is that rather than simply ventriloquizing the post-colonial Other, Pasolini's method anticipated theoretical insights later proposed by the anthropologist James Clifford in *The Predicament of Culture*. Clifford, in his seminal study, attacks both the superficiality of liberal thought — fighting globalization by preserving indigenous cultures in a (failed) attempt to recreate 'artificial aesthetic purifications'[34] — and the orthodox Marxist position which sees local realties and traditions as obstacles on the road to progress (such, for example, is Moravia's stance on the socioeconomic immobility of India which informs his *Un'idea dell'India* [*The Idea of India*], published in 1962). Clifford was not concerned with reserving 'endangered authenticities' but instead with 'mak[ing] space for specific paths through modernity', a new 'inventive poetics of reality' which insist that 'the time is past when privileged authorities could routinely "give voice" (or history) to others without fear of contradiction'.[35] If we can free ourselves from the nineteenth-century notion of culture as an occidental progress, Clifford argues that we can rethink the concept of ethnography as 'writing about culture from the standpoint of participant observation'.[36] At first sight, Clifford's position potentially leads to accusations against Pasolini's global excursions as examples of precisely this traditional notion of ethnography, particularly when considering Pasolini's attempts to impose the forms of ancient Greece upon nascent African democracies in the *Oresteia*, the anything-but-apologetic use of Western visual models in the search for characters in *Notes on a Film about India*, or the use of exotic nudes in *Arabian Nights*. However, the analysis of Pasolini's 'Notes' as an essay film with the revolutionary and experimental valences described above reveals not only the self-consciousness of his own Western ideological trespassing, but also an entirely different goal for the representation of 'the natives'. Unlike the desire to represent other cultures for the orientalist scopophilia of the European spectator, or the desire to understand and translate such knowledge into Western terms, an impetus which typically drives traditional colonial ethnography, Pasolini's works are weapons to be waged in the battles which were taking place in Pasolini's own Italy. His postcolonial thrust developed into a combination of visual experimentalism and comparative anthropology that sought to didactically produce continuous dialectical images with connections to Italy, in such a way as to give points of reference to the Italian spectator, helping to produce

---

34 James Clifford, *The Predicament of Culture* (Cambridge: Harvard University Press, 1988), p. 4.
35 Ibid., p. 5.
36 Ibid., p. 9.

new counter-hegemonic political readings. This only became possible through his experimentation with new visual and narrative techniques that explicitly broke with the modes of ethnographic representation that were honed in the nineteenth century. In this sense, Pasolini's filming style was certainly in dialogue with both Gramsci's notion of counter-hegemony and De Martino's atypical anthropological approach, with the essay film form allowing for artistic openness and co-presences through repeated layering of images, quotations, and multiple temporalities, connecting the archaic with the ultramodern.

Such multiple temporalities are further amplified and made visible when we look at the way Pasolini has been appropriated in more contemporary artistic productions, especially those originating beyond Europe. Malini Guha, in her analysis of the shift from the vision of Empire to the vision of the world in British and French cinema, points to a key text by Homi Bhabha, 'Notes on Globalization and Ambivalence', where he identifies the time of globalization as the 'anxious and impossible temporality, the past-present'.[37] The 'past-present' is the time of the colony, which reappears in every attempt of erasure. It is also the time of the 'great cultural archive' as identified by Edward Said in *Culture and Imperialism*, where the 'rich cultural documents' of the encounter between East and West, periphery and metropole, colonized and colonizer, are continuously reanimated. The reworking of Pasolini's documentaries in Africa and Asia similarly presents an ambitious attempt to negotiate the aesthetic ideologies of the post-war European art cinema with the more radical currents of a postcolonial ethos forged in the heat of armed resistance to the West. As such, these reworkings highlight with particular force the complexities and limitations of Pasolini's original engagement with the Third World, and the legacy of that historical moment within contemporary culture.

I would like to conclude this essay by examining contemporary responses to Pasolini's Third-Worldist works, *Waiting for Pasolini* (2007), directed by Daoud Aoula-Syad and produced by Abderrahmane Sissako, and a short experimental film by Ayreen Anastas, *Pasolini Pa* Palestine* (2005), each of which directly address the issue at the core of the 'past-present'. In addition, I will place these works against the grain of Pasolini's own documentaries with the goal of exposing Pasolini's afterlife. *Waiting for Pasolini* is a fictional account which nonetheless offers a well-informed

---

37   Homi Bhabha, 'Notes on Globalization and Ambivalence', in *Cultural Politics in a Global Age: Uncertainty, Solidarity, and Innovation*, ed. by David Held and Henrietta L. Moore (Oxford: Oneworld Publications, 2008), pp. 36–47 (p. 38).

glimpse into real issues of labour and the impact of Western filmmakers on non-Western countries. *PP*P* rethinks Pasolini's documentary *Sopralluoghi in Palestina* (Location Scouting in Palestine), translating its script into Arabic and using his film survey and location scouting as a map for exploring contemporary Palestine. Both films are important in so far as they allow us to focus on the modalities of production, reception, and dissemination of Western cultural products of *tiermondiste* narratives and to assess their role on a more global and contemporary scale.

Pasolini Pa* Palestine engages with Pasolini's Third World essay films — in particular *Sopralluoghi* — on the level of both form and content. Sponsored by the Al-Ma'mal foundation for Contemporary Art in Jerusalem, this medium-length film opens with a female voiceover asking, 'Should we start?'. The images of Pasolini's film, with French subtitles, are projected over the map of Israel/Palestine, prepared by the artist in her attempt to follow (quite literally) in Pasolini's footsteps as she retraced the route that he took during the production of his film in 1962, as a way of 'visiting [its] places and the ideas', as the voiceover clearly states. The film's opening superimposition, the celluloid projection of Pasolini's film and the map with the highlighted path, creates the first 'past-present' temporal disjunction of the film. Built through a dialogue with five voices — three males (Pasolini, Don Andrea, and the Voice) and two females (the director and the assistant director) — the first scene sets the tone for the film, which begins with Pasolini and Don Carraro looking at a peasant separating wheat from the chaff. The scene is repeated until the voice of the artist interrupts the joyful reconstruction of events, and a split screen appears.

The female voiceover demands that temporal continuity be respected and asks to jump to the actual location in Bethlehem where the movie starts, even though logically this moment would occur at the end of the trip. These sudden breaks in the narrative punctuate the film in order to point out its mistakes and inaccuracies, as well as more generally to mock the teleology of the foreigner who arrived with the intention of superimposing a fundamentally Western narrative upon Palestine. This female voice calls for 'music!' as they ascend Mount Thabor by car and visit the Basilica, as Bach's Passion (a Pasolini staple!) blasts. This Brechtian-infused rewriting of Pasolini, blending issues of gender and geopolitics not addressed in the original film, opens a dialectical relationship with the original, placing Pasolini's own teleological vision of the world in dialogue with a contemporary perspective. The superimposition and split screen used by Anastas are in fact visual citations borrowed from Pasolini's own non-fiction *Appunti* playbook. One could remember the forceful incipit of *African Orestes*, which opens with a profilmic split screen of sorts, with the Italian translation of Euripides on one side and a map of Africa on the other.

The profilmic split screen is followed by a *mise-en-abyme* moment, where we see Pasolini himself holding the camera in a shop window in Dar el Salem, Tanzania. This instant of physical insertion of the filmmaker has been read as a 'personal camera' moment (following, once again, Rascaroli's definition). Following this logic, the insertion of the author in the narrative could be read post-colonially as a superimposition of the Western narrator, and the Western narrative onto the colonial space.

The superimposition is at the heart of Pasolini's own art-making, so much so that his only intervention into the art world was a performance piece he participated in that debuted just few months before his untimely death. This piece, entitled *Intellettuale (Il Vangelo di/su Pasolini)* [*Intellectual (the Gospel by/on Pasolini)*], was created by Fabio Mauri and documented by Antonio Masotti, in May 1975 at GAM in Bologna. The performance was based on Pasolini's physical presence in the museum space as both a medium and object of art: in this piece, the actual film *Gospel According to Saint Matthew* (1964) was projected on its author's white shirt as he was seated at the centre of an otherwise unfurnished room. The Mauri/Pasolini performance spoke directly to the entire corpus of Pasolini's themes and concerns: body, realism, representation, etc. What has often been overlooked in this piece is the fact that what we see is also a superimposition of places: first, Bologna, a breeding ground for young intellectuals; Matera/Palestine, the real and unreal place of the film itself, its physical and symbolic location; and then Pasolini's own body, which a few months later would lay 'in state' on the beach of Ostia in the horrific ANSA images that were printed on every newspaper's first page across Italy.

In *Pasolini Pa* Palestine* the filmmaker is fully aware of the powerful self-inscribing incipit of the *Orestes*, as she re-enacts the opening sequence of the film in front of the shopping window.

However, in this film the male voiceover also mocks Pasolini by appropriating his voice. One of the male voiceover narrators claims: 'After 40 years, I am making the same mistakes', as the image of Anastas appears on screen, this time in colour, asking herself the same question Pasolini asked himself then: 'To film what?'

While *Pasolini Pa* Palestine* makes explicit reference to Pasolini as a father figure for the engaged filmmaker of the elsewhere (hence the *Pa**),

Waiting for Pasolini, a comedy by Moroccan film director Daoud Aoula-Syad from 2012, is infused with both a nostalgia for a better political life that never was, and for European Art Cinema in general. It tells a story set in a village in the middle of nowhere in Morocco, in which satellite dish salesman Thami announces to his fellow villagers the imminent arrival of a troupe of Italian filmmakers who plan to shoot a film there, thus triggering cinema fever throughout the village. The film is a bittersweet comedy, offering many hilarious moments that explore a cross section of a Moroccan village whose only contact with the outside world is through satellite TV, before its sudden collision with the movie-making world. After the announcement by the satellite dish vendor, mayhem erupts in the village, with children running in the streets shouting 'the cinema is coming' while the residents prepare to appear as extras in the film, from the women who rush to put on their make-up, to Fakih, the preacher of the local mosque. Such is the level of excitement that it seems that the arrival of the cinema troupe will solve all the problems in the small village: debts will be repaid, school material will be delivered, houses will be built, and those who were never able to will be able to go on a pilgrimage to Mecca. 'Pasolini will pay amounts which will be sufficient for you, for the lives of your children and grandchildren', Thami tells the citizens of the village, presenting himself as a personal friend of Pasolini. Shot not far from the city of Ouzazarat, in southern Morocco, Daoud Aoula-Syad depicts the disappointment of Thami at the news of the death of Pasolini thirty years before. The man falls on his knees in front of the poster of the Italian artists hanging in his house and asks: 'Why did you die? Why didn't you wait for me?' It gets worse for Thami when he must explain to his fellow villagers why Pasolini will not be arriving after all, and why the Italian troupe dismantles their production and leaves the village after just two days of shooting. In the end, there is nothing left for Thami to do other than to go back to clambering atop roofs to install satellite dishes, with the awareness that Pasolini will never return and that cinema once again belongs exclusively to the TV, as the not-so-subtle finale informs us.

The subaltern rewriting of the history of Italian cinema performed by Aoula-Syad and Anastas finds in Pasolini the ideal figure, as his heretical approach to image-making lends itself to post hoc readings of him as symptomatic of European Art Cinema's pretensions of universalism and progressive politics, as well as of the harsh reality of production and dissemination. By engaging with Pasolini — the most geopolitically aware of Italian art film directors, and the most politically committed — these two films operate as 'contact zones' of a sort (to borrow the postcolonial language of Pratt and Clifford), in the sense that the films as cultural and social objects are social spaces where disparate cultures 'meet, clash, and grapple with each other, often in highly asymmetrical relations of domination and subordination'.[38]

The re-inscription of Pasolini into the transnational networks of artists and filmmakers who form part of a shared history of geopolitically engaged cinema, that same geography that he first engaged with, has, I believe, at least two clear outcomes. On the one hand, this move reconnects the decolonizing efforts of the long '68 with the current anti-neocapitalist struggle via the Western solidarity movement of the European left, and in so doing redeploys all the political weight of countercultural Italian political cinema. On the other, Aoula-Syad's and Anastas's films each highlight the problematic power relations at play both then and now, including the continued exploitation of labour, exclusion for distribution networks, etc.

It seems that in order to make sense of Pasolini — and other engaged political filmmakers — in the contemporary moment, the most useful concept is Néstor García Canclini's *hibridez*, or hybridity.[39] For Canclini, hybridization represents a 'nondialectical heterogeneity', which entails not fusion or integration but speaking from many places at once; and indeed, for him this principle serves as a key gesture of modernity. Heterogeneity stands for Canclini at the conceptual opposite of *mestizaje* or *métissage*, terms which represent a monolithic understanding of national identity, operating under a teleological movement of smooth self-understanding. Rather, hybridization brings to the fore the frictions and hierarchical disparities of the nation-state cultural formation. If Canclini is referring to contemporary artistic practices in Latin America, we can apply its main tenets to understand the globalized cinematic and media practices of today. It is not a surprise, then, if the direction of the movement is now reversed; the engaged filmmaker used to go to the Third World as the space of potential liberation, whereas now the mass of migrants cross the Mediterranean in the opposite direction. And, paradoxically, the discourse has also reversed: much of the debate politically is in fact about the 'archaic' cultural and religious traditions and practices that 'the barbarian hordes' bring with them. This 'nondialectical heterogeneity' has made Pasolini's films both obsolete, as object of a future that never was, and — as proven by their subaltern responses — very necessary.

---

38 Louise Pratt, *Imperial Eyes: Travel Writing and Transculturation* (New York: Routledge, 1992), p. 4.
39 Néstor García Canclini, *Hybrid Cultures: Strategies for Entering and Leaving Modernity* (Minneapolis: University of Minnesota Press, 2005).

EMMANUEL ALLOA

PASOLINI: LOVE AND FEAR OF THE PAGAN

I always liked how, in the *Gospel according to Matthew* (1964), Pasolini had managed to divert the attention from the central figure towards all the other seemingly peripheral ones. Not the actor embodying Christ is in focus — and arguably not even Maria, impersonated by Pasolini's own mother Susanna: the villagers of the community of Matera, in South Italian Basilicata where the film was shot, are the secret heroes of the story. While some of my Marxist friends (suffice it to say: not a single one originating from Southern Europe) repeatedly shared with me their surprise and for some even unease about the fact that a declared atheist and materialist would make such a movie, I have to say I was always very much attracted to Pasolini's inimitable and deeply personal interpretation of the Christian Gospels. For sure, it testifies to a very particular conjuncture, which some like to describe (accurately or not) as the Italian 'catho-communism'.

Let me add that I took the relocation to Southern Italy to be a brilliant idea. Still today, when roving through the *Sassi* of Matera, which were home to cave-dwellers up until the 1950s, we won't find it hard to understand why Pasolini had decided to choose the atmospheric site for shooting his film. As a place continuously inhabited since the Palaeolithic epoch, there is a sense of timeless grandeur in this landscape carved into the rocks. While the inhabitants of the Sassi were forcefully relocated decades ago into hideous rental barracks at the periphery, and the neighbouring landscape is now slashed by high voltage lines and dotted with industrial depots which would have surely incurred the wrath of Pasolini had he lived up until this day, the hills above the troglodyte section of the Matera canyon can give a sense of a landscape immemorial. We are in Lucania, as this region was known since Roman times, and not so long ago, as anthropologists such as Ernesto de Martino have taught us, in the area, witchcraft and healing rituals were still practiced side to side with Catholicism.

More recently, however, I started questioning my own judgment of Pasolini's gesture. Was the idea of relocating a story which supposedly took place in the Near East to an Italian village truly this subversive? Wasn't that what the Church had done for centuries, when nativity sets shift the Middle Eastern narrative to a West European context, or when Renaissance painters such as Ghirlandaio turn the Apparition of the Angel into a mundane event situated among aristocratic Florentine families? It suddenly dawned upon me that bringing back home a narrative to your own cultural framework responds to a strange understanding of Pasolini's self-declared desire for and 'sense of an elsewhere' (*senso dell'Altrove*). But another moment was more decisive in my change of opinion: some years ago, upon venturing into Pasolini's *Location Hunting in Palestine* (*Sopralluoghi in Palestina*) from 1965.

Film still from Pier Paolo Pasolini, *Sopralluoghi in Palestina per il Vangelo secondo Matteo* (1965).

In Palestine: Hypermodernity and Archaism

Between June 27 and July 11, 1963, accompanied by only a very reduced film team that also included a Catholic priest (the Biblist don Andrea Carraro who serves him as a 'fixer'), Pasolini travels to Palestine in order to prospect places that could serve as a stage for his film project on the life of Jesus but also to potentially scout actors or extras. *Sopralluoghi in Palestina* is sometimes referred to as a *making-of* movie: it would be more accurate to describe it as an *unmaking-of*, as it consists in a precise chronicle of a debacle. As it quickly turns out, the real Holy Land doesn't hold up to the imagined one; the Friulan-born filmmaker is deeply dismayed by what he sees as the traces of Israel's hypermodernity and which leave little space for the archaic Biblical landscapes he had fantasized about. As known, upon his return from this field trip the vaguely envisioned alternative idea takes shape to shoot the *Gospel according to Matthew* in the Italian *Meridione*. As the diary of a failure, it might be tempting to discard the *Sopralluoghi* as a mere documentation of a road not taken. However, the fact that he had decided to release the film, one year after his Oscar-nominated *Gospel according to Matthew* had come out, also hints to the fact that this trip to Palestine yields important insights, not the least for Pasolini's conception of primitivism, but also for the relationship it bespeaks towards a fantasized Orient. For sure, the 55 minutes long film deserves a closer inspection: although mostly consisting of roughly cut rushes, the insistent voice-over by Pasolini himself gives it an odd sense of unity.

Film still from Pier Paolo Pasolini, *Sopralluoghi in Palestina per il Vangelo secondo Matteo* (1965).

The thorough bass that the voice-over communicates is that of a total discrepancy between what the atheist Pasolini was expecting and the reality of the sites of the Holy Land, divided between the modern Israeli state and

Jordan. 'Nothing that could be used', is the message incessantly repeated. In a sense though, the auctorial voice leaves no chance whatsoever to the images either, and even though as a spectator, one might find some of the landscapes rather interesting, even from an aesthetic point of view, Pasolini's semi-improvised comment has already pre-emptively deactivated their potential. Wherever the small scouting crew goes, whether the supposed sites of passion around Jerusalem, whether Bethlehem, Tel Aviv, the lake Tiberias, the shores of the Dead Sea, or the crossing of the river Jordan, Pasolini mainly wails about the signs of hypermodernity, of the 'serious' and 'dull' faces of the Israeli urban settlers and of a new Jewish state identity which establishes agricultural technologies that are also to be found anywhere else in Europe. Most striking is the absence of any serious engagement with the Palestinian population.

In the aftermath of the trip, Pasolini publishes a series of poems, some of them establishing disconcerting connections between the architecture of the kibbutz and that of Nazi concentration camps, while in another (*L'alba meridionale*, [*Southern Dawn*]), he describes 'millions of men busy | only to live as barbarians descended | recently on a happy land, strangers | to it, and its owners'.[1] Who are the owners? Are we to fill in 'the Palestinians'? If that is the case, the *Sopralluoghi* hardly indicate any desire to interact with Palestinians. To begin with, they are never called by their name, but just generically referred to as 'the Arabs'. The entire film is traversed by a strange dialectics between what he sees as an Israeli modernity and an Arab premodern archaism. Though while he unceasingly stresses that he is looking for premodern environments, Pasolini hardly ever has any sustained conversation with the Palestinians he meets, as if he preferred to leave his own deep-rooted Orientalism unmodified. Against the settler-colonialist mentality of the modern Israeli state, he plots a conception of the Arab as a happy savage. The strolling Arab youth he meets on a seafront in Tel Aviv (in Yafo?) he compares to destitute populations from Nairobi or Calcutta, all the while celebrating the 'happy [Palestinian] shantytowns' [*le felici bidonvilles*]. Happy fools, that come so strangely close to his own, almost Franciscan reading of Christianity, are however never given to speak. Pasolini prefers engaging in lengthy conversations with kibbutznik in the countryside, who, on top of it all, speak perfect Italian. As if the immediacy he is looking for in his project about Jesus (he claims that only the reading of the Gospels was an experience of 'unmediated [...] 'moral beauty'"[2]) was only possible without

---

[1] Pier Paolo Pasolini, 'L'alba meridionale' (Appendix) [1963–64], in *Tutte le poesie*, ed. by Walter Siti, 4 vols. (Milan: Mondadori, 2009), I, p. 1295.

[2] Pier Paolo Pasolini, 'Letter to Alfredo Bini, 12 May 1963', in *Lettere 1955–1975*, ed. by Nico Naldini (Turin: Einaudi, 1988), p. 514.

ever leaving his own mother tongue and his own cultural framework of reference. Upon entering a Druze village, he first believes he is surrounded by Christians, only to discover that this was due to misunderstanding, and that the youth he had been filming aren't Christians but belong to the Druze faith, a particular version of Islam. No further attempt of a conversation is undertaken, or even to find a translator.

Film still from Pier Paolo Pasolini, *Sopralluoghi in Palestina per il Vangelo secondo Matteo* (1965).

The Arab Animal

The comment Pasolini then makes has been troubling me for long, for years actually, if I think about it carefully. The shots at close range show a succession of faces of the children from the village, and the voice-over adds: *sono facce precristiane, pagane, indifferenti, allegre, animalesche,* 'these are Pre-Christian faces, pagan, indifferent, joyful, animal-like'.[3] The first time, I had to rewind the movie to make sure I had heard properly, so abashed was I by those qualifications. The reduction of the Palestinian to an animal-like creature was hard to swallow. Today, it is difficult not to read into it an anti-Arabic or even anti-Muslim stereotype. I wondered whether Pasolini himself was aware of what he was doing at that precise moment. All I know is that years later, Pasolini seems to feel the urge to defend himself from such suspicion when, in a short newspaper piece in the occasion of the Six Day war in 1967, plainly titled 'Israele', he starts by saying that 'I swear on the Coran that I love the Arabs almost as much as my mother'.[4] On the other hand, there is also a powerful Orientalism guiding these words, as if Pasolini was searching — in a vein not so dissimilar from his contemporary Jean Genet, in his last, testament-like *A Loving Captive* — in the Arabs the representatives of a premodern humanity. When Pasolini later meets the Bedouins, in a stretch of land not far from the river Jordan, Pasolini again celebrates these 'stupid' and yet 'happy' countenances. Around the mid-'60s, Pasolini is actively seeking for non-European embodiments of these figures of humility that films like *Accattone* or *Mamma Roma* had put at the centre. While much has been written about his 'third-worldist' projects in India or Africa, the Arabic Orient seems to pertain to a special category. In a film like *I Fiori delle Mille e una notte* (Arabian Nights, 1974), as authors such as Jalal Toufic or Cesare Casarino have criticized,[5] it is a thoroughly Orientalist projection that is purported, with the fantasy of a world where love and sexuality are still innocently one (as opposed to a Christian vision which opposes the sinful flesh to true Christian *agapé*). So what is the role of the Palestinian Arab in the construction of this 'new prehistory' (*nuova preistoria*) Pasolini was dreaming of?

---

3   Pier Paolo Pasolini, *Per il cinema*, ed. by Walter Siti and Franco Zabagli, 2 vols. (Milan: Mondadori, 2001), I, p. 660.
4   Pier Paolo Pasolini, 'Israele', in *Saggi sulla politica e sulla società*, ed. by Walter Siti and Silvia De Laude (Milan: Mondadori, 1999), p. 144 [originally published in *Nuovi Argomenti*, 6 (April–June 1967)]: 'Giuro sul Corano che io amo gli arabi quasi come mia madre'.
5   Jalal Toufic, *The Withdrawal of Tradition Past a Surpassing Disaster* (Los Angeles: California Institute of the Arts/Forthcoming Books, 2009); Cesare Casarino, 'The Southern Answer: Pasolini, Universalism, Decolonization', in this volume.

Film still from Pier Paolo Pasolini, *Sopralluoghi in Palestina per il Vangelo secondo Matteo* (1965).

There would be arguments to read Pasolini both in a latent Orientalist vein, such as described by Edward Said, as well as in an anti-Arabic fashion, if one reads some of his comments about the little 'Arab animals' too literally. While this passage from the *Sopralluoghi* left me with a deep discomfort, these two diametrically opposed interpretations seemed unsatisfactory too. The only way out of this perplexity, I thought, could come from a better understanding of Pasolini's tormented and yet always continuously renewed relationship to Christianity. In what respect could the Palestinian Semite be seen as the 'Other', as a face standing for a form of life, of existence disconnected from the Christian fate of which Pasolini always states that it is also his own?

> I, for me, am anticlerical (I am not afraid to say it!), but I know that in me there are two thousand years of Christianity: I built the Romanesque churches with my ancestors, and then the Gothic churches, and then the Baroque churches: they are my heritage, in content and style. I would be foolish to

deny the powerful force that is in me, if I left the monopoly of the Good to the priests.[6]

Faces in which the Preaching of Christ Never Passed

Such statements might explain why, in *La Ricotta*, he has the film director impersonated by Orson Welles, who at least in part must be identified as his *alter ego,* speaking about his 'profound, intimate, archaic catholicism'. But if such comments about Pasolini's ambivalent communist Catholicism have often been cited, their connection to his view of the Palestinian Semite remains to be understood. If from the early 1960s on, Pasolini has incessantly been searching for the sites and the figures of an alternative, archaic humanity, whether in India, Yemen or in a film script such as *The Savage Master* about premodern Africa, what about those encounters in Palestine? Why were they 'useless'? There is something deeply paradoxical in the attempt to reread the figure of Jesus Christ as an embodiment of another form of radically simple because 'humane divinity', and of the repeated attempt to place the Arab Palestinian in an altogether different framework. As Pasolini doesn't restrict himself to talk about the 'pagan, indifferent, joyful, animal-like' faces of the children, he also offers a telling for it: 'I have seen the faces of the Arabs; these are faces in which the preaching of Christ has not passed at all'.[7]

It is surprising this statement hasn't attracted more critical discussion in the now infinitely extended body of work on Pasolini. What does a face look like in which the preaching of Christ hasn't passed? And, even more importantly, what does a face look like in which it did pass indeed? The faces of the Palestinians lack the word. The word of Christ. But first of all, they lack their own words. Unlike in the kibbutz near Nazareth, where the filmmaker sits down in the grass with some of its members and has the Nagra microphone going round to capture all their thoughts, the idea never

---

6   Pier Paolo Pasolini, 'Response Letter to Readers', *Vie Nuove* 47, 30 November 1961. Quoted in Pasolini, *Per il cinema*, I, p. xciii: 'Io, per me, sono anticlericale (non ho mica paura a dirlo!), ma so che in me ci sono duemila anni di cristianesimo: io coi miei avi ho costruito le chiese romaniche, e poi le chiese gotiche, e poi le chiese barocche: esse sono mio patrimonio, nel contenuto e nello stile. Sarei folle se negassi tale forza potente che è in me: se lasciassi ai preti il monopolio del Bene'.

7   Pasolini, *Per il cinema*, I, p. 660.

seems to cross his mind that the Druze village children or the Bedouins might have their say too.

Film still from Pier Paolo Pasolini, *Sopralluoghi in Palestina per il Vangelo secondo Matteo* (1965).

The *Sopralluoghi* are all the more important, as they were considered by Pasolini as the starting point of his later essay films, all to be included in the project of the filmic *Notes for a Poem on the Third World* (which would consist of sections in Africa, India, the Arab world, Latin America and the black US ghettoes). Although never realized, it seems as if Pasolini's plan was to apply the linguistic analyses on the 'indirect free discourse' to cinema, something he theorized in the decisive chapter of *Heretical Empiricism*.[8] Freed from the traditional voice of the omniscient narrator, indirect free discourse aims at liberating another kind of expression by a 'return to the origins' and enabling 'the original oneiric, barbaric, irregular, aggressive, visionary quality of cinema'.[9] Pasolini has often been criticized for the scene included in *Notes Towards an African Oresteia* (1970) where a group of African students faces a patronizing Pasolini, who seems to be forcing them to spell out the nature of a true, archaic African identity.

---

8 Pier Paolo Pasolini, 'Comments on Free Indirect Discourse', in *Heretical Empiricism*, trans. by Ben Lawton and Louise K. Barnett (Indianapolis: Indiana University Press, 1988), pp. 79–101.
9 Pasolini, 'The Cinema of Poetry', in *Heretical Empiricism*, p. 178.

I shall leave aside in this context whether the critiques were fully to the point. But what is sure is that in the *Sopralluoghi*, he takes the symmetrical attitude: that of filming muted faces which are never even asked to speak out. In spite of all his love for the subalterns, one might wonder — to pun on Gayatri Spivak's famous essay — whether Pasolini really wants the subalterns to speak, or whether he is not preferring to film their body language and the promise of ingenuity in their faces.

When traveling south, past Beersheba, Pasolini seems fascinated with the faces of the Bedouins.

> These are the same faces we saw in the Druze villages: sweet, beautiful, merry, and a little gloomy, a little funereal; they are full of a totally pre-Christian, animal-like sweetness. The preaching of Christ didn't get here, not even remotely [...].[10]

The voice-over adds that these images speak for themselves, and adds that the images come very close to the representation Europeans have of the Jews crossing the desert. At this point, a convergence seems to take place between the Arab and the Jew, into some nondescript Semitic identity. Where they meet, as it were, is in their incapacity of recognizing the reality of the becoming human of God, and hence their 'uselessness' for a film about the life of Jesus. As if echoing Carlo Levi, whose *Christ Stopped at Eboli* had strongly impacted him, Pasolini seems to apply the trope to the Holy Land now: the 'good news' — the *evangélion* — never reached those individuals, and thus, it would be impossible to locate the story of the gospels here.

The Pagan's A-Historicity: A Heretical Orientalism?

I couldn't help myself finding an echo of it all in the already mentioned poem *Israele*, where the filmmaker-poet contrasts the seriousness of the Israeli settlers he has conversations with and the inarticulate laughs of the Arabs:

> The children of the Arabs, they do laugh | they laugh foolishly | with a poignant stupidity | like our poor men [*poverelli*] | like puppies of the hungry people | the little beasts with the beautiful human eyes | black as gall, filling

---

10 Pasolini, *Per il cinema*, I, p. 663–64.

with smiles | behind the pitch eyelash hedge | like sugar, warmth of flowers | The useless smile, of those born to a single destiny.[11]

Hence a strange hesitation on Pasolini's side: The pagan, pre-Christian faces would embody his ideal of a minor and resistant subjectivity, pretty close to the poverty ideal of the Franciscan *poverello*. But at the same time, a fear exudes from these verses, the fear that the initial destiny will never be undone, that History will never dawn on these faces (he talks of the landscapes as a 'Syrian mountain, ugly as something that remained barren of History'). As if, to imagine a transformative horizon, one first needed to enter the horizon of Christian eschatology, and thus the horizon of an institution set up by names such as Peter and Paul (which are, let's not forget, Pasolini's own first names). Pasolini's attraction to the Non- or Pre-Christian pagan seems to reach its limits here, and his desire for revolutionary change, which makes him part of the cohort of the *tiers-mondistes* intellectuals with Sartre, Fanon, and many others, oddly leads him back to his own, deep-rooted relation to Christianity ('In this respect,' he explains in a public conversation around *The Gospel According to Matthew* 'there is no way to avoid considering Christ as a Revolutionary').[12]

Things slowly started to crystallize. If this hypothesis were true, then the most plausible explanation would be the following: in Pasolini's eyes, what the archaic Semites lack, is the capacity for conversion. If one were ready to take this line of reasoning to the extreme, one might even say that Pasolini comes dangerously close to a very old Anti-Semitic idea, i.e. that of the incapacity of the Jews to recognize the fact of the transfiguration of Jesus of Nazareth. From Saint Paul on, who Pasolini studied so carefully for his own, never realized fragment on *Saint Paul*, and who invented the trope of the 'blindfolded synagogue',[13] all through the Middle Ages and even to figure such as Erik Peterson or Carl Schmitt in the 20th century, the reluctancy of the Jew to recognize the historical event of God made human is associated with the figure of the *katechon*, who holds up time and impedes real change. But even if one resists pushing the plug this far, and accusing Pasolini of surreptitious Anti-Semitism, there is for sure a Christian heritage in his ambivalent primitivism which hasn't been sufficiently acknowledged to this day. Years later, in a short article titled 'What to do with the 'Good savage'?', Pasolini says that the 'good savage'

---

11 Pier Paolo Pasolini, 'Israele', in *Tutte le poesie*, I, p. 1220.
12 Pier Paolo Pasolini, *Le belle bandiere: Dialoghi 1960–65*, ed. by Gian Carlo Ferretti (Rome: Editori Riuniti, 1977), p. 256.
13 II Corinthians 3:13–16.

exists 'objectively', and that he has met him, in Yemen or Somalia.[14] Do we need to add Palestine too?

The trip to the Near East was one of disenchantment for Pasolini, thwarting his dream of a premodern, archaic Arcadia. But maybe there was more to it, or at least, this is what I suspect. It might have stood for the discovery that his search for a stubbornly immanent form of life, which he celebrates on the one hand for its resistance to modern recodifications, coincides with one that lacks what he thinks to have found in the Gospels, and later in the figure of Saint Paul: the potential for radical conversion and change.[15] With the Palestinian Semite, Pasolini seems to have reached his fantasized 'holy land' of sacred primitivism, as the bodies he encounters on which time has no grip, and hence modernity can't contaminate. But these 'timeless bodies', resistant as they are, also appeared to him as bodies incapable of undergoing the radical change required by history. The search for a kind of primitive love, which was guiding the entire film project about the Life of Jesus, placed Pasolini face to face with his own contradictions. When projecting onto the Orient a vision of timeless happiness, and showcasing, in *Arabian Nights*, the nudity of the harems that seem to come out directly from Antoine Galland's 18th century imagination, he repeats a typical Orientalist mindset. On the other hand, the encounter with some Arabic groups in Palestine also seem to elicit a different vision, that of a kind of society that doesn't fully merge with the expansionist ideologies of any kind, from the Roman Catholic Church through colonialism to modern-day capitalism.

With some reason, Luca Caminati dubbed Pasolini's orientalism a 'heretical orientalism'.[16] The idea is attractive to all of those who can't but acknowledge the orientalist traits of Pasolini's poetics, and yet want to save the singularity of his creative mind. Fair enough. For long, I found that idea rather attractive too, or at least, I found some comfort in it. But today, I have grown wary it might just be some self-delusional game. To what extent Pasolini's orientalism really was heretical still awaits an accurate appraisal. One day, we might find out that his kind of orientalism was in fact decidedly more orthodox than many wanted to believe. One thing is for sure: as Church historians know, heresies only exist through and with

---

14 Pier Paolo Pasolini, 'Che fare con il "buon selvaggio"?' [1970], in *Saggi sulla Politica e sulla società*, pp. 217–223 (p. 217).
15 Pier Paolo Pasolini, *Saint Paul: A Screenplay*, trans. by Elizabeth Castelli (London: Verso, 2014).
16 Luca Caminati, *Orientalismo eretico. Pier Paolo Pasolini e il cinema del terzo mondo* (Milan: Mondadori, 2007).

respect to a Church. In that respect, Pasolini's 'heresy' remains profoundly Catholic. The Other can't be seen but as the figure of the pagan: both loved and feared at once. As a pagan, he remains at the threshold of History, as the promise of an outside, but also of a pre-civilizational state of nature. Such need of pitting grace against innocence is and remains deeply Christian. But if we want a confirmation for it, ultimately, we should turn away from the textual and filmic sources, and trust another artist's intuition. Photographer Ernest Pignon-Ernst has probably had the most penetrating understanding of Pasolini's inescapable Christianity, when upon a trip to South Italy, he covered a wall of Matera with his mural of the *Pasolini Pietà*.

Ernest Pignon-Ernst, *Si je reviens [Pietà]*, Installation in situ, Matera (Puglia, Italy), 2015 (Photo: Alloa/Wittmann).

Evan Calder Williams

THE RETURN OF THE DISAPPEARANCE OF THE FIREFLIES

In the essay that will come to be known simply as 'the article about the fireflies', Pasolini's titular insects turn out to remain always just out of reach. To a degree, this is because they appear only as a disappearance [*scomparsa*]:[1]

> In the first years of the Sixties, because the pollution of the air and, more generally, of the countryside, and because of the pollution of the water (those azure rivers and crystal-clear canals), the fireflies [*lucciole*] started to disappear. The phenomena was lighting-quick [*fulmineo*] and dazzling [*folgorante*]. After a few years, there weren't any more fireflies. (They are now a wholly heartbreaking memory of the past: and an old man who could have such a memory can no longer recognize his youth in the new youths, and therefore can no longer even have a beautiful mourning of that time.)[2]

This description serves to haunt the text, and not only because it articulates a sense of that sudden, wrenching passage from flickering presence into an irrecoverable past towards which no new connections can be built. It is also due to the almost perversely tragic compression that the essay offers on a linguistic level: the vanishing of the fireflies — those 'lightning bugs' — is experienced from the outside as if in a flash of lightning (*fulmine*), as if one of their single pulses has exceeded the frame of the organism to become total, immense, and devastating, an electrifying shock [*folgorazione*] riveting the air and earth to erase all the smaller lights and those bodies that housed them.

Yet weapons-grade pathos aside, the *scomparsa* also serves a more analytical function, providing a point through which the argument will loop

---

1   We might also render *scomparsa* more bleakly as 'passing' or, to go straight to the point, as 'death'.
2   Pier Paolo Pasolini, 'L'articolo delle lucciole', in *Saggi sulla politica e sulla società*, ed. by Walter Siti, Silvia De Laude (Milan: Mondadori, 1999), p. 405. All translations from this essay are my own.

to find its loose structure and allowing the central part of the essay to organize itself around the 'Before', 'During', and 'After' of the disappearance.[3] In this way, the *lucciole* appear as a proxy of sorts, less a metaphor than a figure through which to cast negative illumination on what Pasolini in this essay calls simply a '*qualcosa*', a profound 'something' that took place around a 'decade ago' (in the mid-1960s).[4] The text starts with his brief reading of, and disagreement with, Franco Fortini's engagement with Elio Vittorini's language of the divide between 'adjectival' and 'substantive' fascism that appeared in the magazine *Il Politecnico*. Pasolini insists, however, that the distinction no longer pertains as a result of this 'something' that was not only 'unforeseeable in the times of *Il Politecnico* but even a year before it happened' — and, crucially, even 'while it was happening'.[5] Moreover, this *qualcosa* itself underwrites and drives both the collapse of that possible distinction and the birth of something else: the emergence of a new schema, not that of 'fascist fascism' and 'Christian-Democratic fascism', but rather the split 'between fascist fascism and a radically, totally, unforeseeably new fascism that was born from that "something"'.[6] We should note here how the framing is from the start centered on the outmoding and erosion of Christian-Democratic hegemony, as this constitutes a bulk of the essay's focus, building to the idea of *il vuoto del potere*, which gave the essay its original newspaper title and which I would translate as 'power's hollow'.[7]

---

3   I'll note here that I think the hidden interlocutor of this format is Amadeo Bordiga: his writings in *Battaglia Communista* from the early 1950s modeled this again and again, both with its pivot between 'Yesterday' and 'Today' and in the deep links drawn between an ecological and infrastructural reckoning with the consequences of capital and the project of asserting lines of a communist counter-history that could read those against the grain and see them for what they were. (Bordiga's background as a structural engineer gives his texts an especially lucid line of approach to these questions.) They remain some of the most vital but under-acknowledged mid-century attempts at a radical critique of capitalist development.
4   The essay itself stages the term *qualcosa* in quotes.
5   For a long discussion of this debate and Vittorini's original article on this, see my essay, 'The Loss of the Separated World', in *Pasolini Framed and Unframed: A Thinker for the Twenty-First Century*, ed. by Luca Peretti and Karen Raizen (New York: Bloomsbury Academic, 2019).
6   Pasolini, 'Lucciole', p. 587.
7   My reason for this is triple: it preserves the possessive implication present in *il vuoto del potere*; in English, the apostrophe brings a slipperiness between being read both as that possessive (*the hollow core of power*) and as a different assertive phrase (*power is hollow*); and lastly, the extra sense of a 'hollow' as not just a hole but specifically a spatial formation in a landscape (the small valley in a forest as a hollow/'holler'), which gives a sense of the kind of attempted analysis of a

For Pasolini, this is a hollowing out that cannot itself be seen, except for in the attempts to cover it over, most notably in the increasingly unconvincing 'death masks' of those politicians who try to hold on to an already eroded base of power.

It is in this context that the fireflies appear in their disappearance, as a figure to think that *qualcosa* with, and for all its lyrical resonance, Pasolini introduces their *scomparsa* under the sign of this functionality:

> Because I am a writer and I write polemically to, or at least in dialogue with, other writers, allow me to give a poetic-literary definition of this phenomenon [of the disappearance] that happened in Italy a decade ago. It will serve to simplify and shorten our conversation (and also probably let one understand it better).[8]

What, though, is that *qualcosa*, articulated here not as the unforeseeable permutations of a new fascism but the huge structural driver that enabled and engendered them? Unsurprisingly for the relentless bent of Pasolini's writings in the mid-'70s, it is capitalism. More precisely, it is the collective effects of patterns of capital accumulation and circulation, specifically in regards to how those both sever deeply anchored communal values[9] — religious in part, but also archaic and 'popular' — and bring about a mutation that can only be regarded, he insists, as a 'new phase' of human history. Between these and the resulting hollow in structures of governance and control still tuned to already obsolete forms of economic and social management, real power takes place elsewhere, in the banal force of logistics and in new monstrous social cruelties alike. And all the while, the outmoded monsters of Christian-Democracy grin and bear it and try to mime a facade of rule with all the stability of a Hollywood Western's dusty

---

conjuncture as a topography of sorts, reading it for its fault lines and possibilities. This last element in particular opens to an inquiry I won't pursue here: that of the distinct spatial dynamics and logic that marks conceptions of shifting power, from the 'vacuum' to the figures of void and explosive flow, as in Henri Lefebvre's *L'irruption de Nanterre au sommet*. For a discussion of this, see Evan Calder Williams and Alberto Toscano, 'Wrong Place, Right Time:' '68 and the Impasses of Periodization', *Cultural Politics*, 15, 3 (November 2019), 273–88.

8 Pasolini, 'Lucciole', p. 404.
9 In the section 'After the Disappearance of the Fireflies', he begins to enumerate the severity and breadth of this unbinding: 'The "nationalistic", and therefore false, values of the old agricultural and paleocapitalist world suddenly didn't matter. Church, fatherland, family, obedience, order, economy, morality didn't matter anymore'. Ibid., p. 407.

Main Street of rickety theater flats, and with all the ready violence of that film's world itching for an excuse.

Returning to the quieter trauma of the fireflies and their vanishing, though, I don't think the 'phenomenon' and its role here can be reduced to the 'poetic-literary definition' Pasolini suggests, for a few plain reasons. First, even if deployed here as rhetorical device, it is not a familiar figure of speech, legend, or fable, nor is it a generic example of how it might be for a species to disappear. Rather, the claim is that this *happened*, and in the same country and lived spaces where the distinction was being evacuated between modes of fascism. It was a real event, at once part and sign of a historical process, and so too its consequences, given how the sense of shock and loss it may generate gets intimately bound up in private and public memories alike.[10]

Second, the temporal torsion isn't limited to the melancholic feeling of 'an old man' having his memories jolted by the unexpected ripple effect of industrial pollution, as a continual aftermath of the past brings about a present in which this archaic experience of watching the fireflies comes to an end. That is at work here, to be sure, but there's also a more specific element and operation, one we can note in the description: a kind of parallelism, between the *qualcosa* 'around a decade ago' and the disappearance happening in 'the first years of the 1960s'. Because given the essay's publication in 1975, the latter is itself also 'around a decade ago', if just a touch earlier. This means, quite simply, that whatever their link, the vanishing fireflies and the effects of that gargantuan *qualcosa* occur in the same world and at the same time. If they are joined here on the page and in thought, it is to form a bridge between two simultaneous and actual phenomena, albeit of different scale and consequence, neither of which cannot be reduced to a rhetorical figure. Third, what obviously follows from this last point: that the bond is not just one of analogy, metaphor, or even simultaneity. It is a historical one, shot through with tangled forms of causality and effect. Because at its core, the very conditions that produce the disappearance — the devastation of the milieu[11] of the *lucciole*, the

---

10 Moreover, those memories themselves can feed into how other processes get understood and at times challenged — including, perhaps, that very process of capital's transformation of social forms that it was marshaled to help us 'understand better'.

11 This kind of reasoning via a confrontation with animal life devastated by human existence finds a striking instance in Georges Canguilhem's *Knowledge of Life*: 'In Jean Giraudoux's *Electra*, the beggar, the vagabond who stumbles across squashed hedgehogs on the road, meditates on the hedgehog's original sin that

encroaching reach of what Amadeo Bordiga called that 'forest of bayonets and chimneys',[12] and what Pasolini signals here as the 'poisoning' of the soil, countryside, and water — are nothing other than the accelerated ecological symptoms of the *qualcosa*. In other words, they are the side effects of the very something that they might bring closer to the edge of thought.

*

So what are the fireflies doing, stranded somewhere between rhetorical device and actual extinction? One possible sense would be to read them through a lens of indexicality, and specifically in relation to pollution.[13] Read this way, the disappearance of the fireflies becomes what, in its process of becoming invisible, makes visible the reach and saturation of those effects of capitalist industry writ large, a black dye in the engine of the world system and the toxic buildup of its refuse. That kind of analysis is surely compatible with the argument of Pasolini's essay, and it is arguably one of the main reasons that the text has remained influential, insofar as the image of the vanishing *lucciole* holds a mournful potency that is hard to forget. However, that isn't how they actually operate in this essay: they don't appear as an atrocious epitome of a process that genuinely does

---

drives him to cross roads. If this question has philosophical sense, because it poses the problem of destiny and death, it has much less biological sense. A road is a product of human technology, one of the elements of the human milieu — but it has no biological value for the hedgehog. Hedgehogs as such do not cross roads: they explore, in their own way, their own hedgehog milieu, on the basis of their alimentary and sexual impulses. On the contrary, it is man-made roads that cross the hedgehog's milieu, his hunting ground and the theater of his loves, just as they cross the milieus of the rabbit, the lion, or the dragonfly'. Georges Canguilhem, *Knowledge of Life,* trans. by Stefanos Geroulanos and Daniela Ginsburg (New York: Fordham University Press, 2008), p. 22.

12 Amadeo Bordiga, 'Class Struggle and "Bosses' Offensives"', originally published in *Battaglia Comunista*, 39 (1949) <https://www.marxists.org/archive/bordiga/works/1949/class-struggle.htm> [accessed 3 January 2022].

13 A version of this approach can be found in Karen Pinkus' reading of Pasolini's unfinished novel, *Petrolio*, in which she finds both a 'significant rejoinder against placing faith in green washing or green consumerism' and a specific configuration of mythic reactivation, transformation (especially via the model of alchemical thought and processes), and writing as a mode of potentiality that she argues is of particular relevance for thinking this moment and its general framing beneath the banner of Anthropocene. Karen Pinkus, 'Pasolini for the Anthropocene', *Pasolini Framed and Unframed*, p. 196.

result in their disappearance. Rather, they are present almost entirely in *human* terms: the memory of their presence and the disarming experience of their disappearance. This is an experience predicated on being unable to 'foresee', missing something even 'while it was happening', or seeing it too late and after the damage is done. We catch only the after-image, with full awareness that this pulse too will fade in a world that holds no space or support for it.

One way of thinking through this register, then, is to center on the figure of the fireflies and that pulse, reading in Pasolini's use of them the outlines of a distinct and tenuous model of thinking the inconstant possibilities, navigations, and survivals of what hovers on the edge of visibility. As my lexicon already hints, this is the path sketched at length by Georges Didi-Huberman in *Survival of the Fireflies*, which, on the initial ground of Pasolini's letter to a friend and in his extension of how *lucciole* appear in Dante, develops an expansive account of what Didi-Huberman comes to call the 'firefly-image'.[14] I find the attempt generative, in part because of its attention to the survival of images as offering a mode that is 'always spotty, in flickers',[15] and in larger part for a reason not present in the book itself: the way it can open towards social histories of revolt and resistance that quite literally and tactically hinge on these negotiations of bright and dark. To start to navigate those histories would allow us to sketch an inconstant map, one that ranges from attacks on municipal lighting as symbols of policing and rule — how 'since the lanterns were broken and darkness occurred, the royal troops were ordered to withdraw from the insecure streets' and 'darkness thus becomes the medium of the counterorder of the rebellion'[16] — to the specificity of guerrilla tactics to ongoing forms of what Simone Browne refers to as 'dark sousveillance'.[17] It would open the other way too, towards moments when brightness itself becomes a tool to deny the state the dark it wants to orchestrate and control, like when Danish pacifists in 1938 'decided to sabotage three days of blackouts in Copenhagen [and] purchased all the fireworks in their city and planned

---

14   Georges Didi-Huberman, *Survival of the Fireflies* (Minneapolis: University of Minnesota Press, 2018), pp. 71, 74.
15   Ibid., p. 42.
16   Wolfgang Schivelbusch, 'The Policing of Street Lighting', *Yale French Studies*, 73, Everyday Life (1987), pp. 67 and 68.
17   'I use the term "dark sousveillance" as a way to situate the tactics employed to render one's self out of sight, and strategies used in the flight to freedom from slavery as necessarily ones of undersight'. Simone Brown, *Dark Matters: On the Surveillance of Blackness* (Durham: Duke University Press, 2015), p. 21.

to set them off during the blackout, 'to show the whole world that not everybody wants to cooperate in preparations for the next world war'.[18] Or towards moments of startling inversion, when the light of power gets countered by something even brighter, as in the contemporary reinvention of the laser pointer, that banal fixture of business meetings and classrooms, now torqued into a blinding tool that can burn camera sensors, scramble facial recognition software, and point straight into the face shields of riot cops, in a tactic drifting from Hong Kong to Chile and onwards from there.

Like those pointers themselves are starting to become, in the junction between their specific use and the peculiarly cyberpunkish aesthetic that results from the intersection of lasers and tear gas, we could also place the fireflies in such a distinct and dual position, as something that has a discrete material and biological history yet is also written indelibly in a history of human imagination. We find the contours of one attempt to think this dual path in British documentarian Humphrey Jennings' 'imaginative history of the Industrial Revolution'. Titled *Pandaemonium, 1660–1886: The Coming of the Machine as Seen by Contemporary Observers*, it is a book with shades of Walter Benjamin's *Arcades Project* that assembles a set of letters, poetry, documents, excerpts, and fragments that taken together constitute what Jennings calls,

> Images [...] [that] have revolutionary and symbolic and illuminatory quality. I mean that they contain in little a whole world — they are the knots in a great net of tangled time and space — the moments in which the situation of humanity is clear — even if only for the flash time of the photographer or the lightning.[19]

The fireflies, as they appear in Pasolini's text, are themselves one such flash, almost too literally. Yet what consideration of them suggests is just how ongoing and geographically expansive their role of illuminating those 'knots' has been, an archaic image of digital code baked into the memory of our species and arcing across its millennia. It's unsurprising, then, that they rise to the mind, and seem at once under threat and within reach, when it feels like the ground of a human condition, partial as it might be, is shifting under it. Pasolini wasn't the only one to turn towards them when facing this: John Glenn, orbiting the planet in 1962, records his impression

---

18   David Nye, 'Are Blackouts Landscapes?', *American Studies in Scandinavia*, 39, 2 (2007), p. 81.
19   Humphrey Jennings, *Pandaemonium, 1660–1886: The Coming of the Machine as Seen by Contemporary Observers* (New York: Free Press, 1985), p. xxxv.

of 'literally thousands of tiny luminous objects that glowed in the black sky like fireflies'.[20]

Like fireflies, like how the unbinding of traditional memory and social form was *like the disappearance of the fireflies*, like how the Christian-Democrats couldn't recognize the disappearance of their own capacity to read their time, to feel the tectonic forces evacuating power even as they spoke to fill the air. And yet it also is not *like* any of this, because of the fact that these phenomena shared a world and a time. That power changed within a world in which those who might vote for the Christian-Democrats or throw a stone at them — or even one of the politicians themselves, who might step from a council meeting out into the night for a smoke — could notice, however briefly, that the fireflies were not out anymore. So these are pulses of and for the imagination, and they are also resolutely and irrecoverably tangible, a *like* that lives or dies and does not pulse for humans, no matter what they make of it.[21] We could therefore start to narrate this in a quite different way, opening towards what isn't present in Pasolini's own work but which has become more and more familiar in recent years: a story of mutual determination and unexpected crossing points, a co-history of species attentive to how each shapes the other in subtle but immense ways. Such an approach at times shows itself in contemporary versions of flat ontologies, new materialisms, and interest in indigenous cosmologies. However, it also can appear without philosophical dressing, lying instead in the plain fact of trying to trace these sort of junctures and mutations,

---

[20] Quoted in Stefan Ineichen, 'Light into Darkness: The Significance of Glowworms and Fireflies in Western Culture', *Advances in Zoology and Botany* 4, 4 (2016), p. 54.

[21] My recurrent use of the term *pulse* here is intended to stand midway between two other figures of light at play both in discourse on Pasolini's essay and in the histories of describing fireflies and luminescent insects: *flicker* and *glow*. If *glow* suggests a degree of continuity (lacking the particular binary quality of the intermittent signal) and *flicker* conversely conjures the unsteadiness of a power source or flame (i.e. defined by its continued weakness and almost vanishing), *pulse* names both what is rhythmic and what 'beats' out from an organism or technical being, the vital throb (of a *pulsion*/drive) that functions as a sign of life and, in so doing, also forms a fundamental interval that comes to shape a sense of time's passage. We might note here also how much this logic of the pulse shows itself available for capture and cunning use by those who profit from it: Apple notoriously modeled the 'resting' pulse of light when a laptop is 'asleep' on the 'the rhythm of breathing which is psychologically appealing' (see United States Patent 6658577, for 'Breathing status LED indicator'). My thanks to Toni Hildebrandt for his incisive comments about the term *glow*, which has encouraged me to further draw out the particularity of *pulse*.

like the seemingly outsized role that mosquitoes have played in human history or, as the pandemic in which I write this proves, the absolutely real consequences of zoonotic transfer, particularly as a consequence of capital's relentless push into the border spaces between settled areas and zones of comparatively uninhabited jungle, forest, or swamp.

Shifting towards that register of real, rather than rhetorical, intersections between species can go a long way towards accounting for full networks of activity and influence within which human histories unfold. It does this especially in terms of the factors that often get excluded from counting within the terrain of the political — with the exception of those moments, like Pasolini's essay, where they become a trope or figure, an instance lucid or lyrical to try and frame what happens inside that terrain. So the other question we might start to ask is: what does the actual disappearance of the fireflies, and the struggle to witness it, do for the space of thinking politics and what that space cannot contain? One answer might be to think about how that vanishing of the fireflies itself can become part of a political imaginary, a different *qualcosa* to hold against industrial accumulation and certainly worth rioting over. But more precisely, it bleeds out onto another question, one that starts to suggest what happens at the void heart of power's hollow: how do you see a disappearance before it happens, that vanishing waiting in the wings?

*

A preoccupation with disappearance — in the sense both of loss and of the suspension of visibility, however temporary — is hardly limited to the fireflies essay. It marks Pasolini's criticism and poetry through the 1970s, most notoriously in the recurrent language of 'anthropological mutation' and 'cultural genocide'. Both terms mark a thorough reckoning with the loss of what he understood as the vital persistence of the archaic and its energies within popular life, especially as accessed through a bodily register. Yet that corporal thrust means that it also becomes an often tortured heuristic[22] of expressive signs, a quasi-periodization via symptoms, tics, gestures, and styles that keep confirming his worst fears. That approach works at times

---

22 As I've written about at more length, we might note just how much this kind of reading hinges on a vitalism that fixates on the bodies of the 'people', in a register that often loses the more precise sense of archaic transfer (as in Ernesto De Martino or Pasolini's more precise linguistic analyses) and tips instead towards a fetishistic projection of ahistoricity, all the way to the 'innocence of poverty'. See Williams, 'Separated World', p. 143.

through the reading of explicit physical signs or markers (like the long hair of hippies), but more often by picking up on diffuse and often minor linguistic, gestural, aesthetic, and cultural cues that together produce a sneaking sense of, or attunement to, that slippery *qualcosa*, in the mode of *it's just a feeling, but all the same...*

That feeling, as it appears across Pasolini's work, is most frequently one of suspicion and dread, and it feeds directly into his mournful and embittered figuration of loss. Yet the critical consequence of this is not just the substance of what is lost (vitality, deep bonds between meaning and experience, transhistorical pathways joining the present to the long past, and on from there). It is also a crisis of distinction and analysis itself. To be sure, not all is bleak: insofar as this approach hinges on the capacity to pick up on patterns that reveal the trace of historical shifts (even within structures or discourses that desperately try to mask their frictions and weakness), his approach suggests an implicit faith in the human capacity to discern, as well as a belief that this fundamental ability to notice can constitute a necessary ground for that kind of historical reckoning. However, this makes the effects of the 'disappearance' all the more painful, given that it signals the undermining of that very ability, leaving us scrambling to piece together a mesh of mutated gestures and obscure signs into a message that spells anything more than just a confirmation of apocalypse.

'Power's Hollow' itself hinges on this exact operation, because while it offers his familiar astute reading of the broader political and institutional dynamics at work in a conjuncture, it also directs attention again and again to how threatened and weakened the act of paying attention itself has become. Even beyond the central trope of the *scomparsa* (i.e. noticing what no longer can be noticed, other than with the backdrop of memories of a world of nights teeming with bright life), the essay gives one of his most explicit elaborations of this general logic. At times, it still does trust in the lingering possibility of sensing and discerning: 'I have therefore seen "with my senses"', he writes, the power of consumer society and the 'deformation' it wreaks which leads towards an 'irreversible degradation'.[23] The ability to sense these effects is once again qualified and undermined by his persistent sense of the irreversibility of anthropological mutation/degradation, the process that makes continuity amongst generations impossible, unmoors memory from possible collective meaning, and leaves its participants bereft of possible historical comprehension. But despite this weakening, such a grasp of seeing and understanding with 'senses' does

---

23 Pasolini, 'Lucciole'.

suggest a certain automatic and perhaps innate ability. (The hard part being just what to do with what is noticed.) And more potently, at the moment of the essay's turn to power's hollow, it hinges on an appeal to the genuinely *popular* possibility of such noticing: 'All my readers certainly will have noticed the changes in the powerful Christian-Democrats: in just a few months, they have become death masks'.[24]

What, then, of that hollow, the putative focus of the essay? The language of *vuoto* initially suggests a kind of void that could be glimpsed if only the masks might be torn away, in a familiar trope of 'unmasking power'. Yet what is striking about this essay is just how much it refuses that move, or at least refuses any consolation that glimpsing this void would be remotely enough. The reason is that at each stage of his argument, the moment of the possible reveal shows itself to once again name yet another failure of judgment, rather than any novel content. For instance, even with the specific effect gathered under the 'disappearance of the fireflies' (i.e. the metaphorical name for the political phenomenon that underlies the production of power's hollow), the staging of the text itself reveals a crucial aspect. Given that the core of the essay is built around sections of 'Before', 'During', and 'After', one might reasonably expect the 'During' to offer a significant hinge, or at least a clarification of the process.[25] But in that 'During', almost nothing happens *other than the failure to recognize what is happening*. No one, not 'the mass of workers and farmers organized by the PCI', and not the 'most advanced intellectuals and critics [...] realized that the "disappearance of the fireflies" was happening', and none 'could suspect the historical reality that would be the immediate future' (i.e. the reality of the "genocide" that Marx talked about in the *Manifesto*').[26]

Even power's hollow shows itself, in the end, to be nothing other than the result of such a misrecognition. Because what causes the hollowness isn't a crisis of leadership, or an assertion of empty values, but simply the incapacity to recognize that the fireflies have happened: 'the powerful men of Christian-Democracy passed from the "phase of the fireflies" to

---

24   Ibid., p. 409. Arguably the sharpest cinematic version of this logic will come after Pasolini's death, in Elio Petri's *Todo Modo* (1976), in the bunker within which power retreats to its literal void beneath the earth — and finds its death there.

25   This is especially so given that when the text later returns to the idea of a transition between fascisms, it gives the curt definition of the transition as itself 'the disappearance of the fireflies'. For a further elaboration of his periodization via this figure, see his *Corriere della Sera* article that follow the fireflies article by two weeks. Pier Paolo Pasolini, 'Gli insostituibili Nixon italiani', in *Saggi sulla politica e sulla società*, p. 415.

26   Pasolini, 'Lucciole', p. 407.

the "phase of the disappearance of the fireflies" without realizing it'.[27] And it is with this last point that we glimpse a critical part of the argument that remains more implied than actually articulated. Namely, that fireflies and their disappearance aren't even there to mark this particular lack, or crisis of judgement in general. Rather, they mark the contradictions of witnessing a process of transformation from *within* it.[28] The *scomparsa* functions above all as the name for how it is — and how it feels — to lose the ability to recognize tremendous processes that not only remake the world but also us along with it. No vantage point remains outside of the process of mutation that affects even that fundamental capacity of noticing: its contours of perception, structures of attention, experiences of time, and the organization of memory itself.[29] This, then, is the absent substance of power's hollow: not a static void one can point to, but an erosion of the capacity to bind signs to their causes, to recognize and realize and point. The only consolation is that those who hold positions of recognizable power are equally subject to this, unable to foresee the visible effects of shifts already undergone.

The problem, therefore, is how to think in a doubled way that can develop an immense sensitivity to our own perception, in order to detect the traces of that mutation in itself, and also strive to dislocate that perception from its familiar parameters and limits. We might call this latter aspect the hope to perceive *inhumanly*, and I would suggest that it forms a major part of the desire at stake in Pasolini's resurrection and reworking of the Dantean verb *trasumanar* in his unfinished poetry collection *Trasumanar e organizzar* ('Transhumanize and organize'). The verb appears in the first canto of Dante's *Paradiso*, as Dante mimics Beatrice in witnessing God's glory and, having felt in himself the edges of a kind of metamorphosis ('I felt myself becoming | what Glaucus had become tasting the herb'), concludes that,

> Transhumanizing could not be expressed | by words; let this case, therefore, him suffice, | for whom Grace holds experience in reserve.[30]

---

27 Ibid., p. 409.
28 Crucially, this is not limited to a single political stance: even those who benefitted initially from it end up also unable to ride its wave.
29 I won't pursue this here, but it is a small step from this to think more precisely about the deep relation of transforming media structures and image-regimes to these shifts.
30 Dante Alighieri, *The Divine Comedy of Dante Alighieri III: Paradiso*, trans. by Courtney Langdon (Oxford: Oxford University Press, 1921), p. 8.

Pasolini himself explains that his use of 'transhumanization' functions as a shorthand for 'spiritual ascent', at least in its simplest form.[31] Read against the poems that make up that volume itself (as well as essays like 'Power's Hollow'), the urge towards this is unmistakable, given the persistence of a figure of *dehumanization*, as in 'Introduction': 'In dehumanizing myself I shall be free, unrebellious, | and whistle all the while'.[32]

The term itself, especially in its pairing with *organizzar*, comes to designate two tendencies counter to each other. In one regard, a possible reading of those lines from *Paradiso* suggests a standard-order declaration that words aren't up to the task of describing how it was to witness that divine splendor, an operation familiar also from speculative horror fiction that insists that no words can describe *the eldritch terror glimpsed that night*. Yet like those horror stories that warn this and then spend four paragraphs detailing just how tentacular the tentacles were, the fact that this reworking of *trasumanar* appears in a volume of poetry that clearly does not give up on language — in addition to Pasolini's interest in the prospect of a divinity of linguistic signs ('hierosemy', as named in the volume) — means that language's potential is never assumed to be exhausted, no matter the force of the *qualcosa* feeding that dehumanization. On the other hand, however, the pairing of *organizzar* suggests that the work of organizing, and of becoming collective in the process, is both a counterpart to this semiotic pursuit of 'spiritual ascent' and the only way to enact a different sense of transhumanization: the remaking of social conditions so that the restricted boundaries of the human, as corralled into the narrow slots of consumer, individual, and citizen, might be cracked open towards other forms.

Yet what needs to be added to this account is a sense of just how much the source lines in *Paradiso* are themselves not about 'ascending' and exiting the human in general. Rather, they are about moving towards that prospect

---

    It is worth noting what the clunkier translation of these lines by Mark Musa draws out: 'transhumanize' — it cannot be explained *per verba*'. The specific meaning of *per verba*, present in Latin within the original Italian, is less a sense of merely 'in words' but rather of a sort of speech act, given that *per verba* is an expression used commonly to denote marriage 'per verba de praesenti': that is, by words spoken by two people that joined them in legal marriage at that moment by those words alone. See: G. A. Nelson, 'Doing Things with Words: Another Look at Marriage Rites and Spousals in Renaissance Drama and Fiction', *Studies in Philology*, 95, 4 (1998), 351–73.

31 Pier Paolo Pasolini, 'Il Sogno del Centauro', in *Saggi sulla politica e sulla società*, p. 1462.
32 Pier Paolo Pasolini, 'Introduction', in *The Selected Poetry of Pier Paolo Pasolini: A Bilingual Edition* (Chicago: University of Chicago Press, 2014), p. 413.

of perceiving inhumanly. Because what precedes the textual moment of *trasumanar* is an extended meditation of how God unevenly distributed perception itself, with this upper realm being one where 'much more is granted to the human senses | than ever was allowed them here on earth'. Limits still persist ('I could not look for long, but my eyes saw | the sun closed in blazing sparks of light'), and it is only by the imitation of Beatrice (one who no longer is human) that this moment of transindividual exit from limit can happen:

> so, like a ray, her act poured through my eyes | into my mind and gave rise to my own: | I stared straight at the sun as no man could.[33]

In other words, *trasumanar* explicitly names the problem of seeing beyond our limits, and it is a process that cannot be enacted by speech alone, insofar as it needs that temporary passage through an other — and, specifically, an other with profound ontological difference. Brought back to earth from this perceptual storming of heaven, we can see how the prospect of *organizzar* therefore offers a direct extension of that temporary passage, passing through the register not of the divine but of collectivity itself, of being other to ourselves by becoming multiple. There lies the difficulty. Glimpsing God's Glory is one thing, but as to whether this fleeting dislocation of our own perception is enough to let us feel the mutations already at work in our sight and sense: that's another matter altogether.

*

I've gathered these notes under the rather pulp title, *The Return of the Disappearance of the Fireflies*, for a few reasons. First, to speak of the 'disappearance of the fireflies' is almost a tautology, or at least a potential category error, because what defines so much of human interaction with fireflies is nothing but their disappearance — provided, that is, that they reappear again and show themselves to be that rhythmic pulse that together forms a mesh of telegraphic light.[34] In other words, the fireflies are always disappearing, and they're always returning, and on and on.[35] So the *return of the disappearance* names the viewer's experience of this basic cyclical and

---

33 Dante Alighieri, *Paradiso*, p. 8.
34 That is, that they do not become either silence or noise — the sheer scatter being the second and equally disarming possibility.
35 I'm reminded of the joke about someone who's afraid their taillights aren't working, so they ask a friend to stand behind the car and watch while they put the

chemical fact, forming a baseline of repetition against which noise or loss or chaos can be registered, not necessarily through instrument and metric but through the creeping defamiliarization of a pattern that constitutes a literally archaic human memory.

Second, the disappearance returns because the fireflies keep disappearing without actually going extinct, and so their population decline continues to be interpreted as an index of the catastrophic fallout of circuits of capital accumulation. Both a real phenomenon with manifold causes and a mournful harbinger, it's hard to avoid reading such a loss as a perverse apex of the sheer idiocy of human development and its consequences. (It's always almost too much, too terribly ham-fisted a proof, as if even prettiness has no guarantee of survival, and the snuffed-out twinkle spells out a planetary *See, this is why you can't have nice things*.) However, at least compared to how their vanishing is staged in 'Power's Hollow', more recent research around the phenomenon suggests a different set of factors than the 'poisoning of the azure waters', as Pasolini has it, with the prime reason being loss of habitat, followed by the presence of light pollution, and then the use of pesticide.[36]

This second aspect is especially pointed, as a diffuse generalization of technically-produced lighting crowds out the prospect of that ancient biochemical glow. And in this way, to pose the threatened 'flicker' of the fireflies against the bright glare of power, as Didi-Huberman does, leaves out another possibility, the shadows of which moved over and through Pasolini's thought and which I would argue is showing itself to be of accelerating relevance. This is a model of *saturation*. In luminescence, its figure is not the blinding search light or beacon but a diffuse LED twilight that cancels night without the melodrama of its loss. More specifically, it names the collapse of that fundamental binary between the dark and the light, with the firefly as the literally flitting mediator between the two. In its place is this pollution and its drift, one that that does not designate 'matter out of place' so much as the erasure of that kind of spatial clarity, along with the accompanying loss of an ability to read the landscape through its cues. This loss becomes quite literal in the case of the fireflies, because the danger posed by the light pollution, and the hazy always not-night it produces, lies in how it makes the *lucciole* themselves lose sense of both time and direction: in other words, of the basic conditions by which any

---

blinker on. 'Is it working?' asks the driver. The reply? 'Working! Not working! Working! Not Working! Working!'

36   'A Global Perspective on Firefly Extinction Threats', *BioScience*, 70 (2020), 157–67.

navigation of the world is possible. Defamiliarization here is no artistic technique. It is a real experiential and ecological condition in which biologically hardwired capacities — no matter how relatively adaptable over time — enter into spaces where the familiar cues of perception have been untethered from their expected meaning, and the ground falls out from under the feet. Fireflies in this way pose a version of what we see even more starkly with moths, whose behavior in human-built worlds is no joke but marked by a punchline all the same. *Why does the moth fly towards the electric light?* Because it thought it was the moon. That is, the moth navigates by lunar position through transverse orientation, and our bulbs are so many false moons. Unable to distinguish between the impossibly far and the scorching near, the disoriented moth keeps adjusting its angle and batters its wings against the burning electric globe again and again.

What I'm here calling *saturation* is intended to name this double and simultaneous condition. On one side, the proliferation of uncontrollable effects, whether produced as waste or introduced by media and technical forms that actively seek to alter the neurological and experiential grounding of those who use it. These effects continually erode boundaries between body, history, and milieu, and, in this way, they actually — not figuratively — disrupt the base conditions of any possible survival, navigation, and agency.[37] On the other side, the gradual and often imperceptible normalization of such mutations, not because of any ideological hoodwinking but because they also produce effects in the structures of perception and understanding, generating that crisis of the capacity to make sense.[38] As the word *saturation* itself implies, this is a dual process marked both by the all-too pliable upper limit of absorption — what has taken in more and more of something 'other' to it — and the way that this process appears as a vanishing act of incorporation and distribution, like the sponge that makes the water disappear, the haze that diffuses the light, or the lungs that gather coal dust and can't huff it back out.

The problem is how we are ever to see this. How to look from that outside that keeps trespassing inwards, how to *trasumanar* our interiority and glimpse it in real-time, rather than just retroactively when the damage

---

37 Again, the firefly here may well be a model for this: lacking lungs, the oxygen required for the chemical reaction that produces their light passes into the body through tracheole that remain open, so that each flash is the sign of the outside seeping into a body that cannot help but be porous.

38 In both aspects, I intend this as applying both to humans and to other animals alike, even if the human experience of this may be distinct in its attempt to grapple with this under the sign of *history*.

is already done? I'd suggest that one of the longstanding names for such a glimpsing in the present is, simply enough, *horror*. This opens up to the third and most explicit reason for 'the return of the disappearance': the phrase's echo of horror film and literature, especially in its often schlocky versions, a genre that Pasolini never stepped fully into. Obviously enough, the history of horror is full of returns. Something or someone is always coming back, from the grave, from the dead, from the beyond, and also in titles themselves: the return of the wolfman, the return of the mummy, the return of the return, all these most literal ways of naming seriality and the promise that it will happen again. Here I have in mind one particular return, 1985's *The Return of the Living Dead*, a zombie film at once wholly goofy and massively mournful, and one of the strongest instances I know of giving unsteady image to this logic of saturation. Nominally centered around the leak of a toxic military bioweapon[39] that brings the dead back to life, the film is in a quite explicit way about pollution, and crucially differs in this sense from the more familiar logic of such films in which there is either simply a new condition (the dead keep returning to life) or, especially common now, the viral logic of contagion transmitted one-to-one by a bite. In this film, it is the weapon that looses this into the world, but once out, it just keeps spreading, with even the smallest trace enough to continue the chain: a reanimated corpse is cremated and so sends its smoke into the sky, where the rain brings it back to earth, and the dead start screaming in their graves.[40] To deal with the ravenous undead — who pull off a particularly cunning *organizzar* of their own, hijacking an ambulance radio to tell dispatch to 'send more cops' so that they can keep feasting — the government simply nukes the entire town. The mission is declared a success, and all is finished, except for the film's closing detail, as the general mentions no complications other than a bit of 'acid rain'. That is, the explosion has atomized the infected dead and scattered their particles

---

39 The imagined chemical, Trioxin, bears explicit resemblance in its effects to Agent Orange, and in this way, the film also generates a different sense of the post-Vietnam War return of imperial violence. The weapon designed for afar unleashes a contamination that can't be stopped, like a pulp reboot of Aimé Césaire's account of the 'boomerang' effect of colonial subjectivity.

40 Moreover, the effect in this film doesn't confine itself to those who are dead, or at least are aware of having died. The film's immense pathos lies especially in how the two characters who first are exposed to the gas die without realizing that they have: medics inform them that they have no vital signs, and they protest to no avail that they aren't dead. In this, we see again another sharp schlocky expansion of a historical tension, here calling to mind Pasolini's figure in *Lutheran Letters* of those who were 'destined to be dead' but live all the same.

into the atmosphere, the cremation magnified exponentially to start the entire circuit over again, spreading the vitalizing awareness of being dead wider and wider.[41] This nuclear conclusion makes obvious what is already latent throughout it: a long meditation on the figure of *fallout*, which crucially does not name the moment of the blast — the most infamous flash and glare of imperial power in the twentieth century, the light so bright it burns shadows into the wall — but instead a return that cannot quit, as the radiation-soaked dirt that rises up to the sky and drifts, through air and food chains alike, remaining visible only in elevated rates of cancer and in the presence of strontium-90 in baby teeth.

The film is one of the few I know to fully take on the consequences of such an endless, uncontained return. In its most haunting moment, the released gas returns to life even the butterflies that have been pinned to a board as medical display, their wings flapping but unable to get free. (Made into a film of its own, *The Return of the Disappearance of the Fireflies* would surely end with the Lampyridae drawers of the Smithsonian glowing bright with seething reanimation.) In doing this, it offers a fierce vision of those instances where species, spaces, and lives become deeply and strangely chained together in brief and wrenching visibilities of loss, return, and abjection where we can see mutation and extinction at a standstill. Here, too, we open onto histories not held in drive-ins alone, but in struggles against the ongoing fact of these systems. If we consider the silk industry, for instance, we come upon the fact of how millennia of indoor cultivation has led to silkworms that become moths who are unable to fly, even when not pinned to a board, and who are literally desaturated, having lost their camouflage, so that even if they escaped, they stand out vulnerable to predators. Yet if they lost their color, human workers in the same supply chain found it in scalding ways, in the reeking silk dye houses of early twentieth-century New Jersey, where, as 'part of their job, they worked with boiling chemicals — sometimes skin came right off their hands — and even tasted the mixture to determine proportions'.[42] A century on, the most notorious of those dyes they used, Rhodamine B, is now sometimes fed directly to silkworms, so that the silk they excrete is already dyed, their color-saturated bodies turned into small factories themselves.

---

41   I discuss this film — and this sense of the painful knowledge of being dead — at more length in the second chapter of my book *Combined and Uneven Apocalypse* (Winchester: Zero Books, 2010).

42   Steve Golin, *The Fragile Bridge: Paterson Silk Strike, 1913* (Philadelphia: Temple University Press, 1988), p. 24.

How to exit this hell? Perhaps it means refusing any nostalgia or prospect of going backwards, and instead seizing on the horror as a banner for revolt. In the organization of those same New Jersey workers for their immense strike in 1913, while Elizabeth Gurley Flynn spoke and 'tried to explain the meaning of the red flag [of communism], a striking dyers' helper jumped to his feet. "I know! Here is the red flag!" he exclaimed, and held up his right hand, stained blood red from years of working with dyes'.[43] In other words, *trasumanar* and let the stained hands too burn it to the ground.

*

Ultimately, I think it is this *sense* — not even an idea per se, but a feeling in the guts — of saturation and damage that hangs most potently around the figure of the fireflies and the crisis of perception and clarity that their vanishing names. Because we could add a fourth sense of the return of their disappearance. This is the hard and ongoing labor of never letting such a disappearance become un-searing or just one more familiar fade in the landscape. Instead, it raises the prospect of seeking to keep speaking it fresh, along with the enormous challenge of taking on the invisibility of saturation to make a ground on which to organize. Pasolini's work rarely tipped so openly towards an explicitly ecological register as this, but I would argue that what constitutes much of the force and contradictions of his writings in the mid-'70s lies in how they tried to think about saturation.[44] His texts seek again and again to name this, to find its proof in how bodies and their languages seemed to become unknown or unknowable, and those texts mourned and got bitter and spat spleen when that proof showed itself in full. I think the two poles that his approach to this predominately oriented around, that of a vitalist popular nostalgia and of an apocalyptic judgment of new forms on offer, have only revealed their limits more and more in the decades since. But what matters is this

---

[43] The source continues: 'For an instant there was silence, and then the hall was rent by cries from the husky throats as all realized that this humble dyer indeed knew the meaning of the red badge of his class'. Ibid., p. 82.

[44] We could note the simultaneity of this thinking with different strands of extraparliamentary communist theory happening outside party lines and ranks, in circuits that crossed in and out of the fringes of Italian radical discourse, like that of Jacques Camatte, which focused explicitly on this sense of subsumption. (Some of the crossing points for this involve also the links to gay liberation movements, with a complicated intersection on that front. See my introduction to my translation of Mario Mieli's *Towards a Gay Communism* [London: Pluto Press, 2018] for a discussion of this.)

commitment to taking seriously hunches and suspicions, to think with the edges of perception that don't capture Jenning's grand flash of historical illumination but are tuned instead to those smaller shimmers and whiffs that together add up to the subsumption of human activity and processes of experience alike. It matters for how it articulated something that was never reducible to metaphor, no matter how many it deployed, and instead kept insisting, deadly serious, that, *look, this really is mutation, this is doing this to bodies and speech and to how we even can know who or what we are, and how we go on.* Because like those stains that start in the hands and end in the guts a century later, and like the inability of the fireflies to navigate the night, these changes are actual and tangible, neurological and stubborn and chemical.

We come here to my final, and maybe most obvious point: the same actual physical, spatial, and lighting factors that lead to the ongoing disappearance of the fireflies are also factors working on us too, not metaphorically but very physically. Those Christian-Democrats ate grain touched with the same poisons, and those who wanted to drive them from power walked home through streets that forgot how to be dark and so were half-lit by electricity alone. We get no distance from this, and to recognize the subtle changes it produces in our ability to understand and navigate any conjuncture, we have to strain to hold on to those fleeting moments of horror in order to build an interval in which disappearance stutters. I think, simply enough, that this is one of few things that can be fairly expected of art, literature, and cinema, in their own distinct ways: to produce that small interval, one in which to think the suspicion we feel and to become alien to ourselves for a moment, made untimely and holding to the noticing of the dark when it isn't supposed to be there and we feel the shiver of something passing through us. That thickness of effects cannot be reduced to any theater of power and its footlights, and it is immensely more consequential because of how, like fallout, it evades this. And so maybe we start on the edges of sensing itself, there at the boundary between day and night, there with that most basic sense that *qualcosa* has been happening and something is wrong, as wrong as the moth drained of its camouflage, standing out in the unlit forest bright and obscene and vulnerable as snow in summer.

Ara H. Merjian in conversation with McKenzie Wark
RESIDUES OF THE SACRED[1]

Ara H. Merjian: I wanted to start with Pasolini's film theory, because you've written so insightfully and elegantly on its breadth and complexity in a strikingly synthetic way. One of the things that you discuss is this notion of Pasolini's that cinema's technique *is* its philosophy, one which replaces words with actions and things. He quite famously — and polemically — makes the cinema itself the touchstone of a new ontology. For Pasolini, film does not simply record reality, it is part of a reality which is already, in a fundamental sense, cinematic. In your writing you emphasize, rightly, Pasolini's insistence upon human praxis as a kind of cinema. I was wondering if you think that Pasolini's film theory offers us a kind of philosophy in its own right in this vein.

McKenzie Wark: Yes, clearly Deleuze recognized that Pasolini had a philosophy of cinema. I'm not a Deleuze or Pasolini scholar, but there is a good book to be written about how much of the Deleuze's philosophy of cinema actually comes out of Pasolini. There are obviously other sources but that one is fundamental for Deleuze's *The Movement Image*: that it is a philosophy of cinema as a kind of embrace of the world, a love of the world.[2] The extent to which there's an affirming side to it seems key, and I was interested in the way… well, I was sort of reading Pasolini through work I've done on Bogdanov, and the way that, for Bogdanov all philosophies, all worldviews, are overextensions of a particular practice.[3]

---

1 Transcribed by Matthew Zundel, to whom we extend our gratitude. Lightly edited for length and clarity.
2 Gilles Deleuze, *Cinema 1: The Movement Image*, trans. by Hugh Tomlinson and Barbara Habberjam (Minneapolis: University of Minnesota Press, 1986), pp. 27, 72–76. Louis-Georges Schwartz has written eloquently and incisively on Pasolini's importance for Deleuze's film theory, in 'Typewriter: Free Indirect Discourse in Deleuze's "Cinema"', *SubStance*, 34, 3 (2005), 107–35.
3 McKenzie Wark, *Molecular Red: Theory for the Anthropocene* (London: Verso, 2016).

So whatever your particular practice is, you build that out metaphorically as an understanding of the things that you don't have direct experience of, and Pasolini does that out of cinema.

And of course, Pasolini did seven things — why couldn't that bitch leave at least one art form for somebody else, right? She did them all! Had to be good at poetry, *and* journalism, *and* cinema, *and* the novel — come on!

Merjian: Yeah, leave something for the rest of us!

Wark: — and feuilletons, and theatre… But a key part of it comes out of cinema, and I'd wager that there's insight Pasolini has into a kind of theory — rather than philosophy per se — appropriate to a stage in industrial capitalism. The practice of learning and working in cinema immersed him in the kind of technical language of the economic base that was organizing postwar industrial capitalism. As a good vulgar Marxist he was interested in the forces of production. The technics of cinema were of a piece with those forces in a way that the traditional 'literary' arts were not. But then through those modern, neocapitalist techniques he proposes another possibility for life, one that connects to something ancient, even divine. It is almost a theology of what the semiotics of cinema could be, and at the same time a coming to terms with what he's deemed neo-capitalism.

Merjian: Yes, that opens onto a point that I think of all the time, by way of a young Bernardo Bertolucci, who worked as an assistant on the set of *Accattone* (1961) — which was of course Pasolini's first feature film after some work writing scripts for others. Bertolucci said that being on set was like being at the birth of cinema itself: a kind of coming into being of a phenomenon that Pasolini was taking up as a novice, on the fly, without any practical training, and that lack of sophistication necessarily resulted in a kind of theory in extemporaneous practice. And those dimensions nourished each other. The idea of being at the birth of the cinema also confers upon Pasolini an almost religious or creationist kind of power. In your article 'Pasolini: Sexting the World'[4] you remark that Pasolini maintained a religious approach to realism but not a theological one.

---

4   McKenzie Wark, 'Pasolini: Sexting the World', *Public Seminar*, 15 July 2015 <https://publicseminar.org/2015/07/pasolini-sexting-the-world/> [accessed 15 December 2021].

Wark: Yeah, I imagine there's a certain structure of feeling that comes from an unavoidable encounter with Catholicism growing up in Italy in that particular period. But which obviously is also alienating for him on many levels, not least as a homosexual. (To say "gay" seems a little anachronistic.) In Pasolini there's a structure of access to a sense of the divine world through mediating signs, only they're going to be contemporary rather than historical: it's going to happen through cinema, it's going to happen through modern forms of art. Pasolini is also looking at the everyday rural peasant life and subproletarian life in the city as opening onto something that, at least for a moment, escapes commodification.

So to me he is sort of like the dialectical counterpart to Adorno, who finds the non-commodified in these higher forms and only makes occasional gestures to the popular. Whereas Pasolini — and it's partly to do with his homosexuality — is immersed in a kind of everyday non-bourgeois life. He's perceiving a sphere where on the one hand his sexuality is going to connect him to a street life that has an ancient erotic dimension, that has residues of a sacred world that's not theological; and on the other, through a sort of modern technics he's going to attempt to reach backward to try to escape the logic of the commodity. Out of this he tries to find what I think for Pasolini is a culture out of time, the culture of the subproletariat or the rural and marginal as having a different temporality to the specific historical stages of capitalism. Or: rather than the horizontal, modern time of the commodity, he's interested in a divine, vertical time, but one where the vertical arrow doesn't point up to the heavens, but down, to earthy, earthly pleasures.

Merjian: Absolutely. You have a terrific passage where you write about Pasolini's rhetorical question-and-response about the real: 'But is being natural? No, I don't think so. On the contrary, it seems to be miraculous, mysterious, and if anything absolutely *un*natural'.[5] One of the paradoxes (and of course paradox is the sign under which Pasolini works, though he himself calls it 'contamination', and it goes by a number of different names in his work, from pastiche to mannerism to *sineciosis*) is that he is using a wholly modern technological invention to access something untimely, in-actual. Like any modernist worth his salt, he uses strains of atavism

---

5   Pier Paolo Pasolini, 'Is Being Natural?' (1967), in *Heretical Empiricism*, ed. by Louise K. Barnett, trans. by Louise K. Barnett and Ben Lawton (Bloomington: Indiana University Press, 1988), p. 242.

and primitivism as a way to escape the present. But it's never just that in Pasolini, he's not simply an unreconstructed nostalgist.

Wark: Yeah, that's what keeps it fresh. There are a few works that take a bit of critical negotiating in the twenty-first century, like *Arabian Nights*: this sort of reaching for things that are just maybe out of reach. I mean, Pasolini is a Marxist, and a kind of vulgar one in a sense; for him it's still very much about base and superstructure. As Marx writes in the *Preface to The Contribution to the Critique of Political Economy*, the technical forces of production, and the relations of production that organize them, are the base of any social formation, determining in the long run the form of politics and culture that form the superstructure.

Pasolini is roughly contemporary with Althusser, who argues for the 'relative autonomy' of the superstructures, for an autonomous politics or practice in the cultural sphere. And that unleashes a whole set of practices along the lines of 'alright, so I am a cultural worker, so I work in the superstructures'. But Pasolini has this good critique of how that had missed the mark, particularly in Italy's particular historical circumstances. Circumstances in which a relatively new nation was given a whole new kind of national language in the nineteenth century, but one imposed as a superstructural language which tried to shape a national culture (as well as law and politics) from above. After the Liberation the left worked through these superstructures. The cultural work of the postwar Italian left was influential and left us many masterpieces. But Pasolini is aware by the '60s that this is a losing battle. Those superstructural forms are being made obsolete by changes in the forces of production. The world becomes run by technical languages.

His own access to that new language was firstly through cinema, and he has a brilliant theory of cinema as a technical language, of images and gestures, no longer bound by the national, literary written word. But one that could potentially be a part of a different world. And then secondarily through television. To my knowledge he doesn't write directly about this, but also as someone who is interior to the spectacle itself, as someone who is a controversialist, someone constantly interviewed and photographed and a subject of the media in his own right: that to me is also part of his practice.

Merjian: Yes, the knowledge of himself as a subject and as an object of mediatic scrutiny, of endless juridical persecution and process, absolutely informed his sense of a certain kind of powerlessness against something that was developing a momentum that could not be slowed or reversed. With regard to television, though, he was singularly, resolutely, almost maniacally opposed to it. He called it a form of 'cultural genocide', an engine of cultural and linguistic levelling that had no precedence in modern Italy, or in history at large.[6] In part he allowed himself to be a crypto-Catholic because he felt that the Church's actual influence, even its clerical corruption and false pieties, paled in comparison to this new strain of techno-uniformity which television epitomized. His reading of the French philosopher and sociologist Lucien Goldmann [a former student of Lukács] was important here. Goldmann called bourgeois ideology the 'first ideology to deny anything sacred', and the creator of 'the first radically nonaesthetic form of consciousness'.[7] That filters into Pasolini's notion of neocapitalist culture as a new, unprecedented form of totality, a totalitarianism in its own right: one more thoroughgoing in its secular totality than Fascism had ever dreamed of becoming...

Wark: Like nearly all the great Western Marxists, of whom he's more or less contemporary, he's fundamentally a pessimist. And I don't know how this got read as something else by the New Left at the time, but his thought emerges from the same vein as Adorno, Marcuse, Sartre, the later Debord, who are completely pessimistic about what capitalism had become. Although I think he had a far better grasp than his contemporaries of how capitalism was evolving into something else.

Merjian: Yes, a certain negativity in the Adornian sense seems fundamental to aspects of his work. By the late 1960s he starts venturing self-consciously 'unconsumable' and 'unpopular' experiments. His work in the theatre [and his contemporary 'Manifesto for a New Theatre'][8] entails a good deal of wilful opacity, which, if not Adornian per se, certainly

---

6   See, inter alia, Pier Paolo Pasolini, 'Neocapitalismo televisivo', Interview with Arturo Gismondi, *Vie Nuove*, 13, 51 (1958), now in *Saggi sulla politica e sulla società*, ed. by Walter Siti (Milan: Mondadori, 1999), II, p. 1554; and *Pasolini e la television*, ed. by Angela Felice (Venice: Marsilio, 2011).

7   Lucien Goldmann, *Towards a Sociology of the Novel*, trans. by Alan Sheridan (London: Tavistock Publications, 1975 [1964]), p. 14. Pasolini discusses his influence by Goldmann's re-readings of Lukács in a 1965 letter to Marco Belocchio, reprinted in *Pier Paolo Pasolini: Lettere 1955-1975* (Turin: Einaudi, 1988), II, pp. 2802–03.

8   Pier Paolo Pasolini, 'Manifesto for a New Theatre', trans. by David Ward, *Pasolini: Contemporary Perspectives*, ed. by Patrick Rumble and Bart Testa (Toronto: Toronto University Press, 1994), pp. 152-70.

shares some of its elements. But with regard to the New Left, what's so interesting is that at the very moment that he dissented so aggressively from its emergence in Europe, he claimed to find in America (particularly when he visited New York for the first time in '66) the sparks of a new, non-Marxist culture of revolt, which reminded him of Italy's Resistance and its afterlife in the immediate postwar years. The latter had of course been neutralized, subsumed, suborned by the 1960s — not only by an almost uninterrupted Christian Democratic rule since 1948, but even more so by Italy's economic 'miracle' of the late 1950s and the neocapitalist culture that attended it.

Wark: He's a contemporary of prominent critics and philosophers identifying the Black struggle as central to that moment of the late 1960s and early '70s, even in Europe.

Merjian: Absolutely. Pasolini's engagement with 'African America' is complex, fraught, and important.[9] There are some problematic elements to it, to the extent for example that he identifies the entire African-American population at the time as a uniformly 'subproletariat' entity, which of course was not necessarily the case and was in some ways hopelessly essentializing. But it was for him a further space of the 'Third World' that he was desperately turning to at the time. And in America he found it operating within the very model of first-worldism and imperial power, and so for him was even more meaningful as a potential model of resistance to postwar neocapitalist culture, the battle over which he felt had already been lost in Europe.

Wark: It's interesting to me that it's Pasolini and Genet who have a certain instinct about where the actual struggles lay at the time, and I wonder how much that's connected to homosexuality as an experience of everyday life, as an experience — on the level of the body — of how power operates in everyday life. Both articulated political theory and practice out of observing how power is operating in the same spaces where they're looking for 'trade', basically.

---

9   Ara H. Merjian, 'Pasolini's African America: Race, Class, and the Limits of the Analogical Imagination', *SubStance: A Review of Theory and Literary Criticism*, 153, 49, 3 (November 2020), pp. 71–100; and '"Howls from the Left": Pier Paolo Pasolini, Allen Ginsberg, and the Legacies of Beat America', in *Pasolini Framed and Unframed: A Thinker for the Twenty-First Century*, ed. by Luca Peretti and Karen Raizen (London: Bloomsbury, 2019) pp. 37–62.

Merjian: One of the things you write about eloquently is the notion of Pasolini as one of the great practitioners of Marxist thought in action. And one of his more famous lines of poetry borrowed from the American counter-cultural movement at the time he talks about wanting 'To throw my body into the struggle'. Could we say the action in question was, quite often, simply that of fucking and sucking or, being fucked and using his body...

Wark: ... do we know how he liked it?

Merjian: There was evidently a witness whom Barth David Schwartz quotes in his excellent *Pasolini Requiem*. Evidently this tough was hanging out at the bar, I think near Termini, when Pino Pelosi [the man convicted of murdering Pasolini] was discussing with Pasolini whether or not to get in his car that night. Someone else evidently warned him 'don't go with that one, that's Pasolini and he'll try to fuck you in the ass'.[10] Whether or not that's true, you know...

Wark: (Laughs) Can we say he's an unreliable witness?

Merjian: Definitely an unreliable witness...

Wark: It could just be me, but I think there are specific phenomenologies to particular sex acts, so I'm always curious as to, well, 'How'd he like it?'—you know, and how that might have changed how Pasolini thought about the world.
This leads to something I want to ask you about, which is *Petrolio*, about its transsexuality, where both of the novel's double Carlo characters change gender, one of them as a woman who then has sex with twenty men in a field. So how do we read that particular version of sexuality in Pasolini?

Merjian: Well, it's interesting, as I think I mentioned to you, I was just reading again the really inspiring introduction to Stephen Sartarelli's translation of Pasolini's poetry, and he refers to *Petrolio* as a 'transgeneric' novel. That is, 'trans' in the sense of genre rather than gender.[11] And yet there is also, at the heart of the novel, this conceit of transgenderism which

---

10 Barth David Schwartz, *Pasolini Requiem* (Chicago and London: Chicago University Press, 2017 [1992]) p. 38.
11 *The Selected Poetry of Pier Paolo Pasolini*, ed. and trans. by Stephen Sartarelli (Chicago: University of Chicago Press, 2014), p. 3.

is linked to its political indictments and of course the various (horrible) changes that Italy is going through.

Wark: Yeah, probably not in a good sense. You know there's something about the fall of both versions of Carlo that's connected to becoming woman in some weird way…

Merjian: The queer politics of Pasolini's work (or their politics of queerness?) are never going to be satisfying from the place that we're standing in. His queerness seems always to come from a place of, well, if not self-loathing, then some kind of enduring self-doubt which still feels shot through with shame of some sort. I mean, how could it not in Rome for Christ's sake. Though part of that also surely stemmed from a sense, a foreknowledge, that queerness itself would be commodified in short order. And how right he was.

This also bears upon something you were saying earlier about the New Left. For various reasons he wanted nothing to do with their particular refashioning of Marxism after Hungary in 1956, after the Khrushchev speech, after the invasion of Czechoslovakia in 1968. Marxism started organizing itself around something other than a heroic proletariat. But of course that had never been the crux of Pasolini's Marxism to begin with. And he wanted nothing to do with what we would now call a politics of identity. Despite his stubborn dedication to Communism — even despite himself, after the way the party treated him — his connection to the urban working class had always been complicated (maybe even undermined?) by an attraction to its *lumpen* subjects on the level of flesh and language. Who themselves refused the identity of class, in ways maybe comparable to the ways he would refuse the identity of queerness. A *lack* of consciousness — class or otherwise — was always one of Pasolini's redemptive atavisms, a way forward by way of a more worthy past, of a kind of non-knowledge.

Wark: And his eros of the *lumpen* actually then connects to why it would intuitively seem right to him what the Black Panthers are doing at the time, and why any colonial struggles based on something other than the workerist subject would make sense.

Merjian: That's absolutely right. And he meets with some of them in New York, including Stokely Carmichael. His commentary in [the meta-documentary film] *La Rabbia* [Rage] (1963) that after the war 'a new phenomenon explodes upon post-war world: that of color', by which he means, ironically but also elegiacally, race ['*Scoppia un nuovo problema nel mondo. Si chiama colore*'] is prophetic in this sense. I mean the extent to which, compared to a lot of his contemporaries he insisted upon race as a determinant of, well, everything. A whole slew of decolonization projects inform his worldview over the 1950s and '60s, and he was traveling to many of them. Looking for shooting locations but also looking for places outside of bourgeois time.

It's crucial to think about the extent to which, as you were saying, his queerness plays a role in that, because there is obviously an erotics of the anti-colonial in him. I'm not entirely familiar with the ethnic extraction of the 'trade' Genet went in for, but his *voyous* seem always coded as non-white in a certain sense, just as Pasolini's were generally non-northern. Like his great love Ninetto Davoli, whose people came from the Roman *borgata* by way of Calabria. We find it everywhere in Pasolini's work. I was just reading his writing on the paintings of day laborers by his friend, the Sicilian Communist painter, Renato Guttuso. Pasolini wrote this catalog introduction around the same time that they were both collaborating on *La Rabbia*. Which itself takes the 'Third World' as an alternative to the Western neocapitalist present. Pasolini writes about Guttuso's figures that their 'lips and nostrils are big, Sicilian'.[12] It's a quick line but it's telling.

Wark: Oh totally, yeah, there is plenty of that in Genet. And again, those texts don't look that great from a twenty-first-century progressive, intersectional point of view, 'from above', as it were. But Pasolini and Genet were both touching on the milieu of the street because they liked trade. There are forms of interaction with the lumpenproletariat, if we must call it that in Marx's rather Victorian language. Those 'lowlife' figures who embody for them the vulgar in a quite specific but also expansive sense. The two of them are interesting in that way. One can end up in 'the life' due to all kinds of exclusions, of race, region, sexuality, poverty…

Merjian: It's always struck me as funny that Genet said that he never went to movies because one couldn't smoke.

One thing I wanted to talk about because you've written so much and so passionately and incisively on Debord and on the Situationists in general is this notion that for Pasolini, as you write, 'the history of communication can be read critically and retrospectively from the point of view of its

---

12   Pier Paolo Pasolini, 'Twenty Drawings by Renato Guttuso', in *Venti disegni di Renato Guttuso* (Rome: Galleria La nuova Pesa/Riuniti, 1962).

most advanced development'.[13] A couple of things. One: unlike the neo-avantgarde and his contemporaries, Pasolini thought that any attention to the stylistic and technical aspects of language was a kind of empty formalist exercise by this point — the waging of a war that had already been lost, a war against language rather than the social forces that are producing that language. And I think of Debord's notion of the spectacle as something that unites individuals only in their separateness — something that Anselm Jappe writes about really incisively in his biography.[14] And Jappe's first chapter is titled 'Must we burn Debord?'. There has been some similar thinking with regard to Pasolini (I'm thinking in particular of Pierpaolo Antonello's wonderful book *Dimenticare Pasolini* [*Forgetting Pasolini*]).[15]

Pasolini has a wonderful line in one essay from 1967 where he says: 'Whoever loves reality too much, as I do, eventually hates it, rebels against it, and tells it to go to hell'.[16] We might say the same about Debord and Pasolini themselves. How do we use their thinking now? Like Debord's evolving versions of the spectacle, or the names Pasolini coined for something similar (the 'new fascism', an 'anthropological mutation', etc.). Should we still use these but also, eventually, maybe necessarily, also tell them to go to hell, in a sense? Their philosophies are incredibly prophetic, but always inescapably outmoded. And Pasolini would be the first to insist upon that now, I think. What he considered 'totalizing' about culture in the mid-1970s now seems hopelessly quaint, just as Fascism's supposed totalitarianism had seemed to him in comparison to neocapitalism. It's interesting to think about the insidiousness of the Internet — keeping people united in their separateness, apart in their 'connection' —, how do we think Pasolini and Debord might have responded to this? Does it matter? Might there have been any common ground in how they responded to it?

Wark: Debord and Pasolini might from the perspective of our time be the writers of the eulogies of a revolution whose moment was missed. They're delightfully incompatible figures in lots of ways, Debord does come out of a more explicitly avant-garde tradition. Pasolini's relation to the avant-

---

13 Wark, 'Pasolini: Sexting the World'. See also McKenzie Wark, *The Spectacle of Disintegration* (London: Verso, 2013).

14 Anselm Jappe, *Guy Debord*, trans. by Donald Nicholson Smith (Berkeley: University of California Press, 1999).

15 Pierpaolo Antonello, *Dimenticare Pasolini: Intellettuali e impegno nell'Italia contemporanea* (Milan: Mimesis, 2013).

16 Pier Paolo Pasolini, 'Living Signs and Dead Poets' (1967), in *Heretical Empiricism*, p. 252.

garde was a lot more complicated than I thought it was, as I've learned thanks to your book! But that's a whole separate thing we can talk about. It's interesting to note that Debord spent a lot of time in Italy after '68, and his later theory of the 'integrated spectacle' is based on both the Italian and French examples. Debord says somewhere that the goal of the integrated spectacle is to turn secret police into revolutionaries and revolutionaries into secret police. That sense of security apparatus of the state being out of control, those aspects of the paranoid bureaucratic apparatus that we associate with Soviet Union and its satellites, that was also at work in states like Italy and France. The usual: mysterious assassinations, not quite knowing who's actually running various parts of the state apparatus... and of course *Petrolio* [Pasolini's unfinished experimental novel][17] is essentially about this. Among other things it's about the Fascists getting their hands on a bit of the state oil business.

They're sort of thinking similar things, and there's a way you can think Debord's idea about how the spectacle evolves historically as connected to Pasolini's concept of neocapitalism. Spectacle is an historical category in Debord that maybe comes into being around 1917 to 1919 with the failure of both the Russian and German revolutions. When the labor movement itself becomes spectacularized is maybe the beginnings of the society of the spectacle, in both its diffuse (western) and concentrated (Soviet bloc) forms. Debord thinks there's a particular historical stage where aspects of a bureaucratic socialist version of spectacle and the western version have synthesized — that's France, Italy in the '70s and '80s. It's not unrelated, maybe, to the way that Pasolini is trying to think neo-capitalism. They are both interested in the way that both objects and subjects are getting manufactured and the role of the image in the closure of the loop of commodification. Debord has this sublime desire, perennially deferred, for total Revolution. But in the beautiful later texts he is mostly grieving the loss of that as a possibility. Pasolini I think is looking to, well, residues of what's left of a pre-capitalist world, that could point to what might be possible, or might have been possible.

Merjian: Which he thinks — for a time — might be located in the non-bourgeois body, almost as a kind of talisman. The non-'First World' body which could still be found in the *borgate* of Rome, or in Italy's South, or increasingly further afield in India and the dozens of African countries he

---

17 Pier Paolo Pasolini, *Petrolio* (Milan: Mondadori, 2005 [1992; 1972–1975]).

visited in the 1960s, and the ghettos of Harlem and the Bronx. Though later he has to give up even that idea.

Wark: And Debord doesn't make that turn. He's French! He doesn't really have access to that, because Italy has this very different history in terms of development. That is, Italy was never wholly, really part of 'Western' Europe in the same way. Because of the 'southern question' as Gramsci writes about it, and as it filters into Pasolini's thought.

Merjian: That's true. Also by way of the anthropologist and ethnographer Ernesto de Martino in whose work Pasolini was very interested, and maybe connected in roundabout ways to the philosophy of Mircea Eliade in the '60s.

But didn't France have the *banlieue*, and the Algerian presence in Situationism itself?[18] Wasn't there a Third World presence in Debord's Paris which opened up that as a realm of possibility to him and his peers? They're already talking about the problem and the question of decolonization before it gets taken up more aggressively in '68. Which is yet another example of Situationism *driving* politics and history rather than serving — as some would still have it — as some feeble 'art organization'.[19]

Wark: Yeah, it's true, and the Situationists were early critics of the kind of attempts at some sort of bureaucratic state capitalism that happens in places like Algeria. They're somewhat pessimistic about it because it's not a revolution of the totality; and they're pressing about that in certain ways.

---

18 T. J. Clark and Donald Nicholson-Smith call out in particular 'the series of interventions in the evolving situation in Algeria, at the time of Ben Bella and Boumedienne, culminating in the long article "Les Luttes de classes en Algérie" (published in the Situationist journal for March 1966, and then as a wall poster)'. T. J. Clark and Donald Nicholson-Smith, 'Why Art Can't Kill the Situationist International', *October*, 79, Guy Debord and the Internationale Situationniste (Winter 1997), p. 21.

19 See Clark and Nicholson-Smith's meticulous and nuanced dissection of the crude, and reactionary, histories of the Situationist International which patronize the movement's political ambitions. As Clark and Nicholson-Smith write: 'It was the "art" dimension, to put it crudely — the continual pressure put on the question of representational forms in politics and everyday life, and the refusal to foreclose on the issue of representation versus agency — that made their politics the deadly weapon it was for a while'. 'Why Art Can't Kill the Situationist International', p. 29.

T. J. Clark refers to Debord's 'chiliastic serenity', which is a beautiful phrase.[20]

Merjian: 'The real revolutionary knows how to wait', is the Situationist refrain, no? Which maybe connects in some sense to Gramsci's 'war of position'?

Wark: Revolution is all or nothing in Debord, and it becomes, I think, a kind of revolution of nostalgia. There's a way in which Debord and Pasolini are both playing on nostalgia but they don't want to be entirely conservative and reactionary and backward-looking. This sense of attempting to bring into an historical present things that were missed opportunities, past possibilities. For Debord it's doubly the case: it's to continually have a refrain about all of the moments of possibility and defeat so that the moment before the Stalinists take over... the Revolution in 1930s Cataluña, for example, is one of Debord's moments. The other is those moments of pure freedom of the *dérive*, of being outside of commodified time, of experiencing another city for another life. Among a rather different kind of 'lowlife', of bar flies, street people. (Lacking in homosexual adventure also, although Juan Goytisolo writes in passing about nights out with Debord and Michèle Bernstein.) Compared to Pasolini it's very urban and lacking that sense of the kind of rural and pastoral. It's very Parisian. Debord was from the provinces too but forgot all about the provinces when he got to Paris, whereas Pasolini does not.

Merjian: Absolutely. In a sense Pasolini tries to live this Friulian peasant world, which he never really was part of anyway, in Rome. He desperately wants Rome to reproduce elements of a peasant world recusant to the pace and sophistication of the modern city. That's why he loves the Baths of Caracalla (which was still the haunt of prostitutes and johns), and the spaces around the edges of the *borgate*. He was drawn to those spaces in the city that are not even the *banlieue*, that are somehow stubbornly unreadable.

Wark: Yes, and unlike in Paris, the spoken language was still (Roman) dialect. Debord was not a student of language in the same way. Actually Debord comes back around to it in his later work, which his second wife Alice Becker-Ho picks up through underworld language... cant, Romani,

---

20   T. J. Clark, *The Painting of Modern Life: Paris in the Art of Manet and his Followers* (Princeton, NJ: Princeton University Press, 1999 [1985]), p. 10.

the ancient world of Villon. They're looking for those affordances in the margins of what much earlier in France becomes a dominant national language. Whereas in Italy the shift to an official national language is much more recent, and even then an incomplete achievement by the national cultural superstructures.

Merjian: Yes, the French administrative state after the Revolution did away ruthlessly and efficiently with regional languages, with just few marginal cases enduring (Basque and Occitan and such). But of course, for Pasolini, even the Third Republic's banning of other languages — even Mussolini's injunctions against dialect and non-Italian language — were fitful and almost pathetic compared to the technocratic and mediatic sea-change following Italy's consumerist boom. Dialect is for Pasolini the chief sign of difference.

Wark: For their part Debord and Becker-Ho are looking for the linguistic affordances to evade both the commodity and the police in cant, in jargon, you know, in thieves' discourse, in Villon… Whereas Pasolini had living examples of actual dialects, some of which didn't even have written form. And of course he tried to elevate Friulian dialect to a literary form. It's key to his film theory too. Dialect is (usually) spoken-only language. National Italian is spoken-written language. Cinema will be the written form of the gestural language of everyday life in neocapitalism, and beyond all national borders.

Merjian: Yes, and that fixation with idiomatic difference and marginality extended even to what Pasolini called 'dialectal painting'.[21] Even long after he painted peasants and maids and day laborers and young local boys in Friuli. Up until the mid-'70s and almost up until *Salò*, really, he still clung to 'expressivity'. This notion of 'dialectal' visuality as a means of opposing cultural 'homologation'. He even has characters in the *Decameron* speak Neapolitan instead of Tuscan, and that film is quite late in Pasolini's corpus. I think he thought that in the folds and crevices and shaded margins of language he could hold out against what he called the 'frontal and flat'

---

21 See Pier Paulo Pasolini, 'Dialectal Painting' (1954), in *Heretical Aesthetics: Pasolini on Painting*, ed. by Ara H. Merjian and Alessandro Giammei (London: Verso, 2023); Ara H. Merjian, *Against the Avant-Garde: Pier Paolo Pasolini, Art, and Politics* (Chicago: University of Chicago Press, 2020); and Francesco Galluzzi, *Pasolini e la pittura* (Rome: Bulzoni, 1994).

world of the media and its levelling modes of communication. What he called the 'brutal finality' of neocapitalism.

Maybe as a way of concluding, with regard to that term and its outsized presence in Pasolini's work... The 'neo-' was not solely his. In fact it had already accumulated a certain currency by the early 1960s. Italy was even perceived as having helped coin it! At least according to an essay in *Time* magazine at the time.[22] Yet as you've written, Pasolini refused to let new phenomena go by outmoded names and descriptions. He writes in his 'Linguistic Diary' the following year that '[t]he typical operation of common sense is to defend oneself from uncomfortable novelties by making them pass for old'.[23] He insisted on consigning the world of monopoly capitalism to what he called 'paleocapitalism' — something that had to be contrasted (in its partialness, in its still somehow limited seriality and totality) to this new virulent strain of capitalism. (And medical, diagnostic language is always cropping up in his writings and films at the time...)

You have just published a book called *Capital is Dead: Is This Something Worse?*.[24] Were you thinking of Pasolini's own terminological obsessions? And of how these help us think around, or through, theoretical or philosophical problems regarding late capitalism and its effects on culture?

Wark: You know both Pasolini and his Italian context so much better than I do, so thank you for that. Pasolini has been important to me in lots of ways. As a radical queer ancestor, for example, and as someone whose Marxism wasn't genteel, wasn't academic. It came out of a praxis in and against the media forms of his time. Among other things, *Capital is Dead* gestures towards an alternative genealogy of Marxisms that are intelligent, innovative, conceptually rich, but which have a life outside the academic superstructures. Which in some way touch on everyday life, emerging technics, vernacular forms, emerging struggles. Angela Davis is another example I give in that book — surely the most lively inheritor of the Frankfurt school, among other things! I've written elsewhere in

---

22 *Time*, 84, 18 (30 October 1964), p. 109. By the author's account, neocapitalism had 'already made doctrinaire Marxism outdated' by 'raising the standard of living to an undreamed-of level of prosperity'. See also Merjian, *Against the Avant-Garde*, p. 9.
23 Pier Paolo Pasolini, 'Linguistic Diary', *Rinascita*, 6 March 1965; reprinted in *Heretical Empiricism*, p. 39.
24 McKenzie Wark, *Capital is Dead: Is This Something Worse* (London: Verso, 2021).

the Situationists and Platonov in the same vein. There's a whole counter-history or counter-histories of such Marxisms yet to be composed. To have done with the received canon we inherited from the New Left.

I think if one can thread together some of these other Marxisms one can get out of that habit made doubly worse by the conventions of repetitive citation and exegesis where common sense defends us from uncomfortable novelties by making them pass for old. It so often seems that in today's supposedly Marxist writing that capital is an eternal essence. That it changes only in appearances. That's even more depressing than Pasolini's pessimism! So rather than be exegetes of Pasolini's corpus, how can we learn from his living praxis of generating concepts out of engagement with our own distinctive moment in history? There's a lot to learn — even in translation — from how he works and plays with language. The way he makes the forging of new language not an end in itself but a means to articulate the present. Such that we see the past of this present anew and see possible futures anew also.

MICHAEL HARDT
EXPOSURE
Pasolini in the Flesh[1]

For Agamben

La crocifissione

Ma noi predichiamo Cristo crocifisso: | scandalo pe' Giudei, stoltezza | pe' Gentili.
Paolo, *Lettera ai Corinti*

Tutte le piaghe sono al sole | ed Egli muore sotto gli occhi | di tutti: perfino la madre | sotto il petto, il ventre, i ginocchi, | guarda il Suo corpo patire. | L'alba e il vespro Gli fanno luce | sulle braccia aperte e l'Aprile | intenerisce il Suo esibire | la morte a sguardi che Lo bruciano.

Perché Cristo fu ESPOSTO in Croce? | Oh scossa del cuore al nudo | corpo del giovinetto ... atroce | offesa al suo pudore crudo

Crucifixion

But we preach Christ crucified: | scandal for the Jews, folly | for the Gentiles.
Paul, *Letter to the Corinthians*

All His wounds are open to the sun | and He dies under the eyes | of everyone: even His mother | under His breast, belly, and knees, | watches His body suffer. | Dawn and dusk cast light | on His open arms and April | softens His exhibition of death | to gazes that burn Him.

Why was Christ EXPOSED on the Cross? | Oh, the heart shudders at the naked | body of the youth ... atrocious | offense to its raw

---

1 Originally published as 'Exposure: Pasolini in the Flesh', *Canadian Review of Comparative Literature*, 24, 3 (September 1997), 581–87. I would like to thank Gail Hamner, Frank Lentricchia, Michael Moon, Karen Ocaña, Karen Pinkus, and Steve Shaviro for their comments on earlier drafts of this essay. All translations of Pasolini's texts are my own.

... | Il sole e gli sguardi! La voce | estrema chiese a Dio perdono | con un singhiozzo di vergogna | rossa nel cielo senza suono, | tra pupille fresche e annoiate | di Lui: morte, sesso e gogna.

Bisogna esporsi (questo insegna il povero | Cristo inchiodato?), | la chiarezza del cuore è degna | di ogni scherno, di ogni peccato | di ogni più nuda passione ... | (questo vuol dire il Crocifisso? | sacrificare ogni giorno il dono | rinunciare ogni giorno al perdono | sporgersi ingenui sull'abisso).

Noi staremo offerti sulla croce, | alla gogna, tra le pupille | limpide di gioia feroce, | scoprendo all'ironia le stille | del sangue dal petto ai ginocchi, | miti, ridicoli, tremando | d'intelletto e passione nel gioco | del cuore arso dal suo fuoco, | per testimoniare lo scandalo.

modesty ... | The sun and the gazes! The ultimate | voice asked God forgiveness | with a sob of red shame | in a sky without sound, | between His fresh and weary | pupils: death, sex, and pillory.

You must expose yourself (is this what the | poor nailed-up Christ teaches?), | the clarity of the heart is worthy | of every sneer, every sin, | every more naked passion ... | (is this what the Crucifix means? | sacrifice every day the gift | renounce every day forgiveness | cast yourself ingenuous over the abyss).

We will be offered on the cross, | on the pillory, between the pupils | limpid with ferocious joy, | leaving open to irony the drops | of blood from the breast to the knees, | gentle and ridiculous, trembling | with intellect and passion in the play | of the heart burning from its fire, | testifying to the scandal.[2]

---

2   Pier Paolo Pasolini, 'La Crocifissione', in *Bestemmia: Tutte le poesie*, ed. by Graziella Chiarcossi and Walter Siti, 2 vols. (Milan: Garzanti, 1993), II, p. 376–77.

Incarnation

Paul wrote from his prison cell to the Philippians:

> Adopt towards one another, in your mutual relations, the same attitude that was found in Christ. Although he was in the form of God, he did not regard this divine equality as a precious thing to be exploited. Instead, he emptied himself by taking the form of a slave and being born like other human beings. And being in human form, he humbled himself and became obedient to the point of death, even death on the cross.

Abandon me! Incarnation is all about abandonment — abandonment to the flesh. Paul writes that in becoming flesh Christ abandoned the form of God; he emptied himself by taking on a limited materiality. This self-emptying is the exposure of the flesh. It is a kind of slavery that appeared to Paul in prison as liberation. What exactly did Christ abandon when he emptied himself? Certainly he did not abandon divinity as such; rather, he emptied the transcendental *form* and carried divinity into the material. From one perspective this abandoned being might seem precarious, foundationless, cast over the abyss, but really this abandonment testifies instead to the fullness of the surfaces of being. The self-emptying or *kenosis* of Christ, the evacuation of the transcendental, is the affirmation of the plenitude of the material, the fullness of the flesh.

Incarnation is first of all a metaphysical thesis that the essence and existence of being are one and the same. There is no ontological essence that resides beyond the world. None of being or God or nature remains outside existence, but rather all is fully realized, fully expressed, without remainder, in the flesh. Incarnation means that the absolute oneness of all being, infinite and eternal, coincides completely with the constant becoming-different of the modalities of existence. The figure of Christ has often been understood as a point of mediation of the external relationship between divine essence and worldly existence. But the incarnation, the self-emptying of Christ, denies any possible exteriority and hence any need for mediation. Any imagined transcendent substance, separated from the world, is merely a hollow husk, a form emptied of all being. Or better, the transcendent is more properly understood as residing within the material, immanent, as its in-dwelling potentiality.[3] Transcendence, the condition of possibility of being, should not be imagined as above or below the

---

3   See Giorgio Agamben, *The Coming Community*, trans. by Michael Hardt (Minneapolis: University of Minnesota Press, 1993), pp. 14–15: 'The transcendent

material — it dwells, rather, precisely at its very surface. Incarnation is the claim that there is no opposition and no mediation necessary between the transcendent and the immanent, but an intimate complementarity. This immanent transcendence is the innermost exteriority of being, the potentiality of the flesh.

Incarnation is also a theological proposition: The plenitude of materiality, the fullness of existence is divine. But why should we even speak about divinity here, when the form of God has been completely emptied out, abandoned? Because divinity marks the essential vitality of existence. The surfaces of the world are charged with a powerful intensity. Divinity resides precisely in the boundaries or thresholds of things, at their limits, passionate and exposed, as if surrounding them with a halo. Incarnation abandons any notion of a hidden God, any transcendental notion of a divinity that remains 'pure' outside the exposure of materiality. This is the good news whispered to us by the 'impure angel' that Pasolini loves. In the incarnation the divine becomes flesh with an electric vitality; and in turn our innocent limbs become divine, 'con le carni brucianti | di splendidi sorrisi' [with the burning flesh of splendid smiles].[4]

Finally, incarnation is an ethical injunction: empty yourself, become flesh! This is the lesson the poor nailed-up Christ teaches us. (How little we have realized our flesh! We don't even know what flesh can do!) Incarnation is an option of joy and love. And the ultimate form of love is precisely the belief in *this* world, as it is.[5] So be it. (What else could Spinoza have meant by the love of God?) Our belief can finally have no object other than the flesh. Becoming flesh will be our joy.

Christ's life in the flesh plays out this drama. The metaphysical emptying-out which takes place in the incarnation at the beginning of Christ's life is perfectly balanced by the recognition at the end of his life of abandonment on the cross. Or rather, the birth of Christ is merely a formal incarnation, a nominal abandonment to this world. The real incarnation takes place on Calvary. Only hanging on the cross does Christ realize the flesh. When the

---

    is not a supreme entity above all things; rather, the pure transcendent is the taking-place of every thing'.

4   Pasolini, 'Carne e cielo', in *Bestemmia*, p. 341.

5   See Gilles Deleuze, *Cinema 2: The Time-Image*, trans. by Hugh Tomlinson and Robert Galeta (Minneapolis: University of Minnesota Press, 1989), p. 172: 'Only belief in the world can reconnect man to what he sees and hears. The cinema must film, not the world, but belief in this world, our only link […]. Whether we are Christians or atheists, in our universal schizophrenia, *we need reasons to believe in this world*'.

naked body exposed on the cross cries with its ultimate voice, 'Why have you forsaken me?', the question can only be rhetorical. The abandonment took place long before; the incarnation at birth was symbol of the emptying out of any possible addressee. What happens on the cross is that Christ fully fulfills that abandonment in the flesh. Christ was abandoned to the divinity of the flesh, in love and joy.

Exposure

Take me now! Pasolini is fascinated with the immodest offering of Christ's body on the cross. His wounds are open. His entire body — breast, belly, sex, and knees — is burning under the gazes of the crowd and the elements. At the point of death, Christ is all body, an open piece of flesh, abandoned, exposed. This is when Christ's emptied divinity, its radiant surfaces shine forth most brightly.

The exposure of flesh is erotic. The divine charge that courses through the surfaces of being creates this intensity, this excitement. Eroticism, as Georges Bataille tells us, is assenting to life up to the point of death.[6] Christ's incarnation is this pure affirmation of life, even to the point of death on the cross. Death functions here, however, not as the point of fascination nor as an instinct or drive of life, but merely as a negative limit that highlights in contrast life's affirmation. The erotic points us toward the vital continuity extending across the surfaces of being. It breaks down or dissolves the separateness, the self-possession, the discontinuity that exists among individual entities and things. It strips them naked, empties them, and puts them in common. Eroticism is thus a state of communication that testifies to our striving toward a possible continuity of being, beyond the prison of the self.[7] The limits or boundaries of individual entities become open thresholds that feel the pleasures — the rise and the recess — of flows and intensities.

Erotic exposure, paradoxically, does not really involve seeing and being seen. In fact, exposure subverts a certain regime of vision. The exposed flesh does not reveal a secret self that had been hidden, but rather dissolves

---

6   See Georges Bataille, *Erotism*, trans. by Mary Dalwood (San Francisco: City Lights, 1986).
7   See ibid., p. 17: 'The transition from the normal state to that of erotic desire presupposes a partial dissolution of the person as he exists in the realm of discontinuity [...]. It is a state of communication revealing a quest for a possible continuance of being beyond the confines of the self'.

any self that could be apprehended. We not only have nothing left to hide, we no longer present any separate thing for the eyes to grasp. We become imperceptible. In the erotic we lose ourselves, or rather we abandon our discontinuity in a naked and divine communion.

Christ's crucified body is exemplary of this eroticism. For Pasolini, however, in contrast to Bataille, the erotic is not predicated on any kind of transgression. Transgression always functions in relation to (or in complicity with) a norm or taboo, negating the dictates of the norm and yet paradoxically re-enforcing the norm's effects. The transgressive act does not simply refuse the norm, but rather negates it, transcends it, and completes it. It exceeds a limit, but in its excess verifies the limit itself. Transgression always operates through a dialectic of negations. If the norm were destroyed, the transgression itself would lose all value. Pasolini's erotics depend not on transgression but exposure. No norm or taboo forms a negative foundation and no synthesis transcends the opposition. Exposure operates rather on a purely positive logic of emanation. It involves casting off, or really, emptying out all that is external to its material existence and then intensifying that materiality. What is exposed is naked flesh, absolute immanence, a pure affirmation.

Exposed flesh is not transgression but scandal. In other words, exposure does indeed oppose and negate the norms of propriety, but its effect does not depend on that opposition as a support. Violation of the norm is not primary to exposure; the negation is secondary, an afterthought, an accident. It turns its back on the norm — that is its great offence. Exposure operates in ignorance of the norm, and thus conducts, in the only way possible, its real destruction. Christ's body testifies to the scandal, the scandal of the cross.

Crucifixion

In the act of incarnation Christ takes the form of a slave and renounces any divine separation not as a demonstration of ascetic denial but rather in search for the continuity of life and community. This being in common is an escape from prison. Sacrificing the gift is an option of joy. The exposure in the form of a slave that we all share, however, carries with it always and necessarily the potential of the most horrible torments, to the point of torture on the cross.

The effect of torture is always separation and discontinuity even in situations of extreme proximity and intimacy. Often we cannot even recognize our torturers as human; they are irremediably other to us. (We tend to think of them as dogs or beasts, when really those animals never separate themselves in such a way.) And at the same time the torture makes it impossible to recognize the continuity of our own lives. It's not me he's fucking, it isn't me they're burning with that iron prod — they can only touch my body. Torture forces us out of the flesh, it forces us to separate from our bodies, to make ourselves other. The experience of torture is a form of exile, at the most intimate levels of being — an exile from living. Torture makes impossible the exposure of the flesh, even when paradoxically our torturers try to strip us naked.

The miracle of Christ is to take the flesh back from the soldiers of empire who nailed him to the cross. Even in his torment Christ lived the flesh in all its intensity. The critique of torture does not require that we should live in such a way as to avoid all violence and all pain — that would be a life without intensity, always already separated from the violence of experience. Rather, we should refuse the separation from the flesh that torture entails: live the violence of experience in the flesh, make our pain a mode of intensity and joy. This is the miracle that Pasolini sees in the crucifixion. The pain of the crucifixion does not fall back into a private language of isolated individuality, but rather opens up to a common language. Precisely to the extent that they create such a common language and a shared experience of the flesh, pain and violence can be erotic, because the erotic is nothing other than that shared intensity of our experience, that common electric charge coursing through our flesh.

Consider, for example, how authors such as the Marquis de Sade and Leopold von Sacher-Masoch construct a kind of ritual violence through various institutions and contracts in an effort to invent common languages of the flesh. Their ritual and imaginary dramas of victimizer and victim seek to overcome or vanquish the separation that characterizes our daily torture. This violence thus points toward an erotic continuity, an affirmation of life. Pasolini's notion of exposure shares this project to discover an antidote to torture and separation, but it does not create an imaginary plane or a theatre of representation. Representation still implies too much separation. Exposure, then, does not recreate the scene of torture but rather seeks to dissolve its boundaries and its effects of discontinuity. The violence of the exposed flesh does not separate into passive and active roles, but moves united in an erotic affirmation. Through exposure violence becomes again our own as a common language, a vital power of creation, a life force.

Flesh

Abandonment to the flesh is a form of freedom. Exposed, the passions of the flesh are released from any normative structures or organic functions. This is Pasolini's continual call to the utopia of youth: 'Allora la carne era senza freni' [Back then flesh had no brakes].[8] Becoming-flesh is a form of forgetting — a forgetting of self, propriety, discontinuity. Impure carnality, or rather the divine exposure of the flesh enacts its own logic of passions. This abandonment is the joy that Pasolini sees in Christ's example.

In un debole lezzo di macello | vedo l'immagine del mio corpo: | seminudo, ignorato, quasi morto. | E' così che mi volevo crocifisso, | con una vampa di tenero orrore, | da bambino, già automa del mio amore.	In the faint stench of a slaughterhouse. | I see the image of my body: | half-naked, forgotten, almost dead. | This is how I wanted to be crucified, | with a flash of tender horror, | since childhood, already an automaton of my love.[9]

The abandoned body is set free — released from the prisons of separation, immersed in the impurity of this world, or rather in the maniacal love of this world, in the form of a slave, a love automaton.

Even the term 'body' often seems insufficient for Pasolini. It is too caught up in the discontinuous and hierarchical functionings of various organs, too detached from other bodies and things, too implicated in that dialectical coupling with consciousness. Any residues of mind/body dualisms are completely out of place here. Even referring to ourselves as embodied seems too tied to those paradigms, as if we could imagine some spirit or mind potentially separate from corporeality so that we now had to insist on its unity with matter.

Pasolini prefers to think of 'members' and 'limbs' [*membra*] or simply 'flesh' [*carne*]. Flesh is the vital materiality of existence. Flesh certainly refers to matter, a passionately charged, intense matter, but it is always equally intellectual. It is not opposed to or excluded from thought or consciousness. Rather, the paths of thought and existence are all traced on the flesh.[10] Flesh subtends existence; it is its very potentiality.

---

8   Pasolini, 'La religione del mio tempo', in *Bestemmia*, p. 492.
9   Pasolini, 'L'ex vita', in *Bestemmia*, p. 400.
10   See Antonin Artaud, 'Situation of the Flesh', in *Selected Writings*, trans. by Helen Weaver (Berkeley: University of California Press, 1988), p. 110: 'There are intellectual cries, cries born of the subtlety of the marrow. That is what I mean by

Flesh is the condition of possibility of the qualities of the world, but it is never contained within or defined by those qualities. In this sense it is both a superficial foundation and an immanent transcendence — alien to any dialectic of reality and appearance, or depth and surface. It confounds all of these antinomies. Flesh is the superficial depth, the real appearance of existence. That the world is, how the world is, precisely such as it is, is exposed perfectly and irremediably in the flesh. (Is this what Spinoza meant when he said that reality and perfection are the same thing?) The exposure of the flesh is indeed the mystery of life, or rather the miracle of the world.

How do we love in the flesh? What is the flesh's desire? In erotic exposure the boundaries or discontinuities between self and other are broken down and dissolved to open a kind of communication or communion. This love cannot really be conceived as an encounter with the other because the self has already been completely emptied out, abandoned. Similarly, the desire cannot really be conceived as a becoming-other of the self because that too depends on fundamentally stable discontinuities, and implies in the end a return to self. We are only able to love in abandoning ourselves to the flesh.[11] In the flesh I lose track of which is your arm and my arm, your leg and mine, a tangle of limbs and members. Take me! Exposure is anonymous. It brings both an intensification of experience and an undifferentiation of matter. It sets in motion a wild proliferation of erotic zones and modes of intensity across the surfaces of the flesh (the warmth of your lips, the subtle vibration of my tongue), and at the same time brings about a tendential unification or communion. Hence the ecstasy of exposure.

Flesh. I do not separate my thought from my life. With each vibration of my tongue I retrace all the pathways of my thought in my flesh'.

[11] See Gilles Deleuze and Félix Guattari, *A Thousand Plateaus*, trans. by Brian Massumi (Minneapolis: University of Minnesota Press, 1987), p. 199: 'I have become capable of loving [...] by abandoning love and self'.

VEGA TESCARI
RESONANCES[1]

> *Philosophy responds to the question, 'What is in the voice?'*
> *as follows: Nothing is in the voice, the voice is the place of the*
> *negative, it is Voice — that is, pure temporality.*[2]

By following three main paths, which cannot be separated one from the other and which constitute different voices of the same tune, this study proposes a reflection on the notion of 'resonance' in relation to Pier Paolo Pasolini's filmic oeuvre, also considering the conceptual ramifications in his theoretical thought.

The first 'resonant' line is linked to Pasolini's soundscape, in relation to his ideas on dubbing and post-synchronization — opposed to the live recording of voices and sounds —, and in relation to the dimension conveyed by the interplay of silence, words, and natural, environmental sounds. Secondly, I explore what I call 'the resonance of things' from a double perspective. On the one hand there is the resonance of reality and things that must be grasped by the individual so that he can establish a relationship with the surrounding physical world. A perspective that is shown in *Medea* (1969): at a certain moment she must face a reality that does not resound *to* and *in* her, to which she cannot relate, and this provokes a disconnection, a fracture between her and the world. On the other hand, in Pasolini's films there are materials and surfaces that can provoke or evoke a resonance or effects of reverberation. For instance, the metallic sound of armor in *Oedipus Rex* (1967). Lastly, I will underline

---

1 This essay expands a study first presented at the international symposium *Pier Paolo Pasolini: Image, Object, Sound / Immagine, oggetto, suono*, conceived by Ara H. Merjian and Gerhard Wolf, NYU Institute of Fine Arts and Casa Italiana Zerilli-Marimò, New York City, 13 and 14 November 2015.
2 Giorgio Agamben, *Language and Death: The Place of Negativity* [1982], trans. by Karen E. Pinkus with Michael Hardt (Minnesota: University of Minnesota Press, 2006), p. 39.

how Pasolini's 'cinema by analogy' can be read in the light of a poetics of resonance, opposed to naturalism. His films are crossed by echoes, by resonances that make things come to the surface in their essential and archaic, primeval nature, instead of representing them in a mimetic way. In this sense, we can think about the urge that animated Pasolini's quest for 'analogous' places and 'analogous' faces for the shooting of *The Gospel According to St. Matthew* (1964).

During interviews, such as those with Jon Halliday (published in English under the pseudonym of Oswald Stack), Pasolini recalls the reasons behind his choice of dubbing and post-synchronization instead of live recording of voices and sounds. He also details his aversion for naturalism, assigning to dubbing the power to enrich and expand the characters, transforming them into mysterious figures.[3] Pasolini also believes that the language taught and learned at acting academies is a language that does not exist, and for this reason professional actors are the holders of disquieting artificial voices.

If we thoroughly consider the mechanism involved in the practice of dubbing, a more metaphorical and nuanced horizon opens up. By depriving the actor of his voice and giving it back to him only afterwards — so to say — the filmmaker operates a form of subtraction producing a fold, a slight void, a blank space defining the final rendering and perception of the character. The actor — and most of all the character — becomes the holder of this void: during the filming he acts with his own voice, then is deprived of his voice and becomes the receiver of another voice, sometimes his own, and after having undergone a process of dispossession. The final voice will be a sound reaching him, or rejoining him, from the outside, and by which he will be inhabited, instead of being a whole with it. This metaphorical horizon partakes in the structure and texture of Pasolini's characters, thinking for instance of Ettore Garofolo, dubbing himself in *Mamma Roma* (1962); or Franco Citti who was dubbed by another actor (Paolo Ferrari)

---

3   Pasolini: 'Il doppiaggio, deformando la voce, alterando le corrispondenze che legano il timbro, le intonazioni, le inflessioni di una voce, a un viso, a un tipo di comportamento, conferisce un sovrappiù di mistero al film. […]. Detto questo, mi piace elaborare una voce, combinarla con tutti gli altri elementi di una fisionomia, di un comportamento… Amalgamare… Sempre la mia propensione per il *pastiche*, probabilmente! E… il rifiuto del naturale', see Pier Paolo Pasolini, 'Il sogno del centauro. Incontri con Jean Duflot (1969–1975)', in *Saggi sulla politica e sulla società*, ed. by Walter Siti and Silvia De Laude (Milan: Mondadori, 2006), p. 1513.

in *Accattone* (1961), a choice that Pasolini found enriching and capable of raising the character above naturalism.[4]

The aim here is not to go into the technical and effective procedure of dubbing, its occurrences in relation to single films and to their different linguistic destinations, but to look at the theoretical premises, the conceptual — though maybe unpremeditated — implications and possible outcomes deriving from the application of this technique, which can subtly influence the vision and interpretation of Pasolini's works.

The interruption of the link between the physical presence and its voice leads to a suspension, an *epoché*, both in the sense of an interruption, but also, and more meaningfully, in the sense of something 'kept in balance', in an active state, that can be visualized in the form of a tightened and vibrating thread, showing both a temporal and spatial relation: the measure and duration of a distance. The mysterious feature that Pasolini attributes to dubbed characters is also related to and enriched by such a fracture and disconnection. A non-coincidence that stresses the separation between the body and the expression of its actuality in a defined temporal flux. This separation can be regarded as a good representation of the ontological dilemma, which can be synthetized by the fundamental question recalled by Roland Barthes in his *Camera Lucida*: 'I am the reference of every photograph, and this is what generates my astonishment in addressing myself to the fundamental question: why is it that I am alive *here and now*?'.[5] A question directly hinting at the issue of being, and being one's own person, living in a given time and place. But the interruption of the intrinsic link between voice and body can also lead to a liberation of the character from the limits of temporality, and from his being part of a process leading to death. He becomes in this way a meta-temporal figure.

The virtual cancellation of the voice and its symbolic departure from the self — followed by its substitution with another voice — creates an imperceptible fold which becomes a space for mystery, for the longing and yearning for something missing. The individual is no longer the owner of his own voice, but a beholder. In the end it is the self that has gone through a partition, or, in other words, that has become the object of an

---

4   '[…] I think that dubbing enriches a character; it is part of my taste for pastiche; it raises a character out of the zone of naturalism. I believe deeply in reality, in realism, but I can't stand naturalism', see Pier Paolo Pasolini, *Pasolini on Pasolini: Interviews with Oswald Stack* (London: Thames and Hudson in association with the British Film Institute, 1969), p. 39.

5   Roland Barthes, *Camera Lucida: Reflections on Photography* [1980], trans. by Richard Howard (New York: Hill and Wang, 1981), p. 84.

acknowledged irreducible silent division. A technical and material split which creates a metaphorical disconnection; as if saying 'I am here, but at the same time I am the memory of an elsewhere'. Such a gap provokes and allows a *resonance*: an echo of a lost spatial and temporal dimension where voice and body belong together, being in synch one with the other, sharing a simultaneity of space and time.

Going beyond naturalism, then, can also coincide with a different perspective in relation to temporal diegesis. In fact, thanks to the subtle and anti-naturalistic interplay of sounds, voices, and silence, Pasolini's films embrace trans-temporal dimensions that resound through characters and spaces, both becoming in turn the site of a temporal suspension open to timeless and mythical horizons of sense. '[…] I'm not interested in actors. The only time I am interested in an actor is when I use an actor to act an actor', said Pasolini, adding: 'The fact that an actor may depend on his voice is something that interests me very little'.[6] A statement that only erroneously could be intended as a provocation. It is in fact the whole status of acting and of being an actor in the most general sense of the term that is here called into question. For Pasolini actors are the means to express or reveal a stance, a viewpoint on the real. They are messengers of existential, political, and emotional energies, which in some way precede and outdo rational references to individual existence. In this sense actors are not required to interpret someone, but rather to produce a resonance of a condition through their 'being'.

Following the line of this meditation, it is interesting and revelatory to recall Marguerite Duras' approach to actors and to soundscape in the context of *India Song*, the film she realized in 1974. Duras' style is deeply molded by the architecture of sound and voice, and its concrete developments are the result of an intense theoretical meditation. Plunged in a suspended dimension, spectators follow the re-enactment of a love story lived in the 1930s in Calcutta, played by mute characters and told by off-screen voices in a fragmentary and disorienting way. Despite the fictional Indian framework, the film is realized in Paris and its outskirts. This split between the pretended and the real place, together with the overall atmosphere of the film, creates its distinctive mood. Most of the movie takes place in interiors; slow scenes show characters moving through rooms, sluggishly dancing, standing still, looking outside. Nothing seems to happen: the so called 'events' are removed from the film, which is shrouded in an atemporal dimension, characterized by silence — even though music and sounds are

---

6   Pasolini, *Pasolini on Pasolini*, p. 40.

present —, estrangement and a kind of separation from the external world. The gesture of depriving the actors of their voice is not a minor one and provides the film with a spectral and mysterious aura: characters move on the scene as though performing an unknown ritual, of which they are the disembodied beholders. This disembodiment is strictly linked to the deprivation of the voice, which interrupts the adherence between the self and its expression in a definite temporal and spatial dimension. Duras aimed at creating this disconnection; she states that the actors proposed the characters but did not embody them[7] and she describes in detail how she obtained the so called *dépeuplement* (depopulation) of the actors. She recorded the voice of the actors while they were reading the text of *India Song* and then she played their recorded voice during the filming of the scenes, taking advantage of the distraction produced in someone listening to his or her own voice. The effect is just like an echo coming from an unrecognized place, pervading the space and remaining suspended above the bodies on the screen. Michel de Certeau recognized in this practice a technique of detachment which is similar to that implied in spiritual exercises: actors are put outside themselves through an anonymous voice, their gesture is detached from the physical appropriation and so they live an estrangement from themselves.[8]

Even though the style and the poetics of Pasolini and Duras are quite dissimilar, and on a technical level the practice of dubbing does not correspond to the introduction of an off-screen voice, in both cases, and in a more or less marked way, we are faced with a fracture between body and voice and with a non-naturalistic approach regarding sound, space and time. Meaningfully, an alteration of the link between a voice and its source becomes an alteration of one's presence in a given time and place,

---

7   'Dans *India Song*, les acteurs proposaient les personnages, mais ne les incarnaient pas. Le "off", c'est encore le lieu de l'écrit'. In relation to the female protagonist, she says: 'La performance fantastique de Delphine Seyrig dans *India Song*, c'est qu'elle ne se présente jamais à nous comme étant celle nommée Anne-Marie Stretter, mais comme son double lointain, contestable, comme dépeuplé, et qu'elle n'a jamais pris ce rôle comme un manque à jouer, mais, au contraire, comme si sa référence à l'écrit A. M. S. restait intacte', see Marguerite Duras, 'La voie du gai désespoir' [1977], in *Outside: Papiers d'un jour* (Paris: P.O.L. éditeur, 1984), pp. 173–74. For further insights about Duras' oeuvre see: Vega Tescari, *En suspens. Scenari di tempo: Marguerite Duras, Claudio Parmiggiani, Luigi Ghirri* (Reggio Emilia: Corsiero editore, 2018), pp. 19–105.
8   See Michel de Certeau, 'Marguerite Duras: On dit', in *Écrire dit-elle: Imaginaires de Marguerite Duras*, ed. by Danielle Bajomée et Ralph Heyndels (Bruxelles: Éditions de l'Université de Bruxelles, 1985), p. 260.

underlining to which extent language and acts of speech are linked to fundamental ontological dimensions. And this is true both in the case of off-screen voices and in that of dubbing, although with the latter we are facing a less explicit version of these dynamics.

The dubbed actor becomes someone that *is* and *is not* in the place and time where his acting body appears. And thus, his presence resounds with elusive notes that recall the layered and irreducible quality of the real that was part of Pasolini's personal and artistic vision. His use of the dubbing becomes particularly intriguing in those works where an inner questioning, or the dialogue between the self and the real, are at the focus of the plot, or constitute the narrative itself. Such an interpretative light suits especially, though not exclusively, *Oedipus Rex* and *Medea*. Here the treatment of sounds and voices produces manifold effects that deepen and go beyond the aesthetics and acoustic levels. The interaction between the characters, the outside and the objects that are part of the scenario, is also based on the verbal and acoustic realm, as subtle threads linking all the elements comprised in the frame, but also pushing them beyond the limits of the frame, making them resounding in the form of echoes connecting the inside with the outside and vice versa. In this sense soundscapes, dubbed voices, music or noises produced by objects partake in the opening and widening of the filmic frames and of the audience's experience.

Talking about his interpretation of Oedipus, Pasolini says that he wanted to represent the myth in the form of a dream.[9] Such an oneiric dimension is obtained through different devices and among them an important role is played by voice and sounds. Pasolini explains that he used Rumanian folk-music, which he loved because of its ambiguous feature. An ambiguity that is 'qualcosa a mezza via', something in between Slavic, Greek and Arabic chants, which he believed to be indefinable and unrecognizable for the majority of the public.[10] Thanks to this ambiguity, for Pasolini music

---

9   'I wanted to re-create the myth under the aspect of a dream: I wanted all the central part of the film (which is almost the whole movie) to be a kind of dream, and this explains the choice of costumes and settings, the general rhythm of the work. [...] I wanted to represent the myth like a dream, and I could only present this dream by aestheticizing it [...]', see Pasolini, *Pasolini on Pasolini*, p. 122.

10 '[...] I found some folk-tunes which I liked a lot because they are extremely ambiguous: they are half-way between Slav, Greek and Arab songs, they are indefinable: it is unlikely that anyone who didn't have specialized knowledge could locate them; they are a bit outside history. As I wanted to make *Oedipus* a myth, I wanted music which was a-historical, a-temporal', see ibid., p. 126. And afterwards, p. 127: 'Perhaps I was wrong to say it is a-historic, it is meta-historical'.

reflected the timeless and a-historical aspect of the myth. Coming back to the Italian expression *a mezza via*, one can state that it condenses an intrinsic feature of Pasolini's poetics in an eloquent manner, when sound and linguistic issues are called into question. Something that stays 'a mezza via' means that it stands in between two points without choosing one or the other but profiting of this state of suspension. This in-betweenness suits the oneiric and atemporal dimension of the narrative and of the main character. Moreover, in the Italian expression there is also a reference to spatiality, a suggestion of something crossing a distance and measuring it. Similarly, a dubbed voice has experienced in itself a distance, a gap: a voice was cancelled and another one filled a metaphorical void; walking a distance. And it is such a distance that is somehow perceived by the audience and partakes to the particular and fascinating appeal of Pasolini's films.

Music and dubbed voices in *Oedipus Rex* are not the only acoustic presences suggesting an out-of-frame horizon, but also something that goes beyond, as an opening, and a stay-in-between dimension eluding temporal limits. Also sounds from the natural realm and silence play a role in the web that Pasolini wished to create. Obviously, this can be experienced during the vision of the film, but strikingly the complexity of the sound horizon can also be found in the text written about Oedipus. Here we find for instance the reference to the sound of crickets and frogs;[11] a concert, as Pasolini describes it, that will appear again in a scene where such a sound reaches the hearing through an open window.[12] Sleeping sheep, the chant of a nightingale, lark's trills, are cited as well in Pasolini's description of the countryside around Corinth.[13] In the soundscape of the film, silence intervenes as a sacred feature that covers everything, and represents an out-of-time dimension, accompanying for instance what Pasolini calls an 'eternal Summer'.[14] But silence can also be a perturbing, pervading, or 'unnatural' presence, to use Pasolini's word,[15] that is crossed by funereal chants or by Tiresias's flute music. Such an 'absurd' flute sound — again using a Pasolinian term[16] — wanders through the air and provokes a resonance inside Oedipus, who upon hearing it, falls on his knees crying, as

---

11 Pier Paolo Pasolini, 'Edipo re' [1967], in *Per il cinema*, ed. by Walter Siti and Franco Zabagli, 2 vols. (Milan: Mondadori, 2001), I, p. 975. Unless otherwise indicated all translations in English are my own.
12 See ibid., p. 976.
13 See ibid., p. 989.
14 See ibid., p. 1003.
15 See ibid., p. 1005.
16 See ibid.

we read in the written version of the oeuvre.[17] Here the acoustic resonance is a deeply symbolic one: Oedipus' interior voice is awaken and driven by it. He will say: '*Io ascolto ciò che è al di là del mio destino*' [I am listening to what is beyond my destiny].[18] Music becomes the carrier of an omen, putting different and distant times into dialogue, making them resound one into the other. Through music Oedipus sees, or better perceives, something about his future. Such a penetrating and revealing power of sound is confirmed by the fact that in his desperate outburst he will say: 'Avrei dovuto lacerarmi anche le orecchie… per chiudere meglio in me stesso il mio corpo infelice […]' [I should have also torn my ears apart to better enclose my unhappy body inside myself].[19]

The prophetic nature of sounds and music is also present in *Medea*. Considering in this case the written version of the oeuvre, we find a description of Medea when listening her servants' mysterious and premonitory chant,[20] which she listens to in an absorbed and absent state. A note in the text warns about the fact that a sacred music, 'Gregorian chants or something of that sort', writes Pasolini, must always accompany Medea's presence.[21] Thinking about the texture and function of her character, this acoustic remark is a way to stress and reflect Medea's recognition of the world's sacred nature, that one can perceive in the objects inhabiting the real, and that meaningfully will lose their 'voice' when Medea will lose contact with her inner self and her vision of the world, coming into contact with the opposite existential stance of Jason. In Pasolini's words, when Medea goes and prays alone, music will go on obsessively and continuously, though weakened and significantly it will stop and — as in *Oedipus Rex* — an *unnatural* silence will fall on things:[22] the real does not resound and everything remains soundless, isolated and undecipherable.[23] Things surrounding Medea become dead things which do not answer to her gaze. Sacred objects become thus poor and abandoned ones. They do not receive the light, they are in a *penumbra*, as written in the text.[24] Their lack of resonance is accompanied by a lack of brilliance, as they no longer receive or reverberate light. The impossibility to establish a link

---

17   See ibid., p. 1006.
18   Ibid., p. 1007.
19   Ibid., p. 1046.
20   '[…] il loro misterioso e presago canto', see Pier Paolo Pasolini, 'Medea' [1970], in *Per il cinema*, I, p. 1221.
21   See ibid., p. 1225.
22   See ibid., p. 1226.
23   '[…] tutto resta muto, isolato, indecifrabile', see ibid., p. 1227.
24   See ibid., p. 1228.

with the outside is rendered through fragmentary, incomplete acts of speech. It is a 'foolish monologue', as Pasolini describes it,[25] aiming at winning the silence of things. Meaningfully in the written version she will sit, speechless, on a rock,[26] as if this would be the solid and material embodiment of her state. The description of Medea, who is 'closed in her silence as if in a shrine',[27] replies to Oedipus' desire to tear his ears apart and enclose his body inside himself. It becomes therefore clear how much the aural and acoustic dialogue between the individual and the outside is a pretext and a premise to develop a more metaphorical relationship between the self and the real: a resonant reality will be followed by a mute and sealed one.

A visual and acoustic representation of the principle of things possessing a resonance can be found in Pasolini's cinema. The presence of resonant and reverberating materials and objects must not only be taken as part of the setting's aesthetics, but as something with an evocative role, thinking for instance about Oedipus's armor and the resonance it produces through the character's movements. It is a bemusing and layered sound pervading the landscape. A similar effect is produced by the primitive steel weapons, whose trenchant sound cuts the air like an acoustic blade. Pasolini was undoubtedly conscious of the effect created by such scenes greatly pervaded by sound, or noise. And it is also through such an exacerbated acoustic feature that space and landscape suggest openings to further dimensions. Sounds become echoes that move within landscape, going back and forth as boomerangs. Incidentally, it must be remembered that Pasolini speaks of Friulian — the dialect of his mother's region employed in some of his poems —, as a *boomerang*, an unrealistic language, which gave him an access to the real peasant world.[28] Also in the case of Medea (and of other characters of the film), clothes, ornaments and jewelry possess an evocative power, not only because of shiny materials and textiles, but most of all because of a stratification, of something layered that could produce clattering sounds. We could assume that the fact that Jason is almost naked compared to her, could also be read as a visual representation of his more basic, and materialistic vision, deprived of any sacred *weight*.

Natural sounds that cross the landscapes of some of Pasolini's films, convey a feeling of openness and infinitude — thinking about *Medea* or *Oedipus Rex* — exceeding the status of soundscapes to become vectors that go beyond the contingency of the moment, also encouraging a withdrawal

---

25 See ibid., p. 1235.
26 See ibid., p. 1236.
27 '[…] chiusa nel suo silenzio come in una teca', see ibid., p. 1237.
28 Pasolini, *Pasolini on Pasolini*, p. 16.

into one's interiority. As if through the perception of an exterior vastness, an interior one could be recognized and could act as the reflection of the first one. In an essay written in 1945–46 and entitled 'I nomi o il grido della rana greca' [The names or the cry of the Greek frog], Pasolini writes that the infinitude that we feel everywhere, and most of all in ourselves, always reaches a sensitive limit, beyond which we should lie down and remain silent.[29] Further on, he underlines how one's life finds limits at each moment, continuously showing an absolute diversity between where *we are* and where *we are not*. The infinitude he talks about extends beyond everything: moon, clouds, leaves, water, human eyes. And this instant of inhuman clarity, as Pasolini calls it, can be provoked by any thing: lights, sounds, objects and words.[30] A vision that Pasolini synthesizes with Saint Augustine's expression *pulchritudo tam antiqua et tam nova*,[31] meaning that this inner resonance is the trace of something that goes beyond temporal limits, an ancestral memory, old and new at the same time. In thinking about the conceptual line of aural echoes and *resonances*, as well as the possibility for language to go beyond its own temporal limits, one could establish a parallel with what Daniel Heller-Roazen writes:

> Nowhere is a language more 'itself' than at the moment it seems to leave the terrain of its sound and sense, assuming the sound shape of what does not — or cannot — have a language of its own; animal sounds, natural or mechanical noises. It is here that one language, gesturing beyond itself in a speech that is none, opens itself to the nonlanguage that precedes it and that follows it. It is here, in the utterance of the strange sounds that the speakers of a tongue thought themselves incapable of making, that a language shows itself as an 'exclamation' in the literal sense of the term: a 'calling out' (*ex-clamare*, *Ausruf*), beyond or before itself, in the sounds of the inhuman speech it can neither completely recall nor fully forget.[32]

In Pasolini's texts, it is the word and its resonance that are at the center of his meditation. Greek words intensify the real and in the syllables of the Greek word for 'cloud' (Νεφέλη) he recognizes what he calls a 'marble

---

29 'L'infinità che noi sentiamo da ogni parte, ma più ancora in noi stessi, giunge sempre fino ad un qualche limite sensibile. Giunge ad un limite dietro al quale distendersi, tacere', see Pier Paolo Pasolini, 'I nomi o il grido della rana greca', in *Saggi sulla letteratura e sull'arte*, ed. by Walter Siti and Silvia De Laude (Milan: Mondadori, 1999), I, p. 193.
30 See ibid., pp. 193–94.
31 See ibid., p. 194.
32 Daniel Heller-Roazen, *Echolalias: On the Forgetting of Language* (New York: Zone Books, 2005), p. 18.

purity' with a 'blow of wind'.³³ Thus words possess that same infinitude lying in man's interiority and in all earthly things. In Pasolini's view, words are 'natural metaphors', capable of carrying things beyond their mere materiality, into human beings.³⁴

If for Pasolini, cinema obliges as nothing else as to look at things in their materiality and reality, nevertheless it has also the power to express metaphorical dimensions and it can do this through images. In his appendix to *Accatone*'s text, Pasolini underlines that although cinema cannot express metaphors in a direct way, it can create a sort of 'vibrating diapason'³⁵ that resounds in the spectator's head. He adds that the figures that cinema shares with literature are those typical of archaic, religious and childish literature, and music; that is to say anaphora and iteration.³⁶ Two figures that not surprisingly are nurtured by laws of repetition and returns, where the percussive and redundant features often convey a ritualistic and mythic horizon: a sort of absolute image that imposes itself through its vividness and redundancy. Moreover, through repetition time is suspended. Therefore, the reappearance of places or situations in Pasolini's films can be read as a way to suspend temporal diegesis, and to signal the entrance in a mythical horizon. At the end of *Oedipus Rex*, the music heard at the beginning, when the protagonist was a child, emerges anew, marking a repetition, a return, 'that is before and after destiny — the source of everything', as Pasolini writes.³⁷ Music becomes the mean to express a temporal resonance, an echo that crosses time and place. In this sense, the routes of music also stand for the reflection of man's interiority, where memories, thoughts, experiences, and feelings are not stored in a fixed and petrified way, but instead they can resonate, intermingle, and connect different temporal and emotional layers, which are also the expression of a mythical and ontological dimension.

If we consider the principle of resonance in relation to Pasolini's attempt to upset the expectations of an audience addicted to the language of mass media, we can see how the use of sounds, words and music driving the spectator somewhere else and beyond a plain consummation of images, is a way to produce resonances that do not need to be grasped or understood

---

33 See Pasolini, 'I nomi o il grido della rana greca', p. 195.
34 'Le parole sono dunque metafore naturali. E consistono in un portare al di là. Infatti da una parte c'è la natura inconoscibile delle cose, dall'altra la nostra, e le parole aprono il rapporto incredibile tra i due mondi: portano le cose al di là della loro dura esistenza, le portano in noi', see ibid., p. 198.
35 See Pasolini, 'Appendice ad "Accattone"' [1961], in *Per il cinema*, I, p. 146.
36 See ibid., p. 147.
37 Pasolini, 'Edipo re', p. 1052.

rationally, but that first must be felt, heard. Feeling that something echoes something else is already a way to avoid common interpretation, and it encourages a more active and involved participation in the film and in the real. Pasolini's subversive approach consisted in fact in producing oeuvres that could not be easily consumed, that had to be 'difficult'.[38]

The fact that Pasolini claims a devotion to the real in itself and is interested in the real's capacity to speak through its own elements,[39] does not mean that he considers reality as a closed and hermetic entity; on the contrary, it is an absorbing and receptive dimension that through its own elements creates layers that can be heard and perceived. Resonance produces a movement, a dynamic: it tells you that you cannot stop, that you have to listen and look more deeply and move further. So, far from being only an acoustic figure, resonance is also a vector of space and time that interrupts everyday temporality and eludes spatial borders.

It is a productive distance, though a more metaphorical one, that can be recognized also in Pasolini's idea of a 'cinema by analogy'. Taking the distance from naturalistic representation, Pasolini aims at a reconstruction by analogies, rather than a historical reconstruction; and in this process, he does not look for a faithful rendering of sites or of situations, but for an evocation.[40] A place must resonate with another one in its essential features without being its copy. What happens is also that an elsewhere is constantly recalled or makes itself being felt in a sort of spatial syncretism that though not gathering two places in the same image, it metaphorically eludes a spatial distance, avoiding a realistic geographical treatment. His 'cinema by analogy' is at work in the choices of the settings for *Oedipus Rex* and *Medea*. Talking about *Oedipus Rex* in an interview published in 1967 in *Cahiers du Cinéma*, he states: 'I did not want to reconstruct anything from an archeological, philological point of view. [...] I have made everything up [...]'.[41] About the characters' modern outfit he says that he took inspiration

---

38 See Pier Paolo Pasolini, 'Incontro con Pasolini' [1969], in *Per il cinema*, ed. by Walter Siti and Franco Zabagli (Milan: Mondadori, 2001), II, p. 2980.
39 '[...] the cinema represents reality with reality; it is metonymic and not metaphoric. Reality doesn't need metaphors to express itself. If I want to express you I express you through yourself, I couldn't use metaphors to express you. In the cinema it is as though reality expressed itself with itself, without metaphors, and without anything insipid and conventional and symbolic', Pasolini, *Pasolini on Pasolini*, p. 38.
40 See Pasolini, 'Intervista rilasciata a Maurizio Ponzi' [1965], in *Per il cinema*, II, p. 2881.
41 See Pasolini 'Edipo re' [1967], in *Per il cinema*, II, p. 2920.

from ancient photographs,[42] whereas for the part set in the ancient past he says that costumes 'are invented in an almost arbitrary manner', and that he consulted works about Aztec art and Sumerians and some costumes come directly from Africa.[43]

It is interesting to recall Duras' approach to *India Song*, which she shot in a French context to evoke an Indian one. Through this *escamotage* the Parisian mansion where part of the film takes place comes to represent the French embassy in Calcutta. Meaningfully, Duras underlines how this gap between a real embassy, a cinematic one and the place used in her film, marked the whole movie. Most of the action takes place in interiors and even though the external dimension is constantly evoked, the surrounding landscape is not sufficiently characterized to allow a precise geographical reference. It could be India, but also anywhere else, and Duras' intended ambiguity is clearly underlined when she states that all the references to the physical, human, political geography are false and the names of towns, rivers, states and seas of India have primarily a musical sense.[44] If we add to this that the film is built on a continuous dialectics of entries and exits, crossings of rooms, passages from the inside to the outside and silent dialogues with threshold spaces, we face a physical and temporal wandering which blurs the frontiers between real, fictitious, and interior spatiality, as if we are in front of an ontological question, such as: 'where are we?'. And the possible answer could be: 'everywhere and nowhere'; as if space instead of being a realistic data would be valued more as a mental projection, as the result of energies and of thoughts made about it.

Pasolini's approach to *The Gospel according to St. Matthew*, and particularly to the earlier *Seeking Locations in Palestine for the Film 'The Gospel According to St. Matthew'* (1963) is revelatory as well. In an interview with Maurizio Ponzi, Pasolini lists all his analogies: an analogous landscape, analogous environments, analogous faces; all in the line of a poetic cinema, instead of an illustrative one.[45] Writing about his *Gospel* he says that he wants to rebuild Palestinian desert and he is obsessed by

---

42 See ibid., p. 2927.
43 See ibid., p. 2928.
44 'Les noms des villes, des fleuves, des États, des mers de l'Inde ont, avant tout, ici, un sens musical. Toutes les références à la géographie physique, humaine, politique, d'*India Song*, sont fausses [...]', see Marguerite Duras, 'Remarques générales', in *India Song* [1973], *Romans, cinéma, théâtre, un parcours 1943–1993* (Gallimard: Paris, 1997), p. 1209.
45 See Pasolini, 'Intervista rilasciata a Maurizio Ponzi', p. 2881.

the idea of finding a Bethlehem that will be a surrogate of Bethlehem.[46] Similarly, in the draft of a screenplay for a film about Saint Paul, he writes that Jerusalem will be substituted by Paris in the years between 1938 and 1944, that is to say under the Nazi occupation.[47] Moreover, he underlines how the toponymy will be displaced[48] and, for instance, Damascus will be set in Spain, in a space where 'the crossing of the desert becomes the crossing of a symbolic desert'.[49] Compared with the first occurrence of 'cinema by analogy' where a story seeks similar locations to be told in order to convey its message, this second approach gains a further undertone: Pasolini not only searches and finds surrogates of the original state of things, but he gives to this displacement a more pronounced political gesture. Within this framework, the present is the result of the past, history repeats itself and from the comparisons and fusion of temporally distant situations one is encouraged to attain a critical and more conscious vision of the present.

Going back to his text 'I nomi o il grido della rana greca', it is revealing how Pasolini stresses not only how words are linked to the image of the things they refer to, but also to their sound so that image and sound are related.[50] Words possess a visual and an aural resonance, and at the same time this *resonance* exceeds them. Likewise, through the breaking of the simultaneity of voice and body the character gains a mythical distance, an alteration of temporality that allows him to be put outside his mortal temporality and in a way to escape death. His words become the memory of an out-of-time dimension, resonating as an ancient and ever new music.

---

46 Similarly, in conversation with Oswald Stack, he states: 'I knew I would remake the Gospel by analogy. Southern Italy enabled me to make the transposition from the ancient to the modern world without having to reconstruct it either archaeologically or philologically. […] The fact that I made the film by analogy means that I was not interested in exactitude. I was interested in everything but that. […] Besides, along with this method of reconstruction by analogy, there is the idea of the myth and of epicness which I have talked about so much: so when I told the story of Christ I didn't reconstruct Christ as he really was. […] I did not want to reconstruct the life of Christ as it really was, I wanted to do the story of Christ plus two thousand years of Christian translation, because it is the two thousand years of Christian history which have mythicized this biography, which would otherwise be an almost insignificant biography as such. My film is the life of Christ plus two thousand years of story-telling about the life of Christ. That was my intention', see Pasolini, *Pasolini on Pasolini*, pp. 82–83.
47 See Pasolini, 'Abbozzo di sceneggiatura per un film su San Paolo. (Sotto forma di appunti per un direttore di produzione)', in *Per il cinema*, II, p. 1883.
48 See ibid., p. 2024.
49 See ibid., p. 2026.
50 See Pasolini, 'I nomi o il grido della rana greca', p. 197.

Lia Turtas

BADIOU'S PASOLINI
A Poetical Exercise in *Victory*

Novelty and fidelity, local and transhistorical, destruction and subtraction. The work of Alain Badiou is intermittently crossed by unresolved tensions between two different modalities of the event, implying (at least) two corresponding theories of the subject: the Romantic and vitalist against the melancholic and post-revolutionary. Through the analysis of the occurrences of these tensions in Badiou's 'Destruction, Negation, Subtraction' 2007 conference on Pier Paolo Pasolini, I would like to underline the interplay of the two polarities which substantiates his own 'figural realism' (White), and originates the fecund dialectics between the Sartrean 'choice of one's past' and the infinity of the truths always 'to come' at work in his theory of the subject.

In Badiou's reading of the Pasolinian poem *Vittoria,* the two different modalities of event–subject delineated — what we could also call, in Pasolinian terms, the partisan/terrorist and the social democratic — come under the cloaks of 'destruction' and 'subtraction', the left-wing and right-wing 'deviations' that only in their encounter can bring novelty and creative destruction, namely 'true negation'.[1] But these two concepts, so dear to the French philosopher, are just the terminal (or, conversely, starting) points of an entire series of metaphorical chains that I try to unveil. Starting from Badiou's conception of poetry as a sort of laic 'deposition' of the event — 'a negative machinery' that in its cold agency deals with the event's

---

[1] See Alain Badiou, 'Destruction, Negation, Subtraction' (2007), in *The Scandal of Self-Contradiction: Pasolini's Multistable Subjectivities, Traditions, Geographies*, ed. by Luca Di Blasi and others (Wien/Berlin: Turia+Kant, 2012), pp. 269–77 (pp. 269–71). See also Giovanbattista Tusa, '"Finir, commencer": Tra Alain Badiou e Pier Paolo Pasolini', in Alain Badiou and Giovanbattista Tusa, *Alla Ricerca Del Reale Perduto* (Milan: Mimesis, 2016), p. 64: 'Per Badiou la poesia di Pasolini è un "manifesto" della vera negazione, in quanto ogni novità non può ridursi all'oggettività della "situazione" in cui viene a trovarsi, e deve trasgredire una legge a cui rimane comunque legata. In tal senso sin da *L'être et l'événement* Badiou cerca di mostrare come un pensiero "sottrattivo" della negatività possa superare il cieco imperativo della distruzione'.

aftermath and consequences by means of 'subtraction' and 'dissemination' — , I discuss *Vittoria* as one of the many Pasolinian *'deposizioni'* of the Resistenza–Guido event, towards which he would be faithful all throughout his lifetime.[2] Looking at the disseminated metaphors at play in the poem (among which the father–son / father–brother dyads are the most important), I first consider their significance for Pasolini's artistic, political, and amorous life. Then, I argue for their relevance in Pasolini's psychic life too, as the main signs of the split self, divided between brotherhood and paternity, vitalism and melancholy, or, in his own terms, *'rivolta perpetua'* and *'ragione'*, *'passione e ideologia'*.

Afterwards, I come back to Badiou's use of poetry as analysed by Oliver Feltham, who talks about its 'self-reflexivity', as well as of the 'modelling' and 'conditioning' methods adopted by the French philosopher to 'extend' and 'incomplete' philosophy into poetry (and vice versa), but also into heterogeneous fields such as mathematics, politics, art, etc., according to the Marxist tenet of the 'primacy of practice'. In an attempt to embrace Badiou's invitation to perform my own 'poetical exercise', I apply Feltham's suggestions to *Vittoria*'s case. While doing this, the entire 'multiple' of the Pasolinian subject comes to the fore, with all its complexity and contradictions. By following the 'modelling' method, I highlight the emerging, overwhelming role of 'passione', which leads to the dark territories of Badiousian 'terrorist subjectivity'; by following the opposite movement of the 'conditioning' method, instead, I point out the more hopeful (but no less tormented) regions of the Pasolinian split self, of Pauline derivation.

Finally, I argue in favor of the coexistence of these two contrasting interpretations, in the terrain of encounter between Paul and Badiou given by Pier Paolo's body and work. To me, Pasolini works for Badiou as a *figura* — in the Auerbachian sense of 'middle term between *historia–littera* and *veritas'* — either of Badiou, in respect to the 'fulfillment' represented by the latter's thought according to the 'modelling' scheme, or as a prefiguration of Paul in the opposite direction hinted by the 'conditioning' reading. I therefore try to make an argument for a kind of laic, de-theologized use — in Badiou via Paul and Pasolini — of the basic structure of 'figural interpretation', as a privileged militant tool serving the announcement of the 'second coming' of truth(s), and the Badiousian theory of the subject.

---

[2] On the subject as faithfulness to the rupture of the Event in Badiou, also in relation to Pasolini, Paul, and *Vittoria*, see Tusa, ibid., pp. 58–59, and following.

In the opening verses of *Vittoria*,[3] we get to know a Pasolini we do not often meet: both a partisan — even 'terrorist' in Badiou's words — Pasolini, and a social democratic Pasolini. *Vittoria* literally opens up with a declaration of consuming desire for some form of concrete violent action, very quickly disguised as poetry ('bene, mi sveglio per la prima volta in vita mia | col desiderio d'impugnare un'arma. | Il ridicolo è che lo dico in poesia').[4] The old poet talks 'ab joi' (the provençal expression for sheer poetical euphoria) and, for the first time in his life, in the awakening of a grey April morning similar to many others (yet a day of victory, the day of the *Festa della Liberazione*!), would like to take up weapons, and die as a young man, despite the fact that he feels more naturally inclined to the 'violence' of intellectual action ('Dove sono le armi? Io non conosco | che quelle della mia ragione: | e nella mia violenza non c'è posto | NEANCHE PER UN'OMBRA DI AZIONE | NON INTELLETTUALE').[5] He feels ridicule and embarrassed to tell friends, and he needs a poetic form to express that. But, within a few verses, the would-be partisan at dawn will join his fellow countrymen at work, at lunch, in everyday reality, by noon ('Non è la mia che frenesia dell'alba. | A mezzogiorno sarò coi miei connazionali | Alle opere, ai pasti, alla realtà che inalbera | La bandiera, oggi bianca, dei Destini Generali').[6]

If this is the awakening from 'un sogno di gioia' — which alone can bring back to the present 'i vecchi giorni', 'ogni aprile | rosso, di gioventù', and open 'una stagione di dolore armato'[7] — what can possibly be the material of the dream that these first verses are an awakening from? First of all, the event (the vanishing object in Badiou's terms) of Italian *Resistenza*, which for Pasolini was the only historical example of a genuine political fight in Italian history; *Resistenza* that, according to him, has been betrayed by the Italian intellectuals and Communist leaders, and towards which the poet keeps observing an indestructible fidelity, even and precisely, in its present retreat.

---

3   A set of ninety-seven enchained tercets and eight interspersed single verses in third rhyme, *Vittoria* is part of the 1964 *Poesia in forma di rosa* collection, first published by Garzanti, now in Pier Paolo Pasolini, *Tutte le Poesie*, ed. by Walter Siti and Silvia De Laude, 4 vols. (Milan: A. Mondadori, 2003), I, pp. 1259–70.
4   Ibid., pp. 1260–61.
5   Ibid., p. 1259.
6   Ibid., pp. 1260–61.
7   Ibid.

Secondly, together with *Resistenza*, inevitably comes the tragic death of his younger brother Guido Alberto,[8] killed in 1945 while fighting as a partisan in the *azionista* and catholic Osoppo brigade attacked by the communist Garibaldi brigade, as well as the inconsolable mourning of their *dolorosa mater* Susanna.[9] So that *Vittoria* can also be seen as one of the many attempts to deal with the aftermath of the *Resistenza*–Guido event; and (to use a term dear to both Pasolini and Badiou), as a laic, poetical deposition, of both *Resistenza*'s and Guido's phantasmatic bodies.

Finally, it is also the dream of emancipation from their father Carlo Alberto[10] — a military officer seduced by nationalist and fascist myths — and from his symbolic function, therefore (in Robert Gordon's words) from Pier Paolo's 'trauma […] of coming to terms with, and becoming, the father'.[11] The fact that Carlo, the actual father, is never mentioned as such all throughout the poem, but sublimated by other paternal figures, should not come as surprise, being part of that 'strategia del silenzio' with which Pasolini systematically tried to erase his figure — the most striking example of which can perhaps be Guido's funeral oration given by Pier Paolo in June 1945 in Casarsa, where only mothers, brothers and generic 'parenti' are mentioned as sharing the grief.

---

8   Guido Alberto, the second-born child to Carlo Pasolini and Susanna Colussi, was born in Belluno in 1925. As the same Badiou recalls, 'Guido, has been killed in fighting during the war as a partisan, a resistant fighter. And the terrible problem is that he has been killed not by fascists, but by communists of another country, Yugoslavian communists, because of the rivalry between Italians and Yugoslavians concerning the control of some border regions'; see Badiou, 'Destruction, Negation, Subtraction', p. 272. What Badiou defines as 'terrorist subjectivity' in his *Vittoria* reading, is primarily embodied, within the poem, by the figure of Pasolini's younger brother, Guido, who had joined the Italian partisans in 1944, and died while fighting with them the following year. In *Vittoria*, Guido is entirely identified with Italian, and more generally, political resistance.

9   For Susanna's mourning, see for instance Nico Naldini's 'Cronologia', in Pier Paolo Pasolini, *Saggi Sulla Politica E Sulla Società*, ed. by Walter Siti and Silvia De Laude (Milan: A. Mondadori, 1999), I, pp. xli–cviii (p. lxii).

10 Carlo Alberto Pasolini (1892–1958), member of the secondary branch of one of the most important aristocratic families of Ravenna, was a professional soldier and a highly-decorated infantry officer. A fervent supporter of the fascist regime, he commanded his company on the same day of the failed Mussolini's assassination attempt by the young anarchic Anteo Zamboni on October 31, 1926: Carlo himself allegedly identified and arrested the unfortunate attacker. He had chosen to embrace the military career also due to his shaky financial situation, as his father had dilapidated his large patrimony in gambling, see ibid., pp. xliii–xlv.

11 Robert Samuel Clive Gordon, *Pasolini: Forms of Subjectivity* (Oxford: Clarendon Press, 1996), pp. 161–62.

In his contribution to *Fratello Selvaggio,* a volume on Pasolini and youth, Hervé Joubert-Laurencin recounts having counted no less than twenty different occurrences of Guido's story.[12] The recurring emersion of Guido's story in Pasolini's production is a clear sign of an unresolved conflict: it signals the attempt — inevitably destined to failure — on the part of the subject to re-enact a traumatic event and to complete some successful act able to change it. In Pier Paolo's case, this repetition compulsion seems to point at the regret and sense of guilt for the inability to take concrete action, now and then: the once 'partigiano inerme', and 'imberbe', and today's 'inaridito superato, vecchio poeta' share the same, overwhelming feeling of helplessness. As Joubert-Laurencin, again, notes, what is at stake here — as in the case of Gilles Deleuze with his brother, a war hero dead during France's Nazi occupation — is primarily an attempt to justify a non-violent type of action in the face of Guido's sacrifice of life: 'Dove sono le armi? Io non conosco | che quelle della mia ragione: | e nella mia violenza non c'è posto | NEANCHE PER UN'OMBRA DI AZIONE | NON INTELLETTUALE'.[13] The poem would then act as a kind of intellectual weapon to cope with the trauma of exclusion from life.

The awakening in *Vittoria* is that of a post-traumatic and post-eventual subject, one that — like Paul with Jesus Christ — paradoxically, could not witness in person the event that he will always feel compelled to witness. A subject who desperately tries to go back to the scene that binds him to the past in order to overcome it. In Pasolini's case, as we said, the primal scene is like a tragedy that ends in farce, thus inevitably calling for the next repetition. Partisan and faithful to the consequences of the event at dawn, social democratic 'traitor' and reactionary at noon: the split self carries within himself the very division at play in society at large. Faithful to his identification with the Christ figure, the poet takes all the blame and guilt on himself, as in a *Confiteor*: 'Prendo tutta su di me la colpa, prendo (con piacere) su di me la colpa', and represents himself as the link between the oscillation happening in the self, and the division crossing society. Here, the real scandal is not, as one might expect, the division between the old (or new) fascists and the *resistenti*, as much as the division between comrades

---

12   See Hervé Joubert-Laurencin, 'Perdere un fratello: il fantasma di Guido', in *Fratello Selvaggio: Pier Paolo Pasolini tra gioventù e nuova gioventù,* ed. by Gian Maria Annovi (Massa: Transeuropa, 2013), pp. 35–48 (p. 38): 'Ho contato, ma senza aver compiuto una ricerca sistematica, venti occorrenze diversamente modulate della storia di Guido, parziale o completa, nella produzione scritta di Pier Paolo: lettere, discorsi, articoli di giornale, poesie [...]'.
13   Pasolini, 'Vittoria', p. 1259.

and their hierarchies, mostly to be identified with the actual Communist party leaders, and their organic intellectuals.

The social and political dimension is also the one on which Alain Badiou focuses most in his conference on *Vittoria*, introduced by him 'to clarify' the dialectics of 'destruction, negation, and subtraction'.[14] Actually, this is one of the rare examples that Badiou gives of his concept of subtraction. *Vittoria* is heralded as 'a manifesto for true negation',[15] in the Badiousian sense of 'the affirmative part of negation', that is 'something happening as new', which 'cannot be reduced to the objectivity of the situation where it happens',[16] therefore 'affirmation', not just destruction; whereas 'destruction' is the negative part of negation, that is, the violence necessary as a premise to the happening of the affirmative part. As an example in art, Badiou cites Schoenberg's creation of the dodecaphonic musical system, which achieves the 'destruction of the tonal system', therefore being the affirmative part of negation, 'in no way deducible from the destruction of this system':[17] 'subtraction is within the horizon of negation, but it exists independently of the purely negative part of negation [...] so negation is always, in its concrete action — political or artistic — suspended between destruction and subtraction', which amounts to say that 'subtraction is not the negation of destruction, no more than destruction was the negation of subtraction':[18] there should be an alliance between the two in order to allow for what Badiou calls the 'inexistent' to come to the fore.

In the excerpt from *Vittoria* chosen by Badiou, and all over the poem, what he calls the 'situation', the 'state of things', is clearly crossed, instead, by a profound division in two political and semantic fields that cannot communicate, as much as they would be willing — and naturally destined — to. Opposed metaphors of destruction and subtraction proliferate, organized in metonymic chains, such as 'youth' versus 'old age' ('questo esercito — cieco nel cieco | sole — di giovani morti', 'Togliatti, lui, è finalmente vecchio | come per tutta la vita egli ha | voluto'), 'sons' against 'fathers', 'army' against 'chief' ('Se il suo padre, il suo capo, | lo lascia nei bianchi monti'), 'dream' against 'reality' ('Solo un sogno, di gioia, può aprire | una stagione di dolore armato' versus 'Cadono | le ultime foglie della Guerra | e della martire vittoria, sempre più rade, | distrutte a poco a poco da quella | che sarebbe stata la realtà, | non solo della cara Reazione,

---

14 Badiou, 'Destruction, Negation, Subtraction', p. 270.
15 Ibid., p. 274.
16 Ibid., p. 269.
17 Ibid.
18 Ibid., p. 270.

ma della bella | Socialdemocrazia nascente, trallallà'),[19] but also individual versus society, 'scene' versus 'backstage' ('uscendo dalla scena di Brecht, | per ritirarsi nei bui retroscena, | dove impara nuove parole reali l'eroe incerto'), 'white mountains' versus 'serene planes', and so on.

Here, as we said, the personifications of Badiou's destruction and subtraction occupy the scene. On one hand, we have an army of both young, dead warriors and waiting sons (the partisans fallen in the liberation war and the contemporary *sottoproletariato* of Italian suburbs, assimilated to the partisans, some of whom have already succumbed to the State repression),[20] so that there is for Badiou a 'double negation' of young people, both in the past and in the present. On the other hand, we have the chief–father: the leader of the Communist party attached to the 'average honesty of man', who eventually abandons his sons and fails to meet their revolutionary hopes. The hypostasis of subtraction (in the derogatory sense of Badiou's ineffective 'democratic opposition') in the theater of Italian republican politics is the lonely, respectable father/communist leader who acts backstage and speaks a new prose, that of the *'uomo abile'*, able to adapt to different scenarios (the then soon-to-die Palmiro Togliatti, but also the socialist Pietro Nenni, who in 1964 allied with Aldo Moro in a center-left government, against the threat of a right-wing government, and who sat in the front row at Togliatti's funerals).[21]

Therefore, not only has the civil war never come to an end, but it now perpetuates itself separating the (once) brothers, who shared the burden

---

19 Pasolini, 'Vittoria', p. 1261.
20 Pasolini is making particular reference to the 'Strage di Reggio Emilia', where five workers members of PCI were killed by the police authorised by the Christian Democrat government on July 1960, after a period of tensions all over the country, following the formation of the Tambroni government with the external support of MSI (the neo-fascist party). In all, there were eleven victims and hundreds of injured, which caused the resignation of Tambroni.
21 'Chi, alla nuova lotta, li guiderà? | Togliatti, lui è finalmente vecchio | come per tutta la vita egli ha | voluto', in 'Vittoria', pp. 1264–65. Palmiro Togliatti (1893–1964) has been the historical leader of the Italian Communist Party (PCI) — and one of its founding members in 1921 — from 1927 to his death. He has also been an important member of Comintern. After the 1948 elections, he led the party in opposition to the various Christian Democrat and Socialist governments. Pietro Nenni (1891–1980) had been one of the leaders of Italian and international antifascism and socialism during the fascist regime. While militating for the *Liberazione* from Nazi fascism, he fought for the Republican form of government. As the leader of postwar Italian Socialist Party (PSI), he collaborated with Fanfani's and Moro's DC, Saragat's PSDI, and La Malfa's PRI in a number of center-left governments.

of the liberating fight, into father and sons, or, at the least, into cousins and cousins ('E voi, comunisti, miei compagni non compagni, | ombre di compagni, straniati cugini carnali | [...] voi, padri | senza nome').[22] Even more paradoxically, a form of perverted brotherhood is now insinuating itself as complicity between the (once) enemies, the Communist party and the moderates governing the country: 'non riconosci il cuore | che diventa schiavo del suo nemico, e va | dove il nemico va, condotto dalla storia | ch'è storia di tutti due, e li fa, nel profondo, | stranamente fratelli'.[23] According to Badiou, 'We are in a situation where destruction, having been suppressed — the subtraction itself, the opposition, if you want — becomes complicity'. The word 'brother' in its proper and full sense, then, is reserved only to 'mio fratello Guido', in ideal company with 'i giovani Cervi' and 'i ragazzi caduti a Reggio nel Sessanta'. Pier Paolo's elective fathers, as we have seen, are just traitors. Of course for Badiou the result of this division is 'Hate' (for Pasolini the brothers' 'political suicide') and 'Despair' (the fathers' 'loss of hope'). Only if 'allied in an effective negation of the world as it is', they would be able to overcome this stasis.[24]

The conflict between sons–brothers on one side, and fathers–leaders on the other, has been a recurring theme in Pasolini's oeuvre, and an ancient one. As early as in 1942, in the juvenile essay *I giovani, l'attesa*, the poet already devises, at just 20 years of age, a cultural agenda that creates a rift between his generation and that of his intellectual fathers.[25] In his *Forms of Subjectivity*, Robert Gordon has explored the father–son 'dyad' in its recurrence (and ambivalence) all throughout Pasolini's corpus, also putting it in relation with the father–brother dynamic.[26] Such a relationship, well

---

22 Pasolini, 'Vittoria', p. 1261.
23 Ibid., p. 1265.
24 Badiou, 'Destruction, Negation, Subtraction', p. 274.
25 See Pasolini, *Il Setaccio*, 3, 1 (novembre 1942), now in Pasolini, *Saggi sulla politica e sulla società*, pp. 10–14: 'Fatica, estrema autoconoscenza, travaglio interiore individuale e collettivo, saranno gli attributi del nostro nuovo entusiasmo, poiché, ripeto, sia in sede politico-economico-sociale, sia in sede di cultura, succediamo immediatamente a un riscoprimento sulla cui strada dobbiamo proseguire, non già meccanicamente, ma con intenso e lucido approfondimento, che verrà a discriminare nella eredità affidataci — nel nuovo sentimento dell'esistenza — quanto c'è di realmente nuovo e quanto è rimasuglio, avanzo o malafede. Insomma la nostra generazione resterà fissa nella storia con un volto estremamente serio, poiché, già posti, in confronto ai nostri padri — e attraverso il loro insegnamento — in un piano superiore a quello da cui essi, giovani, iniziarono, ci ritroviamo, responsabili, dinnanzi ad una verità rivelata'.
26 See Gordon, '"Mio corpo insepolto": The Body and the Father', in *Forms of Subjectivity*, pp. 161–83.

before being charged of symbolic associations and metaphorical imagery in his work, finds its origin within the very same poet's domestic circle. We cannot expand much here on biographical details, which are nonetheless quite well-known. On one hand, Pasolini's biographers generally emphasize Pier Paolo's profound complicity with his mother against the father. On the other hand, Pier Paolo actually shared with Guido the critical attitude towards the paternal figure, and the political opposition to fascism, so that the father–son conflict always came together with a corresponding sympathetic son–brother relationship. Briefly, Guido Alberto is always described as a passionate character, inclined to disinterested action and constantly exposing himself to life risks: what in Carlo was irrational excess and compulsive tendency to vice, in Guido, corresponded to pure enthusiasm and generosity. Basically, the alliance between the two brothers against Carlo was based on Guido's courage, and on Pier Paolo's intellectual skills. Such a division of roles, according to their cousin Nico Naldini, was tacitly assumed and perpetuated among the family members as a fact, eventually leading to Guido's unfortunate end.[27]

What Badiou fails to notice, or perhaps is not interested in developing, though, is that the division crossing the political arena and epitomized by Carlo's and Guido's different incarnations, also crosses and torments Pier Paolo's poetic (and biographic) self. The father–son–brother dynamic is embodied in him and does not escape the ambivalences of Pasolini's figure. In fact, Pasolini repeatedly conjured up, in his intense public and literary activity, the paternal and fraternal masks in a continuous, unresolved oscillation between the two. Countless examples can be given: from the innovative schoolmaster for young peasants, friends and relatives in Friulian 1950's, with the continuous oscillation of the teacher–disciple

---

[27] See the interview of Enzo Golino with Nico Naldini, 'Ritratto dei due Pasolini da giovani', in *L'Espresso*, 35, 4 September 1997: 'La tacita decisione che uno dei fratelli restasse a casa e l'altro partisse per la guerra partigiana fu come una somma di tutta la loro vita precedente. Spettava a Guido il rosso colore del coraggio: tutto ve lo aveva destinato, anche i conflitti intimi, il rapporto con la madre, con il fratello (che gli era stato maestro di antifascismo), con il padre, il quale, nonostante i difetti, era anche lui un uomo coraggioso. A Pier Paolo toccavano in sorte la tranquillità degli studi, la carriera letteraria e, soprattutto, la protezione dell'adorata madre. [...] Una divisione di compiti così perfetta non lasciava spazio a ripensamenti, rimorsi, pentimenti. Ciascuno dei due fratelli stava facendo la sua parte. Guido, dalla montagna, spediva lettere in cui si firmava Amelia e diceva che si era dato con molto divertimento agli sport invernali. A Pier Paolo chiedeva testi per canzoni che illustrassero il mondo partigiano, e libri di storia moderna e contemporanea'.

roles, to the answers to his readers' letters of the *Vie Nuove* magazine, which alternate paternalistic attitude and fraternal support; from the affectionate advice dispensed to the young poet Bernardo Bertolucci–Guido in 'A un ragazzo',[28] to the debate stirred by *Il PCI ai giovani!!*, the pamphlet–poem in which Pasolini, fearless of incoherence, alternatively and concurrently performed the two roles.[29] Here the students of 1968 are, again, both sons and fathers to him, 'bourgeois father–sons', caught by their double potential as bourgeois and Marxist.[30] But what Pier Paolo projects on the students is his own personal, unsolvable dilemma: becoming the father, or allying with the brother?

For Badiou, Pasolini sides with the struggles of young people: the narcissistic form of love that links him to Guido — due to their similarity of position towards the mother figure — makes him found, to borrow Tracy McNulty's words, a 'fraternal pact of feminine love against the crushing symbolic of the father'.[31] Yet, it is the same necessity of love that lucidly

---

28 'A un ragazzo' (1956-1957) is a poem dedicated to the young Bernardo Bertolucci and also an elegy to his brother Guido, included in *La religione del mio tempo* collection (1957-1959): 'Così nuovo alla luce di questi mesi nuovi | che tornano su Roma, e che a noi altrove | ancorati a una luce d'altri tempi'; 'Al giusto momento, ci lasci, ritorni | alla segreta luce dei tuoi primi giorni: | alla luce che certo tu non puoi dire | né, noi, ricordare, una luce d'aprile'; 'Era un mattino in cui sognava ignara | nei rósi orizzonti una luce di mare: | ogni filo d'erba come cresciuto a stento | era un filo di quello splendore opaco e immenso'; 'Ci togli questa luce che a te splende intera, | ch'è della nuova gioventù ogni nuova sera [...] | Noi invecchiati ora nient'altro diamo | che doloroso amore alla tua lieta fame.'; 'per un anno l'ingenua, eternamente giovane, | povera nostra mamma aveva atteso, e ora | era lì che attendeva, sotto il tiepido sole'; 'Ma l'ombra che è ormai dentro di noi guadagna sempre più tempo, allenta ogni legame | con la vita'; Pasolini, *Tutte le poesie*, pp. 951–58.
29 On this occasion, Pasolini famously attacked the young '68 contestatori as 'figli di papà' and members of a new neocapitalist bourgeoisie asking for power, and counterposed them to the subproletarian police corps.
30 In this respect, Gordon remarks: 'The students of 1968 are, again, both sons and fathers to him. "Il PCI ai giovani!!" develops the polemic, attacking the students for being 'bourgeois father-sons', caught by their double potential as bourgeois and Marxist'; Gordon, *Forms of Subjectivity*, p. 177.
31 As said, Pasolini's biography and Marxism carry a very significant weight in respect to the brotherhood theme. Badiou himself discusses the implications of the filial, fraternal bound theme against the Law of the Father by discussing the Pauline connection in Pasolini. In this regard, see Tracy McNulty, 'Feminine Love and the Pauline Universal', in *Alain Badiou: Philosophy and Its Conditions*, ed. by Gabriel Riera (Albany: State University of New York Press, 2005), pp. 185–212 (p. 198): 'Badiou, in his commentary [to Pasolini's *Saint Paul*], suggests that Pasolini is uniquely poised to appreciate Paul's message, because he understands

recognizes in Carlo 'un amore parziale, che riguardava unicamente il sesso', a partial love, just about sex, and a disconcerting 'affinity for sin and transgressing desire'. So, the link that Badiou institutes between sexuality and politics when referring in his piece to the homosexual 'militancy' of Pier Paolo is valid not only in respect to Guido, but also towards Carlo, therefore showing the two faces of drive, indissolubly linking life and death impulses (as well as the desire–nostalgia for his missing vitality) both to emancipatory and reactionary politics: the narcissistic love for the same, against, and together with, the love as lack and Oedipal castration.

Therefore, the young army and the father–traitor are certainly metaphors for destruction and subtraction, but even more, for the laborious process of individuation of Pier Paolo's self. They unveil the duality forever inscribed in the self, suspended between brotherhood and paternity, partisan militancy and social democracy, or, in his own terms, 'passione e ideologia',[32] 'rivolta perpetua' and 'ragione'. In two words, Carlo and Guido, and their irreconcilable presence in Pier Paolo.

According to Oliver Feltham, Badiou subtly uses poetry in two ways: 1. either as a generic procedure to test the syntax constructed in philosophy in another semantic field (in this case poetry as a form of art), what he

---

that only a militant fraternalism can make way for the universal'. Also, 'for Pasolini, the fraternal pact — guided by "homosexual desire" — annuls the father's "crushing symbolic" and replaces it with maternal love. The passage establishes an implicit analogy between the Pauline polemic against the law and the mother's love, since both defy the inequality of the father's symbolic with the promise of an "egalitarian humanity"' (p. 199). McNulty also reports Badiou's passage from his *Saint Paul* on 'the Greek discourse and the Jewish discourse' as 'both *discourses of the Father*', counterposed to the Pauline–Christian '*discourse of the Son*' as 'the only discourse that has a chance to be universal, detached from all particularity' (p. 46).

32 *Passione e ideologia* is the title of Pasolini's main critical work, which Cesare Segre reads as the opposition between the irrational, the drive, the vital element, the rage, and the conceptual construction, the persuasive and pedagogical commitment: 'prima l'irrazionale, la pulsione, l'elemento vitale, la rabbia; ma poi, anche a dar loro forma e voce, la costruzione concettuale, l'impegno persuasivo e didattico'. While further specifying 'ideologia' as an 'ideological attitude', Segre quotes Pasolini's own definition of it: '[...] atteggiamento d'indipendenza che non può accettare nessuna forma storica e pratica di ideologia: e che insieme soffre come d'un rimorso, d'un indistinto e irrazionale trauma morale, per l'esclusione da ogni prassi, o comunque dall'azione'; see Cesare Segre, 'Vitalità, passione, ideologia', in Pier Paolo Pasolini, *Saggi sulla letteratura e sull'arte*, ed. by Walter Siti and Silvia De Laude (Milan: A. Mondadori, 1999), I, pp. xx–xlvi (p. xxvii and p. xxviii respectively).

terms 'modelling'; 2. or, to the contrary, to test the syntax provided in the particular generic procedure of poetry in the semantic field provided by philosophy (what he calls 'conditioning'). However, what is most important, for Feltham, is not the exact distinction between a method and the other, but their shared 'procedure of incompletion and extension — whether it be termed modelling or conditioning'.[33]

Following Feltham's suggestions, I would like to discuss if such an interpretation of Badiou's method could also be useful for the reading that the philosopher has given of Pasolini's *Vittoria,* and with what results. What Badiou seems to perform and to invite us to do here is, in fact, the 'poetical exercise' that the same Feltham recalls as typical of Badiou's *Theory of the Subject* period, as a 'final twist on the Marxist affirmation of the primacy of practice'.[34]

Modelling seems to prevail in Badiou's reading, as a way of testing a syntax constructed in philosophy in a heterogeneous semantic field — in this case, the brief and tormented Italian Republican history, and within it, Pasolini's life and works —, and finally producing 'a new object of knowledge', namely the Badiousian–Pasolinian 'terrorist subjectivity': Badiou extends the destruction–subtraction dialectic to the present and to the condition of the *banlieues*, applying what he calls the 'terrorist subjectivity' of the army of dead warriors to the desperation of nowadays' rageous youth, which cannot find any proper political outlet in an alliance with the fathers.

Destruction and subtraction are the ultimate signifieds of Pasolini's signifiers/metaphorical chains, while Pasolini's father–son–brother dialectic works as a prefiguration of the Badiousian destruction–negation–subtraction triad (where '→' stands for 'metaphor of'):

---

[33] See Oliver Feltham, *Alain Badiou: Live Theory* (London: Continuum, 2008), p. 133: 'What is at stake in both modelling and conditioning is the production of new knowledge through a logic of incompletion that incompletes a poem or a political movement in order to extend a sequence of thought. It is this procedure of incompletion and extension — whether it be termed modelling or conditioning — that still deserves the name of the dialectic'.

[34] See ibid., p 133: 'To condition philosophy is to stage enduring encounters between philosophy and certain practices [...] philosophy needs to fall in love with the generic. It is just such [...] an articulation of philosophy with generic truth procedures that allows a passage from philosophy through to art or politics or love. Not the least signs of the viability of such a passage are the repeated exhortations on Badiou's part to his readers to perform poetic and mathematical exercises and so to experience the peculiar consistency of an artistic or scientific practice'.

GUIDO–SON–BROTHER–ARMY OF BROTHERS → DESTRUCTION
CARLO–FATHER–CHIEF of the ARMY → SUBTRACTION
PIER PAOLO (CARLO+GUIDO / FATHER+SON–BROTHER)–POET → NEGATION

But if we go back to what this 'terrorist subjectivity' means to the poet, we can actually see the opposite movement — conditioning — at work. If, as I have tried to show with the analysis of Pasolini's 'multiple' and disseminated metaphors, the terrorist subjectivity — well before being the outcome of political and social conflicts — is primarily one of the possible outcomes, or forces at play within the split self, the method of conditioning can be seen employed side by side to modelling, thus pointing backward to a further direction: that of the theory of a (political, artistic and amorous) subject, coming out of the encounter between the syntaxis now provided by the generic procedure of the poem, and tested in the semantic domain (destruction, negation, subtraction...) given by philosophy. In fact, the poem stages the vanishing of the *Resistenza*–Guido event under the surface of social democracy, but also, of the split self. What Badiou attributes to the young dead partisans and subproletariat, as well as to the contemporary, hopeless young men and women, is, as we have already seen, inscribed in the very self of the poet too.

The peril for Badiou in being extended and de-totalized in Pasolini is precisely that, by following his faithful subject Pier Paolo (ideologically faithful to the *Resistenza*–Guido event), he risks to put into indetermination the domain of fidelity with the domain of drives' repetition compulsion that binds the subject to 'reality as it is' under Carlo's paternal form. Therefore, Pasolini's faithfulness to a kind of Badiousian affirmative, constructivist event cannot really be construed without the reference to a negative scheme of void and lack.[35]

---

35 In *À la recherche du réel perdu* (Paris: Fayard, 2015), Badiou talks of an 'affirmative dialectics' of which *Vittoria* is the 'portrait': '[...] la clef de l'accès au réel est à la fin des fins la puissance d'une dialectique affirmative. C'est précisément de cette dialectique que Pasolini fait le portrait dans un autre poème, qui s'appelle *Victoire*'. At the same time, he acknowledges that in Pasolini there is 'une sorte de mélancolie que nous devons surmonter' (p. 59). While attributing such a melancholy to Pasolini's refusal of the end of History, and to the poet's desperate attempt to keep the 'passion of the real' alive at a time of resignation, Badiou tries to affirm the 'joyful' character of such passion: 'Je ne pense pas — et ce sera mon seul point de divergence avec Pasolini — que cette sœur affirmative de la dialectique négative soit par elle-même triste. On sent bien que chez Pasolini, cette sœur de la raison qu'il propose — et qui est bien la raison affirmative — est une sœur triste, parce que pour lui, renoncer à la grâce d'une Histoire favorable est

The 'conditioning' Badiou, instead, gives us an entirely different perspective: it is not only de-totalized by Pasolini's father–son dialectic, but also, looking backwards, recognizes a further antecedent of the Pasolinian (and his own) dialectic: the apostle Paul, with his divided Christian subject, split between flesh and spirit, father/law and fraternal pact of the co-workers/sons in God, and the contradiction brought, within the Church, by the contrasting needs for universalism and organizational structure.[36] As is well known, Pasolini recursively worked, from the 1960s up to the years preceding his death, at the project of a film on *Saint Paul* that he never realized — he only finished the screenplay. Conceived as an actualization in modern times of the Pauline story, it was meant to show the contradictions of the 'founder of churches', at work both in his own spiritual and political lives. Also, it added to the already established Pauline theme of the subject's division the further interpretative layer of homosexuality: for this and other reasons (the common 'apocalyptic message', and mark of diversity and illness),[37] it has been read by Armando Maggi as 'Pasolini's

---

terrible. Mais aujourd'hui, nous devons être convaincus qu'en dépit des deuils que la pensée nous impose, chercher ce qu'il y a de réel dans le réel peut être, est, une passion joyeuse.' (p. 60). In the same work, Badiou says that there was in Pasolini 'une pensée extrêmement violente et un désir illimité' (p. 37).

36 As Badiou himself comments in his *Foreword* to the 2014 English translation of Pasolini's *San Paolo*: 'It is only too natural, in this context, that St Paul should have been a tutelary figure for Pasolini. He saw him, in fact, as the first embodiment of the conflict between political truth (communist emancipation being the contemporary form of salvation), and the meaning this could assume in the weight of the world. In our world, in fact, truth can only make its way by protecting itself from the corrupted outside, and establishing, within this protection, an iron discipline that enables it to "come out", to turn actively towards the exterior, without fearing to lose itself in this. The whole problem is that this discipline (of which Paul is here the inventor under the name of the Church, like Lenin for communism under the name of the Party), although totally necessary, is also tendentially incompatible with the pureness of the True. Rivalries, betrayals, struggles for power, routine, silent acceptance of the external corruption under the cover of practical 'realism': all this means that the spirit which created the Church no longer recognizes in it, or only with great difficulty, that in the name of which this was created'; see Alain Badiou, 'Alain Badiou's Forward to Pier Paolo Pasolini's "Saint Paul: A Screenplay"', *Notebook*, 15 July 2014 <https://mubi.com/notebook/posts/alain-badious-forward-to-pier-paolo-pasolinis-saint-paul-a-screenplay> [accessed 15 November 2021].

37 See, for instance, 'Paul's weakening in Pasolini's script as the growing of an "internal darkening", which culminates in his death', in Besana, as largely evocative of the same Pasolini's final parabola; Bruno Besana, 'Alain Badiou's Pasolini: The Problem of Subtractive Universalism', in *The Scandal of Self-Contradiction: Pasolini's Multistable Subjectivities, Traditions, Geographies*, ed.

most direct and sincere self-portrait, his most explicit autobiography'.[38] Through Pier Paolo, then, the 'conditioning' Badiou is further incompleted in Paul, and the chain of metaphors extend into the sunny territory of truth, opposite to the dark regions of death drive. Destruction, negation and subtraction provide the semantic domain for Pasolini's signifieds Guido, Carlo and Pier Paolo, which, in turn, become metaphors for the Pauline subject's labour and split. Love and grace announce themselves in Pier Paolo through Guido, the pole that bears the stigma of Pauline brotherhood and Christological sacrifice:

DESTRUCTION → GUIDO–SON → SPIRIT
SUBTRACTION → CARLO–FATHER → FLESH

which finally amounts to:

BADIOU ← → PASOLINI ← → PAUL

where Pier Paolo works as a middle 'field/body' of encounters in either way: evental site traversed by the father–son division — torn between faithfulness to the consequences of the Guido–*Resistenza* Truth–Event and paternal adhesion to the order of being —, it can be read both as fulfillment of Paul and prefiguration to the 'modelling' Badiou in an

---

by Luca Di Blasi and others (Wien/Berlin: Turia+Kant, 2012), pp. 209–36 (p. 222).

[38] Maggi emphasizes how the link that Pasolini established between him and Paul is based on the use of analogy 'as a paradoxical rhetorical device that includes both similarity and opposition': 'A first application of analogy is the transposition of Paul's life to our modern times. [...] But an even more interesting analogical level is detectable in the ideological similarities the poet sees between the apostle and himself. Both the Italian poet and the apostle are figures carrying an apocalyptic message. *Saint Paul* is a double biography, of Paul the apostle and of Pier Paolo the artist. Moreover, Pasolini contends that Paul is a divided figure, a figure of internal oppositions. Paul is both a priest, that is, the founder of a repressive institution (the Church), and a prophet who announces the apocalyptic end of that institution'; Armando Maggi, *The Resurrection of the Body: Pier Paolo Pasolini From Saint Paul to Sade* (Chicago: University of Chicago Press, 2009), p. 21. The analogy resides also in their 'view of time and the sacred': 'In Pasolini's interpretation, the apostle lived in a historical era of split between the past of Jesus' sacred time, and the present dominated by a longing for that original manifestation of the sacred' (p. 21). A time of the event's retreat, then. On Pasolini's Paul, see also Luca Di Blasi, 'Split and Conversion in Pasolini's *San Paolo*', in *The Scandal of Self-Contradiction*, pp. 189–207 (pp. 191–92): 'This tension between eternity and present time is accompanied by another, much more difficult and complicated, one — the tension within Pasolini's Paul. As was the case in other adaptations of classical subjects [...], Pasolini obviously used his own inner disruptions as a key for the interpretation or construction of Paul. The saint is thus — like Pasolini — a deeply divided or split man'.

'onward' movement, and as fulfillment in respect to Badiou, and figure of Paul 'backwards', so that:

DESTRUCTION → ← GUIDO–SON → ← SPIRIT
SUBTRACTION → ← CARLO–FATHER → ← FLESH

What I am trying to argue for is, as elsewhere in Badiou,[39] the secularized reuse of a theological structure, in this case one of capital importance not only to the Sacred texts' exegetical field, but also in literary studies on realism, as best represented by the German philologue Erich Auerbach: figural interpretation.[40] In the great critic's words,

> Figural interpretation establishes a connection between two events or persons, the first of which signifies not only itself but also the second, while the second encompasses or fulfills the first. The two poles of the figure are separate in time, but both being real events or figures, are within time, within the stream of historical life. [...] promise and fulfillment are real historical events, which have either happened in the incarnation of the Word, or will happen in the second coming.[41]

---

39 See, for instance, Besana, 'Alain Badiou's Pasolini', p. 230, on the difference between Paul's 'second coming', and the idea of 'resurrection' or 'reactivation' in Badiou, also in note 78, pp. 234–35. Also, see Meillassoux on the 'blurred line between the Badiouian conception of truth and the Christian conception of the Incarnation. [...] Because if Christianity is founded on a fable, according to Badiou, its force stems from having, if not the content, then at least the real form of all truth: [...] Badiou is here very faithful — to the structure, if not the content — of Christian eschatology. And he would not dream of denying it, he who declared Paul the "founder of universalism", the one who was the first to understand the militant nature, and not the erudite nature, of truth'; Quentin Meillassoux, 'History and Event in Alain Badiou', *Parrhesia*, 12 (2011), 1–11 (pp. 9–10).

40 As Hayden White claims in 'Auerbach's Literary History: Figural Causation and Modernist Historicism', in *Figural Realism: Studies in the Mimesis Effect*, ed. by Hayden V. White (Baltimore, MD: Johns Hopkins University Press, 1999), pp. 87–100 (p. 95): 'The Christian schema of the figure and its fulfillment (used by Christian thinkers to interpret the relation between the Old Testament and the New, between Judaism and Christianity, between this world and the beyond, between the present and the future, and [in Dante] even between paganism and Christianity) is grasped by Auerbach as itself a figure that will be fulfilled in the modern idea of history. Indeed, Auerbach holds that history is precisely that mode of existence in which events can be at once fulfillments of earlier events and figures of later ones. Such a schema provided him with a way of characterizing the peculiar combination of novelty and continuity which distinguished historical from natural existence'.

41 Erich Auerbach, *Scenes From the Drama of European Literature* (Minneapolis: University of Minnesota Press, 1984), p. 53.

Figura, which comes from the same root of *fingere/fictio*, is originally a 'plastic formation';[42] then it later becomes synonimous with *typos*, i.e. 'scheme', 'mold'.[43] It is then defined in opposition both to a 'fullfillment or truth' (*veritas*), and to *historia* or *littera* as

> the literal sense of the event related; *figura* is the same literal meaning or event in reference to the fullfillment cloaked in it, and this fullfillment itself is *veritas*, so that *figura* becomes a middle term between *historia–littera* and *veritas*.[44]

Figurae, for the purpose of this paper, are reciprocally Paul and Pier Paolo, as well as Badiou in respect to each of them. It is notable to consider that Paul is, in a way, the inventor of figural interpretation, which would be born out of a strict militant concern, as a specific tool serving the fight for the doctrinal justification of Christianity in respect to Ancient Scriptures. As the same Auerbach recalls, Paul elaborated the use of *typoi–figurae* as a way to reread the Old Testament 'in terms of figural prophecy'.[45] Figural interpretation is then the chief instrument for Paul's 'as if', his capacity to create and announce a new world, the 'fiction' of truth that annuls the normative validity of Old Testament's law by declaring it 'shadow and *typos*' of grace. In sum, says Auerbach, Paul's 'thinking [...] eminently combined *practical politics* with *creative poetic faith*', and 'what the Old Testament thereby lost as a book of national history, it gained in *concrete dramatic reality*'.[46]

---

42 Ibid., p. 45.
43 Ibid., pp. 44, 45.
44 Ibid., p. 47. Despite the profound differences, one cannot help but think about Badiou's definition of the subject in *Being and Event*, trans. by Oliver Feltham (London: Continuum, 2006), p. 406: 'the subject is the finitude of the generic procedure, the local effects of an eventual fidelity'.
45 Auerbach, *Scenes From the Drama of European Literature*, pp. 49–50: 'The Church Fathers often justify figural interpretation on the basis of certain passages in early Christian writings, mostly from the Pauline Epistles. [...] Those passages in the Pauline epistles which contain figural interpretations were almost all written in the course of Paul's bitter struggle on behalf of his mission among the Gentiles'. Alongside Pasolini's interest in figural interpretation, see Toni Hildebrandt's 'Allegories of the Profane on Foreign Soil in Pasolini's Work after 1968', *Estetica. Studi e ricerche*, 2 (2017) <doi:10.14648/88229>, for the poet's use of allegory as a means to 'open(s) up the discursive space of modernity and put(s) trust in novel constellations' through his exploration of non-European cultures.
46 Auerbach, *Scenes From the Drama of European Literature*, p. 51 [emphasis mine].

Pier Paolo as a figure is then, as I previously anticipated, middle term between *historia–littera* and *veritas*, being and event, Badiou and Paul. He is the kind of 'present suspended between two events' of which Besana talks with regard to Pasolini's Paul.[47] Pasolini, himself a fervent reader of Auerbach, according to Hervé Joubert-Laurencin is no less than the creator of a kind of Auerbachian filiation of the figural interpretation, the so-called 'figural integration' (*'integrazione figurale'*), which he defines as a 'post-Auerbachian, heretical figurism', meant to de-theologize figural interpretation, applying it to the world of humans and opening it to a revolutionary use.[48]

Figura — in this heretical sense — would therefore serve as the par excellence representation of Badiousian thought (and subject), with its kind of 'figural realism' suspended between (Pauline) truth and world(s), logic of Being and logic of being, and itself figure of, and prefiguration to the 'second coming'-fulfillment of communism.[49] Badiou's destruction and subtraction, in the modelling and conditioning's shared logic of 'incompletion and extension', are both metaphors and procedures of the Badiousian fidelity to the event Paul (the Christian divided subject, the split into the whole set, the multiple in the one–*ecclesia*). In a peculiar declination of the Sartrean *choisir son passé* (and relative ancestors),[50] Badiou is fully immersed in the 'purely retrospective' logic of *figura* as a genealogical — 'neither causal nor genetic' — link established between

---

47 Besana, 'Alain Badiou's Pasolini', p. 229: 'Each revolutionary subject thus necessarily stands in between two events: [...] and this in-betweenness constitutes what I would call "Paul's limbo"'. Also, see note 78, pp. 235–36, which discusses Agamben's reading of the second coming as the 'in between' itself: 'in this sense, the Pauline second coming and the Badiousian time of the subject, stretched between two events, share a similar logic, as they both are times "in between", and somehow thinkable only in retroactive terms'.

48 Hervé Joubert-Laurencin, 'Figura Lacrima', in *The Scandal of Self-Contradiction*, pp. 237–54 (pp. 249–51).

49 As the same Badiou says in his *Foreword* to the 2014 English translation of Pasolini's *San Paolo*: 'Paul is one of the possible historical names of the tension between fidelity to the founding event of a new cycle of the True (*metaphorically*, the resurrection of Christ; *actually*, the communist revolution) and the rapid exhaustion, under the cross of the world, of the pure subjective energy (holiness, or totally disinterested militancy) that the concrete realization of this fidelity would demand' [emphases mine].

50 Jean-Paul Sartre, 'Mon passé', in *L'Être et le Néant: Essai D'ontologie Phénoménologique* (Paris: Gallimard, 1943), pp. 577–85.

historical events, in the fiction of the (Pauline?) 'as if'.[51] In his *Figural Realism*, Hayden White has so described figural fulfillment in terms evocatively resonant, to the reader of Badiou, of his performative concept of faithfulness to the event:

> *Erfüllung* must be here understood as a kind of anomalous, nondetermining causal force or ateleological end. [...] the kind of *Er-füllung* envisaged by Auerbach is the kind suggested by such synonymous prefixed lexemes as English *per-formance, con-summation, com-pliance, ac-complishment,* and the like, all of which are suggestive of the kinds of actions of which morally responsible persons are thought to be capable, actions such as fulfilling a promise, cleaving to the terms of an oath, carrying out assumed duties, remaining faithful to a friend, and the like. [...] And so it is with the relationships between the kinds of event we wish to call historical as against, say, natural events. A given historical event can be viewed as the fulfillment of an earlier and apparently utterly unconnected event when the agents responsible for the occurrence of the later event link it "genealogically" to the earlier one.[52]

Pasolini's *figura* as a middle term between Badiou and Paul, allows the opposite and concomitant movement of the de-totalising modelling and conditioning methods, which put the three 'events–thoughts' in reciprocal co-extension. This way, Badiou's poetical exercise in *Victory* becomes one of the many sites in which the genealogy of a Pauline–Badiousian dialectic comes to the fore. Working as a *figura* suspended between two historical facts, and internally split into fulfilment–fidelity to an earlier event and prefiguration of its possible resurrection(s), *Vittoria*'s dramatization of the 'terrorist subjectivity', traversed by the Pauline–Pasolinian father–son dialectic, is an ideal evental site for the *laica rappresentazione* of Badiou's theory of the subject.

---

51   For White's use of the 'as if' formula, see for instance White, *Figural Realism*, p. 89, and Hayden V. White, 'What Is a Historical System?', in *The Fiction of Narrative: Essays on History, Literature, and Theory, 1957–2007*, ed. by Hayden V. White and Robert Doran (Baltimore, MD: Johns Hopkins University Press, 2010), pp. 126–35 (p. 132).
52   White, *Figural Realism*, pp. 88–89.

BARBARA VINKEN

PASOLINI'S SACRIFICIAL DEATH

> *Ma essere è naturale? No, a me non sembra, anzi, a me sembra che sia portentoso, misterioso e, semmai assolutamente innaturale.*
>
> Pasolini[1]

> *De la question du sacrifice, il est nécessaire de dire qu'elle est la question dernière.*
>
> Bataille[2]

> *Er lässt uns seine leichen / Zum pfande letzter gunst.*
>
> Gryphius[3]

A Loss of Reality: The Author as Seer

Pasolini is not the poet of the natural, but of the holy. Through the destruction of the natural, the real comes to light. This moment of illumination unveils the holy. For Pasolini, the natural or, in its superlative form, the most natural, stands opposed to the real. The bourgeoisie's logic killed the real in the name of the natural.

Pasolini is anti-Rousseauism, anti-enlightenment, anti-rational. That does not mean that he is a sentimental nostalgic.[4] Pasolini does not believe

---

1   Pier Paolo Pasolini, 'Essere è naturale?' (1967), in *Empirismo eretico* (Milan: Garzanti, 1977), pp. 242–47 (p. 244).
2   Georges Bataille, '"La Limite de l'utile", version abandonnée de "La Part maudite"' (1949), in *Œuvres complètes* VII (Paris: Gallimard, 1976), pp. 181–280 (p. 264).
3   Cited after Walter Benjamin, *Ursprung des deutschen Trauerspiels* (1928), in *Gesammelte Schriften* I (Frankfurt am Main: Suhrkamp, 1974), p. 392.
4   The limitations of this reproach, which is often formulated from a rationalistic position, were shown particularly convincingly by Gert Mattenklott in

in a goodhearted savage, who's natural goodwill could be mourned and restored in a distant future. While Pasolini may long for a rural Catholic culture, as in his home region of Friuli, for the ancient Catholic renaissance orgies of the *Decameron* and *Canterbury Tales*, or for *Arabian Nights*, as magnificently staged in *The Trilogy of Life*, and while he may love the roman 'borgate' subproletarian culture depicted in *Ragazzi di vita* or in *Accattone*, or while he may withdraw more and more frequently to third world countries: all of this is not because these worlds might stand for a nonviolent, peaceful world of free, natural, naive love, and of an authentic self.[5]

Completely to the contrary, they stand for a world, in which violence is not natural, but holy, a world of meaningful, ritual sacrifices, which opposes another world of mechanical, natural crime. Thus, the subject of *Medea* is this collapse from a holy, ritual society based upon sacrifice, in which 'nothing is natural and all is holy', as the centaur says, into a rational, natural society, where nothing is holy anymore, but instead everything is natural and because of this violence is criminal.[6] Pasolini's 'golden age' is illuminated by the Passion of Christ; it shines blood-red in the light of violent sacrificial death. Pasolini's emblem for the real is the human body and its sex. But not every human body and every sex. The bourgeoisie created a new type of civilization. It removed the real from the human body, so that the body has become a mask: 'À présent, les bourgeois, créateurs

---

conversation with Karsten Witte, 'Kennwort "Pasolini": Ein Dialog', in *Kraft der Vergangenheit: Zu Motiven der Filme von Pier Paolo Pasolini*, ed. by Christoph Klimke (Frankfurt am Main: Fischer Taschenbuch, 1988), pp. 97–116. For Pasolini's 'nostalgia' see Anna Panicali, 'L'ultima gioventù', in *Perché Pasolini: Ideologia e stile di un intellettuale militante*, ed. by Gualtiero De Santi, Maria Lenti, and Roberto Rossini (Florence: Guaraldi, 1978), pp. 203–13. Hans Ulrich Reck gives a critique of Pasolini's so called 'irrationalistic-postmodern' position that does not appear as much in the body of work as in the reception, 'Mythische Verweigerung und totale Person: Zu Werk, Leben und Rezeption Pier Paolo Pasolinis', *Merkur*, 38 (1984), 165–71. In contrast, Philippe Soller's article 'Pasolini, Sade, Saint Matthieu', in *Pasolini. Séminaire dirigé par Maria Antonietta Macciocchi* (Paris: Grasset, 1980), pp. 109–19, shows subtlety with great casualness.

5   See Cesare Casarino, 'The Southern Answer: Pasolini, Universalism, Decolonization', *Critical Inquiry*, 36 (2010), 673–96, for 'sexual orientation and sexual Orientalism' in 'the conflation of Roman proletariat and Third World, Italian and Global South'.

6   Michel Covin, 'Médée, la violence et le symbole', *Revue d'esthétique*, 3 (1982), 59–64, originating from René Girard, *Des Choses cachées depuis la fondation du monde* (Paris: Grasset, 1978).

d'un nouveau type de civilisation, ne pouvaient qu'en arriver à déréaliser le corps. Ils y sont parvenus, en effet: ils en ont fait un masque'.[7] In this fashion, the body, and more precisely the body of the lowliest worker, the subproletariat, the sole abode of that which is real, disappears in the new civilization. 'Ainsi l'ultime lieu où habitait la réalité, à savoir le corps ou plus exactement le corps populaire, a lui aussi disparu.' Pasolini suffers with and through his body, he suffers existentially under the loss of a reality that shapes the consumer society to a previously unknown degree:

> La consummation consiste, en effect en un pur et simple cataclysme anthropologique; et je vis, existentiellement ce cataclysme qui, du moins pour l'instant, n'est que dégradation; je le vis chaque jour, dans les formes de mon existence, *dans mon corps* [...]. C'est de cette expérience, existentielle, directe concrète dramatique, corporelle, que naissent en conclusion tous mes discours idéologiques.[8]

For Pasolini, the transformation of rural or sub-proletarian society through bourgeois-ization into consumer culture[9] is an unparalleled degradation, an anthropological mutation. The change constitutes the radical extermination of any difference, it consists of a standardization and normalization. 'La *matrice* che genera *tutti* gli *italiani* è ormai la *stessa*.'[10] All identify themselves, without history and faceless, with the same figure. Pasolini drastically calls this levelling of all cultural and historical differences a genocide. The new society is hedonistic, permissive, and tolerant; sex is the society's favorite consumer good. The family is the privileged place of consumption, monopoly-like, and finds its utmost expression in the act of coitus. (Pasolini's infamous polemics against abortion stem from this point.)[11] Eroticism is no longer a subversive power, on the contrary, it possesses the strongest leverage in favor of standardization; dissociations between life and eroticism take the place of tabus. The obligatory

---

7 Pier Paolo Pasolini, 'Thétis', *Revue d'esthétique* 3 (1982), 5–8 (pp. 7–8); revised edition of a contribution to an exhibition of 1973 [Italian version in *Erotismo, eversione, merce*, ed. by Vittorio Boarini (Bologna: Cappelli, 1974)].
8 On body and reality, love and life in Pasolini's work, see Alberto Moravia, 'Il poeta e il sottoproletario', in Pier Paolo Pasolini, *Ragazzi di vita* (Turin: Einaudi, 1975), preface to the new edition, pp. 3–12.
9 For a particularly impressive, early representation of the topic see Elsa Triolet's novel *Roses à crédit* (Paris: Gallimard, 2009).
10 Pier Paolo Pasolini, 'Studio sulla rivoluzione antropologica in Italia' (1974), in *Scritti corsari* (Milan: Garzanti, 1975), pp. 50–56 (p. 53).
11 Pasolini, 'Il coito, l'aborto, la falsa tolleranza del potere, il conformismo di progressisti', in *Scritti corsari*, pp. 131–32.

heterosexuality of the couple does not signify freedom. Instead, this obligation is the most effective machine for conformity. The society, a 'universo orrendo' has even transformed death into one giant consumer good.[12] Pasolini views Italy after World War II as a continuation of fascism using more effective means; television is the most effective tool of all.

In its last stage of development, the bourgeoisie infects all the other social classes. It celebrates its last triumphs as modern consumer society. According to Pasolini's diagnosis, the bourgeoisie is not primarily a socioeconomic phenomenon, but rather an epistemological and ontological category: a state of complete oblivion of being. The bourgeoisie persists through the extermination of the very concept of reality. The world can no longer be experienced; 'naive and sensual love' is no longer possible. For Pasolini, reality is not a once and for all given, but something that evades itself, that is endangered and could disappear; in the new all-devouring bourgeoisie's triumph, reality is buried. Fundamentally, in order to appear, reality needs revelation. But without reality there is no life, and because of this, all in this society are living dead, having the appearance only of living. Pasolini places his 'disperata vitalità' against this death, which has already set in. This despairing liveliness does not aim to conserve its own life, but to sacrifice it and thereby live.

Restauration of the Real: The Sacrificial Author

The other economy's protagonist, against whom Pasolini opposes the bourgeois economy, is the author. The author's ability predestines him to a different exertion than that of consumption: the exertion, which in its highest form becomes sacrifice. By taking on the burden of sacrifice, the author lives, while others, who in a desperate endeavor cling to life, are already dead while living. In this society concerned only with preservation, it is the author, whose mission it is to overcome the instinct to survive. This is the author's freedom. In an article titled 'Il Cinema impopulare', that was published in the journal *Nuovi Argomenti*, run by Pasolini, he devotes himself to a problem posed by a film congress that took place in Assisi under Catholic auspices: 'Libertà dell'autore e liberazione degli spettatori'[13].

---

12   Gian Carlo Ferretti, *Pasolini: L'universo orrendo* (Rome: Riuniti, 1976).
13   Pier Paolo Pasolini, 'Il Cinema impopolare', *Nuovi Argomenti* 20 (1970), later published in *Empirismo eretico*, pp. 269–76 (pp. 270 ff.).

The author's purpose and the purpose of the link between martyrdom and authorship is most concisely and fundamentally formulated as follows:

> Anche la natura è d'accordo: e, per aiutarci, ad essere amorosamente attaccati alla vita, ci fornisce dell' 'instinto di conversazione'. Senonché [...] natura è ambigua: e infatti eccola fornirci anche dell'istinto opposto, cioè quello del desiderio di morire. Questo conflitto, che non è contraddittorio — come vorrebbe la nostra mente razionale e dialettica — ma oppositorio e quindi non progressivo, non capace di sintesi ottimistiche, si svolge nel fondo della nostra anima: nel fondo inconoscibile, com'è ben noto. Ma gli 'autori' sono gli incaricati a rendere come possono manifesto ed esplicito tale conflitto. Essi hanno infatti la mancanza di tatto e l'inopportunità necessarie a rivelare in qualche modo di 'desiderare di morire' e di venir meno quindi alle norme dell'istinto di conservazione: o, più semplicemente, di venir meno alla CONSERVAZIONE. *La libertà è dunque un attentato autolesionistico alla conservazione.* La libertà non può essere manifestata altrimenti che attraverso un grande o un piccolo martirio. E ogni martire martirizza se stesso attraverso il carnefice conservatore.

And somewhat later:

> Vorrei accentuare la parola esibizione. La vocazione alle piaghe del martirio che l'autore fa a se stesso nel momento in cui trasgredisce l'istinto di conservarsi, sostituendolo con quello di perdersi, non ha senso se non è resa esplicita al massimo: se non è appunto esibita. In ogni autore, nell'atto di inventare, la libertà si presenta come esibizione della perdita masochistica di qualcosa di certo. Egli nell'atto inventivo, necessariamente scandaloso, si espone — e proprio alla lettera — agli altri: allo scandalo appunto, al ridicolo, alla riprovazione, al senso di diversità, e perché no?, all'ammirazione, sia pure un po' sospetta.

In the displayed wounds of martyrdom, something is brought to light, that is fundamentally concealed, and that becomes completely disguised in our dialectically rational, optimistic approach. The conflict in the indiscernible depths of the soul becomes visible through self-sacrifice.[14] The task of the author is to reveal and manifest a desire that lies in the depth of the soul, the desire to die in freedom to sacrifice oneself. The author does this through the act of overexerting invention. Self-preservation and consumption are linked; on the other hand, there is consumption in the sense of self-consumption, destruction, and sacrifice. In this sense, Pasolini's films can

---

14 On Pasolini's 'La crocifissione' compare with Michael Hardt's 'Exposure: Pasolini in the Flesh', in this volume.

only be 'unpopular', they close themselves off to consumption. The poet does not consume to keep himself alive; instead the poet devours himself in the act of production. Also, the poet does not produce something able to be consumed, but something devouring. To this end, Pasolini's filmography is 'cinéma d'élite'.

The text is determined by the antithesis of sacrifice versus the preservation of life. The transgression of the normality of preservation to self-sacrifice is an act filled with fear, an act in which pain and desire mix. In the self-inflicted wounds the author attests to his faithlessness towards the principle of preservation, in a certain way the principle of life. But just only in a certain way because life can only be loved in an 'amore desinteressato' when it is dedicated to death. All humans fundamentally are potential authors: despite all efforts to preserve themselves, they are controlled by that which Pasolini calls a death drive [*Todestrieb*]. Solely because of this, it is possible to overcome the dark threat, that comes in inexplicable fashion from the rejection of a communicative exchange pertaining to the author and surrounds the author with a storm of panic and scandal. In martyrdom, the author acts upon the human's concealed truth and hidden desire; the author acts upon the human's 'ignoto e inconfessato istino di morte, per definizione anti conservatore'. Through the realization and acting out of this desire, the reality shines through a 'holy' and therefore indefinable act between audience and author, 'sotto il segno ambiguo degli istinti e sotto il segno religioso (non confessionale) della carità'.

Reality is produced through the sadomasochistic act of creation and reception. In a sadistic transgression the author violates the code, he destroys, in masochistic fashion, the principle of his own life. The audience either passionately takes part in the sadistic aggression, that always also contains masochistic components because it concerns the principle of life itself, or they insult and condemn the author for this orgy of transgression. As a result, the author is punished for termination of the 'fraternal code' and his masochistic desire is again satisfied. The full purpose of this operation, however, does not lie in the acting out of a desire, but in the revelation of truth, in the production of a reality, a reality that only shines through the act of violation, that is also always a violation of a principle which protects life:

> Solo nell'attimo in cui si è a tu per tu con la regola da infrangere, e Marte è ancipite, sotto l'ombra di Tanatos, si può sfiorare, la rivelazione de la verità, o della totalità, o insomma di qualcosa di concreto: operata la trasgressione — che si realizza in una nuova invenzione — cioè in una nuova realtà costituita — la verità, o la totalità, o quel Qualcosa di concreto, si vanifica perché non può

essere vissuto né stabilizzato in nessun modo. È per questo infatti che il Potere, ogni Potere, è cattivo [...]. Se è pensabile un Potere 'meno peggio' degli altri, questo potrebbe essere solo un Potere che, nel conservare o nel ricostituire la norma, tenesse conto delle apparizioni o delle possibili riapparizioni della Realtà.

This process can never be concluded; norms and rules need to be present so that they can be violated, and every new violation leads to the establishment of a new rule, that once again needs to be transgressed, so that reality can once again shine through. Where everything is transgression, transgression is pointless, because it is without danger. This is Pasolini's reproach to the avant-gardists. The confrontation with power, the instance of struggle against the norm is decisive: 'il momento della lotta, quello in cui si muore, è al fronte'. This being because, 'solo la morte dell' eroe è uno spettacolo; e solo essa è utile'. One only needs to be careful not to be carried away by the hero's 'slancio vittorioso verso il martirio', but instead to stay at the heart of the struggle. Pasolini compares the sadistic and masochistic components of the struggle with the instance of violence in the sex act: 'io stesso provo in moviola [...] l'effetto quasi sessuale dell'infrazione al codice, come esibizionismo di qualcosa di violato'. In the end, this violence is always treated with the respect, that one has for one's parents. For Pasolini, the world is 'un insieme di padri e di madri'[15], he loves and admires. Therefore, he must commit sacrilege, a rape against them — for which he will then be punished. The last and determining form of this violence must be incest, as highlighted in *Teorema*.

Is the talk of martyrdom, the death of the hero at the front line, the talk of the displayed wounds, the desire which is experienced in the sadomasochistic act, and the pain, is it metaphorical? In Pasolini's language one can observe a peculiar smooth movement between structural conceptions of an 'infrazione del codice-operazione necessaria all'invenzione stilistica' and a 'religious-erotic' code, which seamlessly merge into one another. The violation of the code is simultaneously an exhibition of the violation of the 'conservazione' and therefore 'l'esibizione di un atto autolesionistico: per cui qualcosa di tragico e di ignoto scelto al posto di qualcosa di quotidiano e di noto (la vita)'. The state of being an author and inventing is not a metaphorical self-sacrifice, but a self-sacrifice full of fear and desire.

Pasolini refers to Freud in the conflict between death drive and self-preservation; but the antitheses his text constructs, contradicts Freud. Freud's death drive has nothing to do with martyrdom and with a

---

15 Pasolini, 'Battute sul cinema' (1966), in *Empirismo Eretico*, pp. 227–36.

displayed, almost public, ritual sacrifice. Besides, Pasolini's opposition is resolved paradoxically because one who safeguards slaughterers who sacrifice is a 'carnefice conservatore'. In the image of the butcher, the sacrificial death, the burden which the martyr takes upon himself, becomes apparent. The figure who has self-sacrificed, the figure who willfully nears a self-alienation, is after a maximal exhibition of exertion. This maximal exhibition of exertion turns the author into a scandal in the society that surrounds him. This does not reference Freud, but Bataille.

Pasolini's semiotically formulated goal becomes clear when viewed in the context of his idiomatic concept of reality, even if this goal is hard to understand within the semiotic frame: to portray reality through reality, or 'attraverso la realtà'. Christian Metz, Jean Dufflot, or even Umberto Eco could make little of the concept. In Pasolini's work, the type of cinema that pursues this objective is not a cinema-verità; Pasolini always protested his work being categorized as cinema-verità or neorealismo. Contrary to neorealismo, he speaks of cinema-poesia and implies a non-naturalistic, non-natural, and therefore real cinema. One of his alienation techniques consists in *not* recording the voices of the actors, but later synchronizing them with their own or a foreign voice.[16] Characteristic of this movement against the grain is the principle of a 'real' montage, that runs contrary to the naturalistic frame sequence. Being 'real' means for Pasolini an aggressive relationship with that which is real; this violence against the real stems from an 'allucinato, infantile e pragmatic amore'.[17] Reality finds expression in a religious, as well as a sexual fetishism, that aims to affix objects, to make things stand still: 'Il mio amore feticistico per le "cose" del mondo, mi impedisce di considerarle naturali'. These objects are removed from the flow of time, they are knocked out of their surroundings, are examined in isolation, and outside of any narrative structure, delivered to the idolatry which they request.

The reproduction of nature, that, in Pasolini's cinematic work, seeks to create reality, occurs through the rape of the naked naturality. 'Ma cos'è che rende la realtà "naturalistica", cioè irreale?' The true nature of reality, that in the outside world becomes disguised and thus unreal because of narration and its own naturalistic effects, is restored in film. The frame sequence, which is produced by montage, is the appropriate technique. Pasolini thus compares montage, filled with aggression and desire, to death:

---

16 Anselm Haverkamp on 'Non-Construction' in Barthes' conception of photography, 'The Memory of Pictures: Roland Barthes and Augustine on Photography', *Comparative Literature*, 45 (1993), 258–79.
17 Pasolini, 'Battute sul cinema', pp. 229 ff.

> *La morte compie un fulmineo montaggio della nostra vita*: ossia sceglie i suoi momenti veramente significativi [...] e li mette in successione, facendo del nostro presente, infinito, instabile e incerto, e dunque linguisticamente non descrivibile, un passato chiaro, stabile, certo, e dunque linguisticamente ben descrivibile (nell'ambito appunto di una Semiologia Generale). *Solo grazie alla morte, la nostra vita ci serve ad esprimerci*. Il montaggio opera dunque sul materiale del film [...] quello che la morte opera sulla vita.[18]

The real nature of the objects, their suggestive archaic, eidetic form only starts to shine through when this type of montage is used. And in this sense, the sacrificial death is nothing but a montage that violently intervenes in the naturally occurring life (flowing as time flows), to conquer a true reality. Mythical reality can thus shine through in film. Technology does not promote the rational, but the myth.

Damnation's Blessing: Pasolini and Bataille

The relationship between Bataille's and Pasolini's work is manifold.[19] Thematic overlapping is the first thing that catches the eye. Both authors believe that a systematic dissemblance of reality is arising in the modern world. They state a loss of the holy. The rational and moral is deified, while God is moralized and rationalized. The moral and the rational do not pertain to a world of the real (as Pasolini would say), or to a world of intimate immanence (as Bataille would say), but to a world of preservation, a world of objectification. Morality proclaims rules that universally arise from the mundane world, rules that guarantee the world's consistency. However, reason is only the universal form of objects.[20] Numerous connections between Bataille and Pasolini result from what they see as an increasing dissemblance and misjudgment governing the modern world. Both Bataille and Pasolini commit to a nondenominational religiousness, combined with sadomasochistic eroticism and Passion. Their commitment to communism goes hand in hand with a categorical rejection of late capitalist consumer society. They both analyse fascism as a perversion of the holy sacrifice. They both emphasize poetry, especially Rimbaud, the 'violent poet'.

---

18 Pier Paolo Pasolini, 'Osservazione sul piano-sequenza' (1967), in *Empirismo eretico*, pp. 237–41 (p. 241).
19 See Philippe Lacoue-Labarthe's 'Pasolini, an improvisation (of a Saintliness)', in this volume.
20 Georges Bataille, 'Théorie de la religion' (1974), in *Œuvres complètes* VII, pp. 281–351 (p. 325).

Pasolini and Bataille share the conviction that poetry 'leads to the same place that every form of eroticism (and of violent sacrifice) leads to: to the indistinguishability, the amalgamation of different things. It leads us to eternity, to death, and through death to continuity. Poetry is eternity. The sea, that orbits with the sun'.[21] Alongside this major theme, there are a variety of small details, (going as far as similarities in formulations,) which indicate Pasolini's lifelong intimate knowledge of Bataille's works. Like in Bataille's work, Pasolini's formulations are marked by the same awkwardness of being unable to speak of — or only able to speak of — sacrifice and violence, of ecstasy and passion. Bataille confesses this embarrassment writing, 'Il me faudrait parler comme parlent les poètes', and, marking the necessarily violent desecration, a rape of the parents, Pasolini says: 'Beh, son cose che si dicono in quello straordinario genere letterario che è un'intervista'.[22] Bataille sees laughter as giving consent to that which destroys us; Chaplin's slapstick humor is a fitting example. Pasolini uses Bataille's example when he puts Chaplin's 'gag' to the test as 'pure realism' in cinema.[23] Thus, the best interpretation of Pasolini's *Accattone* is given via Bataille's phrase: the forgery which is the capitalistic society is exposed through the scoundrels' splendor.

> *À cet égard, la société actuelle est une immense contrefaçon, où cette vérité* de la richesse est passée sournoisement dans la *misère*. Le véritable luxe et le profond *potlach* de notre temps revient au misérable, je veux dire à celui qui s'étend sur la terre et méprise. Un luxe authentique exige le mépris achevé des richesses, la sombre indifférence de qui refuse le travail et fait de sa vie, d'une part une splendeur infiniment ruinée, d'autre part une insulte silencieuse au mensonge laborieux des riches. [...] nul ne saurait désormais le sens de la richesse, ce qu'elle annonce d'explosif, de prodigue et de débordant, s'il n'était la splendeur des haillons et le sombre défi de l'indifférence. Si l'on veut, finalement, le mensonge voue l'exubérance de la vie à la révolte.[24]

Pasolini brings together Sade and Buchenwald in the way Bataille had prophesied. Isn't Pasolini the one, who "peut lire les Cent Vingt

---

21 Georges Bataille, *L'Érotisme* (Paris: Les éditions de Minuit, 2011), citation from Rimbaud's *Poésies*.
22 Pasolini, 'Battute sul cinema', p. 229.
23 Pasolini, 'La "Gag" in Chaplin' (1971), in *Empirismo eretico*, p. 256; Bataille, 'La limite de l'utile', p. 277.
24 Georges Bataille, 'La Part Maudite', in *Œuvres complètes* VII, pp. 17–179 (p. 79).

Journées en reconnaissant son monde"?[25] Was it not Pasolini, who showed the perversion of the holy sacrifice, perversion of holy eros and sacred sadomasochism that took place in fascism because the Passions were not unleased with the emotion of fear, but came under the sign of reason and its cold, alienating light? Pasolini does not strive for this perversion, but for epiphany's shining, blinding light, that his role model Caravaggio staged in an unmatched fashion. It is not by accident that it was Pasolini's teacher Roberto Longhi, who rediscovered the works of Caravaggio — long interpreted as 'naturalistic' —, instead celebrated Caravaggio's use of light as the invention of cinematic lighting.[26]

Pasolini's work is a commentary on, and homage to Bataille's work. He literally succeeded Bataille. He did not only write his work according to Bataille. Through his 'spectacular death' as with his 'maximally exposed' sacrificial death, he also lived and completed Bataille's work.[27] Pasolini brings Bataille's written protagonist to life. Let us focus on what was not only for Bataille, but also for Pasolini the 'last question', the question of sacrifice. What links sacrifice, eroticism, and poetic contemplation? What makes the sacrifice holy? What reveals itself as final truth, a glory, which shines through a horror? I will confine myself to outlining Bataille's basic ideas to the point at which Pasolini's work and his death become apparent as a projected consequence of Bataille's work.

The principle of life justifies an economy of abundance determined by 'consommation' and in accordance with the sun model. This economy is structured towards a consumption of overflowing resources and not towards production. The human history is one of increasing decay, of increasing dissemblance of a being with which humans once were intimately interconnected. Discontinuity and objectification are, within a large current of cultural criticism, the passwords for both Pasolini and Bataille. When we subjugate ourselves to the world of production, we lose the intimate relationship with life's continuity. We objectify ourselves in

---

25 Georges Bataille, 'Le Mal dans le platonisme et le sadisme', in *Œuvres complètes* VII, pp. 365–80 (p. 373).
26 On the intricate metaphysics of light that is crucial for Pasolini's technique see Helga Finter, 'San Pier Paolo oder "Alles ist Paradies in der Hölle" (Sade)', in *Der Körper und seine Sprachen: Über Fichte, Duras, Pasolini, Bellmer, Artaud*, ed. by Hans-Jürgen Heinrichs (Frankfurt am Main/Paris: Qumran, 1984), pp. 61–92.
27 Pasolini, 'Il Cinema impopolare', p. 275, with an unacknowledged citation from Bataille's *Érotisme*. The 'imitative' reenactment of iconic photos of cadavers has been highlighted by Georges Didi-Huberman, 'Abgioia: Tanz der Angst und des Konflikts', *Zeitschrift für Medien- und Kulturforschung*, 0 (2009), 119–31, here on *La sequenza del fiore di carta* (1968).

a world of objects. 'La nature devient la propriété de l'homme mais elle cesse de lui être immanente.'[28] Bataille considers that the society of his time has achieved the pinnacle of the rational — and therefore rational's possible tipping point. Real life and its economy did not go astray in archaic societies. In civilized societies, the religious sphere compensates for the complete loss of real life and for the loss of its most important device: sacrifice.

In sacrifice, the life's lost intimacy, continuity and immanence are restored for a moment, a moment in which the truth of life shines through. Sacrifice is necessarily violent. In sacrifice, the 'cursed part', the part destined for 'consummation violente', is destroyed through the destruction of life in its objectification. Its true being can shine through the horror of destruction, the being of the victim, our being. 'Mais la malédiction l'arrache de l'ordre des choses; elle rend reconnaissable sa figure, qui rayonne dès lors l'intimité, l'angoisse, la profondeur des êtres vivants.'[29] The moment the continuity of the being manifests itself in death is the holy. In the sacrificial death, the victim enters life through death. Life's glory, abundance, and exuberance can only be achieved through the greatest horror; on the verge of life stands the greatest fear.

> Et dans l'extase de cette angoissante vision, il en est comme si vraiment le vieil homme était broyé: la vie de la personne étroite se perd dans une réalité beaucoup plus vaste, comme la vague qui éclate se perd en retombant dans le flot qui l'entoure.[30]

Bataille refers to the conversion topos, which is here atrociously literalized. The human lives by giving his life, ceding it, and dying — not in transcendence, but in intimacy, in the immanence that the sacrifice conquers. Through the sacrificial victim, death becomes an epiphany of holiness. Without a doubt, this immersion into intimacy occurs only seldomly through actual death. The erotic union, laughter, and writing are not necessarily lethal forms of sacrifice. What unites these forms is the 'agreement unto death'. 'Que signifie l'érotisme des corps sinon une violation de l'être des partenaires? Une violation qui confine à la mort? Qui confine au meurtre?'[31] As in love, as in death, the author consumes him

---

28 Bataille, 'Théorie de la religion', p. 305.
29 Bataille, 'La Part Maudite', 64.
30 Bataille, 'La Limite de l'utile', 259.
31 Georges Bataille, 'L'Érotisme', in *Œuvres complètes* X (Paris: Gallimard, 1987), pp. 7–270 (p. 23).

by writing: 'Personnellement, je ne suis rien auprès du livre que j'écris: s'il communique ce qui m'a brûlé, j'aurai vécu pour l'écrire'.[32] Although death does not directly ensue through writing, writing is 'l'ébauche — ou l'image, ou le commencement' of this fearful becoming one with rampant life; Pasolini would say a becoming one with reality, a reality that suspends the state of things.

A Barred Conversion: The Author as Demonstrator

TEOREMA means that which comes to view, that which becomes visible.[33] This becoming visible is already subject of Pasolini's *Divina Mimesis*, this fundamental essay written in 1963 and publicized posthumously as a fragment in 1975.[34]

The newer meaning of the word 'teorema' testifies to the transition from the older meaning of epiphany to a scientific demonstration, to an

> enunciato sommario d'una proposizione contenente una verità che si intende dimostrare e che costituisce la conclusione (tesi) cui si giunge, attraverso un procedimento logico deduttivo in cui ci si avvale di postulati o verità dimostrate, della premessa iniziale.[35]

Within the title *Teorema*, Pasolini indicates the technical achievement of film to create revelation. *Teorema* was also made into a book which begins with a clear framework of characteristics of scientific discourse and is divided into small parts, which each stage proofs. As a book about light, sun, and the colors they cause, *Teorema* is engaged in a project of scientific standards which in many regards stays paradoxical. Therefore, its execution must be directed more towards a visible demonstration of this paradox than towards its scientific resolution. An epiphany remains the objective of the project. Scientific proofs fail in the face of this objective, but their failure itself cries out for epiphany.

This is because this piece, which is about a 'making visible' of 'truth' and whose silent protagonist is the sun, ends with a scream. What becomes visible is not something that could have been logically deduced, but rather something that clings tenaciously to the godly-holy, to the holy-sexual.

---

32   Bataille, 'La Limite de l'utile', p. 270.
33   Pasolini, *Teorema* (Milan: Garzanti, 1968).
34   Pasolini, *La Divina Mimesis* (Turin: Einaudi, 1975).
35   *Grande Dizionario della lingua italiana* (Novara: De Agostini, 1990).

Despite the almost scholastic structure, nothing is more distant to it than a logical deduction of a theorem. Pasolini speaks of his text, *Teorema*, as a data collection ('enunciare: formulare un principio di cui ci si accinge a dimostrare la verità con una serie di argomentazioni matematiche') and in the same breath, he claims that this 'teorema' is painted against a gold background and gives this 'teorema' a motto out of the Old Testament that engraves the Christian Aura with an inscription of the preceding prophecy. Scientific discourse is amalgamated with religious discourse in the talk of a 'manualetto laico', as this book should be a manual for a lay person. From the first glance on, scientific and religious discourse collide.

Teorema is the story of a family from an exclusive residential area of Milan. Ideologically, they belong to the petty bourgeoisie; economically they are definitely part of the grand bourgeoisie.[36] The family consists of a father, mother, son, and daughter, as well as a service maid named Emilia, coming from the identically named region to which she will return as a spring goddess of antiquity. As an angel of annunciation, the mailman aptly called Angelino proclaims the arrival of a stranger — the advent of the divine in a bourgeois, and thus unreal, world. Within this God, antique and Christian elements mix: Plato's *Symposium* and Old and New Testaments are the most evident sources.[37] The stranger's scandalous beauty shines in blinding fashion in the Milanese reception room's Sunday tea party, where natural and artificial light mix. The stranger will continue to appear in such heavenly, supernatural light, which shines from his blue eyes, and in Caravaggio's style, rests upon the head and genitals. Like Eros who is praised by Agathon in *Symposium*, the stranger is beautiful, supple, graceful, delicate, blissful.[38] Every family member, including the service maid, burn with love for him. What follows is the description of five sex acts. It is hard to overlook these sex scenes as a counterfactual Annunciation. The holy spirit comes as sacred sex. First the service maid, then the son, mother, daughter, and father all encounter the guest's genitals ('sesso sacro'). The grace revealed is sexual. His 'immaculate lap' grants sexual fulfillment without a word becoming flesh. The revelation, of a peculiarly priapic nature, becomes visible in the young man's erotic, carnal beauty, his flesh. The camera remains directed towards the lap of Terence

---

36 See summary review of *Teorema* in Naomi Greene, *Pier Paolo Pasolini: Cinema as Heresy* (Princeton: Princeton University Press, 1990), pp. 130–248.
37 Explicit reference to Plato's *Symposium* in Pasolini, *Teorema*, p. 102.
38 On lighting in film E. Maakeroun, 'Pasolini face au sacré ou l'exorciste possédé', *Études cinématographiques*, 53, Special Issue: *Pasolini: le mythe et le sacré* (1987), 109–11.

Stamp, who sits or lies with his legs spread. (*Teorema* showed the first male nude). His underwear is of a flawless, supernatural white; the 'immaculate briefs' radiate like a holy relic.

The story, a 'parable', is not written realistically in chronological order. Probability, as well as the categories of space and time are suspended; this is evident well before the elevated service maid hovers over the roof of the farm. The time sequence is suspended: even though it is either spring or fall, we have a midsummer sun. It is impossible that Emilia and the poor old woman accompanying her can walk from the Bassa to the suburbs of Milan in a timespan as brief as 'shortly before sunrise'. Both the rational and the realistic-psychological register are crossed out by an omnipresent religious register of miracles. The characters of the story do not just play roles, but cite all kinds of aesthetic genres: the simple mailman with the heavenly name Angelino is a 'buffone'; the mother with the light filled name, Lucia, is an 'eroina popolare', who speaks like a character in a tragedy; the son Pietro, upon whom the father, Paolo, cannot build a church, harkens to 'Charlot' of the silent film era; Odetta, the bourgeois daughter displays befittingly the humor of societal comedy (these characteristics put together in part two under 'additional specifications'). All in all, an allegorical travesty of dramatic citations is at work in this bourgeois buffa tragedy.

'Poetic', 'prosaic', 'artificial', and 'natural' discourses collide with one another. Originally a 'pièce en vers', then transformed into 'artistic prose' or 'poetic prose', *Teorema* displays a large amount of 'discours indirect libre', for Pasolini the classic bourgeois style.[39] The genre of the press or television interview appears next to these two styles. Side by side with this low, tabloid genre, not only 'cheap, but vulgar', are sublime, free rhythms of monologue. Realistic stories such as Tolstoy's *The Death of Ivan Illich* alternate with the hymnal style of Rimbaud and citations from the Bible. The model for these harsh style breaks is Rimbaud, in whose work the grotesque, strange, and obscene collides with the sublime and sacred. The allegory provided in the piece for this stylistic method is the mixture of the sound of bells with the sound of sirens, and the mysterious mixture of electric light and sunlight. The overwhelming beauty of the foreign guest radiates in cinematic lightning.

The guest is announced intertextually, namely through a citation from the Old Testament, as a seductive and overwhelming God (Jerimiah 20:7 and 20:10). As Mary is immersed in the reading of the Bible at the moment

---

39   Pier Paolo Pasolini, 'Intervento sul discorso libero indiretto', in *Empirismo erotico*, pp. 81–103.

of her Annunciation, he is immersed in the reading of Rimbaud. With the character of the young Gerasim in *The Death of Ivan Illich* yet another annunciation is alluded to. All three annunciations, emptied out of all sublimity, appear now in a manifestly sexual, homosexual light. Pasolini's early novel *Amado mio* showed already this cunny sense for a latent sexual, homosexual twisting. The phrase from Goethe's Erlking: 'mich reizt Deine schöne Gestalt, und bist Du nicht willig, so brauch ich Gewalt' is placed into a clearly homosexual context.

His Eros comes with an obscene twist, that is, although always averted, always evoked: oral sex in the case of the daughter Odetta, for the guest's immaculate lap appears on the height of her mouth. In the case of Pietro, the son, there is a vacillation between comradery and homosexual codes. The mother Lucia plays in the masochistic register; she is uplifted by the 'voyeuristic-debasing, violating' guest's glance, which she — in infernal flirtatiousness — meets with a shameless invitation. The maid, who pulls her dress up, offers a vulgar image despite all helplessness. And in the end, the godly beautiful guest, sprawled as lasciviously as innocently, legs wide spread, awaits the head of the family.[40]

The guest gives and loves, without regard to person, understandingly with a pinch of irony — he is after all but a medium. One could almost say he acts in the holy trinity of the mother, father, and son. In a hugely grotesque contrafaction, under the banner of Rimbaud and with his methods, violence is inflicted upon a discourse: The religious expression of the revelation of God and the expression of an almost mystic-loving encounter with God is raped by turning towards that which is low instead of that which is high, a reversal of a sublimation. That which is revealed as holy through this act does not appear as a cosmic new order, but as a chaotic power which overturns and destroys not only the bourgeois and religious order, but also the order of aesthetic styles. The act of love bears all characteristics of a *conversio* which occurs to the characters concerned. But they do not find themselves in God, but lose themselves for good. All are beside themselves, enraptured, overwhelmed. They are possessed, hysterically or mystically and do not own themselves anymore. Their thoughts turn to prayers. They move like automata that do not know, what they are doing. Exit the autonomous, self-confident, self-determined, self-controlled subject. Normality, rationality, and morals are destroyed. After the sex acts, the guest is called off to yet another annunciation — a promiscuous affaire.

---

40   Pasolini, *Teorema*, p. 86.

According to the prophecy from the Old Testament which prefaces *Teorema*, God has come to guide the family, in the footsteps of the people of Israel, out of captivity into the desert. This is a detour through an a-topos, an inexistent space at an inexistent time. This space shows the father Paolo the truth in the light of a revelation:

> Come già per il popolo d'Israele o l'apostolo Paolo, il deserto mi si presenta come ciò che, della realtà, è solo indispensabile. O, meglio ancora, come la realtà di tutto spogliata fuori che della sua essenza così come se la rappresenta chi vive, e, qualche volta, la pensa, pur senza essere un filosofo.[41]

The final monologue has hymnal aspects, but the genre of the hymn is distorted as is the perception of the desert, where the hymn is brought into words and where it ends in the introspection of a scream. Only this one figure arrives in the desert which is 'opposed to the nature of man'. His path crosses over the body which has undergone the reverse sublimation, a body no longer paranormally alienated from itself. But the new Paolo experiences a paradoxical revelation of another nature.

This revelation is the modern antithesis to the ancient return of the maid, Emilia, who literally represents the return to the pre-Christian wellspring of a primeval revelation. Paolo's revelation reveals the aporia; the misguided *imitatio Christi* of his family falls victim to the mirage-like hallucinations of that aporia in different forms and patterns.

The conversion, the illumination is staged in the artificial light of a staged demonstration, for which the cinema is an allegory, but the text is the pattern of demonstration's paradoxical decipherment. In a fundamental re-reading of one own's life in the light of a revealed, illuminating truth, Pasolini's protagonists cast the old human aside. With conversion, Pasolini remains within the religious paradigm only to turn it upside down. It is surely no accident that Pasolini's next film should be about saint Paul, his name saint. Paul, struck to the ground by an illuminating lightning, has become the paradigm of conversion. In *Teorema*, conversion leads to destruction; nothing is left of their reality. The mother, Lucia, recognizes the family's life as distorted by naturalness, and, like all naturalness, a fake construction:

---

41 Ibid., p. 197.

> Come ogni epoca storica, anche la nostra | ha ricostruito la natura, e quindi la naturalezza. | Da grande borghese dell'Alta Italia | mio marito Paolo ha vissuto la sua natura con naturalezza.[42]

That which is natural is the opposite of an 'interesse oggettivo, puro e culturale per l'esistenza', an 'interesse puro e pazzo'; it is the opposite of a life of devotion, *religio*. Contrary to the classic topos of a conversion, in *Teorema,* no new self in God is found after the casting away of the old man, but only total alienation. Out of a quite bearable, even normal situation, in which, although they misjudged themselves, they were able to live in this misjudgment with the image they made of themselves, they arrive in a more real, but unbearable situation. A greater insight into the unreality, the naked naturality of their previous being, amounts from the *conversio*. But this insight is a threat, to which no liberation follows. For the mother and her two children, like later in the film *Medea*, the attempt to find God leads to a conversion *à rebours*.

Nevertheless, 'truth' and another reality shine through for a moment in the destruction. The question of this reality, the question of this new truth radicalizes itself for all in the latency of incest. As the most severe madness, the greatest sacrilege, the absolute transgression, incest is the epitome of reality's impossibility. In the impossibility, incest is, as all protagonists implicitly agree, their most appropriate reality. Life can only be recognized in this immorality and irrationality; life can only be recognized in this absolute transgression: 'fuor dell'ordine e dal domani'. For this reason, incest is the symbol for the real life. The most unbearable exception that is incest symbolizes reality, a reality which is represented as excluded.

So, what is the result of the appearance of the godly in the demonstration of Pasolini, the author? The result is in bourgeois terms the family's complete ruination. They leave the house and follow the guest as figures of a reversed *imitatio*. The daughter lands in a psychiatric hospital, frozen in a catatonic lifelessness. The son becomes a crazy, completely infantile painter. The mother picks up lovers that resemble the stranger, only to then fall back into her abstract, incorporeal religiousness. The father gives his factory to somebody, strips himself naked at the train station, and leaves this world through the desert. The service maid returns to the farm where she lived in the Bassa. In the tradition of the village, she becomes a saint, heals pustules, is elevated, now only eats stinging nettle, and all the way to the burned tips of her hair — in a fully grown, permanent wave — she

---

42 Ibid., p. 101.

becomes slightly green. In the end she allows herself to be buried alive in a foundation ditch in one of the industrial suburbs of Milan. A small creek that heals the wounds of the injured workers arises from her tears. The conversion looks more like a metamorphosis. Mother, daughter, and son lose or betray their God. Father and maid obtain what is to be obtained by not choosing the bourgeoisie-conform versions of this death in life (psychiatric hospital, avant-garde, religiousness after a detour through excess), but by choosing to lose their life in spectacular fashion.

It never comes to incest, the unthinkable resolution. The protagonists primarily differentiate themselves from each other through the failure of their attempted substitutes, through the failure of metaphors. Emilia, the service maid is the only one to completely renounce any pictorial representation. The service maid withdraws herself to a time preceding the modern age, a time standing still, saturated with art and culture, and appearing as a time of folklore and legends, in a region which magnificently shines in the red of Pontormo. There, she becomes a godless saint, who, without godly presence and in complete hopelessness, is capable of doing that which the saints once could do. Her death is no different from a metamorphosis in Ovid, she nourishes the subproletariat stratum of popular fantasies.

Unlike the simple child who unintentionally revives the dead treasure of folklore, Odessa — who stands for the memory that keeps, and incorrectly cites Proust's *In Search of Lost Time* in her name — searches for representations and fishes out her photo album, which contains several photos of the guest.[43] She cannot but fall for the light of these photos; she cannot but fall for the deceptive shadow of the image and the portrayed reference. Here too, the 'referential fallacy' is, as incidentally always, a 'fallacy' which holds onto the phallus. When her hand touches the through-image-recorded genitals, the hand cramps up to a fist, and Odetta keeps this closed fist in the madness when she no longer moves. Things do not go any better for her brother, Pietro; he stands for the misunderstanding of the artistic avant-gardists.[44] He tries to create an image of the guest by starting to paint that which has evaded him. He fails grotesquely. The mother ultimately focuses on similarity. She looks for boys that resemble the godly guest, in order to repeat the experience with the guest. This attempt

---

43 On Pasolini's name Noel Purdone, 'Pasolini: The Film of Alienation', in *Pier Paolo Pasolini*, ed. by Paul Willemen (London: British Film Institute, 1977), p. 44.

44 Pier Paolo Pasolini, 'La Fine dell'avanguardia. Appunti per una frase di Goldmann, per due versi di un testo d'avanguardia, e per un'intervista di Barthes' (1966), in *Empirismo eretico*, pp. 122–43.

is condemned to fail, as one can easily deduce from the briefs of the first young man. For his 'mutadine', contrary to the guest's immaculate white, 'forse non del tutto immacolate, coi tristi segni della vita'.[45]

The grotesque runs rampant; it becomes absorbed in and implemented into the rampant-running symptoms of a burlesque mishappening, symptoms of renewed bourgeois decay in contrast to Emilia's rural homecoming in Emilia.

The mother will betray the wanted original to a false likeness, a Christ with blue eyes. Emilia's speechless, metamorphic homecoming corresponds with nothing but the tragic delusion of symbolic values that have not been understood, a conversion which remains hysterical from the side of the bourgeoisie — with exemption of Paolo. He is not, as is his wife, led by the eyes filled with false blue light. He is not led to leave his body behind. Lucia had taken off her body from herself and left it like a cover. In Paolo's case such a separation does not occur; he resists the temptation of repeating the love act with a (false) image of the guest, a boy with blue eyes; rather, the gaze of the boy makes him take off the clothes of the old man and to pass, naked, into the desert.

> Ormai estraneo a tutto, Paolo continua, imperterrito e assorto lontano, a spogliarsi di quello che ha addosso, quasi egli non sapesse più distinguere la realtà dai suoi simboli; oppure, forse, come se egli si fosse deciso a valicare una volta per sempre i vani e illusori confini che dividono la realtà dalla sua rappresentazione. Cosa, insomma, che fanno gli uomini che qualche fede distacca per sempre dalla loro vita.[46]

That's 'how it looks' for Paolo and those who are willing to follow him, and he sees it himself. In the final monolog which, in refined, free rhythms, presents the outlasting own uncertainty as a continuance of an unarticulated scream, Pasolini leaves no doubt towards facts with much doubt: 'The one who searches on Milan's streets' and 'now' recognizes this search as a search 'on the paths of the desert', realizes something different to the revelation that his family misses in mistaken *imitatio*: 'IO SONO PIENO DI UNA DOMANDA A CUI NON SO RISPONDERE. | Triste risultato [...] | questo significato nuovo, mi resta indecifrabile'.[47] The indecipherable new steers the gaze back to a mediality which is no longer transparent; towards a mediality that even reality itself does not

---

45 Pasolini, *Teorema*, p. 164.
46 Ibid., p. 191.
47 Ibid., p. 198.

have. The 'story' itself in whose 'days' he once lived was 'so much less beautiful and pure as its depiction' the monologue continues. So, the new, additional meaning is no new meaning, but a further one; the meaning cannot be searched for in meaning, but is perceptible in the oscillation of the difference, that the desert is as a 'non-place' of all meaning. The sun's light changes to blackness, blackness' symbol is a scream that alone shall be able to outlast its surroundings. In spite of — and only in spite of — that, 'which the scream could signify' the scream — only the scream — is 'predestined to outlast every possible end' (END): '[...] che qualunque cosa | questo mio urlo voglia significare, | esso è destinato a durare oltre ogni possibile fine. | FINE.'[48]

All this is there to be read and to be seen. The film's FINE repeats the text's 'fine'. Pasolini the author succeeds in staging this end, in the medium of the consulted discourse from Caravaggio to Rimbaud and Bataille, in a new fashion. *Qu'est-ce qu'un auteur?*[49] The author is to be understood starting at the end like life is to be understood; as the end of life requires writing (to depict it), the author's end requires the inscription of the sacrifice. The author's end and fulfillment is the sacrificial death, that alone is capable (citing the sacrifice according to Bataille, who was himself in the end not able to follow his citation) to in the end chant a revelation with the aura of authentic experience, a revelation that has been cinematically staged, commentated in books and whose alienation has been made subject: A scream which should persevere.

Tail Piece: Qu'est-ce qu'un auteur?

On November 2, 1975, on the beach of Ostia, in the night from All Saints' Day onto All Souls', Pasolini was beaten to death by a male prostitute. At dawn, his corpse was found, streaming with blood and horrifically disfigured. Pasolini had found his butcher. The photograph of the corpse appeared on the same day on the Italian front pages and made headlines around the world — a spectacular death, effectively exposed. A death, that he himself had long prophesied and which fulfilled his theory into every detail. The most compelling example of this prophecy of his own death is the advance warning of the death of the author, that Pasolini dictated

---

48 Ibid., p. 200.
49 Michel Foucault, 'What is an author?', in *The Foucault Reader*, ed. by Paul Rabinow (New York: Pantheon Books, 1984), pp. 101–20.

to his publisher, Einaudi, in the posthumously published *Divina Mimesis*' introduction: 'egli è morto, ucciso a colpi di bastone, a Palermo l'anno scorso'. A slightly dis-placed dead notice: the place of death indeed was not Palermo, but Ostia. Pasolini took the burden of the role of the 'poète maudit' upon himself and let himself be murdered by society. But Pasolini not only felt he was damned to be the sacrifice, but that he was chosen to experience the highest fear and most terrible horror and pain. In his being a sacrifice, he fulfilled his mission. As Bataille put it: 'En un sens le cadavre est la plus parfaite affirmation de l'esprit.'[50]

Inscribed in a hagiography, in a tradition of exempla, Pasolini followed the law of the genre and let his hagiography peak with his death. Christ and Paul, Dante and Proust, Nietzsche and Klossowski, Baudelaire and Rimbaud appear in this canonical tradition, but Bataille was to Pasolini what John was to Christ. Like the prototype, whose fulfillment Pasolini approximated, Caravaggio, the inventor of cinematic lighting in painting, Pasolini met with a violent end at the hands of a male prostitute.

It is remarkable that this death immediately opened up an interpretation vacuum and that, to this day, has remained a touchstone of analysis. Two reactions are easily distinguished: For some, in this death a depraved life finds its exemplary end; an individual comes, who avenges the other seduced and corrupted individuals.[51] Others do not emphasize the personal factor of the tragedy of passion, but the public nature of the 'execution'. The murder of Pasolini is interpreted as a political murder in which Pasolini's 'vice' is not punished; instead a hypocritically veiled truth of the society comes to light through the dismembered corpse: 'une société s'était vengée. La haine déchaînée contre Pasolini trouve, en effet, son expression "sociale" dans la façon même dont fut accomplie le crime: une exécution politique effectuée de manière spectaculairement sanguinaire pour que chacun voit et comprenne', writes Macciocchi.[52] 'Affirmant le fond de transition perverse du lien social en tant que, *c'est-à-dire intrinsèquement homosexuelle*, il est devenu, de ce fait même, le sujet italien le plus menacé, parce que le moins homosexuel. Ce paradoxe est la logique même. Pasolini a été tué pour que le nœud social homosexuel refoulé reste inconscient, qu'il soit scellé dans

---

50 Bataille, 'Théorie de la religion', p. 305.
51 Titles such as 'Tragedia di un corruttore' or 'Un Eroe sporco' suggest this; see Pio Baldelli, 'Il "Caso" Pasolini e l'uso della morte', in *Perché Pasolini: Ideologia e stile di un intellettuale militante*, ed. by Gualtiero De Santi, Maria Lenti, Roberto Rossini, (Florence: Guaraldi, 1978), pp. 153–68 (p. 164).
52 Maria Antonietta Macciocchi, 'Esquisse pour une biographie de Pasolini', in *Séminaire*, pp. 13–60 (p. 56).

le sang de quelqu'un qui pouvait le *dire*. Il s'agit d'une demande sauvage d'aphasie', was Macciocchi's verdict. Next to the political interpretations of the murder, an almost aesthetic interpretation following the scheme of Pasolini's life and work appears. Pasolini's biographer E. Siciliano asks: 'Pasolini chiese a se stesso di morire? Il suo assassinio fu un suicidio per delega?'[53] Pasolini's carefully staged death, following the model of Christ, turned masochistic, is supposedly his most perfect work. In and through his death, Pasolini survives:

> Dans aucun de mes livres dans aucun de mes films je ne m'étais montré à la hauteur de mes ambitions. Mais maintenant je m'en allais tranquille, ayant organisé dans chaque détail ma cérémonie funèbre et signé ma seule œuvre assuré de survivre à l'oublie.[54]

---

53 Enzo Siciliano, *La Vita di Pasolini* (Milan: Rizzoli, 1978), p. 389.
54 Thus, the biographical novel by Dominique de Fernandez, *Dans la main de l'ange* (Paris: Grasset, 1982), p. 455. Giuseppe Zigaina, a painter who was a friend of Pasolini's, contributed a most affectionate testimony in *Pasolini e la morte: Mito alchimia e semantica del 'nulla lucente'* (Venice: Marsilio, 1987).

Alessia Ricciardi

PASOLINI FOR THE FUTURE[1]

Although 'the future' may represent an ever hazier notion in the cultural and political imagination, public figures in Italy lately have invoked the concept with increasing frequency. Since their rift with the governing coalition led by Silvio Berlusconi, the members of Gianfranco Fini's right-wing party have taken to calling themselves 'the Futurists' [*i futuristi*] and have established the 'MakeFuture Foundation' [*Fondazione Farefuturo*] to propagate their ideological views. Berlusconi himself recently has declared the intention of renaming his own party from 'Let's Go, Italy' [*Forza Italia*] to the more progressive-sounding 'Forward, Italy' [*Avanti Italia*].

At the same time, it appears that loss of hope regarding the future has become integral to our sense of our own late modernity in the field of critical thought. Among only the most current examples, the French anthropologist Marc Augé has announced that he is about to publish a book with the telling title *Where Did the Future Go?* [*Où est passé l'avenir?*].[2] The Italian strain of the attitude may be traced back at least to Giacomo Leopardi, who in the nineteenth century identified the narrowing down of

---

1 Previously published as 'Pasolini for the Future', *California Italian Studies*, 2, 1 (2011).
 This paper was presented at the symposium 'Pier Paolo Pasolini and the Multiplicity of the Italian Language' at the University of Chicago in October 2010. I would like to thank Armando Maggi in particular for inviting me to contribute to the proceedings. I also would like to express my appreciation to the students who attended my graduate seminar at the University of California Berkeley in the spring of 2010, especially Rossella Carbotti, Viviana Cois, Tinley Ireland, Jennifer Mackenzie, Marina Romani, and Iulia Sprinceana. Their lively discussion inspired much of the thinking in this essay.
2 According to an interview in *L'Unità* of October 7, 2010, with Flore Murard-Yovanovitch, Augé will analyze the emergence of what he calls 'non-time' analogous to the idea of non-places that he introduced in his book *Non-lieux*, a non-time that ultimately would coincide with an eternal present; see Marc Augé, *Non-lieux, introduction à une anthropologie de la surmodernité* (Paris: Seuil, 1992).

life to the present tense as one of Italy's most problematic tendencies, a trait that led him to characterize the nation as 'without the prospect of a better sort of future, without occupation, without purpose'.[3] Reflecting from the vantage point of the early twentieth century on Italy's responsiveness to the weight of its long history from classical Rome to the present, Antonio Gramsci contended that among his compatriots the future always is passively expected 'as it seems to be determined by the past'.[4]

The literary, critical, and cinematic *auteur* Pier Paolo Pasolini may not look at first glance exactly like a figure who was galvanized by the future. An outspoken critic of the changes that were taking place in Italy during his lifetime, he embodied a melancholic devotion to the past that was tempered only partially by a dialectical, modern attitude. In a poem that Orson Welles famously recites in Pasolini's short film *La Ricotta*, the Italian director defined himself as 'a force of the past' [*una forza del passato*] who paradoxically also views himself as 'more modern than all the moderns' [*più moderno di tutti i moderni*]. However, some readers — and on this score I think particularly of Andrea Zanzotto — have interpreted his fascination with the past and his insistence on a simpler agrarian or subproletarian vitality as rhetorical or encoded ruses for speaking of a new beginning.

On the other hand, Georges Didi-Huberman lately has criticized Pasolini's supposedly apocalyptic tone in what is, in my opinion, a beautiful if fundamentally 'incorrect' book, *The Survival of the Fireflies*.[5] Didi-Huberman's title is a nod to Pasolini's controversial opinion piece in *Il corriere della sera* of February 1, 1975, 'The Void of Power in Italy' [*Il vuoto di potere in Italia*]. Pasolini's treatise subsequently was re-titled 'The Article of the Fireflies' [L'articolo delle lucciole] for the volume *Corsair Writings*, as if to identify its future poetic legacy with a single synecdoche. In the essay, he dates the beginning of the end for Italy in anthropological and cultural terms to the contemporary disappearance of fireflies from the Italian countryside due to the advancing ecological crisis produced by industrialization: 'In the first years of the '60s, because of pollution in the

---

3   See Giacomo Leopardi, *Discorso sopra lo stato presente dei costumi degli italiani* (Milan: Feltrinelli, 1991), p. 52: 'Or la vita degl'italiani è appunto tale, senza prospettiva di migliore sorte futura, senza occupazione, senza scopo e ristretta al solo presente'.
4   Pier Paolo Pasolini, *Heretical Empiricism*, trans. by Ben Lawton and Louise K. Barnett (Washington: New Academia, 2005), p. 201.
5   Georges Didi-Huberman, *La survivance des lucioles* (Paris: Les Éditions des Minuit, 2009).

air and, in the country, particularly of the water, the fireflies have started to disappear. The phenomenon has been sudden and traumatic. After a few years, there were no more fireflies. They are now a rather crushing souvenir of the past'.[6]

Yet as a tiny, frail, and fleetingly luminous natural phenomenon, the firefly, as I argue in my own book *The Ends of Mourning*, also may be viewed as an emblem of Pasolini's 'spectropoetics', an art that he practiced in poems such as 'The Ashes of Gramsci' and in his films, where he sought to reinvent his chosen media in ways that allowed him to envision past and future at once.[7] Indeed, we might argue in a broad sense that Pasolini's very determination to pursue a career as a filmmaker after having achieved early success as a poet and novelist bespeaks his commitment to an experimental, multimedia creative ethos that resists nostalgia for the artistic ideals of the past and turns decisively to the horizon of the future for inspiration. Accordingly, I wish to reflect in what follows on the particularities of Pasolini's ethical engagements with the future. Although Pasolini's later works often strike an apocalyptic note, I am not convinced that our focus on this tendency should be taken to its bitter, logical conclusion à la Didi-Huberman.[8]

On this point, I follow in the wake of Carla Benedetti, who interprets Pasolini's most paradoxical propositions as signs of his refusal to adopt the cynical, postmodern stance of ironic detachment.[9] What is at stake in this reading is nothing less than the recognition of what it means today in the heyday of the society of spectacle, when we confront the perpetual present of mass media on a '24/7' basis, to engage critically with the future. Of course, it is important as well to recognize that, while Pasolini may have

---

[6] See Pier Paolo Pasolini, *Saggi sulla politica e sulla società*, ed. by Walter Siti and Silvia de Laude (Milan: Mondadori, 1999), p. 405: 'Nei primi anni sessanta, a causa dell'inquinamento dell'aria, e, soprattutto in campagna, a causa dell'inquinamento dell'acqua [...] sono cominciate a scomparire le lucciole. Il fenomeno è stato fulmineo e folgorante. Dopo pochi anni le lucciole non c'erano più. Sono ora un ricordo abbastanza straziante el passato [...]'. [*Translation mine*]

[7] See Alessia Ricciardi, 'Heretical Specters', in *The Ends of Mourning: Psychoanalysis, Literature, and Film* (Stanford, CA: Stanford University Press, 2003), pp. 123–65.

[8] There are other readers as well who have raised questions about Didi Huberman's project. See in particular Roberto Fai, 'Didi Huberman, da Pasolini ad Agamben', *e-mmaginale*, 18 October 2010, and Alain Naze, 'Ni liquidation, ni restauration de l'aura: Benjamin, Pasolini et le cinéma', *Revue Appareil* (online), 14 January 2009 <http://journals.openedition.org/appareil/711>.

[9] See Carla Benedetti, *Pasolini contro Calvino: Per una letteratura impura* (Turin: Bollati Boringhieri, 1998).

been preoccupied with the future, he was not in the slightest way hopeful about it. He in fact disparaged hope itself as a form of hypocrisy that under certain circumstances encourages our emotional blackmail. According to his view, as he expressed it in his weekly column '*Il Caos*' in 1968, every régime of power including Nazism mantles itself in the alibis of faith and hope, which, however, turn 'monstrous' when divested of charity.[10] Pasolini thus ought to be perceived as wishing not for a hopeful future but rather for a charitable one, in keeping with what Filippo La Porta describes felicitously as an overriding concern for 'the fragility of the present'.[11] Although unconvinced of his regard for the future, La Porta calls attention to Pasolini's fierce dedication to uncovering the meaning of an ongoing or 'eternal' present. For La Porta, it is this unwavering devotion that makes Pasolini our contemporary.[12]

First of all, we ought to observe how, from the early days of his artistic and intellectual career onward, Pasolini drew visionary inspiration from the future. We well might note, for example, that his magisterial poem 'The Tears of the Excavator', which was published in 1956, culminates with the ringing assertion that 'the light of the future does not cease for even an instant to wound us' [*la luce del futuro non cessa un solo instante di ferirci*]. This is a light that the poet claims 'burns in all of our daily deeds' [*che brucia in ogni nostro atto quotidiano*], including the 'Gobettian impulse' of solidarity with the workers around us who 'silently raise [...] their red rag of hope' [*che muti innalzano...il loro rosso straccio di speranza*].[13] The elegiac outlook of *The Ashes of Gramsci*, the volume in which 'Tears of the Excavator' initially was collected, is counter-balanced by the forward-thinking vitality of the city, which runs like an undercurrent throughout Pasolini's poetry, most especially in his depictions of the subproletarian boroughs that he viewed as nerve centers of erotic and political energy.

Moving from the 1950s to the 1960s, Pasolini increasingly pinned his hope of a brighter future on the liberation movements in Africa, a continent that he invokes in the poem 'Fragment on Death' [*Frammento alla morte*]

---

10 See Pasolini, *Saggi sulla politica e sulla società*, p. 1122.
11 La Porta thinks that his investment in the fragility of the present in the end rendered Pasolini insensitive to the 'warmth' of the future. If we take our cue from Pasolini himself, however, we might conclude that the future implies the possibility of a rebirth, which also ultimately means the future's annihilation, as he pointed out in *Appunto* 84 of *Petrolio*; see Filippo La Porta, *Pasolini: Uno gnostico inamorato della realtà* (Florence: Le Lettere, 2002), pp. 52, 68.
12 Ibid., p. 93.
13 Pier Paolo Pasolini, *Poems*, trans. by Norman MacAfee with Luciano Martinengo (New York: Farrar, Straus and Giroux, 1996), pp. 52–53.

in the collection *The Religion of My Time*, with the apostrophic outcry 'Africa! my only alternative' [*Africa! Unica mia alternativa*].[14] The outlines of an apocalyptic, redemptive metaphysics in Pasolini's thought indeed may be derived from his historical optimism toward non-western cultures, which moved him to shoot a number of films outside of Europe including *The Gospel According to Matthew*, *Notes for a Film on India*, *The Walls of Sana'a*, *Arabian Nights*, and *Notes for an African Orestes*.[15] In the last of these productions, he reinterprets the transformation of the Furies into the Eumenides in *The Oresteia* as an allegory for the fulfillment of the future through the synthesis of 'Africa antica' with a 'new Africa'. This new Africa, according to Pasolini, is 'modern and independent, free', and its spirit is best exemplified by an intellectual and political figure such as that of Léopold Senghor.[16] *Notes for an African Orestes* ends with a wedding scene that seems designed to evoke Pasolini's earlier documentary *Love Meetings* [*Comizi d'amore*]. As the scene unfolds, a narrator intones in voiceover: 'A new nation is born, and its problems are infinite, but problems cannot be solved, should be lived. And life is slow. Proceeding toward the future is a continuous task. The work of a people knows neither rhetoric nor hesitation. Its future is in its anxious anticipation for a future; and its anxiety is a great patience'.[17]

Pasolini makes something of a concession to the critical trends of the day in the collection *Heretical Empiricism*. In these writings, he affirms his admittedly melancholic preference for the future anterior as a way

---

14   Pier Paolo Pasolini, *Bestemmia: Tutte le poesie* (Milan: Garzanti, 1993), p. 580.
15   For a nuanced but not always convincing interpretation of Pasolini's cinematic orientalism, see Luca Caminati, *Orientalismo eretico: Pier Paolo Pasolini e il cinema del terzo mondo* (Milan: Mondadori, 2007). Gian Maria Annovi links Pasolini's interest in North African cultures to his alleged 'immaginario mediterraneo pasoliniano'; see Gian Maria Annovi, 'ISTAMBUL KM. 4.253: attraverso il Mediterraneo di Pier Paolo Pasolini', *CIS* (online), 1, 1 (2010) <http://escholarship.org/uc/item/92v0p4wz> [accessed 13 January 2022]. Giovanna Trento takes up the topic of Pasolini's relation to Africa within a specifically postcolonial critical framework in *Pasolini e l'Africa, l'Africa di Pasolini: Panmeridionalismo e rappresentazioni dell'Africa postcoloniale* (Milan: Mimesis, 2010).
16   Pier Paolo Pasolini, *Per il cinema*, ed. by Walter Siti and Franco Zabagli, 2 vols (Milan: Mondadori, 2001), I, p. 1194.
17   See Ibid., p. 1196 : 'Una nuova nazione e nata, i suoi problemi sono infiniti, ma i problemi non si risolvono, si vivono. E la vita e lenta. Il procedere verso il futuro non ha soluzioni di continuità. Il lavoro di un popolo non conosce ne retorica ne indugio. Il suo futuro e nella sua ansia di futuro; e la sua ansia e una grande pazienza'.

of criticizing the linear temporal logic of conventional historicism, thus taking up a problem made famous by Lacan in psychoanalysis and Lyotard in philosophy. It is particularly in the celebrated essay 'Observations on the Sequence Shot' that Pasolini elaborates on his own terms the idea of the future perfect as a projected recognition of the itinerary of becoming. Here he asserts that 'death effects an instantaneous montage of our lives [...]. It chooses the truly meaningful moments and puts them in a sequence, transforming an infinite, unstable, and uncertain present into a clear, stable, certain, and therefore easily describable past. It is only thanks to death that our life serves to express ourselves'.[18] According to Didi-Huberman, however, Pasolini's impatience with precisely the 'infinite, unstable, and uncertain' play of the present and bias in favor of the perfect hindsight of retrospection comprise one of his worst lapses in reasoning, a blunder that Giorgio Agamben allegedly recapitulates: 'There is with these two thinkers a very great impatience with the present, but it is forever bound up with an infinite patience for the past. In this, they are necessary for us, since they regard the contemporary world with a violence always buttressed by a profound searching into the thickness of time'.[19] The advantage of this attitude in other words is its ability to offer a three-dimensional, layered view of our modern-day culture, a 'thick description' in anthropological and philosophical terms.

This perspective definitely helps to produce what Didi-Huberman calls a 'not incorrect diagnosis' when it comes to the society of the spectacle and its all too literal incarnation in Italy,[20] Yet he nevertheless accuses the two thinkers of depriving us of a cultural afterlife, a *Nachleben*, in order to attain for their reasoning the irrefutable status of a final, apocalyptic truth.[21] However, I wish to take issue with this idea that Pasolini had no patience for the present. The evidence of his writings and films indicates, if anything, that he was mesmerized by his time and, under the influence of the philosopher and anthropologist Ernesto De Martino, undertook in his last years to become a sort of anthropologist of the present. Simply put, to accept such a calling often meant to come to grips with the realities of his

---

18 Pasolini, *Heretical Empiricism*, pp. 236–37.
19 Didi-Huberman, *La survivance des lucioles*, p. 92: 'Il y a chez ces deux penseurs une très grande impatience quand au présent; mais elle est toujours liée à une infinie patience quant au passé. En cela, ils nous sont nécessaires puisqu'ils regardent leur monde contemporain avec une violence toujours étayée par d'immenses recherches dans l'épaisseur du temps'.
20 Ibid., p. 86.
21 Ibid., p. 87.

day as the symptoms of a cultural emergency, to embrace ferociously the devastated circumstances in which he lived, to be heard.

After repudiating the cinematic aesthetics that he developed in *The Decameron*, *The Canterbury Tales*, and *Arabian Nights* between 1969 and 1972, a change of heart that he recounts shortly before his death in 1975 in the essay 'Disavowal of the Trilogy of Life' [*Abiura dalla Trilogia della vita*], Pasolini seems to have relinquished any claim to dialectical method in order to face more directly the contemporary disaster that, at various times, he referred to as the 'anthropological mutation' or 'cultural genocide'. The upheaval that he chronicled in his articles mostly for *Il Corriere della sera* and *Il mondo*, which subsequently were collected in *Corsair Writings* and *Lutheran Letters*[22] apparently revealed itself to him as an apocalypse without palingenesis or 'eschaton'. The line of investigation leading to this awareness can be traced back in a genetic sense to De Martino, who published an article entitled 'Apocalypses Cultural and Apocalypses Psychopathological' in a 1964 issue of the literary magazine *Nuovi argomenti*, which was founded by Alberto Moravia and featured Pasolini among its editors.[23]

To understand Pasolini's increasingly dire sense of historical calamity in his later years, in other words, we should look more closely at De Martino's work of the 1960s. In an essay from *Corsair Writings* titled '*Gli uomini colti e la cultura popolare*', Pasolini laments that De Martino's investigations have produced an anthropology focused strictly on agrarian or 'peasant' culture at the expense of the urban, clearly hinting that he saw his own contributions in some way as a complement to De Martino's.[24] Of particular importance for Pasolini would have been De Martino's idea of a

---

22 See Pier Paolo Pasolini, *Lutheran Letters*, trans. by Stuart Hood (Manchester, UK: Carcanet Press, 1983).

23 Pasolini was familiar with De Martino's contributions to *Nuovi argomenti* and in fact made several references to them. For example, he mentions De Martino's work in some of the essays collected in *Scritti corsari* such as 'Limitatezza della storia' and 'Gli uomini colti e la cultura popolare'. In 'Il caos', the weekly column that he wrote for *Il tempo*, he mentions De Martino to support his view that drug use was a response to the feeling of loss of 'presence'; see Pasolini, *Saggi sulla politica e sulla società*, pp. 321, 469, and 1168.

24 See Pasolini, *Saggi sulla politica e sulla società*, p. 469: 'Non poteva evidentemente essere altrimenti, e quindi non è il caso di recriminare: ma è veramente un peccato che De Martino anzichè occuparsi della cultura popolare della Lucania non si sia occupato della cultura popolare di Napoli. Del resto nessun etnologo o antropologo si è mai occupato, con la stessa precisione e assolutezza scientifica usata per le culture popolari contadine, delle culture popolari urbane'.

'cultural apocalypse', which the anthropologist identified as the uniquely contemporary manifestation of an older mode of historical cataclysm that already encompassed theological, post-colonial, and Marxist varieties.[25] As De Martino observed, the traditional Christian notion of apocalypse established by John in the Book of Revelation coincides with an unveiling of the future, with the end of the human world at the advent of the New Jerusalem. In his eyes, however, what is peculiar to the modern form of apocalypse is its severe restriction of any hope of regeneration, its dismissal especially of the prospect of a future shaped by communal human intervention.[26] For De Martino, the withering of faith in the idea of a cultural homeland and the resulting impossibility of social reintegration deprive present-day narratives of catastrophe of any redemptive promise. The cultural apocalypse that has emerged in the most recent epoch, then, threatens to be a radical crisis for human nature.[27]

According to this view, to belong to a culture means to possess a structuring ethos, the loss of which dooms humanity to being plunged into social disarray and thus marks the end of the world as a historically specific domain.[28] Given Pasolini's familiarity with the anthropologist's work, it seems likely that he was thinking of De Martino when he proposed in his later writings the concept of 'anthropological mutation' to describe the spread of social and intellectual conformism under the pressure of Italy's spectacular brand of consumerism. It is worth noting, in this connection, that Pasolini went so far as to characterize this transformation in *Lutheran Letters* as an 'apocalyptic picture' [*quadro apocalittico*].[29] Interestingly, however, De Martino dedicated a large share of his attention to studying literary and creative representations of the apocalypse and took pains to identify several modern-day authors of such works, including Sartre and Camus among the French and Pavese and Moravia among the Italians — but not Pasolini.[30] This omission begs the question to what extent was Pasolini

---

25 Ernesto De Martino, *La fine del mondo: Contributo all'analisi delle apocalissi culturali*, ed. by Clara Gallini, intro. by Clara Callini and Marcello Massenzio (Turin: Einaudi, 2002), p. ix.
26 Ibid., p. 479.
27 Ibid., p. 471.
28 Ibid., p. 475.
29 Pasolini, *Lutheran Letters*, p. 15.
30 In his book, De Martino dedicates a large share of his attention to what he calls the crisis of bourgeois society and the consequent loss of a 'cultural homeland'. De Martino maintains that modern literature is dominated by the idea of apocalypse, albeit an apocalypse without eschaton. According to his view, two antithetical terrors inform the modern age: the fear of 'losing the world' and the fear 'of being

truly an apocalyptic thinker, in the nihilistic sense that the term conveys today?[31] All of his gadfly pursuits — his tireless editorial interventions in Italian newspapers, his deliberately provocative ideas and controversial artistic productions, his condemnation of the *Democrazia Cristiana*, and his meticulous critical attention to the anthropological mutation of life in Italy — all of these vital engagements with his time would seem to point toward an anti-cynical temperament and a rejection of fatalist thinking.

Yet there is no denying that Pasolini at times adopted a strident and unforgiving tone. On this score, it is helpful to consider his recurring use of the theme of genocide in his writings. In his essays, for example, he refrains neither from depicting the materialism of Italian society as the 'real, immense genocide of the new fascism' [*immensi genocidi del nuovo fascismo*], and thus in a serious sense anticipating Agamben's designation of the camp as 'the "nomos" of the modern', nor from comparing the young people of Italy, who in his eyes have become incapable of smiling or laughing spontaneously, to 'Fascist emissaries of concentration camps' [*inviati fascisti di un Lager*].[32] In a retrospective discussion of his 1961

---

lost in the world'. In this context, De Martino regards it as unsurprising that Sartre is obsessed with nausea or Moravia with the so-called 'malady of objects' or that Pavese desperately tries to renew the 'domesticity of the world'; see De Martino, *La fine del mondo*, pp. 466–79.

31   In what follows, I will use the term 'nihilistic' or 'nihilist' to refer to the modern attitude of resistance to the idea that life has intrinsic meaning or value. Nihilism often is associated in the cultural domain with the radical skepticism toward social convention expressed in the nineteenth-century Russian novel, notably Turgenev's *Fathers and Sons* (1862), and in the philosophical domain with Nietzsche's espousal of 'the transvaluation of all values' in *The Antichrist* (1895) and emphasis on perspectivism throughout his oeuvre. Properly speaking, the nihilist outlook ought to be distinguished from an apocalyptic way of thinking insofar as apocalypse is an overtly religious concept that originates in the Christian eschatology articulated by John in the Book of Revelation.

32   For the two quotes from the essay 'Unhappy youths' [*I giovani infelici*] see respectively Pasolini, *Lutheran Letters*, pp. 16, 14, and *Saggi sulla politica e sulla società*, pp. 547, 545. For the argument behind Agamben's definition of modernity, see Giorgio Agamben, 'The Camp as the "Nomos" of the Modern', in *Homo Sacer: Sovereign Power and Bare Life*, trans. by Daniel Heller-Roazen (Stanford, CA: Stanford University Press, 1998), pp. 166–80. It is interesting in this regard to note Pasolini's contempt for the Italian youth of 1968. Their acceptance of the culture of consumption on the one hand and 'purely verbal' progressivism on the other represented in his eyes a 'loss of values' [*una perdita di valori*] so extreme that it made young people look to him like 'the *proletarian* troops of the SS' [*le truppe* proletarie *delle SS tedesche*]; see Pasolini, *Lutheran Letters*, p. 56 and *Saggi sulla politica e sulla società*, p. 608.

film *Accattone*, he claims along similar lines that between 1961 and 1975 a 'genocide' took place that transformed the young boys of the working class into 'Hitler SS' who are deprived of all meaningful values and social models.[33] In his most extensive and despairing elaboration of this view, he invokes Marx as a witness to earlier attempts to exterminate the proletariat and invites his ideological patron to abandon all belief in progress in favor of acknowledging what he defines as the apocalyptic '*fait accompli*' that has taken hold in Italy.[34] His skepticism toward the possibility of social communion even through sex reaches a masochistic level of disgust that prompts him in the 'Disavowal of the Trilogy of Life' to declare, 'I now hate bodies and sex organs' [*ormai odio i corpi e gli organi sessuali*].[35] He thus gives voice to a sentiment that may be understood to achieve its fulfillment in *Salò*, his searing vision of murderous, Sadean cruelty under the fascist régime of the Republic of Salò, the German-occupied puppet state that was established in Northern Italy toward the end of Mussolini's reign.

We well might note that Pasolini also found the logic of mass violence useful in explaining not only the workings of Italian social relations but also the political and economic relations between western and non-western societies. In one of his most prophetic interventions, a long sequence of pedagogical epistles entitled 'Gennariello', he relates the exploitation of the people, historical monuments, and natural resources of North Yemen by the Chinese and European corporations who represent the global forces of modernity, a predicament that he witnessed in 1970 while scouting locations for *The Gospel According to St. Matthew*:

> Yemen is still only a small, even pathetic market for [these] industries. Thus it is despised and even ridiculed. The fact that it requires a renunciation by the Yemenis seems quite natural to the German and Italian speculators: the Yemenis need to be completely complicit in their own genocide: cultural and physical [...] as in the concentration camps.[36]

---

33 See Pasolini, *Lutheran Letters*, pp. 101–02 and *Saggi sulla politica e sulla società*, p. 676.
34 See Pasolini, *Lutheran Letters*, p. 104 and *Saggi sulla politica e sulla società*, p. 680.
35 Pasolini, *Lutheran Letters*, p. 50 and *Saggi sulla politica e sulla società*, p. 600.
36 Pasolini, *Lutheran Letters*, p. 32 and *Saggi sulla politica e sulla società*, p. 572: 'Gli yemeniti devono essere del tutto consenzienti a proposito del loro genocidio: culturale e fisico, anche se non necessariamente mortale, come nei Lager'.

Yet out of this starkly pessimistic view of the plight of the Yemenite poor, he managed at the same time to make a positive historical difference by shooting the fourteen-minute documentary *The Walls of Sana'a*, which vividly exposed the destruction of the medieval architecture of North Yemen's capital city to make way for the modernization required by 'neocapitalist policies'. The film ends with a poignant sequence of shots panning across the ancient walls of Sana'a, while Pasolini's voice intones a plea to the United Nations to take action: 'We call upon UNESCO in the name of the true, if also unexpressed, will of the Yemenite people. In the name of simple men whom poverty has kept pure. In the name of the grace of obscure centuries. In the name of the scandalous revolutionary force of the past'.[37] With this call to conscience, Pasolini enlists the memorial power of film, its ability to evoke 'the revolutionary force of the past', as a means of holding the current institutional order accountable to the promise of the future. In this sense, The *Walls of Sana'a* powerfully exemplifies what I have called in *The Ends of Mourning* the director's 'spectropoetics'[38] and, more broadly, his critical and political concern for the future. In fact, it was not until 1986, some fifteen years after the release of the film and eleven years after Pasolini's death, that UNESCO granted the city of Sana'a status as a World Heritage site.

In many ways, Pasolini reserved his most apocalyptic rhetoric for his discussions of Italian culture. He was quick to concede that in the representative urban centers of other capitalist nations — say, in New York, or Paris, or London — the people could take comfort from the effective operation of at least some of their institutions, as the industrialization and acculturation of these societies had occurred in ways that were very different from what was happening in Italy.[39] The author and editor Pier Giorgio Bellocchio places an illuminating emphasis on the role that Pasolini played in his native milieu by describing him in an introduction to the volume *Essays on Politics and Society* [*Saggi sulla politica e sulla società*] as 'desperately Italian' [*disperatamente Italiano*].[40] In this context,

---

37   Pasolini, *Per il cinema*, II, p. 2110 : 'Ci rivolgiamo all'UNESCO, in nome della vera, seppure ancora inespressa, volontà del popolo yemenita. In nome degli uomini semplici che la povertà ha mantenuto puri. In nome della grazia dei secoli oscuri. In nome della scandalosa forza rivoluzionaria del passato'.
38   See Ricciardi, *The Ends of Mourning*.
39   See Pasolini *Lutheran Letters*, p. 104 and *Saggi sulla politica e sulla società*, p. 680.
40   Piergiorgio Bellocchio, 'Introduction', in Pasolini, *Saggi sulla politica e sulla società*, p. xiii–xxxix.

it is worth reflecting on the resonances and implications of a *cri de cœur* that Pasolini voiced in an article in *Il corriere della sera* of September 28, 1975, just a few days before his murder, in which he ardently declares that Italians want to know what the limits of the new culture are and 'what future it has in mind'.[41] If we consider this challenge to his readers in light of his published proposals in the same year to eliminate the state school system and television from Italian pedagogy altogether, the impulse behind his thinking seems more Rousseauvian then nihilistic.[42]

In 'Two Modest Proposals for Eliminating Crime in Italy', he introduces an almost pragmatist tone into the essays collected in *Lutheran Letters*, a volume whose very title more sharply suggests the need for a sober reformation inspired by an intellectual who refuses to traffic with worldly interests and 'courtiers' than for some convulsive upheaval.[43] And in 'Drugs, an Italian Tragedy', which was published initially in the *Corriere*, Pasolini relates the increase of drug addiction in Italy to the 'great phenomenon' of moral and cultural loss resulting from the expansion of the neo-fascist order of corporate and governmental power. He adds in summation that 'one needs a great deal of vitality to love culture', thus re-deploying in a hortative register a key term that he already had adopted as a kind of credo or emblem, albeit with a more paradoxical twist, in the title of his celebrated poem, 'A Desperate Vitality'.[44] Far from inciting his reader to embrace the Dionysian excess of consumerism in a nihilist gesture of welcome to the apocalypse, Pasolini painfully diagnoses in his last works the demise of grace and style, indeed of a way of life, from Italy's overall social ecology. Culture, he adds, does not belong to the elite but expresses

---

41 Pasolini *Lutheran Letters*, p. 98 and *Saggi sulla politica e sulla società*, p. 672: 'Gli italiani vogliono ancora sapere che cos'è, che limiti ha, che futuro prevede, la "nuova cultura" [...]'.
42 In an interview about television with Arturo Gismondi published in *Vie Nuove*, Giulio Sapelli reminds us that Pasolini decried contemporary society's tendency to encourage young people to forget the present and to pay no attention to the future; see Giulio Sapelli, *Modernizzazione senza sviluppo: Il capitalismo secondo Pasolini* (Milan: Mondadori, 2005), p. 85.
43 See Pasolini, *Lutheran Letters*, pp. 105–08 and *Saggi sulla politica e sulla società*, pp. 687–92.
44 See Pasolini, *Saggi sulla politica e sulla società*, p. 612: 'Perchè la cultura — in senso specifico o, meglio, classista — è un possesso: e niente necessita di una più accanita e matta energia che il desiderio del possesso'. More broadly, see Pasolini, *Lutheran Letters*, pp. 58–62 and *Saggi sulla politica e sulla società*, pp. 611–17.

'the knowledge of a way of life, of a country in its totality' [*il sapere e il modo di essere di un paese nel suo insieme*].[45]

In 'Gennariello', as I noted earlier, he experimented with pedagogy, thus adopting a rhetorical strategy that by definition addresses the future of the younger notional reader. He sets out, in this series of didactic letters, to identify how the future itself in some ways has changed as a class concept in Italy, while suggesting there is still the basis for a version of solidarity: 'Vitality is always a source of affection and candor. In Naples both the poor boy and the middle-class boy are full of vitality'.[46] He observes that before the arrival of the anthropological mutation, which may be seen to coincide with the economic boom following World War Two, the poor wished for 'a different future', but that the 'future [was] slow in coming', so that tomorrow wound up being for them very much like today: the product of a 'lazy revolution'.

After the mutation, however, the very tempo of change has accelerated to the point that the future threatens simply to renew class conflict, arriving as a universal and unbearable shock: 'The right of the poor to a better existence had a counterpart which has ended by degrading them. The future is imminent and apocalyptic'.[47] Pasolini concludes his lesson by observing that his talk is not a panegyric to the past, which, he slyly adds, he did not much like when it was the present. 'They are talks', he asserts, 'in which conservation and revolution no longer have meaning' and concludes in parenthesis 'so you see I am modern too'.[48] The attitude surely is a familiar one; as Carla Benedetti has remarked, striking a note reminiscent of Zanzotto, Pasolini generally claimed to examine the past only in order to criticize the present.[49]

As an index of the rapid alteration of Italy's social fabric, Pasolini noted not only the disappearance of the fireflies but the 'loss' of another highly

---

45 Pasolini, *Lutheran Letters*, p. 60 and *Saggi sulla politica e sulla società*, p. 613.
46 Pasolini, *Lutheran Letters*, p. 18 and *Saggi sulla politica e sulla società*, p. 553: 'La vitalità è sempre fonte di affetto e di ingenuità. A Napoli sono pieni di vitalità sia il ragazzo povero che il ragazzo borghese'.
47 Pasolini, *Lutheran Letters*, p. 36 and *Saggi sulla politica e sulla società*, p. 579: 'Il diritto dei poveri ad un'esistenza migliore ha una contropartita che ha finito col degradarla. Il futuro è immimente e apocalittico'.
48 Pasolini, *Lutheran Letters*, p. 37 and *Saggi sulla politica e sulla società*, p. 580: 'Sono discorsi diversi da tutto ciò che oggi da parte di un uomo della mia età si possa dire; discorsi in cui "conservazione" e "rivoluzione" sono appunto parole che non hanno piu senso (come vedi sono, dunque, moderno anch'io)'.
49 Carla Benedetti, 'Pasolini celebrato o tradito?', *Italian Culture*, 24–25 (2006–2007), 141–51.

visible phenomenon: church icons of Madonnas were no longer weeping at election times, as they had in past decades. The secularization of society, in other words, had made it impossible for conservative Catholic politicians to drum up support among superstitious voters, particularly in campaigns against the Communist Party, through the carnival trick of a staged miracle.[50] It is evident in this case that Pasolini does not exactly mourn the passing of a somewhat ludicrous Italian political custom. When taken together with 'The Article of the Fireflies', however, what becomes evident is how much attention he dedicated to looking for signs of change in the prevailing forms of cultural and political life — signs that in fact ranged from the sublime in the case of the fireflies to the bathetic in the case of the weeping Madonna icons.

Contiguous with his efforts as a filmmaker and poet to deconstruct à la Derrida the relation between the specters of the past and those of the future, there appears an aspect of Pasolini's overall project that may be defined as an attempt to trace the emerging anthropology of the contemporary or, borrowing Paul Rabinow's expression, to 'seize the ratio of modernity'. According to Rabinow,

> The ethos of the contemporary contrasts with that of the modern; it is not fascinated by the new per se but concerned with the emergence and articulation of forms within which old and new elements take on meaning and functions. Today there is no doubt that one site of such problem is: how might we forge a way of life that does not make a sharp and brutal separation between what used to be called nature and culture.[51]

In the late writings that are gathered in *Corsair Writings* and *Lutheran Letters*, Pasolini tries very hard to understand the new political phenomenology and its articulation of old and new: from the failure of the so-called 'historical compromise' that was intended to unite the Italian Communist Party and the Christian Democracy, to the crimes of the old Christian Democracy party, the new operations of the church in a consumer society, and even the procedures of referendums and elections. Far from being hopeless in outlook, he was frantic to take in the whole picture. If it cannot be granted that Pasolini was a consistent voice for the future, he certainly was relentless in his scrutiny of the contemporary.

---

50   See Pasolini, *Lutheran Letters*, p. 46 and *Saggi sulla politica e sulla società*, p. 593–96.
51   Paul Rabinow, *Marking Time: On the Anthropology of the Contemporary* (Princeton: Princeton University Press, 2007), pp. 24–25.

In another recent book dedicated to the topic, Agamben defines the contemporary as

> the person who perceives the darkness of his time as something that concerns him, as something that never ceases to engage him....To perceive, in the darkness of the present, this light that strives to reach us but cannot — this is what it means to be contemporary. As such, contemporaries are rare. And for this reason, to be contemporary is, first and foremost, a question of courage.[52]

It is telling that what distinguishes the contemporary in Agamben's eyes is a potential for illumination that is missed or fails to reach us, at least within the bounds of historical time. Yet by the same token precisely this anachronism or untimeliness gives urgency to the engagement of the contemporary with the obscure conditions of the present, thus making possible the very glimpse of the light traveling toward us through the darkness. In his view, what is contemporary is inscribed in the present and always already marks it as archaic, so that only someone who can discern the indices and signatures of the archaic in the latest phenomena can be truly contemporary.[53] The coexistence of the archaic with historical becoming, like an embryo that encompasses the shape of the mature organism, is certainly a vision that Pasolini would have embraced.[54]

As has been well established, Pasolini had a taste for what in art history is known as the technique of the *non finito* or unfinished. This predilection surfaces in a recurring impulse to assign the title of *appunti* [notes] to certain films (*Appunti per un film sull'India*, *Appunti per un poema sul Terzo Mondo*, *Appunti per un'Orestiade Africana*). His penchant for the *non finito* appears as well in the chaotic, fragmentary style of the novel *Petrolio*, which he left incomplete at the time of his death, his unfinished

---

52   Giorgio Agamben, *What is Apparatus? and Other Essays*, trans. by David Kishik and Stefan Pedatolla (Stanford, CA: Stanford University Press, 2009), pp. 45–46. See also Giorgio Agamben, *Che cos'è il contemporaneo?* (Rome: Nottetempo, 2008), pp. 15–16: 'Colui che percepisce il buio del suo tempo come qualcosa che lo riguarda e non cessa di interpellarlo [...]. Percepire nel buio del presente questa luce che cerca di raggiungerci e non puo farlo, questo significa essere contemporanei. Per questo i contemporanei sono rari. E per questo essere contemporanei e innanzitutto una forma di coraggio'.
53   See Agamben, *Che cos'è il contemporaneo?*, p. 21 and *What is Apparatus*, p. 50.
54   Agamben thus may be of help in assessing the philosophical resonances of the archaic in Pasolini's work. For a more general exploration of this issue, see Noa Steimatsky, 'Archaic: Pasolini on the Face of the Earth', in *Italian Locations: Reinhabiting the Past in Postwar Cinema* (Minneapolis: University of Minnesota Press, 2008), pp. 117–65.

modernization of the first four cantos of Dante's *Inferno* entitled *La divina mimesis*, and ultimately in the body of unrealized film concepts that he accumulated over a span of more than thirty years including his scenarios for a film on Saint Paul and for the sprawling allegory *Porno-Teo-Kolossal*. Pasolini himself appears to recognize in his own fascination with the *non finito* a form of devotion to the ideal of intellectual work as process when in 1963 he gives one of his most celebrated and emblematic poems the title *Progetto per opere future* [*Plan of Future Works*].[55] As Carla Benedetti has pointed out, his attachment to the notion of a work that ought to be kept in a state of potentiality is an important key to understanding Pasolini's last endeavors in particular.[56] One might well notice that Pasolini's interest in the poetics of potentiality finds a philosophical counterpart in Agamben's thought, where the concept plays a pivotal role.[57] Although this is not the place to pursue an in-depth comparison between the two authors' poetic and philosophical interpretations of potentiality, the topic clearly reflects a shared concern that could provide the basis of a discussion of Pasolini's and Agamben's aesthetic and political affinities with each other, beyond the all-too-reasonable criticism à la Didi-Huberman of their mutual tendency to apocalyptic rhetoric.

At the moment of his death in 1975, Pasolini left behind an unfinished scenario for the film project titled *Porno-Teo-Kolossal* that propounds a surprisingly comic vision of apocalypse, an image of the end time that finally is most remarkable for its sweetness and, to invoke a Pasolinian term, charity.[58] Armando Maggi helpfully calls attention to the fact that the director may have taken the idea of a 'porn-theology' from an article by Gilles Deleuze entitled 'Pierre Klossowski et le corps-langage' that

---

55 See particularly Pasolini, 'Ideas, Subjects, Treatments' [*Idee, Soggetti, Trattamenti*], in *Per il cinema*, II, pp. 2585–2757.
56 See Carla Benedetti, 'La forma — progetto', in *Pasolini contro Calvino*, pp. 158–70.
57 See Agamben's *Potentialities*, especially the essay 'Bartleby, or on contingency', in *Potentialities: Collected Essays in Philosophy*, trans. and ed. by Daniel Heller Roazen (Stanford, CA: Stanford University Press, 1999), pp. 243–75. For a superb analysis of the concept of potentiality as a running *fil rouge* in Agamben's work, see Leland de la Durantaye, *Giorgio Agamben: A Critical Introduction* (Stanford: Stanford University Press, 2009).
58 For a perceptive close reading of Pasolini's scenario, see Armando Maggi, 'The Journey to Sodom and Gomorrah and Beyond: The Scenario *Porn-Theo-Colossal*', in *The Resurrection of the Body: Pier Paolo Pasolini from Saint Paul to Sade* (Chicago: University of Chicago Press, 2009), 107–57.

was published in *Critique* in March 1965.⁵⁹ Not only was Pasolini well acquainted with Deleuze's work, but he listed Klossowski's *Sade, mon prochain: Le philosophe scélérat* in the 'Essential Bibliography' for *Salò* that he incorporated into that film's opening title sequence. By appending the term 'Kolossal' to the concept of a porn-theology in the title, the filmmaker amusingly underscores the grandiose rhetoric of the society of spectacle that conventional Hollywood movies adopt in their recounting of historical events. The adjective puts a clownish exclamation point on the philosophically ponderous valences of the title, ultimately reframing the notion of revelation that seems implicit in the expression 'porn-theology' as an overblown and somewhat grotesque spectacle.

According to Gian Carlo Ferretti, Pasolini intended to shoot *Porno-Teo-Kolossal* immediately after *Salò* and before *Saint Paul*, the other unfinished project that was in the planning process when he died.⁶⁰ The surviving scenario recounts the picaresque wanderings of an aging Neapolitan Magus named Eduardo (played by the well-known Neapolitan actor and playwright Eduardo de Filippo) and his younger Roman servant Ninetto (played by Ninetto Davoli) as they pursue a quest to find the newborn messiah after witnessing the appearance of a comet in the sky. In the first scene of the film's prologue, which is set in Naples, Pasolini situates Eduardo and Ninetto 'in the darkness and silence of the heights of the cosmos' [*nel buio e nel silenzio delle altezze cosmiche*].⁶¹ The logic of Pasolini's fantasy, however, soon compels our two protagonists to leave home on their journey through a succession of allegorical dystopias beginning with Sodom, an entirely gay version of 1950s Rome that appears to be an enlightened metropolis of tolerance and democracy, but that eventually is destroyed by violence. Eduardo and Ninetto then proceed to Gomorrah, a brutal Milan that threatens to crush diversity, where a naked homosexual man is hooked

---

59 Maggi elucidates Deleuze's motivating question, 'Is the theology that becomes a total art a prodigious theo-pornology?' [Est-ce la théologie qui devient un art total, une prodigeuse théo-pornologie?], in terms of the French philosopher's insistence on 'the linguistic nature of the body' in the essay on Klossowski and adds that Pasolini may be viewed along similar lines as interested in 'the image of a body miming the "gesture" lying at the center of its life'; See Maggi, *The Resurrection of the Body*, p. 111.

60 See Gian Carlo Ferretti, 'Sedici anni di ricordi, 1959–1975', in *L'ultima intervista di Pasolini*, ed. by Colombo Furio and Gian Carlo Ferretti (Rome: Avagliano, 2005), p. 34. To Ferretti's testimony, Maggi adds that of the writer Uberto Paolo Quintavalle, who was one of the four libertines in *Salò*; see Maggi, *The Resurrection of the Body*, p. 109.

61 Pasolini, *Per il cinema*, II, p. 2697.

to a helicopter in front of the Duomo and shot while lifted into the air in a macabre parody of the opening of Fellini's *La dolce vita*. Like Sodom, Gomorrah meets with an abrupt and devastating end. The next episode in the two characters' travels takes place in Numanzia, which is to say Paris, a socialist city on the verge of being occupied by the fascists. The city collectively and 'democratically' decides to commit mass suicide rather than surrender.[62]

In the final segment, Eduardo and Ninetto, who now have been given the theologically resonant names Epifanio and Nunzio, finally arrive in the Middle Eastern city of Ur in a jumbo jet, still in search of Jesus. As it nears its conclusion, the narrative becomes increasingly comical and surreal until finally Epifanio is told in a Kafkaesque epilogue that too much time has elapsed since he first set out on his mission, which means that the Messiah is now dead and forgotten. Desperate at this news, Epifanio takes his last breath and dies, only to reawaken in the afterlife to the discovery that Nunzio has become 'a true and proper angel of the Lord' [*un vero e proprio Angelo del Signore*].[63] The two protagonists, reunited as disembodied souls, set out for Paradise: 'The two, increasingly happy, climb up and up through the cosmic expanses (the same in which our poem started)' [*i due, sempre più felici, salgono di buona lena su su, per gli spazi cosmici (gli stessi in cui era cominciato il nostro poema)*].[64]

After losing patience as the pair cannot find their destination and exclaiming 'I cannot take this anymore' [*non gliela faccio più*], Epifanio gradually begins to listen attentively to the voices, noises, and chants emanating 'from the world map' [*dal mappamondo*].[65] The playful choice of '*mappamondo*' rather than a more pompous word for the earth in Pasolini's scenario bespeaks the Chaplinesque absurdity of his characters as they fulfill their apocalyptic fates in the hereafter. What follows in the final moments of the tale continues in this gently ludicrous vein, as

---

62 See ibid., p. 2741. According to the critic Laura Salvini, the three cities stand respectively for the past, the present, and the future, but I find this neat partition to be questionable in light of the end of Numanzia. The most convincing of these analogies is between Gomorrah and the present (the Italy of the 1960s and 1970s), which highlights the kind of heterosexual conformity, terrorist attacks, and quotidian violence that Pasolini also examined in his unfinished novel *Petrolio*; see Laura Salvini, *I frantumi del tutto: Ipotesi e letture dell'ultimo Progetto cinematografico di Pier Paolo Pasolini, Porno-Teo-Kolossal* (Bologna: Clueb, 2004), p. 73.
63 Pasolini, *Per il cinema*, II, p. 2751.
64 Ibid., p. 2752–53.
65 Ibid., p. 2751.

Epifanio arrives at the realization that 'it is only through illusion that, in the world, he has been able to know reality' [*ma è stata quell'illusione che, del mondo, gli ha fatto conoscere la realtà*] while he pauses 'to take a piss' [si mette a pisciare].[66]

Although he recognizes that, like all such would-be divine miracles, their *cometa* or guiding star has turned out to be a 'load of crap' [*stronzata*], Epifanio gazes at the world 'with sympathy' [*con simpatia*]. Unexpectedly, he finds himself moved to 'certain mysterious tears of gratitude' [*certe misteriose lacrime di gratitudine*] for having known life on the earth, from which he can hear the growing sounds of revolutionary struggle:

> From down below arrive confusedly the voices and noises of daily life — chants of poor people, fashionable chants, and finally revolutionary chants.... The chants, the revolutionary chants down below become increasingly sharper'.[67]

In response to Epifanio's disquiet, Nunzio delivers the Beckettian final lines of the drama: 'Let's wait. Something will happen' [*Aspettamo. Qualche cosa succederà*].[68] In Pasolini's disenchanted epic, which distils the apocalyptic voices of modernity from Cervantes to Kafka and Beckett, the two unlikely heroes appear at the end to have found, if not Paradise, then at least a shared space of gratitude and perhaps even of mercy.

The scenario may be said to recur to the original etymology of the word 'apocalypse' in Saint John, which according to André Chouraqui connotes contemplation rather than the punishment of the sinful.[69] If Epifanio can do no more than listen from afar to our worldly clamor, thus resembling the poet of 'Plan of Future Works' [*Progetto di opere future*] who declares that 'the revolution is now just a sentiment' [*la rivoluzione non e più che un sentimento*], *Porno-Teo-Kolossal* nonetheless imagines the apocalypse

---

66 Ibid., p. 2753.
67 Ibid., p. 2753: 'Da laggiù arrivano — confusi tra le voci e i rumori della vita quotidiana — canti di povera gente, sciocchi canti di moda, e, infine, canti rivoluzionari [...]. I canti — i canti rivoluzionari — laggiù si fanno sempre più nitidi'.
68 Ibid.
69 For an extended discussion of the meaning of apocalypse according to Chouraqui, see André Chouraqui, *Un Pacte neuf: Lettres, Contemplation de Yohanân*, trans. from the Hebrew by André Chouraqui (Paris: Desclée de Brouwer, 1977). See Derrida's comments on Chouraqui in Jacques Derrida, 'On a Newly Arisen Apocalyptic Tone in Philosophy', trans. by John Leavey Jr, in *Raising the Tone of Philosophy*, ed. by Peter Fenves (Baltimore: Johns Hopkins University Press, 1993), p. 119.

as a domain where contemplative gratitude for humanity's noisy activity is privileged over the punitive task of judgment.[70] Pasolini's narrative thus challenges the conventional wisdom that apocalyptic visions must always necessarily be greeted with enlightened, rational skepticism. Both Pasolini and Agamben in this sense raise an important ethical question for readers: must we always reject the apocalyptic manner in works of art and thought as a means of giving voice to irrational and politically irresponsible views [granted that in Agamben the mode sometimes verges on messianism], albeit with occasional protestations of sympathy as in Didi-Huberman's case?[71]

On this question we may find it useful to turn to Derrida's essay, 'On a Newly Arisen Apocalyptic Tone in Philosophy' [*D'un ton apocalyptique adopté naguère en philosophie*], the title of which alludes to Kant's 'On a Newly Arisen Superior Tone in Philosophy' (1796) [*Von einem neuerdings erhobenen vornehmen Ton in der Philosophie*].[72] As a way of examining more closely 'the hypothesis or the program of an intractable demystification', Derrida calls on us to 'nuance the praise' that readers reflexively give to Kant for having the audacity to 'denounce a *manner* of

---

70 See Pasolini, *Poems*, pp. 202–03. My interpretation of the scenario on this point diverges from Armando Maggi's more pessimistic conclusion: 'The end of *Porn-Theo-Colossal* alludes to a renewal, which is apocalyptic in that it manifests an eternal waiting. The two enlightened men are "out of this world", and the revolution seems something perennially announced but never realized'; see Maggi, *The Resurrection of the Body*, p. 155.

71 On Agamben's interpretation of messianic time in relationship to the apocalypse, see Giorgio Agamben, *The Time That Remains: A Commentary on the Letter to the Romans*, trans. by Patricia Dailey (Stanford: Stanford University Press, 2005). Agamben regards Saint Paul's interpretation of messianic time as the fundamental one of the messianic tradition. The messianic in this light becomes a figure not related to the naïve idea of a future to come, but rather to the present time or 'the time of the now'. On this reckoning, Paul faces all the contradictions of the 'remaining time' that represents the real messianic time. Indeed, the temporal experience to which messianic time gives access seems based on a reversal of the relationship between past and future. Although my rapid synopsis cannot do justice to the intricacy and complexity of Agamben's argument, I wish to note that the Italian philosopher has written an original genealogy of apocalyptic and messianic time that repositions hope in a new temporal economy of past and future. As messianic hope does not address an indefinite future, but the time of now, the time that remains, the urgent critical pathos of Agamben's thought is not necessarily in contradiction with his interpretation of messianic time.

72 See Jacques Derrida, 'On a Newly Arisen Apocalyptic Tone in Philosophy', pp. 117–71; Derrida's lecture was first delivered in 1980.

giving oneself airs' that coincides with the apocalyptic tone in philosophy.[73] According to Derrida, Kant's criticism of this 'tone' is grounded in a suspicion that 'the oracular voice' of apocalyptic thought 'covers over the voice of reason', which is to say that the prophetic view mistakes 'the *Geheimnis* of practical reason, the sublimity of moral law' for the inspirational 'mystery of vision and contact, whereas the moral law never gives itself to be seen or touched'.[74] Yet such a debate is doomed to remain confined within the terms of phallogocentrism, as both sides, in their fear of castration, bind themselves to the same movement of reason, of the mastery of presentiment.

On this score, there is no metalanguage to which we may have recourse to mediate the question of eschatology, because 'each of us is the mystagogue *and* the *Aufklärer* of an other'.[75] To the extent that the oracular impulse itself represents a 'desire for clarity and revelation', Derrida points out, Kant's attempt 'to demystify or, if you prefer, to deconstruct apocalyptic discourse' in the name of *Aufklärung* must be understood as itself apocalyptic.[76] As the French philosopher aptly puts it, 'The question remains and comes back: what can be the limits of demystification'?[77] Derrida's observations are especially pertinent to taking stock of a certain genre or regimen of criticizing apocalyptic thinkers such as Pasolini and Agamben. Although it may be productive and necessary at times to call into question the rhetoric of the uncompromising and the unreasonable, the critics who undertake such a line of attack too often leave us with the impression that they operate ultimately in the name of a conservative wish for mastery.[78] Precisely with the danger of this wish in mind, Derrida concludes his essay by asking a last question that comes close to ventriloquizing the voice of reason itself: 'To what ends do you want to come when you come to tell us, here now, let's go, come, the apocalypse, it's finished, I tell you this, that's what's happening'.[79]

It may be said, then, that many of Pasolini's more demystificatory or skeptical readers have not succeeded in resisting the self-regarding

---

73 Ibid., pp. 156, 123.
74 Ibid., pp. 131–33.
75 Ibid., p. 142.
76 Ibid., p. 148.
77 Ibid., p. 159.
78 See Ibid., p. 159: 'Shall we thus continue in the best apocalyptic tradition to denounce false apocalypses? [...] Nothing is less conservative than the apocalyptic genre'.
79 Ibid., p. 168.

enjoyment of their own principles. In so doing, they have refused to see the Pasolini who, *malgré lui*, stood for the future, albeit for a future achieved through apocalyptic lucidity, through a refusal to accept complacently the given state of affairs, through the repudiation of indifference. Moreover, such readers have failed to recognize that, if there is one Italian intellectual of the twentieth century who may claim to have had a 'future', it is Pasolini. From Nanni Moretti to Roberto Saviano, the most courageous minds in Italy have dedicated their own works to Pasolini in the years that have followed his death.[80] A Gennariello for our times, Saviano may even have been thinking of *Porno-Teo-Kolossal* when he gave his celebrated denunciation of Neapolitan organized crime the fittingly Pasolinian title *Gomorra*.

---

80   Pasolini also continues to inspire a steady series of critical titles in Italy. Two of the most recent additions that are worth considering are Marco Belpoliti's *Pasolini in salsa picante* (Parma: Le Fenici Rosse, 2010), which attempts to emphasize the question of Pasolini's queer identity while downplaying his more traditional political engagements, and Giorgio Galli's far-more convincing *Pasolini comunista dissidente: Attualità di un pensiero politico* (Milan: Kaos, 2010).

Thomas Macho

PASOLINI'S METABOLIC CRITICISM[1]

There is a fundamental criticism of power that targets eating practices. This has to do not only with the ongoing debate about animal welfare, but with an attitude towards the world. The person eating wants to take in, to appropriate, to assimilate: to as it were, erase the difference between self and world. Eaters see themselves as containers to be filled as quickly as possible. In his key work *Crowds and Power*, Elias Canetti writes,

> Everything which is eaten is the food of power. The hungry man feels empty space within himself: He overcomes the discomfort which this causes him by filling himself with food. The fuller he is the better he feels.[2]

A different attitude is characterised by caution, wariness, refusal: here the world is alien to the eater. In order for something to enter the body, seals of quality, indications of origin and lists of ingredients have to be scrutinised, almost as if food items needed to apply for asylum before being permitted to pass through mouth and gut.

The first attitude could be described as inclusion, or to borrow the terminology of psychoanalysis, introjection; the second can be described as exclusion, an attempt to follow the dictates of ideal immunity: asceticism yearns for purity. A third, and perhaps older, attitude sees eating as an exchange with the world, as metabolism — from the Greek word μεταβολή 'change'— as a kind of communication. Siberian hunter peoples are believed to have ritually assured the beasts they killed that they in turn would serve their prey's own species as food; the hunters assuaged the guilt of killing by symbolically anticipating their own death. In the Shatapatha-Brahmana, an ancient Indian treatise on sacrificial rituals, it is

---

[1] Previously published as 'Pasolini's Metabolic Criticism', *Electra*, 13 (2021), 145–54.
[2] Elias Canetti, *Crowds and Power*, trans. by Carol Stewart (New York: Seabury Press, 1978), p. 219.

said of the hereafter, which takes the form of a picture puzzle of this world, 'For whatever food man eats in this world will eat him in the next'.³ Elias Canetti formulates this succinctly as, 'The thing which is eaten eats back'.⁴

But metabolic exchange does not need to be conceived of as radically as it is in Eurasian hunter rituals or ancient Indian sacrificial treatises; it also occurs in the daily routine of shared mealtimes, in which a mutual giving and taking of food is practised. In this sense, Jacques Derrida emphasises that,

> 'One must eat well' does not mean above all taking in and grasping in itself, but *learning* and giving to eat, learning-to-give-the-other-to-eat. One never eats entirely one's own: this constitutes the rule underlying the statement, 'One must eat well.' It is a rule offering infinite hospitality.⁵

The ideal of gathering around a table — from the Platonic symposium to the Christian Last Supper — has often been cited as a political symbol of peace and integration. However, Canetti would presumably have had doubts about Derrida's 'law of never-ending hospitality', because he dreamed of another world, one in which 'people laugh instead of eat',⁶ and 'of a land in which people cry over their meals'.⁷ And he asks, with an almost gnostic undertone, 'A creation based on eating — how could it succeed?'.⁸

Death *and the Full Stomach*

Pier Paolo Pasolini was a keen critic of the prevailing power structures, and especially of consumer society, which he saw as a continuation of fascism by other means. Eating is consumption in its most basic form, and in this respect, it is hardly surprising that, especially in his films, Pasolini

---

3   Quoted from Herman Lommel, 'Bhrigu im Jenseits', in *Paideuma*, Mitteilungen zur Kulturkunde (Bamberg: Melsenbach, 1950), IV, pp. 93–110 (p. 101).
4   Canetti, *Crowds and Power*, p. 357.
5   Jacques Derrida, '"Eating Well," or the Calculation of the Subject', in *Points*, ed. by Elisabeth Weber, trans. by Peter Connor and Avital Ronell (Stanford: Stanford University Press, 1995), pp. 255–87 (p. 282).
6   Elias Canetti, *Die Provinz des Menschen: Aufzeichnungen 1942–1972* (Munich/ Vienna: Carl Hanser, 1973), p. 231. [*Translation mine*]
7   Ibid., p. 157.
8   Elias Canetti, *The Secret Heart of the Clock: Notes, Aphorisms, Fragments 1973– 1985*, trans. by Joel Agee (New York: Farrar, Straus and Giroux, 1989), p. 46.

also commented on eating practices with a sensitivity and attention that could be characterised as an attitude of metabolic criticism. This commentary pays attention to processes of exchange, of the conversion of life and death, of the internal correlations between a gathering at a table and sacrificial ritual. Indeed, following its opening credits to the music of Johann Sebastian Bach and an epigraph from Dante's *Divine Comedy*, Pasolini's very first film, *Accattone* (1961), begins around a table. The first sentence to be uttered refers to the end of the world, and before long, the subject turns to death. First of all, the flower-seller describes the company around the table as resembling 'something out of the morgue', and then the story is told of poor Barbarone, who had bet that he could swim across the river with a full stomach and drowned in the attempt. In the course of the squabble, Accattone makes the same bet: he stuffs himself with food, hastily crosses himself and jumps off the bridge into the water. Much of *Accattone* is taken up with joyous meal scenes celebrated with almost mime-like perfection, bits of food occasionally spilling out of a crammed mouth. While a kilo of spaghetti is being cooked, Accattone reflects, 'What is hunger anyway? Nothing but imagination, a dangerous vice, a stupid habit. Our parents should never have got us used to eating in the first place'. He lifts a little boy onto his lap, 'And who was it who taught you to eat? No doubt it was that starving wretch your father'.

The full stomach represents death; thus in *Accattone* the belly of the drowned Barbarone is described as being 'swollen like a drum'. And the motif of swimming on a full stomach also crops up in Pasolini's first novel, *Ragazzi di vita* [The Street Kids] (1955), in which suburban youths organise a kind of test of courage in the river. One of these boys, Begalone, nearly comes to grief during the attempted swim,

> Finally he plunged in, and swam for a while with half strokes in the middle of the river, but he felt even worse: his head was spinning like a top on a string, and he seemed to feel something like a dead cat in his stomach. He was near fainting. Frightened, he swam, gasping, toward the shore [...] That morning, because he had eaten nothing the day before, he had had, poor boy, half a bowl of bread and pork rind: it must have given him indigestion, and now he was throwing up his soul, too.[9]

Another boy, Genesio, drowns during the next attempt to swim across the river.

---

9   Pier Paolo Pasolini, *The Street Kids*, trans. by Ann Goldstein (New York: Europa Editions, 2016), p. 411–12.

Every so often he sank under the surface of the current and then re-emerged a little farther down; finally when he was almost at the bridge, where the current broke and foamed over the rocks, he went under for the last time, without a cry, and all that could be seen was his small black head coming up for a moment.[10]

Pasolini had originally planned to have Accattone drown too, as Sergio Citti, the elder brother of the *Accattone* actor Franco Citti, reports:

> The death of Accattone caused Pier Paolo some serious concern. According to the screenplay, he was to drown in the river, but the seasons were well advanced and the water was ice cold. So he said to me, 'You know what, if it's very cold when we film, we'll simply have him die under a motorbike. I don't want him catching pneumonia'.[11]

While there is no doubt that exposure to icy water can be dangerous, the conventional wisdom that one should not go swimming on a full stomach is merely a myth. What is more interesting, however, is how intuitively convincing such views are. Why should a full stomach be incompatible with swimming? The answer may appear obvious: our movements in water remind us of our metabolisms before we began eating, when as babies we were still swimming in amniotic fluid; or of the 'oceanic feeling' on which Sigmund Freud passes such critical judgement in his treatise *Civilization and its Discontents* (1930). Accattone knows it was our fathers who 'taught us to eat' rather than our mothers, and only with eating does the metabolic transformation begin that is associated with death and guilt, but is also associated with the eschatological yearning for a creation that is not 'founded on eating'.

Last Supper with Ricotta

A year after *Accattone*, Pasolini filmed *Mamma Roma* (1962) with Anna Magnani in the leading role. The title refers implicitly to Rome's founding

---

10 Ibid., p. 432.
11 Pier Paolo Pasolini, *Lichter der Vorstädte*, ed. by Franca Faldini and Goffredo Fofi, trans. into German by Karl Baumgartner and Ingrid Mylo (Hofheim: Wolke, 1986), p. 43 [*Translation mine*]. This anthology is based on the two following Italian editions: *L'avventurosa storia del cinema italiano, raccontata dai suoi protagonisti 1960–1969* (Milan: Feltrinelli, 1981), and *Il cinema italiano d'oggi, raccontata dai suoi protagonist 1970–1984* (Milan: Arnoldo Mondadori Editore, 1984).

myth, a story that starts familiarly with the twins Romulus and Remus being abandoned on the banks of the swollen Tiber. The basket containing the babies washed up beneath a wild fig tree, the *Ficus Ruminalis*, which was still standing there on the Palatine under Emperor Augustus. In ancient times, the fig tree was known as the suicide tree —Timon of Athens is supposed to have announced in a speech that he was planning to have a fig tree near his house felled, so anyone who was tired of life should get a move on and put an end to it. According to the Greek philosopher Plutarch of Chaeronea (a staunch opponent of meat eating and a supporter of vegetarianism), the children lying under the tree were soon tended by a she-wolf 'who gave them suck', and a woodpecker came to help in feeding them and to watch over them. But they were then discovered by a swineherd called Faustulus, who handed them to his wife to nurse. According to other sources, explains Plutarch, it was the name of this woman that,

> [...] by its ambiguity, deflected the story into the realm of the fabulous. For the Latins not only called she-wolves 'lupae', but also women of loose character, and such a woman was the wife of Faustulus, the foster-father of the infants, Acea Larentia by name. Yet the Romans sacrifice also to her, and in the month of April the priest of Mars pours libations in her honour, and the festival is called Larentalia.[12]

From this, other authors have sought to establish a connection with the Lares or ancestral spirits. Anna Magnani, one quickly realises, is the very embodiment of this Lupa. She turns up at the wedding of her former pimp Carmine — played by Franco Citti — with three pigs on leashes, wearing bows. She sings a song deriding marriage, while the wedding table is reminiscent of painted depictions of The Last Supper.

The following year Pasolini made *La Ricotta* [The Ricotta] (1963), a 35-minute anthology film segment starring, among others, Orson Welles. It was soon banned, and Pasolini was convicted for blasphemy, even though *La Ricotta* could be described as one of the most devout films ever made. It depicts the filming of a version of the Christian story of the Passion, which is emphasised by Pasolini in the opening credits of *La Ricotta* as the 'greatest event' that has ever taken place. The film operates on two levels. On the one hand, as a film within a film it is a travesty of the Passion story, with reference in part to various paintings. However, on the other hand, it portrays the Second Coming of Christ in the guise of

---

12   Plutarch, *Lives*, trans. by Bernadotte Perrin (New Haven: Harvard [Loeb Classical Library], 1914), I, pp. 99–101.

Stracci, a poor, starving extra played by Mario Cipriani, whose role in the story is that of the Good Thief. Stracci's attempts to find something to eat initially come across as comical. He fails several times before eventually managing to devour a ricotta while on a short pause from filming. He is observed by the film team, who make fun of him and pelt him with all kinds of food with which, as they laugh at him, he rapidly stuffs himself. The collective meal thus mutates into a ritual of contempt and aggression, a variant of the widespread practice of hurling eggs or tomatoes at those who have fallen from favour. Stracci is almost forced to fill his stomach, and a little later dies on the cross. The director (Orson Welles) stands at the foot of the cross, repeatedly calling 'azione, azione!' before it dawns on him, and the crowd, that a genuine Passion — 'passione, passione' — has occurred.

So Stracci also dies of a full belly, albeit in a different way to the characters in *Accattone* and *Ragazzi di vita*. The metabolism of the consumer society devours its protagonists; even as we eat, we are eaten. 'One must stop letting oneself be eaten when one tastes best; this is known by those who want to be loved for a long time', writes Nietzsche in praise of the 'sacred nay-sayer' in his plea for a 'free death';[13] but perhaps the point of the story of the Last Supper derives from the reversal of the metabolic logic of consumption. Can we only 'learn to give food to the other' by allowing ourselves to be eaten? The Last Supper scene in Pasolini's *Il Vangelo secondo Matteo* [The Gospel According to St. Matthew] (1964), dispenses with art-historical allusions such as those in *Mamma Roma* and *La Ricotta*. The disciples sit together around their meal rather than in a row down a long table; they eat pieces of bread and meat with their fingers — seriously but not solemnly. The supper only develops out of the defending of the woman who rubs oil into Christ's hair, then through the naming of the person who will betray the host, with voices echoing the words 'sono io?', and finally through the sharing of bread and the passing of the wine cup: my body ['*mio corpo*'], my blood. The images of the disciples drinking are repeatedly intercut with the smiling face of Jesus; his union with the company around the table has clearly succeeded.

---

13   Friedrich Nietzsche, *Thus Spoke Zarathustra: A Book for All and None*, ed. by Adrian Del Caro and Robert B. Pippen, trans. by Adrian Del Caro (Cambridge, UK and New York: Cambridge University Press, 2006), p. 54 f.

The Utopia of Harmony in the Animal World

For Pasolini, who had so often lamented the decline of rural life in Italy, the Last Supper was an event that could only have taken place within an agrarian culture. There is no pelting of food which has to be rapidly gulped down as in *La Ricotta*. Rather, there is a calm giving and taking. But why is it the bread that Jesus reaches for in order to share with the others and declare it his body? On the table there is also — in Pasolini's film at least — a dish containing pieces of meat. And is not Jesus himself identified in numerous liturgical texts with the sacrificial lamb? Meat, however, is a food rarely eaten in agrarian cultures. Animals are simply too valuable as beasts of burden and draught animals, as providers of milk, butter, cheese and wool, to be eaten at every opportunity. Therefore, meat was often only eaten within the context of sacrificial feasts. It is known that the feast of Passover, commemorating the deliverance of the Israelites from slavery in Egypt, was imminent. The Pessach lambs had already been slaughtered, although they were not supposed to be eaten until the day of the feast itself, which is why the Gospels make no mention of lamb being on the menu of the Last Supper. Bread and wine, on the other hand, are symbolic foodstuffs, and feature prominently in the day-to-day life of rural society. And metabolic criticism always asks *what* is being eaten and how it can be shared. The sharing of meat is complicated. Who gets the best pieces? And who has to make do with bones or fat? This is treated in ancient myth, for example in the story of Prometheus's deception over sacrificial meat, while even the etymological roots of the words for bread in different languages refer to the practice of sharing and — as in *compain* in old French, *Kumpan* in German and *companion* in English — friendship.

The utopia of a creation 'not founded on eating' also aims at a renunciation of meat, slaughter and sacrifice. It harks back to the eschatological vision of peace among animals expressed by the Prophet Isaiah,

> Then the wolf shall live with the sheep and the leopard lie down with the kid; the calf and the young lion shall grow up together; and a little child shall lead them; the cow and the bear shall be friends, and their young shall lie down together. The lion shall eat straw like cattle; the infant shall play over the hole of the cobra, and the young child dance over the viper's nest. (Isaiah 11: 6-8)

Such a utopia of humans and animals living in a peaceful, paradisiacal community is considered in Pasolini's film about the large and small birds, *Uccellacci e uccellini* [The Hawks and the Sparrows] (1966). This film unfolds in two time sequences: firstly the present, in which a father (Toto) and son (Ninetto Davoli) wander through the suburbs accompanied by a talking raven; and secondly in the time of St Francis of Assisi, who gives two monks the task of carrying to a conclusion his preaching to the birds, 'starting with two very different types of bird: the high and mighty hawk and the unassuming sparrow'. Brother Ciccillo (Toto) learns the screeching of the hawk, to whom he preaches the gospel of peace among birds. From time to time, Ninetto casts a glance heavenwards, to the garden of paradise containing every species of animal, but also to a table laden with food. God urges him to eat as much as he wants, and he stuffs his mouth full of — ricotta. The long wooden table bears loaves of bread, cheese and melons, but no meat. Their ensuing ministry to the sparrows turns out to be more complicated, until it dawns on Ciccillo that with sparrows one communicates not by chirping but by hopping. And so they hop the following dialogue, which again revolves around food. 'We are the servants of the Lord, we bring you Good News', begins Ciccillo. 'At last!' answer the sparrows, 'We've been waiting so long for it'. The monk is delighted: 'Really? That's wonderful', he says, whereupon the sparrows reply, 'Yes, especially in winter, when snow blankets the ground and in the countryside we can't find a crumb to eat'. The man of God is irritated, 'Wait a moment! What kind of Good News are you expecting then, my friends?' — and he is told, 'The tidings of heaps of millet and tender wheat for us so that we can grow as fat as thrushes!'.[14] But this will not do — the sparrows also need to love like the hawks — and to fast.

In the present day, Toto and Ninetto are taught by the speaking raven that 'Europe is haunted by the spectre of a crisis of Marxism'.[15] The continent is being led back into a pointless cycle of production and consumption, and also to violence,

> War between India and Pakistan; war over Trento and Trieste! […] And so Gandhi was right! Like Gandhi we must always triumph without violence! You should have conducted yourselves more like Gandhi! […] And in a single act of gentleness you could have brought the Communist Revolution and the Gospel into harmony![16]

What should Marxists do about the crisis of Marxism, asks the raven — and answers with Pasolini,

---

14 *Uccellacci e uccellini*, dir. by Pier Paolo Pasolini (Italy, 1965).
15 Ibid.
16 Ibid.

Hold your governments up to ridicule, make martyrs of yourselves in the cause of a never-ending revolution, that power may be decentralised until the ultimate goal, anarchy, is achieved, that mankind may renew itself through continual revolution, that the red carnations of hope may eternally bloom![17]

However, yet again, making a martyr of oneself means allowing oneself to be eaten. For the 'teachers are there in order to be eaten in a spicy sauce', comments the raven, adding that 'those who eat and digest them will also become something of a teacher themselves'.[18] And indeed at the end of the film the bird has its neck wrung and is eaten by its companions — all that remain are a few feathers, claws, some tiny bones and its beak.

In the Pigsty

At the centre of Pasolini's *Teorema* [Theorem] (1968), possibly his best-known film, released two years after *Uccellacci e uccellini*, is another variation on the banquet. A Milanese industrialist family receives an unexpected visit from a guest played by Terence Stamp. This guest — the descendant of a Greek god or the French poet Arthur Rimbaud, whose works he reads — is his own gift to the host family. He shares his body through sexual relationships with every member of the family, from the housekeeper Emilia, the daughter Odetta and the son Pietro, to the mother Lucia and the father Paolo. He then abandons the family, who are left in a state of utter bewilderment. The catatonic Odetta is taken away to a psychiatric clinic; Pietro starts to paint abstract pictures — splatter and piss paintings in the style of Jackson Pollock; Lucia seeks serial sexual encounters with young men; Paolo hands his factory to his workers and removes his clothes on Milan station before wandering around the bleak wilderness we see during the opening credits. Meanwhile Emilia (played by Laura Betti) chooses the path of asceticism and martyrdom. After returning to her home village, she eats nothing but stinging nettles and is suddenly seen hovering over the rooftops like an angel glued to the sky. After this, she has herself buried alive, and a sacred stream springs from her tears. She translates the antique vision of the guest into a Christian logic of renunciation, imitation, self-sacrifice and the performing of miracles. The chosen exit routes — Odetta's insanity, Lucia's promiscuity, Pietro's piss paintings, Paolo's nakedness and Emilia's sanctity — are nevertheless

---

17   Ibid.
18   Ibid.

incapable of reciprocating the young man's gift or of evoking his return. It is the story of a failed Communion: according to Pasolini, the consumerism of bourgeois society is doomed.

The following year Pasolini made a dark, allegorical film based on his plays *Porcile* [Pigsty] (1966) and *Orgia* (1968). Despite its modest budget, this production, set partly in a pigsty and filmed in just a few weeks, brought together a cast of prominent actors from *Nouvelle Vague* circles: Anne Wiazemsky, Robert Bresson's heroine in *Au Hasard Balthazar* [Balthazar] (1966), who had already played Odetta in *Teorema*, Truffaut's favourite actor Jean-Pierre Léaud, Ugo Tognazzi, and Marco Ferreri, who, four years later, would help portray a related subject, a suicide pact based on unrestrained eating in *La Grande Bouffe* [The Grande Bouffe/Blow-Out] (1973). *Porcile* is about eating and being eaten. The film has two interwoven storylines: that of a young man (Pierre Clementi), who prowls a volcanic wasteland, becomes a cannibal and is ultimately sacrificed to wolves (Alsatians in the film), and that of a household in the Federal Republic of Germany which exemplifies the contrasts between the protest movement and the new alliance between capitalists and Nazi criminals. Julian (Jean-Pierre Léaud), the protagonist in the second story, shuts himself off from both sides, withdrawing even from Ida (Anne Wiazemsky), a girl who declares her love for him. In the end he is eaten by the pigs who were the sole objects of his erotic inclinations. The director regarded the film as an autobiographically inspired, cruel-but-tender parable, a 'Petrarch sonnet on a theme of Lautréamont'. He summed up its 'simplified message' as follows, 'Society, every society, devours its disobedient children as well as its children who are neither obedient nor disobedient'.[19] For Pasolini, the pigs symbolised on the one hand the bourgeoisie (in the sense of Brecht or George Grosz), and on the other, an archaic counterworld able to stand firm against industrialisation and capitalism. For him the pigs were associated with the ambivalence of barbarism — as a world both *post*- and *pre*-civilisation.

Opposition to capitalism manifests itself as cannibalism,

> Cannibalism is a semiological system. We need to restore it here to its full allegorical significance: as the symbol of a revolt seen through with the greatest possible rigour. The secret of the second hero, which allows him to communicate with the mystical universe and by means of which he is able to partially withdraw from the influence of his bourgeois family, the authority of his father, the captain of industry, is his love of the pigs. It is a symbolic love,

---

19   Pasolini, *Lichter der Vorstädte*, p. 121. [*Translation mine*]

a symbol analogous to cannibalism. With one difference: cannibalism is the symbol of absolute revolt, which comes close to the most appalling conditions of sanctity, whereas the love of pigs — a love that is after all possible — stops halfway.[20]

The pigsty symbolises society and simultaneously the wilderness — a site of resistance, martyrdom, sacrifice and consent to oneself being eaten. Pasolini's metabolic criticism is directed against a consumerism that ultimately sentences us to autophagy. In the unconscious eating that ignores the self-evidence of metabolic exchange we begin to eat ourselves — as in the almost unbearable scenes in Pasolini's last film *Salò o le 120 giornate di Sodoma* [Salo, or the 120 days of Sodom] (1975), in which the victims of those in power are forced — in a parody of the dinner party — to consume their own excrement. No longer is it the thing eaten that eats back but the eaters themselves, in a gesture of permanent suppression of any metamorphosis, from the first mouthful unto death.

---

20   Ibid., p. 123. [*Translation mine*]

Marcus Döller

PORNOGRAPHY AS PHILOSOPHY
Reflections on Pasolini's 'Petrolio'

Pasolini's last poetical work, 'Petrolio', is at once a novel and a gesture of resistance to the form of the novel. It is a novel only insofar as it resists, in its very form, being what a novel could be: this is why this 'novel' is a fragment. For the form of the novel, this means that the novel must resist what it means to be a novel. 'Petrolio' does not take the form of a novel; the reader only finds cursory hints of what the novel could be. In order to understand the 'birth of a new form',[1] we must first understand that the novel resists being a novel, and this manifests itself in the way in which these cursory remarks constitute the possibility of a novel in the reader's experience while, at the same time, the fragmentary notes make the reader experience that there is a resistance against of what it is to be a novel.[2]

In the following, I will describe an internal tension between the way in which the novel shapes the experience of subjectivity, on the one hand, and the way in which the aesthetical form of the fragment manages to deal with sexual transgression, on the other hand.

To be a subject means to have certain capacities: this is what constitutes subjectivity. To have certain capacities means to have specific abilities to perform certain acts. At the same time, however, these abilities not only have the structure of the subject's potential, they have a tendency to become naturalized. The form in which naturalized capacities to act manifest themselves in actions is the *mechanism*. The mechanism consists only of the empty repetition of something which the subject is able to do.[3]

---

[1] Armando Maggi, *The Resurrection of the Body: Pier Paolo Pasolini from Saint Paul to Sade* (Chicago: The University of Chicago Press, 2009), p. 157.
[2] This is why Giorgio Agamben talks about a 'possible or virtual book' in characterizing 'Petrolio', Giorgio Agamben, 'From the book to the Screen: The Before and the After of the Book', in *The Fire and the Tale* (Stanford: Stanford University Press, 2017), p. 94.
[3] Regarding this reading of the mechanism in Hegel, see also: Christoph Menke, 'Zweite Natur: Der schwerste Punkt', in *Autonomie und Befreiung* (Berlin: Suhrkamp Verlag, 2018), pp. 119–48.

But at the same time, the mechanism is able to open itself up to something which does not have the structure of pure mechanical iteration. I call this dialectical tension the *liberation of subjectivity*. In order to understand the liberation of subjectivity, we must grasp both moments involved: we have to understand how the pure mechanical structure resists liberation, and we have to understand how the transgression of the pure mechanical structure is part of the process of liberation. Pasolini's 'Petrolio' demonstrates how subjectivation works in this very dialectical tension between mechanization as a structuralized order of repetition, one the one hand, and a transgression of this mechanistic structure of repetition as an interruption, on the other.

My method will be to show how the transformation of subjectivity and transgression of the aesthetic form are internally connected to each other. The way in which the novel shapes the experience of the subject is also the way in which the novel creates a language that differs from the language of the form of subjectivity which it is trying to represent. In a close reading of 'appunto 55', I will be able to describe how Pasolini's novel approaches two different movements at the same time. One movement is the movement of the mechanization of subjectivity; the other movement — the counter-movement — is the transgression of a pure form of mechanism. — This is the way in which the two movements appear on the *level of subjectivity*. The other movement is the transgression of social-class borders within the social structure, while the counter-movement consists of the reproduction and restitution of social-class borders. — This is the way in which the two movements appear on the *level of social reproduction of the order*. Both movements — on the level of subjectivity and on the level of social structure — show a similar dialectic. On the level of the representation of subjective formation, we see how the subject is constituted through the form of mechanism, but, at the same time, this mechanical structure is never fully mechanical. On the level of the description of social structure, we see how social-class domination is constituted not against but rather through the transgression of the borders between the 'working class' and the 'bourgeoisie'. Both levels — the subjective and the social — entail an internal dialectical conjuncture in which the novel is able to create a consciousness of their mutual entanglement for the reader during the process of reading the text.

The significant experience of 'appunto 55' is as follows. The main character, Carlo, who doubles as two characters during the various annotations, is a middle-aged engineer in the beginning. Later, after his rebirth, Carlo transforms himself into a woman. In the following scene, Carlo meets some teenage boys and younger men behind a hill in a landscape situated between the urban space and the countryside.

The most striking aspect of 'appunto 55' manifests itself precisely in this dialectic conjuncture of the mechanism, on the one hand, and the transgression of the mechanism, on the other. This structure is not only an inner experience of subjectivity as perceived by Carlo in the novel, it is simultaneously a reflection on and transgression of the poetical form. The poetical form of prose represents how the young working-class men talk, while, in its capacity as a counter-movement to this working-class language captured in quotation marks, also representing the bourgeois language and the romantic description of nature as an ironic gesture, which demonstrates to the reader how class difference manifests itself in the smallest subconscious 'movements' and 'gestures' of subjectivity.

In the beginning, Carlo describes what he does as pure mechanical repetition. When the narrator describes the first encounter between Carlo and Sandro, he focuses on the way in which Carlo reduces his actions to the pure mechanical form of the performance.

> He looked at him without any expression, like one preparing to perform a duty that has to be reduced, if I can put it this way, to pure technique; that, besides, has already been determined and agreed on in advance. 'All that remained was to /carry it out'/, so to speak.[4]

Important here is the term 'senza espressione' — 'without any expression': The term is created in order to describe the pure mechanical repetition of what Carlo does in performing the sexual behavior of a prostitute.

> But Carlo's looks and actions — from the beginning, with the first one [...] — gave no sign that he was a participant. In sum, one immediate feature of Carlo's behavior was an imitation of the hurried services of a prostitute, who must not admit to doing what she does for pleasure, in addition to the money. If she revealed here pleasure, she could no longer ask for money. Thus Carlo, almost without having planned it, went down on his knees before Sandro and waited, expressionless and as if detached, to perform them diligently, and also with a complicit thoughtfulness.[5]

---

4 Pier Paolo Pasolini, *Petrolio*, trans. by Ann Goldstein (London: Secker & Warburg, 1997), p. 167.
5 Ibid.

The narrator describes that Carlo attempts to perform what it is to act like a prostitute. To act like a prostitute means to perform the pure form of mechanism. The form of the mechanism is nothing but an empty repetition. The mechanical form of repetition can only connect external relations of actions with each other. In the mechanical form of repetition, actions are only externally related because the subject has no inner relation to them. The term 'senza espressione' is able to articulate that the inner relation of the subject to the performance of his behavior is not possible. The subject is reduced to the pure external repetition of the movements in action. At the same time, however, the subject cannot entail only an external relation to the actions he performs. Exactly this is the dialectical counter-movement to the description of the mechanical form. The dialectical counter-movement is expressed in two ways: in the description of Carlo's experience of 'tenderness' when attempting to perform purely mechanical actions and in Sandro's 'shyness' in the state between sexual intercourse and his first contact with Carlo. Both counter-movements are internally related to the mechanical form in which Carlo's actions shape the experience of subjectivity.

> Sandro was, for his part, a little shy. But at that time boys had a code of behavior in common, even for a feeling as private and personal shyness. There was a smile for shyness, there were words for shyness, there were gestures for shyness. Of course, it was a slight shyness and therefore easily masked.[6]

The narrator describes how shyness is a form of subjectivation. The gestures and actions of shyness have a common form: they are produced by a social regime of subject formation. The way in which Sandro expresses his shyness is not a performance of individuality, rather, it is the performance of a common subject formation of a working-class boy with a 'good education'. For a complete understanding of the sexual transgression, this would mean that even the sexual transgression is constituted by a formation of subjectivity that is the presupposition of the transgressive act.

In these passages, the narrator develops a theory of what he calls 'gesti "codificati"' — 'codified gestures' — this concept is a concept which makes us able to understand that gestures are not prelinguistic and meaningless movements but an effect of 'good manners' and the formation of what it is to be a subject. Shyness is not situated between natural instincts and social achievements as signified performances. Rather, the gesture is produced and created by the way in which subjectivity is formed.

---

6   Ibid.

From the perspective of Carlo, this means that even he cannot perform 'the behavior of the prostitute' purely mechanically. The narrator makes us aware that Carlo is somewhat too affectionate in his performance.

> And from the beginning he did it mechanically, because that was precisely an aspect of the behavior of the 'prostitute', who forces the client to be content with the mechanicalness of the act she is paid to perform. But then, as if more and more /enamored of/ that infantile yet already overbearingly paternal penis with its knotty hardness and its tenderness, he began to /'put more feeling into it'/. Which gave him the overwhelming joy of hearing Sandro, slightly bent over him say, 'Bravo'. This word threw him into an abyss of tenderness, and tears nearly filled his eyes.[7]

The concept for this inability to reproduce 'the behavior of the prostitute' — the purely mechanical repetition — is 'tenderness', which breaks out of the logic of the mechanism. In Pasolini's annotation, the narrator always describes a slight tension within language. Not only does he articulate Carlo's inability to reproduce the sexual action purely mechanically as a form of 'tenderness', he also quotes the conventional 'working-class language' used to describe the performance of this action in terms of 'putting more feeling into it' at the same time. What the text does here is a twofold operation. First, it mentions Carlo's own bourgeois perspective; second, it mentions the 'working-class perspective' of the younger boys. In this description, the text is a movement and a counter-movement at the same time. It reproduces the hegemonial middle-class vocabulary while simultaneously quoting the 'working-class' language of the teenage boys. Both perspectives, the middle-class language and the working-class language, make us aware of the shift that is taking place between the purely mechanical reproduction of the sexual performances of what it is to act like a prostitute and the slight transgression of what it would mean to perform those actions purely mechanically. It is exactly in this tension that Pasolini's *appunto* provides an insight into how the dialectics between the transcendence of social-class borders, one the one hand, and the restitution of these class borders, on the other, must be conceptualized in their structure of movement and counter-movement.[8]

This tension between two different and opposed movements within the text has two contrasting temporal structures. Whereas the younger working-

---

7 Ibid., p. 169.
8 For these dialectics, see also Didier Eribon, *Returning to Reims*, trans. by Michael Lucey (Los Angeles: Semiotext(e), 2013).

class boys or men want to perform the sexual act they enjoy as fast as they can, Carlo on the other side tries to extend the act for as long as possible. But exactly this very desire to extend the act is a counter-movement to what the conventional movement in the actions of a prostitute would be. My claim is, that this tension characterizes the bourgeois perspective which the text is trying to destabilize or undermine. Both characters — Carlo and Sandro — feel a social pressure to perform the act as it would be a 'duty', but each perceives this pressure in a different way. It is exactly this difference that marks the class differences. The two different and opposed temporal regimes of the inner perspective of subjectivity in Carlo and Sandro collapse, however: because Carlo wants to perform the actions as mechanically as he ought to, but he does so too affectionately. Sandro wants to perform the act as fast as he can, but he feels pleasure when Carlo extends the act by performing it somewhat too affectionately. This tension is exactly the way in which a transgression of the class boundaries takes place.

When the act ends with Sandro's expression 'Bravo' the act has still not ended for Carlo. This is why Carlo's own inner perspective is described as 'abyss of tenderness',[9] which contradicts the interruption and standstill of the purely mechanical performances described as the conventional behavior of the prostitute earlier in the text. The tension within the text describes a double movement: Carlo's effort to perform the act purely mechanically and his inability to do so in a purely mechanical way at the same time. The mechanism is both: it is the purely external relation of subjectivity to the way in which the subject performs the social, even though the subject is not fully able to perform the social role of a prostitute in a purely mechanical way. This is the moment in which the class difference reproduces itself. Both moments, the movement of the mechanical performance of the act and the counter-movement of the affectionate non-performance of the act, articulate an inner tension in the way in which subjectivity is constituted thought the act. In Carlo's effort to control his performances in a purely mechanical way, reduced 'to pure technique'[10] in the repetition of his actions, something breaks out of the purely mechanical repetition. This 'something' cannot be planned or intended. It is the counter-movement within the movement of mechanical repetition. Exactly this tension marks the gap for a transgression within the sexual act. The text manages representation of these two opposed movements in showing that there is

---

9   Pasolini, *Petrolio*, p. 169.
10 Ibid., p. 167.

a mechanical reproduction produced by the normative order, on the one hand, and Carlo's inability to reproduce the mechanical form due to an inner experience within the application of the rules that does not fit into the rules, on the other.

> This time, the technique of a good whore was explicitly demanded of Carlo. The job of giving the cock an erection, something that falls within a norm better covered /by the rules/, apparently, than that of the two preceding cases. Carlo therefore tried to demonstrate his patient skill. This time, too, his heart was in a tumult, because the cock always appeared in the form of a miracle [...].[11]

The inner experience is described as 'tumulto' of his heart. It is his inner experience, his stance and his attitude towards his performance that gives birth to his counter-movement to the sheer mechanical imitation of a prostitute's behavior.

In his polemical writings about gay identity, Christian Maurel shows how homosexual desire is internally connected to the reproduction of class domination in the way in which the sexual act reproduces race stereotypes of 'Arab' masculinity by criss-crossing the difference between the masculine and feminine. What interests me in Maurel's analysis is what he calls 'homosexual behavior' insofar as it is 'bourgeois' in reproducing the form of mechanism in the sexual act.

> Almost all homosexual behavior is bourgeois, and I do not mean that in the moral sense that the labor movement intends when it condemns the class spirit of the bourgeoisie or their petty-bourgeois prejudices. I mean it in terms of mechanical repetition: instead of being invented, desire is recited by heart. This has to do with the fact that this desire is directed exclusively at the sex and not at the whole body. After all, it is not so clear that the anus does not know a gender difference and that its replacement weakens the great phallic signifier. The libidinal use of the anus — no matter how shameful it may be — calls on the phallus no less than the socially orthodox use of the vagina.[12]

Maurel describes here the 'mechanical repetition' and the 'recited' desire in opposition to the creative form of desire that could be invented in its performance. The bourgeois form of desire is repetitive because it is 'directed exclusively at the sex and not at the whole body' in its form. The bourgeois form is nothing but the pure form of mechanism. It is precisely

---

11 Ibid., p. 173.
12 Christian Maurel, *Für den Arsch*, trans. by Tobias Haberkon (Berlin: August Verlag, 2019), p. 25. [*Translation mine*]

in its mechanical structure that 'homosexual behavior is bourgeois' in reproducing class-differences in the very moment in which they are transgressed within the sexual act. Beyond this, Pasolini's work tells us that the purely mechanical reproduction of the sexual performance is not possible: it opens itself up for something that transgresses mechanical reproduction. The name of this radical interruption is 'the holy' — it is the name for a transgressive experience.

> Only after the last drop of semen was squeezed out did Sandro loosen his hold and free Carlo's head. Carlo pulled away and looked at Sandro's cock, a few inches from his nose: in that condition, already a little soft, it seemed even bigger; and then there was the translucence of the semen and the saliva, which gave a kind of bestial and obscene lividness to the color of his skin; and yet there was something sacred in that oily liquid. Carlo raised his eyes to Sandro's face again for an instant. It was another instant equal to a century of contemplation.[13]

After the actual sexual act between Sandro and Carlo there happens on the side of Carlo the experience of 'something sacred' in the sheer temporal extension of a moment. The expression 'a century of contemplation' makes use of the term of 'contemplation' ironically in order to articulate Carlo's inner experience. The text achieves two things here: it shows how the experience of 'something sacred' is able to transcend the conventional bourgeois order but at the same time the transcendence takes place only in Carlo's inner perspective; in this moment, it reproduces class separation. The reader never actually learns anything about the inner perspective of the working-class men. Only when they are able to talk in a reduced way, the reader gains an insight into how these men deal discursively with their desire. The inner experience of the working-class men is completely withdrawn from the reader.

The text aestheticizes the materiality of the body in the structural extension of time. This shapes the experience of 'something sacred' in the inner perspective of Carlo's experience. Later, one of the men rapes him. In this very moment, Carlo is able to experience the absolute. 'The cosmos viewed with eyes glued to the ground was even more absolute: a single flat expanse divided from the luminous strip of the sky by an almost perfect line.'[14] Of course, this is an ironic gesture of the text, but, at the same time, the text describes Carlo's experience of inner transcendence.

---

13 Pasolini, *Petrolio*, p. 170.
14 Ibid., p. 175.

The text is very careful in describing gestures and movements that are almost unrecognized by the subjects themselves. The strategy of the textual descriptions consists in the detailed conscious observation of these withdrawn elements by showing how these withdrawn elements constitute iterations of a mechanical structure of subjectivity. This mechanical structure is, at the same time, the reproduction of the social class-order.

> At the same time, the gesture a boy makes when he is alone — in order to pee against a bush or a wall or any solid structure […] as the rules recommended […] xxx xxx xxx xxx xxx — was made with completely natural care. Thousands of times that gesture […] /is/ hidden, removed from all profane curiosity, out of sight of the stare of strangers, men or women; and now in a situation so different it remained perfectly the same […].[15]

What the text describes is a hidden gesture, a gesture completely withdrawn from any perception. At the same time, however, there is a structurally similar feature of repetition in every performance of this gesture; this defines the gesture as a performance of the gesture. The gesture is nothing but an identical repetition of an action in its very performance. The text describes how a gesture that is supposed to be a gesture of intimacy is actually the repetition of a conventional form and the normalization of subjectivity. There is no difference in the performance of the act, whether observed or unobserved. The text not only describes an observation, the text connects this observation to something that is not observable, namely, the innermost intimacy of withdrawn gestures. But when the hidden form of the gesture becomes observable, the gesture does not change: the gesture is still exactly the same, because the gesture is only constituted through a mechanical repetition.

In this movement, the text reproduces the difference between the inner and the outer. This is the most basic ontological difference for political liberalism and liberal subjectivity. In establishing the difference between the inner and the outer, however, the text also subverts this very difference. There is a 'hidden' element 'removed from all profane curiosity' on the one side, and there is something resisting 'against the mysteriously dark skin of his abdomen'[16] on the other side. But the text does not reproduce the difference he refers to. In the very iteration of this difference, the text shows that the difference is, in fact, an indifference, resisting and criss-crossing the

---

15 Ibid., p. 191.
16 Ibid.

difference he refers to in the iteration of that difference. To be sure, the text draws a distinction between 'hidden' gestures and observable gestures, but, in making this distinction, the text shows that both forms of gestures are fundamentally the same. This is what it means to understand the mechanical repetition of gestures in their performance. The mystery has become profane, which means that the mystery has the structure of repetition.

In order to designate this structure, Pasolini uses the concept 'gesti "codificati"',[17] which refers to the idea that gestures are expressions of codified behavior. Codified behavior has the structure of mechanical repetition. The form of mechanical repetition is the way in which class-domination reproduces within subjectivity. This is important because Carlo — who represents the bourgeois perspective — is not only able to break out of the purely mechanical form in the repetitive performance, he is also able to make innermost transgressive experiences of 'something sacred' and the 'absolute' in his attempts to imitate a prostitute's behavior. But it is precisely this inability to behave like a prostitute that marks his class-position. Because his inability to reproduce the mechanical behavior of a prostitute shows that his sexuality is able to open itself to transgressive experiences. The working-class men, in contrast, are integrated into the repetitive order because here, too, gestures are codified and integrated into an order marked by the disciplination and normalization of subjectivity.

Through the term 'gesti "codificati"', the text is able to make the reader experience that the gesture is not only an interruption of repetitive action structures. The gesture is also integrated into the social form of class domination in which subjectivity is shaped and defined. The gesture is not only an interruption within the action 'as a kind of stalled action' that is able 'bring to a halt forms of violence accepted',[18] the gesture is simultaneously integrated into the structure of the action and able to reproduce violence and class difference. What Pasolini's text describes here is the form in which the subject is integrated into the class order. To be integrated into the class order means both, it means to be able to transgress the order and suspend the order, but transgression and suspension of the order is the way in which the order reproduces and stabilizes itself. This is why the experience of 'the holy' as an experience of the absolute is only possible for Carlo from his own bourgeois perspective. But this experience of the absolute as an interruption within the innermost experience must be thought at the

---

17   Ibid., p. 168.
18   Judith Butler, 'When Gesture becomes Event', in *Inter Views in Performance Philosophy*, ed. by Anna Street, Julien Alliot, and Magnolia Pauker (Basingstoke: Palgrave Macmillan, 2017), pp. 178 and 182.

same time as the other side of the integration of the normalized subject in and through the transgressive sexual intercourse. The concept 'gesti "codificati"' is able to articulate this truth. It makes the reader aware of the fact, that inherent to the repetition of the withdrawal there is something, a social positivity, that never really dissolves or disappears through the experience of negativity in the sexual intercourse, the experience of negativity is rather something that is able to reproduce the social formation in its class-division all the way through. But this does not mean that all negativity is able to be integrated into the social formation. For at least one moment in time, the ordinary flow of temporality is suspended. This brief moment of rapture expands time to its extreme. The rapture expands time to eternity, and eternity manifests itself within the present.

At the very end of 'appunto 55', the text develops his own theory of how the 'flesh' is inscribed in the social order of class domination.

> An hour is a hole. Where time that is not consecutive accumulates. He [Carlo] did not love Pietro only for that gigantic piece of flesh that he had in his mouth, smooth and hard, with its shapes that were as if /created/ by a mold, although they were so overwhelmingly themselves, new, /never/ seen: with their heat, their odor, and that lividness, almost abjectness — that is, something not innocently animal — which oozed out. He loved that boy also for what he did not give him and could not give him; for example, that he, Carlo, was unable to enjoy the act completely — without/other thoughts, which sought/the reasons for his enjoyment. That he was there only for the time purely necessary to obtain that pleasure which to boys seem so important and which they cannot resist. That he was about to leave and disappear forever, taking away with him all that he had given. As soon as that piece of flesh had come out of Carlo□s mouth and, still swollen and dripping, had been put back sideways inside the briefs and then closed up inside the pants that would be buttoned up tight again, he would become that untouchable and mysterious thing he was by nature, by the decision of society. Pietro□s return, soon, to his own life was the resealing of a social pact. And what he returned to was poverty, the world of work. For this reason Carlo liked in him, besides his naked, powerfully revealed sex, the smell of grease from the shop that he had about him, the absolute, innocent casualness of his clothes, the expressive force of those overalls, and, especially, the fact that he was there for a short while, that he was ready to disappear; because all this, in spite of being so obvious and irrelevant, so transparent in itself, was on the other hand the symbol of a profound social difference: the world of the other class, which was almost the world of another life. It was that which made Pietro, and all the others, dear; and their love of money, even if money was only a pretext, derived from a whole way of life, a whole economy.[19]

---

19   Pasolini, *Petrolio*, pp. 193–94.

This final passage develops both a theory of subjectivity and a theory of social class division in a nutshell. What is decisive here is that social-class difference is embodied in the flesh of the subject. The 'gigantic piece of flesh' is not completely meaningless, it is inscribed in the social order and the social order is an order of class domination. Of course, the 'gigantic piece of flesh' appears to Carlo as something 'new' or 'never seen' but, at the same time, it is social-class difference inscribed in the flesh. Not as something positive, but rather as negativity. This is why Carlo's desire, then, is constituted by 'what he did not give him and could not give him'; it is the negativity of the desire with regard to the other. But the lack in the desire with regard to the other is not an abstract withdrawal; it is, rather, a withdrawal constituted through class division. Carlo 'was unable to enjoy the act completely' because he is aware of the fragile, episodic character of the experience. This is why he tries to expand the act in its temporal structure. The formulation that interests me here is that the 'flesh [...] would become that untouchable and mysterious thing he was by nature, by the decision of society' — this formulation entails a fundamental dialectical thought. From Carlo's perspective, there is something 'untouchable and mysterious' in the 'flesh' of Pietro, the working-class man. But this 'untouchable and mysterious thing' is only the appearance of the 'flesh' in his desire. At the same time, Pietro's 'flesh' is constituted through nature, and this nature takes the form of a *created* nature, because it is the nature of the social order. The text goes very far in making the reader aware about the way in which what appears to the bourgeois perspective as an 'unteachable and mysterious thing' is, in fact, 'a decision by society'. Society creates nature. It is this very creation of nature that produces the 'untouchable and mysterious thing' for the bourgeois desire. The creation of nature is nothing more than the creation of the 'untouchable and mysterious thing' for the bourgeois perspective. It would be wrong to claim that the mystery no longer exists in modernity. The mystery is existing as an ideological effect of society, which produces and reproduces class-domination. But it is precisely this ideological effect that creates an 'unteachable and mysterious thing' which cannot be controlled fully by the bourgeois desire. The creation of nature by and through society is the creation of a withdrawal. But the withdrawal is the return to the order.

Jun Fujita Hirose

PASOLINI AGAINST THE CINEMA OF POETRY
Pasolini and Deleuze

Cinema of Poetry and Neocapitalism

In the chapter on the 'perception-image' in *Cinema 1: The Movement-Image* (1983), Gilles Deleuze concludes his reading of Pier Paolo Pasolini's conference paper entitled 'The "Cinema of Poetry" [*Il 'cinema di poesia'*]' and pronounced in June 1965 at the first International Exhibition of New Cinema in Pesaro, by saying:

> Of Pasolini's very important thesis we retain only this: that the perception-image might find a particular status in 'the free indirect subjective shot', which would be like a reflexion of the image in a camera-self-consciousness.[1]

If so, what does the French philosopher *not* retain of the text, in which the Italian film director contemporaneously testified to the emergence of what he called 'cinema of poetry', characterized by using the 'free indirect subjective shot [*soggettiva libera indiretta*]'?

What Deleuze doesn't take up from Pasolini's paper is its remark on the 'pretextuality [*pretestualità*]' of the free indirect subjective shot in the cinema of poetry.[2] Pasolini argues:

---

1 Gilles Deleuze, *Cinéma 1: L'Image-mouvement* (Paris: Éditions de minuit, 1983), p. 110 [*Cinema 1: The Movement-Image*, trans. by Hugh Tomlinson and Barbara Habberjam (Minneapolis: University of Minnesota Press, 1986), p. 76]. [*Translation mine*]

2 We have a very important previous study by Maria Rosaria Gioffrè ('Deleuze e Pasolini: Un discorso indiretto libero', *Agon*, 1 (June 2014)). Our text is particularly inspired by her following argument: In 'the cinema of poetry defined by Pasolini as realm of the free indirect subjective shot', 'the latter is however — we shouldn't forget it — only a pretext for the author's personal expression. It is probably this attribution of a poetic character to the tendency, observable in the film-makers taken in consideration by Pasolini, to telling about one's self rather than about the other, through a strong and insisting expressivity, that interdicted the Italian film-maker from recognizing other forms of free indirect subjective

> The 'cinema of poetry' [...] has the characteristic of producing films of a double nature. The film which we normally see and receive is a 'free indirect subjective' one [...], due to the fact that the author makes use of the 'dominant psychological state of mind in the film' — which is that of an ill, not normal protagonist — to make a continuous mimesis of it [...]. Under such a film runs the other film, that is, the one that the author would have made even without the pretext of *visual mimesis* with his protagonist: a totally and freely expressive-expressionistic film.[3]

Determined by its tradition historically formed as that of a 'language [*lingua*] of narrative prose', the cinema, in practice, cannot allow itself direct access to the 'language [*lingua*] of poetry',[4] even though it's the latter that corresponds to the cinema's 'original oniric, barbaric, irrelugar, aggressive, visionary quality'.[5] If the cinema of poetry employs the free indirect subjective shot and organizes in it the visual mimesis of the author with his protagonist, it's only because the 'traditional narrative convention',[6] always in force in the realm of production of films, obliges it to do so for the purely pretextual purpose. In short, what the cinema of poetry expects from using the free indirect subjective shot is not more than 'some narrative alibi'[7] or 'pseudo-tellings [*pseudoracconti*]'.[8]

It's well known that in the paper in question, Pasolini analyzes the works of Michelangelo Antonioni, Bernardo Bertolucci, and Jean-Luc Godard as examples of the cinema of poetry. On *Red Desert* (*Deserto rosso*, 1964), he writes:

> [Antonioni] has finally succeeded in representing the world seen by *his* eyes, because *he has substituted, in whole, his own delirious vision of aestheticism for a neurotic woman's vision of the world*: a substitution in whole justified by the possible analogy of the two visions.[9]

---

    shot, i.e., more authentically 'plurivocal' forms, such as those pointed out by the French philosopher: the idea that a true plurivocality, a heterogeneity of not pretextual gazes, cannot proceed from the poetic genre, but probably [it's] necessarily tied, in Bakhtinian way, to the narrative prose [...]'.

3   Pier Paolo Pasolini, *Empirismo eretico* (Milan: Garzanti, 2000, third edition), pp. 191–92 [*Heretical Empiricism*, trans. by Ben Lawton and Louise K. Barnett (Washington, DC: New Academia Publishing, 2005, second English edition), p. 182]. [*Translation mine*]
4   Ibid., p. 180 [p. 172].
5   Ibid., p. 187 [p. 178].
6   Ibid.
7   Ibid., p. 195 [p. 85].
8   Ibid., p. 194 [p. 184].
9   Ibid., p. 189 [pp. 179–80])

Still, Pasolini points out that Antonioni's 'delirious vision of aestheticism' is technically constituted of a set of 'obessive framings',[10] and asserts that it goes beyond its presupposed 'possible analogy' with the neurotic heroine's vision, in the sense that its excessive obsessiveness 'contradicts not only the norm of common cinematic language [*linguaggio*], but also the very internal regulation of the film as "free indirect subjective" one'.[11] The 'substitution in whole' takes place by transgressing or ignoring what 'justifies' it. What are purely pretextual in a film of cinema of poetry are not only the free indirect subjective shot and the visual mimesis of the author with his characters, but also the characters in person and their psychological illness.

Actually, Pasolini considers that the neurotic characterization of personages in the cinema of poetry is a straight outcome of the bourgeois ideology, in which should live and work the authors such as Antonioni, Bertolucci, or Godard. That ideology deprives them of 'class consciousness'[12] and makes them 'identify [themselves] with all of humanity in an irrational interclassism'.[13] It means that from those authors' point of view, their characters 'can only be chosen from [their] own cultural circle: therefore analogous to [them] by culture, language [*lingua*] and psychology'.[14] If it's through their mimesis with a *different* vision that the authors obtain a 'poetic freedom',[15] what provides them with such differentness in the world of *sameness*? It's nothing but the illness as anomaly supposedly produced by accident in such a totally homogenized, leveled world. In the cinema of poetry, the authors forge their neurotic characters as 'exquisite flowers of the bourgeois class'.[16] Throughout the paper, Pasolini never questions if the neurosis really exists in the bourgeois world, but he does insist on the fact that it functions as a bourgeois concept of differentness, and goes so far as to affirm: 'If [the pretextual characters] belong to the other social world, they are mythicized and assimilated through the typification into the anomaly, the neurosis, the hypersensibility, etc.'.[17] The cinema of poetry not only creates fictitious neurotic characters *ex nihilo*, but also comprehends the really existing proletarians and subproletarians in an irrationally imagined

---

10   Ibid., p. 189 [p. 179].
11   Ibid., p. 192 [p. 182].
12   Ibid., p. 185 [p. 176].
13   Ibid., p. 195 [p. 185].
14   Ibid.
15   Ibid., p. 189 [p. 180].
16   Ibid., p. 195 [p. 185].
17   Ibid.

interclassist or, rather, *monoclassist* world, by categorizing them into psychological or sensitive anomalies.

The cinema of poetry is a bourgeois or capitalistic product, not only for its monoclassism on the free indirect subjective level, but also for its 'neo-formalistic researches'[18] on the poetic level, where 'the language [*linguaggio*] frees itself of function and presents itself as 'language [*linguaggio*] as such', as style'.[19] If its monoclassist aspect comes from the ideological nature of the bourgeoisie, its neo-formalist one, in turn, corresponds to the contemporaneous 'evolution — that we can call anthropological — of the bourgeoisie [...] along the lines of an "internal revolution" of capitalism, that is, along those of neo-capitalism'.[20] In the text entitled 'New Linguistic Questions [*Nuove questioni linguistiche*]' and originally published in the PCI's official organ *Rinascita* on December 26th, 1964, i.e., six months before the conference at Pisaro, Pasolini explains that evolution in the following terms: 'the paleo-industrial bourgeoisie becomes neo-capitalistic, at least *in nuce*, and the boss' language [*linguaggio padronale*] is substituted with the technocratic language'.[21] What he means by neo-capitalistic 'technocratic language' is the Tayloristic managerial language, formed with 'scientific' or 'technical' conceptions of the production. Pasolini parallels the ongoing poetic turn of cinema with such a technocratic turn of bourgeois language, considers both of them as historical returns to formalism, and puts forward that the former is an integral part of the latter. In 'The "Cinema of Poetry"', he sociohistorically contextualizes the 'tendency of the most recent cinema [...] toward a "cinema of poetry"',[22] by arguing that it 'appears as a sign of a strong and general resumption of formalism, which constitutes the average and typical production of the cultural development of neo-capitalism'.[23] For him, it's the very capitalism, turned technocratic, that 're-attributes to the poets a late-humanistic [*tardo-umanistica*] function: the myth and technical consciousness of form'.[24] If Godard's cinema, for example, consists in demonstrating that '[e]verything that is fixed in movement by a camera is

---

18   Ibid.
19   Ibid., p. 192 [p. 182].
20   Ibid., pp. 195–96 [p. 185].
21   Ibid., p. 20 [p. 17].
22   Ibid., p. 183 [pp. 174–75].
23   Ibid., p. 195 [p. 185].
24   Ibid., p. 196 [p. 185].

beautiful',[25] such a 'technicistic [*tecnicistico*]' formalism[26] shows nothing but a poet's subordination to the command of capitalism in transformation.

That said, Pasolini goes beyond discerning the above mentioned double implication of the cinema of poetry in the bourgeois or capitalistic culture. Actually, what Pasolini was witnessing in the 1960s is the veritably 'antholopogical' process in which the bourgeois ideological or *ideal* monoclassism came to be socially *materialized* through the technocratic-formalistic turn of capitalism, especially in Italy. The word was tending to turn into flesh. In 'New Linguistic Questions', he notes:

> [W]hile the big and small bourgeoisie of paleo-industrial and commercial type never has succeeded in *identifying itself with the entire Italian society* and has made the literary Italian its class language [*lingua di classe*] by imposing it from above, the nascent technocracy of the North hegemonically identifies itself with the entire nation and elaborates, then, a new type of effectively national culture and language [*lingua*].[27]

The bourgois monoclassist linguistic and cultural subsumption of society remained *formal*, i.e., only formally national, when the paleo-industrial and commercial bourgeoisie was imposing the literary language [*lingua*] on the society, but tends to turn *real*, i.e., 'effectively national', when the bourgeoisie becomes neo-capitalistic and begins to make its technical or technicist language [*linguaggio*] penetrate into the society: '[T]he Italian as national language [*lingua*] is born',[28] when 'what is at the helm of the language [*lingua*] [is] not the literature any more but the technique'.[29] The anthropological evolution of the bourgeoisie produces an anthropological leap of the entire Italian society. The cinema of poetry actively engages in this shift. With its monoclassist and neo-formalist praxises, the cinema of poetry 'forms a part of the general movement of recuperation, by the bourgeois culture, of the territory lost in the battle with Marxism and with its possible revolution',[30] namely, of the proletariat as the class which Marxist movement has created by bipolarizing the bourgeois society and has been maintaining by continuously provoking and organizing the class conflict.

---

25   Ibid., p. 191 [p. 181].
26   Ibid., p. 192 [p. 181].
27   Ibid., p. 20 [p. 17].
28   Ibid., p. 21 [p. 17])
29   Ibid., p. 22 [p. 18].
30   Ibid., p. 195 [p. 185].

Free Indirect Subjective Cinema and Renewed Marxism

The most important point to note in Pasolini's paper on the cinema of poetry is the fact that the author places himself *against* that cinema and considers that his own cinematic work does *not* form a part of it. In the concluding part of the text, Pasolini says by referring to Franco Fortini's contemporaneous observation of 'the end of the [writer's] social mandate' such as defined by Mayakovsky: 'Naturally, there is the reserve, due to my moralism as Marxist, of a possible alternative: that is, of a renewal of that writer's mandate which at this moment appears expired'.[31] The writer's renewed social mandate formulated by Fortini himself consists in 'prefiguring the party within the society' where 'the Party is not the party any more', by 'working [...] *as if* that body that we still call Party existed as a whole [...], as if it really occupied its own place, which is between the individual and the class'.[32] This is not the one that Pasolini has been imposing to himself as film director since his first film *Accattone* realized in 1961. He bets, rather, on the fact that the neo-capitalistic real subsumption of society has not been completed yet in Italy in the 1960s: if the proletariat has already been recuperated by the bourgeois culture, the subproletariat still remains intact. The film-makers' renewed social or, better, *political* mandate, for Pasolini, must consist in their entering a visual mimesis with the really existing subproletarians.

What opposes Pasolini to the cinema of poetry the most is his categorical rejection of any 'pretextual' use of the free indirect subjective shot. Here the Italian filmmaker rejoins the French philosopher, who reads his paper on the cinema of poetry without taking into account its remark on the triple pretextuality in that cinema, namely, those of the free indirect subjective shot, of the visual mimesis in it, and of the 'problem of the neurosis by alienation'[33] affecting the characters. What Deleuze aims in his reading of Pasolini's text is to extract a theory of *free indirect subjective cinema* out of it. For this purpose, Deleuze doesn't only leave out of account any pretextuality noted by Pasolini in the cinema of poetry, but even actively *de-pretextualizes* what Pasolini finds pretextual in it. For example, commenting on the above quoted passage in which Pasolini argues the 'substitution in whole' of the author's own aesthetic vision for his heroine's neurotic one in *Red Desert*, Deleuze writes: 'It is good, in fact, to have the

---

31 Ibid., p. 195 [p. 185].
32 Franco Fortini, 'Mandato degli scrittori e limiti dell'antifascismo, III: La fine del mandato sociale', *Quaderni piacentini*, 17–18 (July–September 1964), 5–10.
33 Pasolini, *Empirismo eretico*, p. 189 [p. 179].

neurotic character for further highlighting the difficult birth of a subject in the world'.[34] This doesn't correspond at all to how Pasolini presents Antonioni's neurotic protagonist: as we've already seen, he considers her as a purely 'pretextual character', whose supposed difficult becoming-subject hardly interest the author, and besides, as a purely ideological product of bourgeois monoclassism. De-pretextualizing its protagonist by *existentializing* the anomalous state in which she is caught, Deleuze represents Antonioni's work as an example of the free indirect subjective cinema and not of the 'cinema of poetry' as defined by Pasolini.

In other words, Deleuze *reverses* the primacy of the poetic over the free indirect subjective in the cinema of poetry. And, by doing so, he turns the latter into free indirect subjective cinema, which corresponds to his concept of 'double becoming' and to the 'modern political cinema' that he theorizes based on that concept. Actually, what Deleuze finds in the 'modern political cinema', especially in the Third World cinema, is the 'substitution in whole' in its *reversed* version. In the pages dedicated to the Quebecois film director Pierre Perrault's *'cinéma du vécu* [living cinema]' in *The Time-Image*, he writes by paraphrasing Pasolini's passage on *Red Desert*:

> What the cinema must grasp is not the identity of a character, whether real *or* fictitious, through his objective and subjective aspects. It is the becoming of the real character when he himself starts on 'making fiction [*fictionner*]', when he enters 'into the act of legend-telling [*légender*]' and so contributes to the invention of his people. [...] He himself becomes another [*un autre*], when he starts on fabulating [*fabuler*] without ever being fictitious. And the filmmaker for his part becomes another, when he 'takes as his intercessors [*s'intercède*]', in this way, real characters who substitute, in whole, their own fabulations [*fabulations*] for his own fictions. Both communicate in the invention of a people.[35]

In the free indirect subjective cinema, the author lets his really existing characters substitute, in whole, their fabulous or legendary vision for his fictitious vision, as opposed to the cinema of poetry, in which the author substitutes, in whole, his own poetic vision for his fictitious characters' anomalous vision. Deleuze calls 'double becoming'[36] what Pasolini calls

---

34 Deleuze, *L'image-mouvement*, p. 108 [p. 74].
35 Gilles Deleuze, *Cinéma 2: L'Image-temps* (Paris: Éditions de minuit, 1985), p. 196 [*Cinema 2: The Time-Image*, trans. by Hugh Tomlinson and Robert Galeta (Minneapolis: University of Minnesota Press, 1989), p. 150]. [*Translation mine*]
36 Ibid., p. 289 [p. 223].

'visual mimesis', in the sense that the author *becomes* his character *becoming* a people to come.

It's such an acrobatic reversing (*de-poeticizing* and *politicizing*) reading of Pasoloni's text on the cinema of poetry that allows the French philosopher to suggest: 'To his list of examples, Pasolini might have added his own example' over and above those of Antonioni, Bertolucci, and Godard.[37] Pasolini's cinema is a free indirect subjective one and forms, as such, a part of the modern political cinema or even of the Third World one, as the Italian filmmaker himself says of his subproletarian characters from Roman suburban slums [*borgate romane*] or from Southern Italy that they 'are simply characters from the Third World'.[38] Southern Italy belongs to the Global South, and Roman suburban slums are enclaves of the latter in the Global North. Pasolini calls himself a 'realist', in the sense that he believes that 'the cinema expresses the reality with the reality',[39] so that he 'avoids the fiction'[40] by 'choos[ing] the actors for what they really are'.[41] His subproletarian characters are played by real subproletarian people, including the professional actors. Still, the realism of his Third World cinema is far from being limited to making a social denunciation of misery or underdevelopment. Pasolini says in an interview realized in the same month at his conference at Pisaro:

> My cinematic inspiration, emerged in the heart of the 1950s, was born from Gramsci's poetics and his idea of a great national-popular literature. This made me overcome the positions of Neo-realism, which were too strictly lyrical and documentary [...]. I gave realism a personal twist which I would define as mythical or epic.[42]

Pasolini's Gramscian inspiration leads his cinema to a quadruple front: against the cinema of poetry, which neither sees the people as they exist, nor is interested in the constitution of a nation; against Neo-realism, which has well grasped the existing popular reality, but without posing the national question; against the paleo-industrial bourgeoisie, which has constituted the nation only on a rhetorical level (Gramsci calls it 'rhetoric-nation

---

37   Ibid., p. 109 [p. 75].
38   Pier Paolo Pasolini, *Polemica politica potere: Conversazioni con Gideon Bachmann*, ed. by Riccardo Costantini (Milan: Chiarelettere, 2015), p. 36.
39   Pasolini, *Empirismo eretico*, p. 141 [p. 124].
40   Pasolini, *Polemica politica potere*, p. 55.
41   Pier Paolo Pasolini, *Pasolini su Pasolini. Conversazioni con Jon Halliday* (Parma: Ugo Guanda, 2014), p. 79.
42   Pasolini, *Polemica politica potere*, p. 38.

[*nazione-retorica*]' in opposition to 'people-nation [*nazione-popolo*]'[43]); and against the emerging neo-capitalistic bourgeoisie, which is constituting a people-nation by subordinating the people to its hegemonic technocracy. Pasolini's national-popular cinema consists in letting the really existing subproletarian or popular characters substitute, in whole, their mythical or epic vision for the bourgeois author's intellectual vision: the author becomes-popular at the same time as his popular characters themselves become-nation, so that he enters the foundational process of a nation with them.

The subproletarian characters get out of their identity by forging a mythical or epic vision of nation and withdraw, at the same time, the bourgeois author from his identity by bringing him into a visual mimesis with them. In their double becoming, Pasolini and his characters vision their nation as what they are *before* or *after* the historical determination of their social identities. It's in this sense that Pasolini evokes his *innate* gaze by distinguishing it from the *acquired* one:

> When I see the things, I have a rational, critical gaze [*sguardo*], learned from the laic, bourgeois and then Marxist culture. There is a continuous critical exercise of my reason over the things of the world, but my veritable gaze, the most ancient and archaic one, which I have from my birth [...] and, therefore, which is my original [*originario*] gaze, is a sacral gaze.[44]

Here is the possibility of speaking of an 'interclassism' peculiar to Pasolini's political thought and having nothing to do with the bourgeois ideological monoclassism. The innate gaze, as preceding to any historical determination, is an interclass or, rather, *trans-class* faculty, necessarily common to the bourgeois author and his subproletarian characters. It's with such an innate and common gaze, and not with the acquired or historically formed one, differentiated as being proper to their class identity, that the characters make their fabulous or legendary vision of the world. And it's not by any 'possible analogy' but by the transverse sharing of a same gaze that Pasolini enters a visual mimesis with them. If the innate gaze is called 'sacral', it's because it surpasses or, better, dodges the historical by directly connecting the prehistorical to the post-historical: the nation that we are *after* our historical determination is to be found in what we are *before* it, in

---

43 Antonio Gramsci, 'Quaderno 3 (maggio–ottobre 1930)', *Quaderni Miscellanei (1929-1935)*, ed. by Giuseppe Cospito, Gianni Francioni and Fabio Frosini (Roma: Istituto della Enciclopedia Italiana, 2017), p. 390.
44 Pasolini, *Polemica politica potere*, p. 41.

an archeological manner. That's actually what Deleuze says about the 'real characters' of Jean Rouch's *Dionysos* (1984) in the pages on the modern political cinema:

> [T]he image of industrial society which brings together a Magyar mechanic, an Ivorian riveter, a West Indian sheet metal worker, a Turkish carpenter, a German mechanician woman, plunges into a Dionysian before [...], but this before is also an after, as the post-industrial horizon where the workers have respectively become a flautist, a tambourine player, a cellist, a soprano, forming the Dionysian procession which reaches the forest of Meudon.[45]

Welcome to the Desert of Physical Reality

In the paper entitled 'Tetis' and pronunced in 1973 at the conference on 'Erotism Subversion Merchandise [*Erotismo Eversione Merce*]', organized by the *Mostra Internazionale del Cinema Libero di Porretta*, Pasolini comes to state that the neo-capitalistic bourgeoisie has now accomplished its revolution in Italy by finally subordinating the subproletarian or popular classes, i.e., the South or the Third World, to its technocracy: 'At the end of 1960s, Italy has moved into the era of Consumerism and Subculture, loosing thus all reality, which has survived almost uniquely in the bodies and precisely in the bodies of the poor classes'.[46] His conjunctural analysis of the development of Italian capitalism obliges him to admit and declare the end of his Third World cinema or the disappearance of its material condition of possibility. He concludes his conference at Porretta Terme by saying:

> Until a few years ago (when I was thinking of *The Decameron* [*Il Decameron*, 1971] and the subsequent *Trilogy of Life*), the people [i.e., the popular classes] were still almost completely in possession of their own physical reality and the cultural model according to which it was configurated [...]. If [now] I wanted to continue with films like *The Decameron*, I couldn't make them anymore, because I wouldn't find anymore in Italy — especially among the youth — that physical reality [...] which is the content of such films.[47]

---

45   Deleuze, *L'Image-temps*, p. 198 [p. 152].
46   Pier Paolo Pasolini, 'Tetis', in *Saggi sulla politica e sulla società*, ed. by Walter Siti and Silvia De Laude (Milan: Mondadori, 1999), p. 261 ['Tetis', trans. by Patrick Rumble, *Pier Paolo Pasolini: Contemporary Perspectives*, ed. by Patrick Rumble and Bart Testa (Toronto: University of Toronto Press, 1994), p. 247]. [*Translation mine*]
47   Ibid., pp. 261–64 [pp. 246–49].

Pasolini's Gramscian national–popular project has been defeated by the neo-capitalistic bourgeoisie's technocratic one, after a decade of confrontation or rivalry.

Where are we to find the possibility of reactivating Pasolinian sacral realism after that definitive 'disappearance of the fireflies [*lucciole*]' under the technocratic light [*luce*] of neo-capitalism? As we've already seen, what distinguishes the neo-capitalistic bourgeois monoclassist subsumption of society from the paleo-industrial one consists in the fact that the former is real, while the latter was only formal. If the paleo-industrial bourgeoisie imposed the values like 'Church', 'Family', or 'Discipline' on people only on the formal or rhetorical level, the neo-capitalistic bourgeoisie promotes a set of subcultural or technical 'human models'[48] and makes people *desire* to assimilate themselves always more to those models by means of endless consumption of merchandises. Among such models, Pasolini pays particular attention to that of 'sexual freedom' and says: 'The conformistic anxiety to be sexually free transforms the young people into miserable neurotic erotomaniacs [...]'.[49] The same thing is true with all the other neo-capitalistic human models. Might such neurotic subjects, now coming into real existence in Italian society, serve as new intercessors for Pasolini? His answer is absolutely negative, because he considers the neurosis as the *normal* or *normative* state of desire in the neo-capitalistic society and not as an anomaly in any way. If the neurotics were fictitious 'exquisite flowers of the bourgeois class' in the paleo-industrial era, we are all really neurotic in the neo-capitalistic era.

The neo-capitalistic revolution is an anthropological one, in the sense that it has neuroticized all of the human bodies by its direct action on the libidinal economy. 'In this way', says Pasolini in his conference paper of 1973, 'the last place that reality occupied, namely the body, or the popular body, also disappeared'.[50] If his cinematic work had not been interrupted by his sudden death in November 1975, Pasolini should have had nothing to film but the very desert of physical reality. This is exactly what Deleuze finds prefigured in Pasolini's existing films. In the closing pages of *The Time-Image*, the philosopher writes: '[T]he deserts of Pasolini [...] make prehistory [...] the "essence" co-present with our history, the archaean base which reveals an interminable history beneath our own'.[51] In the new society where the subproletarian or popular bodies have completely disappeared

---

48   Ibid., p. 263 [p. 248].
49   Ibid.
50   Ibid., p. 264 [p. 248].
51   Deleuze, *L'Image-temps*, p. 317 [p. 244].

into their neuroticization, Pasolini should have intended to enter a visual mimesis with such a depopulated land, which now constituted the only physical reality remaining for his cinema of sacral realism.

Jay Hetrick
PASOLINI AND STRATEGIES OF RE-ENCHANTMENT

> *Reanimating the past is not a matter of resurrecting it as it was, of dreaming to make some 'true', 'authentic' tradition come alive. It is rather a matter of reactivating it, and first of all of learning to feel the smoke in our nostrils ... to activate memory and imagination regarding the way we have learned the codes of our respective milieus.*
>
> Isabelle Stengers[1]

Pier Paolo Pasolini's *La Rabbia* (1963) is self-described as 'an essay in film journalism'. Pasolini was of course highly suspicious of journalism — which he derides as 'false', 'moralistic', 'uncreative', and 'poorly stitched together' — and restated his intention to in fact 'invent a new film genre'.[2] While Georges Didi-Huberman rejects the latter claim, and instead situates this work firmly within the history of documentary editing, he does so by also bringing to mind Pasolini's idea of the cinema of poetry:

> The operation claimed by Pasolini in *La Rabbia* delegates to something like *visual poetry* — but also verbal, of course, since poems will be uttered by way of commentary on the images — the power to carry out a necessary *critical essay* on newsreel material of the 1950s and early 1960s. The critical virtue of such editing is possible, in Pasolini's eyes, only if an 'ideological decoding' is accompanied by a poetic power, a power that makes it possible to *see something else* in everything that the consensual images of film journalism show.[3]

---

[1] Isabelle Stengers, 'Reclaiming Animism', in *Animism: Modernity through the Looking Glass*, ed. by Anselm Franke (Cologne: Walter König, 2010), p. 187.
[2] Pasolini quoted in Roberto Chiesi, 'La Rabbia', in Pier Paolo Pasolini, *The Anger* (Minneapolis: RaroVideo, 2011) [on DVD].
[3] Georges Didi-Huberman, *Sentir de Grisou* (Paris: Minuit, 2014), p. 45. [*Translation mine*]

The idea of reanimating images of the past — by redeploying memory and recoding received meanings, in order 'to render sensible' the heterotopic gaps in history 'that have escaped us until then but that regard us directly'[4] — lies at the core of Didi-Huberman's political turn since at least the fourth volume of his *The Eye of History*. But before we turn to that, we should linger a bit further on the consensus, between Pasolini and Didi-Huberman, that *La Rabbia* should be understood as a cinematic essay which verges on poetry.

For Theodor W. Adorno, the essay is a hybrid form that 'provokes resistance because it is reminiscent of the intellectual freedom that, from the time of an unsuccessful and lukewarm Enlightenment all the way to the present has never really emerged, not even under the conditions of formal freedom'.[5] Although this article, completed five years before the first screening of *La Rabbia*, has been sufficiently commented upon in the literature, it may be useful for reconfiguring the main theme of this film: the possibilities for freedom, or at least resistance, in the post-Enlightenment period, which is marked by 'a disenchantment of the world' and 'the extirpation of animism'.[6] The essay form is important, for Adorno, not simply because it gives expression to — that is, represents — independent voices. It's critical value — with respect to a 'repressive order', which presupposes 'that all knowledge can potentially be converted into science' — is primarily due to its capacity to formally present an 'anachronistic eclecticism':[7]

> In the essay, the persuasive aspect of communication [...] is alienated from its original goal and converted into the pure articulation of presentation in itself; it becomes a compelling construction that does not want to copy the object, but to reconstruct it out of its conceptual *membra disjecta*.[8]

The essay resists an easy continuity of thought that would represent — like journalism — coherent self-identical things interacting with each other and with the world in a harmonious way. The essay form thus annuls 'the theoretically outmoded claims of totality and continuity'. It is necessarily

---

4   Georges Didi-Huberman, 'To Render Sensible', in Alain Badiou et al., *What is a People?*, trans. by Jody Gladding (New York: Columbia University Press, 2016), p. 85.
5   Theodor Adorno, 'The Essay as Form', *New German Critique*, 32 (1984), p. 152.
6   Theodor Adorno and Max Horkheimer, *Dialectic of Enlightenment,* trans. by Edmund Jephcott (Stanford: Stanford University Press, 2002), p. 2.
7   Adorno, 'The Essay as Form', p. 156.
8   Ibid., p. 169.

discontinuous because 'reality is fragmented' and does not function according to a higher rational order. Formally, it must be constructed by highlighting gaps and fissures rather than attempt to 'smooth them over [...] in such a way that it could always, and at any point, break off'.[9] *La Rabbia*, with its nearly incoherent presentation of discontinuities[10] — between image and text, between times and places, between sound and music, between documentary and poetry — certainly stands out as an exemplary expression of the cinematic essay. But, beyond a quick reference to the Early Romantics, Adorno doesn't present a workable picture of our fragmented reality. That is, he doesn't really offer us — here or elsewhere — a political ontology beyond a vague resistance to scientific comportment.[11] On the contrary, Maurizio Lazzarato very clearly articulates, not only Pasolini's pessimistic view of the shards of neoliberalism, but also how a cinema of poetry can be strategically deployed within it. More specifically, Lazzarato's work allows for a different interpretation of the dreadful scream that echoes from *La Rabbia* all the way to Pasolini's firefly article in the year of his death.

For Lazzarato, neoliberalism is marked primarily by a shift from war to wars, *ad nauseam*, the concatenation of which can be continuously seen, felt, and heard for the duration of *La Rabbia*. This is because 'the war machine of capital has, since at least the early 1970s, definitively integrated the state, war, science, and technology, clearly declaring the strategy of contemporary globalization [...] by attacking everywhere and with all means available the conditions of reality of the power struggle that imposed it'.[12] That is, in neoliberalism money functions as an apparatus of machinic enslavement. But, quite remarkably, Lazzarato understands cinema itself as a kind of 'war machine' that can be redirected against our contemporary society of the spectacle. This is because both capital and cinema function not only on the level of signifying signs — the recognizable and easily representable world of words and images — but also on the plane of what

---

9   Ibid., p. 164.
10 'A rather confused montage of film footage commenting on political issues of postwar Europe'. Mira Liehm, *Passion and Defiance: Film in Italy from 1942 to the Present* (Berkeley: University of California Press, 1984), p. 352.
11 For more on this, see my 'The Uses and Abuses of Bergson in Critical Theory', *Cosmos & History*, 17, 1 (2021), 99–136, especially the section on the Frankfurt School.
12 Marizio Lazzarato and Éric Alliez, *Wars and Capital*, trans. by Ames Hodges (Los Angeles: Semiotext(e), 2016), p. 28.

he calls, after Félix Guattari, 'asignifying signs'.[13] This point is crucial since at the core of Pasolini's own conception of the cinema of poetry is the idea that 'the semiology of cinema should be understood as no more than a chapter of the General Semiology of reality'.[14] This General Semiology, which he sometimes refers to as the 'Code of Reality', consists of different registers of signs that have the capacity to move us well beyond the received *logos*. This is important for Pasolini since 'not all thought is verbal'.[15] What he calls image-signs and gesture-signs are 'irrational, elementary, and barbaric, forced below the level of consciousness'[16] and therefore able to express events 'on the border of what is human'.[17] Such a widening of the field of semiology — for example, by taking into consideration the system developed by Charles Sanders Peirce[18] — is therefore necessary since 'all of "scientific" linguistics, including structuralism, has always ignored this original magic moment'.[19] We will come back to the two other main characteristics of Pasolini's cinema of poetry — its biunivocal nature and its use of free indirect style — in relation to *La Rabbia*. First, it may be useful to explore Lazzarato's further articulation of the ontology and semiology of cinema. This may help us to better grasp the kind of cinematic discontinuity at work in this film as well as give a more nuanced sense of its title.

Lazzarato more or less inherits Gilles Deleuze's film-philosophy and Guattari's semiotics, and renders them more explicitly political through slightly different readings of the works of Dziga Vertov and Walter Benjamin. Cinema is subsequently understood as 'a discontinuous movement of bodies that render sensible new matter, new affects, and new forces',[20] and 'cine-language becomes a powerful tool for the repudiation of the imperialism of signifying semiotics'.[21] As in Pasolini, this ontology

---

13 Jay Hetrick, 'Lazzarato's Political Onto-aesthetics', in Maurizio Lazzarato, *Videophilosophy: The Perception of Time in Post-Fordism*, ed. and trans. by Jay Hetrick (New York: Columbia University Press, 2019), p. xix. See also Maurizio Lazzarato, *Signs and Machines: Capitalism and the Production of Subjectivity*, trans. by Joshua David Jordan (Los Angeles: Semiotext(e), 2014), p. 109.
14 Pier Paolo Pasolini, *Heretical Empiricism*, trans. by Louise Barnett (Washington: New Academia Publishing, 2005), p. 238.
15 Ibid., p. 261.
16 Ibid., p. 172.
17 Ibid., p. 171.
18 Ibid., p. 280.
19 Ibid., p. 262.
20 Lazzarato, *Videophilosophy*, p. 21.
21 Ibid., p. 30.

and semiology of cinema reflects reality to such an extent that the universe is *itself* described as a 'metacinema'.[22] In Deleuze's *Cinema 1*, the universe of things — including humans — is presented as a Bergsonian flux of signaletic matter-images that connect and disconnect through the intervals, or gaps, between them. In the theoretical move from *Cinema 1* to *Cinema 2*, Deleuze's Leibniz — operated upon by Nietzsche — intervenes such that these gaps become discontinuous, irrational cuts which 'have a disjunctive and no longer conjunctive, value' and which stand on their own as primary sites of productive difference.[23] Here we move from Adorno's simple, fragmented discontinuity — expressed with the phrase *membra disjecta* — to a more 'disjointed and divergent' movement of re-animation, a 'disjunctive synthesis' that Deleuze calls *membra disjuncta*.[24] I argue elsewhere that this logic of disjunction, which Lazzarato builds upon with the work of Gabriel Tarde, functions as a non-Hegelian dialectic — beyond identity and negation — in which seeming continuity is *produced* out of a more profound movement of discontinuity.[25] I also show that it is incorrect to say that such 'political vitalism' simply obfuscates the movements of contradiction, opposition, or antagonism. Deleuze already anticipates this kind of misunderstanding in the preface to *Difference and Repetition*: 'the greatest danger' of thinking this new onto-logic is a Romantic collapse back into the 'beautiful soul […] far removed from bloody struggles'.[26] This is the context in which Lazzarato is able to introduce his latest book, co-authored with Éric Alliez, with the provocative phrase 'To Our Enemies'.[27] In any case, this discontinuous conception of the 'cinemachinic universe'[28] brings us back to both the form and the content of *La Rabbia*. This is because 'the genetic element of the image, the differential element of movement' is 'the *clinamen* of Epicurean materialism'.[29] That is, the differential, and seemingly aleatory, inclination of the swerve not only determines the

---

22   Gilles Deleuze, *Cinema 1: The Movement-Image*, trans. by Hugh Tomlinson and Barbara Habberjam (Minneapolis: University of Minnesota Press, 1986), p. 59.
23   Gilles Deleuze, *Cinema 2: The Time-Image*, trans. by Hugh Tomlinson and Robert Galeta (Minneapolis: University of Minnesota Press, 1989), p. 248.
24   Gilles Deleuze, *Logic of Sense*, trans. by Mark Lester (New York: Columbia University Press, 1990), p. 179.
25   See Jay Hetrick, 'The Uses and Abuses of Bergson in Critical Theory'.
26   Gilles Deleuze, *Difference and Repetition*, trans. by Paul Patton (New York: Columbia University Press, 1994), p. xx.
27   Lazzarato and Alliez, *Wars and Capital*, p. 11.
28   Anne Sauvagnargues, *Artmachines*, trans. by Suzanne Verderber (Edinburgh: University of Edinburgh Press, 2016), p. 55.
29   Deleuze, *Cinema 1*, p. 83.

continuity of its subsequent trajectory.[30] It is also the cause of collisions between atoms that ultimately produce recognizable things. It is precisely the violent encounter *between* two matter-images, the discontinuous break 'between two actions, between two affections, between two perceptions, between two visual images, between two sound images, between the sound and the visual' that 'renders sensible the indiscernible'.[31]

This reference to Epicurean philosophy is doubly significant since, in the second half of Book V of Lucretius' *On the Nature of the Universe* — between his account of the emergence of the *logos* from the cacophony of 'various noises' (1045) and the origin of the 'storms of war' (1290) — we read, for the first time in Classical Latin, the root of the term *rabbia*:

> When Molossian dogs first draw back | their large flabby jowls, expose hard teeth, | and start to growl with anger, their rage then | menaces with a very different sound from | when they merely bark and, with this noise, | fills every space around them. (1065)

Rabbia is not simply anger, as the English translation of Pasolini's film would have it, which is much too specific. It is rather a menacing — nearly rabid — noise that fills every space. The proto-Indo-European roots of the term even point to an unspecified impetuous passion, force, desire, or zeal. It is closer to the non-logocentric, inhuman rabble expressed by Pasolini's image-signs and gesture-signs, which are 'irrational, elementary, and barbaric'. In English, rabble refers not only to incoherent, rambling speech but also to the disorderly crowd of barbarians who go on saying 'bar, bar, bar…' For a political theorist like Thomas Hobbes, the rabble was another name for the multitude who acted at the threshold of lawlessness. *La Rabbia* is therefore best understood as a generalized, menacing scream — rather than a mere bark — that verges on pure noise. It is subtended not by a singular, well-formed emotion like anger — which readily links up 'with the models of social action and transformation theorized by Hobbes'[32] — but rather to a 'vague and atmospheric' affect[33] that 'foregrounds a failure of emotional release (a form of suspended action) and does so as a kind of

---

30 In *Difference and Repetition*, Deleuze directly associates his discontinuous logic of differentiation with the concept of *clinamen*. Deleuze, *Difference and Repetition*, p. 184.
31 Deleuze, *Cinema 2*, p. 180. [*Translation modified*]
32 Sianne Ngai, *Ugly Feelings* (Cambridge: Harvard University Press, 2007), p. 5.
33 Lazzarato, *Signs and Machines*, p. 99.

politics'.[34] I'd like to now explore further the contours of this politics of suspended action. As Antonio Negri points out, reading Spinoza, the sad affects 'diminish or arrest the body's capacity to act'.[35] With this in mind, it is all too easy to understand Pasolini's last completed film *Salò* (1975) as simply an attempt to stage 'the capacity to resist reduced to near-zero'.[36] The problem with this statement is that, already in the mid-1960s — as Deleuze says in conversation with Negri — we moved 'toward "control" societies that are no longer exactly disciplinary', for which the historical conception of political action is no longer relevant.[37] Rather, what is necessary now is 'finding a characterization of "war machines" that have nothing to do with war but with a particular way of occupying, taking up, space-time, or inventing new space-times'.[38] This precisely is why art and philosophy are already micro-political. In any case, Spinoza himself claims that the sad affects 'follow from the same necessity and force of Nature as all things' and are therefore 'equally deserving of our attention'.[39] This opens up for Deleuze a different reading of Spinoza, which is again partly inspired by Lucretius: 'Something in the world forces us to think. This something is not an object of recognition but of fundamental encounter. It may be grasped in a range of affective tones'.[40] Despite their shared allegiances, there are huge theoretical and practical differences between these two readings. Whereas Negri tends to wager on the future joys of a coming communism, Deleuze lingers with the potentials inherent to the nearly anarchic moment of a collision, which 'moves the soul, perplexes it — in other words, forces it to pose a *problem*: as though the object of encounter, the sign, were the bearer of a problem'.[41] Here any deliberate action — that is, one that moves

---

34   Ngai, *Ugly Feelings*, p. 9.
35   Antonio Negri, 'Nécessité et liberté chez Spinoza: Quelques alternatives', *Multitudes*, 2 (May 2000), <https://www.multitudes.net/Necessite-et-liberte-chez-Spinoza/>. [*Translation mine*]
36   Howard Caygill, *On Resistance* (London: Bloomsbury, 2013), p. 165.
37   Or again: 'a redefinition of historical conflict is needed, not intellectually but vitally' because 'the front line no longer cuts through the middle of society; it now runs through the middle of each of us'. Tiqqun, *This is not a Program*, trans. by Joshua David Jordan (Los Angeles: Semiotext(e), 2011), p. 12.
38   Gilles Deleuze, *Negotiations*, trans. by Martin Joughin (New York: Columbia University Press, 1995), pp. 174, 172.
39   Spinoza, 'Ethics', in *Complete Works*, trans. by Samuel Shirley (Indianapolis: Hackett, 2002), p. 278.
40   Deleuze, *Difference and Repetition*, p. 136.
41   Ibid., p. 140.

us beyond our everyday habitual tendencies — must begin with discord, with discontinuity with regard to the power of recognition. It is a matter of discovering 'more in the body than we know and hence more in the mind than we are conscious of'.[42] This is not a program — even less a collapse into passive contemplation — but rather a strategy that demands that action ensue from an already reconfigured space-time, that is, from a situation that has been problematized and has 'forced thought to develop from the *sentiendum* to the *cogitandum*'.[43]

We see this already in Antonio Gramsci, who appropriates from Henri Bergson the concept of intuition, which he gives a political rather than aesthetic or philosophical determination. For Gramsci, political intuition is a form of knowledge that connects 'seemingly unrelated facts, rousing the passions of men and directing them to a determinate action'. It is the ability of a leader — which can be an individual or a collective — to grasp the complexity of a given situation through a range of cognitive faculties from affect to perception to the intellect. This somewhat vague operation is what Didi-Huberman calls — in relation to *La Rabbia* — 'sensing the firedamp', whose unrecognizable yet 'catastrophic force we have to feel, see or foresee, or anticipate each time'.[44] For Gramsci, the subsequent 'expression of the leader' is ultimately an action that is adequate to this situation, which has been reconfigured and therefore rendered legible. In his discussion of this process, Gramsci quotes extensively from Bergson's *Creative Evolution*. Remarkably, in Deleuze's discussion of intuition as method, the reciprocal interplay of problems and solutions is explained through Karl Marx's statement — in the preface to *A Contribution to the Critique of Political Economy* — that 'humanity only sets itself problems that it is capable of solving'.[45] Gramsci translated this text into Italian and, furthermore, often cited or paraphrased this very sentence numerous times

---

42   Gilles Deleuze, *Spinoza: Practical Philosophy*, trans. by Robert Hurley (San Francisco: City Lights, 1988), p. 90.
43   Deleuze, *Difference and Repetition*, p. 145.
44   Didi-Huberman, *Sentir de Grisou*, p. 13. [*Translation mine*]
45   Marx quoted in Deleuze, *Bergsonism*, trans. by Hugh Tomlinson and Barbara Habberjam (New York: Zone Books, 2011), p. 16. Many of the themes in *A Contribution to the Critique of Political Economy* (1859) are anticipated in draft form in Marx's 1841 doctoral dissertation on Epicurean philosophy, which he attempts to revive after Hegel's negative assessment. For example, the idea of *clinamen* introduces spontaneity into the seemingly mechanistic movement of atoms. This (meta-)physical view allows him to conceive *praxis* as a free activity through which humans construct themselves and their historical world.

throughout his notebooks.[46] We might therefore reclaim from *Gramsci's Ashes* a concept of intuition that re-appropriates Marx through Bergson and thus recovers historical materialism — with a non-Hegelian dialectic that still allows contradictions — for so-called political vitalism.

> The scandal of self-contradiction — of being | with you and against you; with you in my heart, | in the light, against you in the dark of my gut. | Though a traitor to my father's station | — in my mind, in a semblance of action — | I know I'm bound to it in the heat | of my instincts and aesthetic passion.[47]

If the sense of mixed affects is not immediately apparent here, in 1957, five years later — just before the release of *La Rabbia* — Pasolini writes:

> I drink down the light's | nightmare like a dazzling wine. | Nation without hope! Exploding outside | people's consciousness in the melancholy | Italy of the Mannerists, the Apocalypse |has killed them all — look at them: shadows | oozing gold in golden agony.[48]

In Bergson's notes on Lucretius — aptly entitled *Philosophy of Poetry* in English — he claims that 'Latin literature offers nothing superior to the last half of Book V'.[49] He also claims that

> A pervasive melancholy is the most striking characteristic of Lucretius' work. *De Rerum Natura* is sad and disheartening. What is the point of living? Life is monotonous; it is a treadmill that leads nowhere, a desire that never finds fulfillment. Pleasures are deceptive, no joy is untainted; the bitterness that stifles us when we are surrounded by perfumes and flowers reeks from the very seat of our desires.[50]

For Bergson, it is precisely this melancholy that accounts for the poetic quality of the work, which, in turn, is what marks Lucretius' originality beyond Epicurus. But what is the source of this melancholy? To be sure, the

---

46   Antonio Gramsci, *Prison Notebooks*, ed. and trans. by Joseph Buttigieg (New York: Columbia University Press, 1996), II, pp. 176, 555.
47   Pier Paolo Pasolini, 'Gramsci's Ashes', in *The Selected Poetry of Pier Paolo Pasolini*, ed. and trans. by Stephen Sartarelli (Chicago: University of Chicago Press, 2014), p. 177.
48   Pier Paolo Pasolini, 'Poem in the Shape of a Rose', in *The Selected Poetry of Pier Paolo Pasolini*, p. 315.
49   Henri Bergson, *Philosophy of Poetry: The Genius of Lucretius*, trans. by Wade Baskin (New York: Wisdom Library, 1959), p. 23.
50   Ibid., p. 44.

philosophical recognition of the 'rigidity of natural laws [...] obsesses and saddens the poet'.[51] But Bergson also points to the political and social strife that pervaded Lucretius' world, during the decline of the Roman Republic:

> We can be certain that the spectacle of civil wars left a dark imprint on Lucretius. At an early age he witnessed the bloody struggles that stemmed from the rivalry between Marius and Sylla. That was but a prelude to the violent upheavals that were to darken the Roman Republic. The poet could foresee them, and as a result he suffered cruelly. His first lines are a prayer to Venus, begging her to have her Mars bring about peace and harmony.[52]

Of course, these two causes are not separable since the very nature of things is to continuously decline. This is precisely why there is 'no indignation and no trace of anger' to be found in the poem.[53] Quite remarkably, Bergson then argues that, for Lucretius, 'the one who screams out is the one who has managed to convince himself even for an instant that resistance is possible'.[54] We will come back to the figure of the scream. For now, we should begin to unravel what all this could mean for *La Rabbia*.

What is the source of Pasolini's own melancholy? Like Lucretius, he was witness to a society in decline: a cultural genocide, as he expresses it — following Marx — in the firefly article. According to Lazzarato, Pasolini was one of the first thinkers to grasp the nature of neoliberalism, which was appearing at precisely the same moment that the 'disappearance of old cultural' forms was producing — in the face of a new sun — 'frustration, violence, and guilt' in Italy.[55]

> A scorched earth whose blaze, extinguished | this evening or a few millennia ago, | is an unending circle of rose-colored ruins, | whitening coals and bones, scaffoldings | bleached by rain and then burnt | by a new sun. The radiant Appia | teems with thousands of insects |— today's human beings — the neorealist | madmen of News in the vernacular.[56]

Strangely, all this seems to have already happened 'a few millennia ago', says Pasolini. Or better yet, has happened again and again in an 'unending circle' as the ruins and bones continue to pile up. The Appian Way, 'the

---

51 Ibid., p. 51.
52 Ibid., p. 46.
53 Ibid., p. 49.
54 Ibid., p. 52.
55 Lazzarato, *Signs and Machines*, pp. 131–32.
56 Pasolini, 'Poem in the Shape of a Rose', p. 313.

queen of long roads',[57] here becomes a metaphor for the sad trajectory of Italian history, understood as the seemingly eternal return of perpetual declines. It was constructed amidst the Samnite Wars as a military road, at a time in the early Roman Republic when large parts of Italy began to become subsumed under its rule. It is also the site — during the third slave uprising, when Lucretius would have been in his mid-20s — along which nearly 6000 members of Spartacus' army were crucified. At the end of WWII, it was the site of the prolonged Battle of Anzio during the Republic of Salò in which — amidst the malarial mosquitoes of the Pontine Marshes — the allies eventually captured Rome. In Pasolini's time, during the so-called 'post-war' period, these virulent pests have come to signify, not the coming spectacle of Augustus at the end of the Republic, not the coming spectacle of the atomic bomb at the end of WWII, but the coming society of spectacle: a new sun, which is itself 'the terrifying specter of unlimited production for unlimited war'.[58] These are amongst the direct causes of Pasolini's sad affects. In the opening scene of *La Rabbia*, just before the cacophony of machine gun fire, we hear in voice-over: 'Why is our life dominated by discontent, by anguish, by the fear of war, by war?'. Furthermore, this series of questions becomes the constellation of the problem that the film consciously sets out 'to answer [...] following no chronological, nor perhaps even logical line, but only my political reasoning and my poetic feeling'. The first politico-poetic expression of this problem is: 'freedom has become a sorrow'.[59]

Pasolini argues that cinema, like literature, has a 'double nature [...] there is a language of poetry and a language of prose'. Historically, however, even 'art films' have tended to employ narrative conventions in order to impose a logical progression over 'the fundamentally irrational nature of cinema'.[60] Pasolini consciously chose not to provide a chronological or logical trajectory for *La Rabbia* making it, in the first instance, 'a magnificent example' of the cinema of poetry.[61] Nonetheless, the notes for the script of *La Rabbia* indicate that, at the level of spoken word, two very different voices form a major part of the film's elaborate soundtrack. The voice of prose, read by the painter Renato Guttuso — who's images are themselves the only color elements of the film — is the critical voice, 'the

---

57 Statius, *Silvae*, ed. and trans. by D.R. Shackleton Bailey (Cambridge: Harvard University Press, 2003), p. 123.
58 Lazzarato and Alliez, *Wars and Capital*, p. 20.
59 Pasolini, *The Anger*.
60 Pasolini, *Heretical Empiricism*, p. 174.
61 Didi-Huberman, *Sentir de Grisou*, p. 81. [*Translation mine*]

voice of political conscience'[62] that confronts and reconfigures the official, journalistic narrative that accompanied the original found footage. The voice of poetry, read by the poet and essayist Giorgio Bassani is, however, 'the most important in the film, in every respect',[63] but most of all because it most directly conveys the 'expressionistic'[64] quality of the film. Pasolini was well aware of the apparent discontinuity involved in presenting a 'Marxist denunciation of the society of the time [...] in verse'.[65] Indeed, he was asked by a journalist for *Il Giorno* in 1966 to elaborate on the seeming ridiculousness of 'getting enraged in Alexandrian poetry'. Pasolini explained that

> an 'artistic war' must be waged on two fronts simultaneously, which sometimes means being cursed by the 'pure poets' on the one hand and the 'pure revolutionaries' on the other. Furthermore, the poetic forms of the past [...] may very well appear as 'novelties compared to more recent codifications or conventions'.[66]

We will come back to this important point. It has been noted that *La Rabbia* — a poem with the same name, penned by Pasolini in 1960 — employs a prosodic structure found in Petrarch's *Rerum Vulgarium Fragmenta*. Is it impossible to imagine that, three years later, Pasolini might have been inspired by Lucretius' *De Rerum Natura*? Interestingly, Bergson claims of Lucretius: 'His ability to grasp the two-sided character of things is the source of the incomparable originality of his poetry, his philosophy and, to sum up everything in one word, his genius'.[67]

The last important element of Pasolini's cinema of poetry is its use of free indirect style, in which the artist 'disappears' into a character.[68] The subsequent displacement of a single source of enunciation pushes the cinema of poetry even further 'toward undefinable irrational ambiguities'.[69] Pasolini discusses the use of free indirect style in avant-garde literature and art, but only hints at a cinematic equivalent. Deleuze develops Pasolini's

---

62 Ibid., p. 47. [*Translation mine*]
63 Ibid., p. 47. [*Translation mine*]
64 Pasolini, *Heretical Empiricism*, p. 172.
65 Pier Paolo Pasolini, *Pasolini on Pasolini: Interviews with Oswald Stack* (Bloomington: Indiana University Press, 1969), p. 70.
66 Pasolini quoted and paraphrased in Didi-Huberman, *Sentir de Grisou*, p. 75. [*Translation mine*]
67 Bergson, *Philosophy of Poetry*, p. 80.
68 Pasolini, *Heretical Empiricism*, p. 177.
69 Ibid., p. 106.

theory for cinema in two ways. First, what he calls free indirect images blur the distinction between the categories of objective and subjective — breaking the law of the excluded middle — and thus become the ontological ground of cinematic subjectivity. He quotes directly from Bergson in order to claim that, in this cinematic *cogito,*

> two different egos [*moi*] one of which, conscious of its freedom, sets itself up as independent spectator of a scene which the other would play in a mechanical fashion. But this dividing-in-two never goes to the limit. It is rather an oscillation of the person between two points of view on himself, a hither-and-thither of the spirit.[70]

Second, and more important for us here, Deleuze highlights the ethical and political potential of free indirect style. Already in Pasolini, free indirect style points not simply to a blurred relation between artist and character. In the example he cites from *Don Giovanni*, the use of the infinitive reverts back not to the voice of the artist but to an unnamed collective, that is, to a '*sociological consciousness*'.[71] In the best cases, collective enunciation should involve a heightened consciousness of 'neocapitalism'.[72] More generally, free indirect style opens up the possibility of other modes of expression beyond the dominant discourse and, therefore, should itself be understood as a form of 'resistance'.[73] For Deleuze, we find the best examples of free indirect images in certain post-war documentaries. In such films, for example Jean Rouch's *Les maîtres fous*, 'the distinction between what the character saw and what the camera saw vanishes [...] because the camera entered into a relation of simulation ("mimesis") with the character's way of seeing'.[74] The use of the word mimesis is provocative since, with free indirect images, we can no longer depend upon any recognizable concept of truth. Rather, the images in these films constitute an assemblage that can only be called a 'pseudo-story', a term that Deleuze borrows from Pasolini.[75] Quite remarkably then, the construction of *cinéma vérité* primarily involves an act of 'story-telling', which has important social and political functions for both Benjamin and

---

70 Bergson quoted in Deleuze, *Cinema 1*, p. 74.
71 Pasolini, *Heretical Empiricism*, p. 82. Remarkably, Deleuze also calls this collective enunciation a 'kind of truly cinematographic *Mitsein*'. Deleuze, *Cinema 1*, p. 72.
72 Pasolini, *Heretical Empiricism*, p. 185.
73 Ibid., p. 85.
74 Deleuze, *Cinema 2*, p. 148.
75 Ibid., p. 149.

Bergson that Deleuze builds upon. Or, as Bertolt Brecht says about his *War Primer*, there cannot be a simple reproduction of reality — whatever that might mean — but only something that is constructed artificially. Furthermore, and we will come back to these points, cinematic free indirect style 'produces collective utterances, as the prefiguration of a people who are missing'.[76] In the remainder of this essay, I will discuss how *La Rabbia* uses free indirect style in order to render sensible a collective scream that is 'constantly becoming another and is no longer separable from a becoming that merges with a people'.[77]

During the first five minutes of the film, in the midst of a montage of clips from various political rallies in different cities, we hear the following poetic voice over:

> If you don't scream 'long live freedom' humbly, | you aren't screaming 'long live freedom'. | If you don't scream 'long live freedom' laughing, | you aren't screaming 'long live freedom'. | If you don't scream 'long live freedom' with love, | you aren't screaming 'long live freedom'. | Scream with contempt, with anger, with hatred, 'long live freedom'.[78]

In a lamenting voice, the film concludes with the following words as we see an image of the earth without borders from above:

> A civilization triumphed down there. | Now I announce its death-agony | and bear witness to a new sun.[79]

The film is therefore framed by politico-poetic screams or cries that ultimately announce the death-agony of human civilization but — as we know from Pasolini's other work from the same period — also the disappearance of tradition, of resistance, of the avant-garde, of fireflies. True to its title, *La Rabbia* is — as a whole — a menacing scream that verges on pure noise, a cacophony of disjunctive layers of texts, images, sounds, and silences. This is a scream that, through a 'dysposing' method of montage, reveals the 'heterogeneous temporalities' and 'discontinuities at work in every historical event'. It reanimates and thus renders sensible

---

76   Ibid., p. 188.
77   Ibid., p. 152.
78   Pasolini, *The Anger*. For the sake of consistency in the following, I have rendered the Italian *grido*, the French *cri*, and the English *cry* as 'scream'.
79   Pasolini, *The Anger*.

the *membra disjuncta* of 'our dark history'.[80] Also true to its title, this scream carries with it a polyphony of different emotions, from love to contempt. Didi-Huberman, following Deleuze, notes that 'emotions do not say "I", but always tread the line between community and singularity'.[81] Etymologically, emotions move us beyond ourselves and therefore already shift the center of enunciation away from a singular *cogito*. The scream of *La Rabbia* is not simply Pasolini's own, but the collective scream of humanity. He achieves this effect more concretely through the use of free indirect style. Not only do we hear the above lines in the voice of another, their center of enunciation is visually displaced and dysposed, throughout the film, onto the multitudes of oppressed proletarian and subproletarian peoples. Although it is beyond the scope of this essay to demonstrate this fully, free indirect style thus provides a way in which to rethink the question 'can the subaltern speak?' beyond the dichotomy of self and other and beyond the logic of representation.

A bit further into the film, the critical voice then announces that 'a new *problem* bursts out in the world [...] color'. In the first place, it is clear that this refers once again to 'the enslaved peoples of the subproletarian world'.[82] But we can also understand this problem formally. Color cinema and broadcasting weren't standardized in Europe until the mid-1960s and Pasolini didn't produce a color film until *Oedipus Rex* in 1967. Most of the footage of *La Rabbia* is therefore necessarily black and white. The only instances of color we see in the film are the politically conscious, expressionist paintings of Renato Guttuso. Around half an hour into the film, we are presented with a detail of one of these paintings, which frames in close-up an image of a boy screaming, which immediately brings to mind the famous scream from Sergei Eisenstein's *Battleship Potemkin* (1925) that influenced Francis Bacon's *Study After Velazquez's Portrait of Innocent X* (1953). Just prior to this image, we see footage of people viewing social realist art in a soviet museum. The critical voice then speaks from the position of the museum guide:

> I go on doing my guide's duty and say to you, | as if speaking like a father the first time about love: | In these pictures there lies an error. | We should take these pictures from the walls, | put them in the basement! | We must start all

---

80 Georges Didi-Huberman, *The Eye of History: When Images Take Positions*, trans. by Shane Lillis (Cambridge: MIT Press, 2018), p. 239.
81 Georges Didi-Huberman, *L'Œil de l'histoire 6: Peuples en larmes, Peuples en armes* (Paris: Gallimard, 2016), p. 55. [*Translation mine*]
82 Pasolini, *The Anger*.

over, | from where there's no certainty | and the sign is desperate | and the color shrill | and the figures writhe.

Pasolini therefore seems to be formally highlighting this shrill scream — writhing with uncertainty — and through it immediately returns us, using free indirect style, to the figure of the global subaltern fighting for freedom. It is useful to note that, at the end of *Cinema 2*, Deleuze writes 'free, indirect style' with a comma, emphasizing that such figures are always on the side of freedom:

> We're not in Moscow or Leningrad | but in the factories where | the class struggle is fought. | We are Italian, Spanish workers, | French intellectuals, Algerian partisans | and in the deserts of the colonies | fighting for freedom.[83]

This color sequence also highlights the power of images to reanimate hope in the midst of an existence that has become nearly intolerable, even if this hope can only produce a shrill scream. This scream 'organizes pessimism' — to use a phrase Didi-Huberman borrows from Benjamin — 'within the historical world by discovering an "image space" in the very depths of our "political action"'.[84] The ultimate source of Pasolini's melancholy therefore seems to lie in the recognition that, while traditional Marxist action is impotent in the post-war period (we must put it in the basement and start over), the flittering glimpses of color we are able to reanimate — the firefly-images — are simply not enough.[85] It is not by chance that *La Rabbia* begins with clips from the Hungarian Revolution against Soviet rule.

In the 1966 interview for *Il Giorno*, Pasolini was asked, 'seriously, what is the difference between an *arrabbiato* and a *rivoluzionario*?'

> Pasolini's physical reaction: 'He runs his hand over his face and half-closes his eyes, like someone suffering from a permanent migraine'. Then he

---

83 Pasolini, *The Anger*.
84 Georges Didi-Huberman, *Survival of the Fireflies*, trans. by Lia Mitchell (Minneapolis: University of Minnesota Press, 2018), p. 68.
85 The idea of starting over beyond Marxism brings to mind a rather provocative claim made by Benjamin, which also returns us to the 'irrational, elementary, and barbaric' potential of the cinema of poetry: 'Barbarism? Yes, indeed. We say this in order to introduce a new, positive concept of barbarism. For what does poverty of experience do for the barbarian? It forces him to start from scratch; to make a new start'. Walter Benjamin, 'Experience and Poverty', in *Selected Writings*, ed. by Michael Jennings, 4 vols. (Cambridge: Harvard University Press, 1999), II, p. 732.

comes to an answer in two parts. First, Pasolini admits that the revolutionary wants to bring about a 'real' change in the existing political system, while the enraged never ceases to encounter the limits of a system in which he considers himself to be enslaved. Second, the revolutionary's aim is to substitute another system for the existing one, which the enraged person has every reason to fear will retain what Pasolini calls the 'moralism' and 'conventionalism' of any established system. The revolutionary (whose type, in Pasolini's eyes, is Lenin) would be simply waiting for a new conformism, while the enraged (whose type would be better illustrated by Socrates) suffers from all possible conformisms in all possible systems.[86]

We might humbly suggest again that Lucretius, rather than Socrates, should be put forward as the conceptual personae of *La Rabbia* since the logic of his system disallows in advance this type of conventional systematization. Rather, the dysposing and reanimating movement of the *clinamen* ensures the perpetual creation of new worlds and new forms:

> atoms 'decline' perpetually, but their fall in this infinite *clinamen* allows exceptions with unforeseen consequences. An atom may diverge only slightly from its parallel trajectory, yet enough that it may collide with others, a collision from which a world may be born. Such then, would be the essential *recourse of decline*: bifurcation, collision, the 'ball lightning' crossing the horizon, the invention of a new form.[87]

Didi-Huberman also reminds us, with a nod to Benjamin, of the 'special vitality of periods in so-called decline' since such decline — which is very different from disappearance — is the natural order of things.[88] Bergson adds that the *clinamen*, which 'obeys no law and is unpredictable',[89] gives rise to a conception of 'nature as animate'.[90] Furthermore, this conception determines an ethics — and potentially a politics — since the soul is itself composed of atoms. When the soul moves by engaging the natural capacity

---

86 Didi-Huberman, *Sentir de Grisou*, p. 74 [*Translation mine*]. A move beyond Leninist conformism would necessarily entail 'the refusal of authoritarian disciplines, formal hierarchies, orders of priorities decreed from above, and compulsory ideological references, which should not be seen in contradiction with the obviously inevitable and desirable establishment of *centers of decision* that use the most sophisticated technologies of communication'. Félix Guattari, 'The New Spaces of Freedom', in Félix Guattari and Antonio Negri, *New Lines of Alliance, New Spaces of Liberty* (New York: Autonomedia, 2010), p. 124.
87 Didi-Huberman, *Survival of the Fireflies*, p. 66.
88 Ibid., p. 65.
89 Bergson, *The Philosophy of Poetry*, p. 73.
90 Ibid., p. 55.

to decline, it is 'active and takes advantage of its freedom'. Otherwise, it remains 'passive'.[91] But where does the scream — the most important figure of *La Rabbia* — fit in to all of this?

Deleuze develops a concept of the scream from Wilhelm Worringer's writings on expressionism and argues that it is, in fact, 'the only expression of expressionism'.[92] For Deleuze, any creative act — in science, art, philosophy, or indeed politics — must begin with a scream, which attests to the fact that *praxis* must be reconfigured in the midst of an unrecognizable situation. The scream is the necessary initial reaction — which hovers uncomfortably between activity and passivity — to a 'catastrophic force we have to feel, see or foresee, or anticipate each time'.[93] It is the natural expression of Gramsci's intuition, Didi-Huberman's sensing the firedamp, and Deleuze's seer. What is *La Rabbia* in this context? Pasolini answers that it is, above all, the expression of a 'state of emergency' that is simultaneously a 'state of emergence'.[94] That is, Pasolini's scream — and ours — is the painful expression of the *process* of rendering sensible the dark layers of our history, the *process* of formulating a problem. As Isabelle Stengers states in the epigraph to this essay, in order to reanimate and recode these layers, we need to first learn how 'to feel the smoke in our nostrils'.[95] This requires something like hope — or, in Deleuze's terms, a 'belief in this world';[96] or again, following Guattari, a 're-enchantment of subjectivation'[97] — which Pasolini, at the end of *La Rabbia* and elsewhere, claims he could no longer foster. He tried to find even the smallest joy in his situation, but it always revealed an even deeper, 'inextinguishable terror, in a thousand parts of the world, in a thousand parts of the soul'.[98] But hope or belief does not necessarily involve the overly dramatic and utopian emotion of joy. Rather, it is the affirmation of decline as well as the affirmation of the variety of affects that emerge from that initial affirmation. *La Rabbia* should be understood as a cinematic scream, as the initial expression of such a confusing and confused affirmation.

---

91 Ibid., pp. 75–76.
92 Deleuze, *Cinema 1*, p. 225. For more on this, see my 'The Ethico-Aesthetics of the Figure', in *This Deleuzian Century: Art, Activism, Life*, ed. by Rosi Braidotti and Rick Dolphijn (Leiden: Brill, 2014), pp. 205–35.
93 Didi-Huberman, *Sentir de Grisou*, p. 13. [*Translation mine*]
94 Pasolini quoted in Didi-Huberman, *Sentir de Grisou*, p. 38. [*Translation mine*]
95 Stengers, 'Reclaiming Animism', p. 187.
96 Deleuze, *Cinema 2*, p. 188.
97 Félix Guattari, *Chaosmosis: An Ethico-aesthetic Paradigm*, trans. by Paul Bains and Julian Pefanis (Bloomington: Indiana University Press, 1995), p. 105.
98 Pasolini, *The Anger*.

When Lazzarato argues that the construction of new forms of action must first pass through 'machinic animism' — a concept he develops from Guattari — he doesn't simply mean a nostalgic return to the 'sacred' and 'animated' world of 'peasant culture' that has disappeared.[99] Rather, he is referring to the visionary moment of Gramscian intuition, which is able to affirm and therefore *reanimate* the dark layers of history. Furthermore, this affirmation becomes the foundation for an entirely different political ontology that functions — through a disjunctive and divergent onto-logic, for example, a cinemachinic logic of the *clinamen* — beyond the strictures of Enlightenment thinking, which is itself marked by 'a disenchantment of the world' and 'the extirpation of animism'.[100]

For Deleuze, the genius of Lucretius was precisely the affirmation of sadness, beyond the negative, and beyond contradiction.[101] But the moment of intuition and affirmation — that is, of belief — is necessary but not sufficient. This is simply because images — even firefly-images or scream-images — 'do not rise up'.[102]

> if we scream, it is always as victims of invisible and insensible forces that scramble every spectacle that even lie beyond pain and feeling [...]. These invisible forces, the powers of the future, are they not already upon us, and much more insurmountable than the worst spectacle and even the worst pain? It is within this new visibility that the body actively struggles [...] as if combat had now become possible.[103]

Belief in the world must be subsequently translated into action, albeit an action that is also completely reconfigured to the point, perhaps, of being nearly unrecognizable as such.[104] As Deleuze says in conversation with Negri, 'if you believe in the world you precipitate events [...] engender new space-times [...] resist control [...]. Utopia isn't the right concept: it's more a question of "fabulation" [story-telling] in which people and art

---

99   Pasolini quoted in Lazzarato, *Signs and Machines*, p. 136.
100 Adorno and Horkheimer, *Dialectic of Enlightenment*, p. 2. In an interview with Lazzarato, Eduardo Viveiros de Castro provocatively claims that 'machinic animism is the ontology of societies against the state'. Angela Melitopoulos and Maurizio Lazzarato, *Assemblages*, 2010, video installation.
101 Deleuze, *Logic of Sense*, p. 279.
102 Jacques Rancière, 'One Uprising Can Hide Another', in *Uprisings*, ed. by Georges Didi-Huberman (Paris: Gallimard, 2016), p. 68.
103 Gilles Deleuze, *Francis Bacon: The Logic of Sensation*, trans. by Daniel Smith (Minneapolis: University of Minnesota Press, 2003), pp. 51–52.
104 'We hope for the emergence of a new type of barbarism in which power-time opens an incommensurable field of action'. Lazzarato, *Videophilosophy*, p. 226.

both share. We ought to take up Bergson's notion of fabulation and give it a political meaning'.[105] Even in Bergson, fabulation must ultimately be 'consummated in action'.[106] Stengers argues that 'creating new means of grasping a situation' — the moment of sensing the firedamp — necessarily 'leads to the production of new ways of acting', a new type of strategic *praxis* that refuses generalities as well as predefined or programmatic ends.[107] This is what Deleuze calls the fabulation of 'people who are missing'.[108] While the former, expressionist, moment of the scream may appear spontaneous, the latter involves a painstaking machinic constructivism.[109] 'We haven't yet found an effective mode of organization [...] we have to figure it out [...] we do see new forms of subjectivation, new fields of experimentation, but maybe we need some more time'.[110] It is precisely the machinic and constructivist character of this strategy that makes it 'completely contrary to some ode to spontaneity'.[111] Rather, it is the immediate demand for developing a clear and distinct program that should be understood as all-too-spontaneous since it might not be able to sufficiently see and consider all the unknowns of a situation, which would return us to the kind of '"moralism" and "conventionalism" of any established system' that Pasolini warned against.[112]

> One must refuse to pass from the *scream* 'another world is possible!' to a *program* describing 'this other world that we want'. Because this program would have either to appear utopian or to take no notice of the primordial unknown of every situation: the difference that the event by which people seize hold of a problem that concerns them can create.[113]

---

105 Deleuze, *Negotiations*, pp. 176, 174.
106 Henri Bergson, *Two Sources of Morality and Religion*, trans. by Ashley Audra and Cloudesley Brereton (Notre Dame: University of Notre Dame Press, 1977), p. 212.
107 Isabelle Stengers and Philippe Pignarre, *Capitalist Sorcery: Breaking the Spell*, trans. by Andrew Goffey (Basingstoke: Palgrave, 2011), p. 77.
108 Deleuze, *Cinema 2*, p. 188.
109 Another way of describing this two-phased strategy of action, beyond the demand for a concrete program, might be: 'organization is spontaneity reflecting upon itself'. Antonio Negri, *The Factory of Strategy: Thirty-Three Lessons on Lenin*, trans. by Arianna Bove (New York: Columbia University Press, 2014), p. 32.
110 Lazzarato, *Videophilosphy*, p. 237.
111 Félix Guattari, 'Institutional Practice and Politics', in *The Guattari Reader*, ed. by Gary Genosko (Oxford: Blackwell, 1996), p. 128.
112 Didi-Huberman, *Sentir de Grisou*, p. 74. [*Translation mine*]
113 Stengers and Pignarre, *Capitalist Sorcery*, p. 105.

Pedro A.H. Paixão

THE TESTAMENT
(Open Letter to Jean-Marie Straub)

Dear Jean-Marie,

It has been fifteen years since we met — in September 2004 — in the *borgata* Petrelli, in the suburbs of Rome, where you lived. The reason for that meeting was to invite you to take part in a film I was developing with a friend. It was a project about Pier Paolo Pasolini's unfinished *San Paolo*.

At the time, the intention was for us to adopt the same method that Pasolini used for his project and, with that in mind, to ask you to take the place of Paul of Tarsus — possibly reading the text that Giorgio Agamben had agreed to write for us, an epistle similar to those of the Apostle, but for an ineffable notion of community, a 'coming community' without assumptions, to be read in the film.

Before such contingencies, therefore, and the occasion of our meeting in Rome, we contacted you by telephone, as you perhaps recall, so that we could get to know you and present you with the challenge.

[I knew, unless I am mistaken, that Danièle Huillet and Jean-Marie Straub had moved to Rome at the end of the sixties; continuing an exile that had lasted eleven years, beginning in Munich after Straub's conviction by the military tribunal in Metz for having refused to get involved in the war in Algeria and thus become a direct accomplice of what he called 'institutionalized torture'. And even when amnesty was granted, it was in Italy, based in Rome, that they both preferred to live, first in the heart of the city, then in a workers' *borgata* in the suburbs, where we visited him.]

In the second of our telephone conversations, you told us that you had three things to say on camera and, some days later, a forty-minute train ride from the centre, we met you in a café near your house. You wanted to get to know us first and see whether we were serious about our proposal.

Then, at your house, moments later, you showed us the spot in the garage of the building where, perched on the edge of a flowerbed, you were planning to be filmed. There was a drizzle in the air and some rain dripping on leaves in the background.

Of the three things you had to tell us, the third was decisive for me. 'C'est mon testament', I heard you say at one point. Your 'testament' was nothing more than a passage from *Der Tod des Empedokles* by Friedrich Hölderlin, quoted from memory.

I knew well how special this tragedy was to you and Danièle and that, of the three versions left unfinished by the German poet, you had directed, on film, the first — in four different editions — and the third.

[It is well known that in his tragedy Hölderlin freely adapted the fragmentary biographical tradition passed down, in particular, by Diogenes Laërtius in the 18th book of *Lives and Opinions of Eminent Philosophers*. For example, Hölderlin only wrote about the final phase of the life of the philosopher in question, in the 5th century B.C.E., shortly before his legendary suicide in the crater of Mount Etna. More specifically, Hölderlin dealt with the years of exile by situating them in a rustic cabin at the foot of the volcano and not in the Peloponnese, as per the accepted historiography.
As for the ancient philosopher Empedocles, the central figure of the tragedy, it is said that he was banished from Agrigentum for his 'arrogance' or 'hubris', or — in the words of his adversary, the priest Hermocrates — for having claimed to have 'ascended' Mount Olympus in life and, in correlation with this insolence, for having wished to free himself of human time. These pretensions, as legend tells us, were fundamental in the fusion of death with life, the result of which is said to be immortality, which the philosopher believed he would find in the incandescent lava of the volcano.
His condemnation to exile was also rooted in the cowardice of a former friend, Critias, the archon of Agrigentum, the representative of earthly law, who was incapable of standing up to the will of the people, the Agrigentans, who had succumbed to Hermocrates' jealousy and slander.
Eventually, except for Hermocrates, who remained alone with his envy, Empedocles would reconcile with those who had expelled him, including his old friend Critias.]

When we met, I had no idea how crucial this was to our meeting; I was merely astonished by how the third thing you had to tell us was so important to you — 'C'est mon testament' — as well as that it should be filmed anew, on a shooting that was merely preparatory.

Your 'testament' included a very precise moment from the first version of the tragedy; specifically, it placed us at the end of Scene 4 of Act 2, the moment when Empedocles, now in exile, receives the Agrigentans, who implore him to return to the city. Had we come to you for the same reason? I wondered, days later, already home in Milan, when I re-read the passage from the tragedy, and understood the magnitude of the event.

Present before Empedocles in that passage are his loyal friend and disciple Pausanias, the archon Critias, representing civil power, the priest Hermocrates, representing religious power, as well as three deputies, representing the bourgeoisie.

If your intention were to create an analogy, which of these six would we be, my friend and I? I'm conscious that this passage from the tragedy was no arbitrary choice. With this scene, you constructed so simply and precisely the 'ceremonial stage' for our meeting in Rome, as well as for future viewers of the [definitive] recording you left us.

[In a text about resistance in film, from 1994 I think, Straub had written that

> the job of every director should be to know the reciprocal relationships of the distances revealed between characters and objects, to get to know the relationships of strength, of class and of feelings in that specific moment or in that situation.

In other words, as I will now demonstrate, it seems Straub had placed us all in a very precise layout within the topological context of the written tragedy.]

To perfect the operation, you simply withheld from the German poet's text the initial part of the passage, in which Empedocles addresses each of those in front of him by name. You wouldn't reveal to whom you were referring, which of his six or other addressees we would be... It was up to each one alone to decide it.

With the scene set — with the ceremonial stage of our meeting now open —, you addressed us with the same lofty gaze with which Empedocles would have addressed his interlocutors, whichever of the six or others they were. And you said,

> *...und schon — o Luft, | Luft, die den Neugeborenen umfängt, | Wenn droben er die neuen Pfade wandelt, | Dich ahnd ich, wie der Schiffer, wenn er nah | Dem Blütenwald der Mutterinsel kömmt, | Schon atmet liebender die Brust ihm auf | Und sein gealtert Angesicht verklärt | Erinnerung der ersten Wonne wieder!*

[The arrangement of the meeting orchestrated by Straub — to receive us that early autumn morning — spilled over the physical boundaries of the screen. We, my friend and I, just like any future spectator, whether disciple, friend, rival or mere citizen, had come to meet him to ask for who knows what, for 'words', for his return to the common space, or merely for recognition and for expressions of wisdom, clues or even vanities. The truth is that the place of great simplicity in which he received us and orchestrated our encounter seemed now to depend on the intimacy and presence of each of us alone. We were there, but before whom? And who were we? What did we want from our interlocutor and which of us were his? Creating a completely open cinematographic interstice for a dialogue between the philosopher–poet–director and his interlocutors, Straub made it possible for us to be anyone, Pausanias, Critias, Hermocrates, or any other representative (or not) of the people. Only each of us alone (we and future viewers) would know whom.

However, it was the 'air' embracing that newborn that gave our meeting atmosphere; it was that 'air' — which, in a cosmic respiration, circulates through every being —, showing us that the order of the day was one of ethics and not of aesthetics. Eager or loving in the face of the authority or love of an ancient, the unexpected opportunity of this encounter allowed us to understand that we would receive nothing more than that which Empedocles had already conveyed to Hölderlin and the poet to Straub: the 'air' embracing the newborn, who bears the memories that can transfigure the face with the innocence of the first delights.]

Milan, October 12th, 2019

Fig. 1
Pedro A.H. Paixão, *The Testament*, 2019, video audio, 3'52 min. loop., courtesy of the artist.

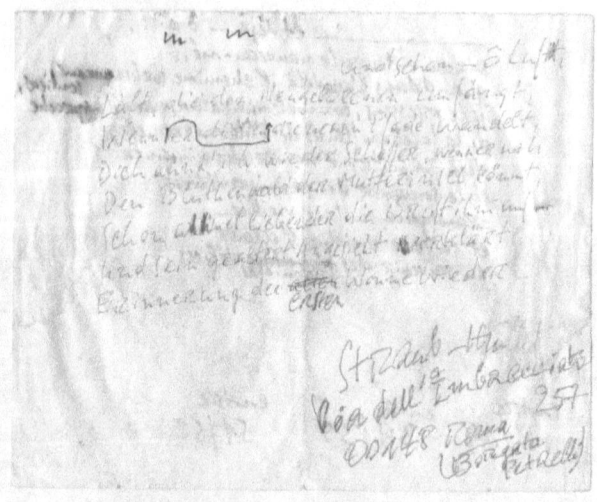

Fig. 2–3
Written note (recto and verso) by Jean-Marie Straub given to Pedro A.H. Paixão and François Bucher after their meeting in Rome, in 2005.

Fig. 4
Pedro A.H. Paixão, *The Testament*, 2019, courtesy of the artist.

Alain Badiou
DESTRUCTION, NEGATION, SUBTRACTION[1]

The abstract content of my lecture is very simple. I can summarize it in five points:
1. All creations, all novelties, are in some sense the affirmative part of a negation. 'Negation', because if something happens as new, it cannot be reduced to the objectivity of the situation where it happens. So, it is certainly something like a negative exception to the regular laws of this objectivity. But 'affirmation', the affirmative part of the negation, because if a creation is reducible to a negation of the common laws of objectivity, it completely depends on them with respect to its identity. So the very essence of a novelty implies negation but must affirm its identity regardless of the negativity of negation. That is why I say that a creation or a novelty must be defined paradoxically as the affirmative part of a negation.

2. I name 'destruction' the negative part of negation. For example, if we consider Schoenberg's creation, at the beginning of the previous century, of the dodecaphonic musical system, we can say that this creation achieves the destruction of the tonal system, which had dominated musical creation in the Western world for three centuries. Similarly, the Marxist idea of revolution is one of achieving the process of immanent negation of capitalism through the complete destruction of the machinery of the bourgeois State. In both cases, negation is the evental concentration of a process through which is achieved the complete disintegration of an old world. It is this evental concentration which realizes the negative power of negation, the negativity of negation. And I name it destruction.

3. I name 'subtraction' the affirmative part of negation. For example, the new musical axioms which structure the admissible succession of notes in a musical work, for Schoenberg, outside the tonal system, are in no way deducible from the destruction of this system. They are the affirmative laws

---

[1] First delivered as a lecture at the Art Center College of Design in Pasadena on February 6, 2007.

of a new framework for musical activity. They show the possibility of a new coherence for musical discourse. The point that we must understand is that this new coherence is new not because it completes the process of disintegration of the system. The new coherence is new to the extent that, in the framework that Schoenberg's axioms impose, musical discourse avoids the laws of tonality or, more precisely, becomes indifferent to these laws. That is why we can say that musical discourse is subtracted from its tonal legislation. Clearly, this subtraction is within the horizon of negation, but it exists independently of the purely negative part of negation. It exists apart from destruction.

It is the same thing for Marx in the political context. Marx insists on saying that the destruction of the bourgeois State is not in itself an achievement. The goal is communism, that is, the end of the State as such, and the end of social classes, in favour of a purely egalitarian organization of civil society. But to come to this, we must first substitute for the bourgeois State a new State, which is not the immediate result of the destruction of the first. In fact, it is a State as different from the bourgeois State as the experimental music of today can be from an academic tonal piece of the nineteenth century, or a contemporary performance can be from an academic representation of the Olympic gods. For the new State — which Marx names 'dictatorship of the proletariat' — is a State that organizes its own vanishing. A State which is, in its very essence, the process of the non-State. Perhaps as for Adorno 'informal music' is the process, within a work, of the disintegration of all forms, so we can say that in the original thought of Marx, 'dictatorship of the proletariat' was a name for a State that is subtracted from all the classical laws of a 'normal' State. For a classical State is a form of power, but the State named the 'dictatorship of the proletariat' is the power of un-power, the power of the disappearance of the question of power.

In any case, we name subtraction this part of negation that is oriented by the possibility of something which exists absolutely, apart from that which exists under the laws of what negation negates.

4. So negation is always, in its concrete action — political or artistic — suspended between destruction and subtraction. That the very essence of negation is destruction has been the fundamental idea of the previous century. The fundamental idea of the century that is beginning must be that the very essence of negation is subtraction.

5. But subtraction is not the negation of destruction, no more than destruction was the negation of subtraction, as we have seen with Schoenberg or Marx. The most difficult question is precisely that of maintaining the complete concept of negation from the point of view of

subtraction — as Lenin, Schoenberg, or Marcel Duchamp, or Cage, or Mao Zedong, or Jackson Pollock maintained the complete concept of negation from the point of view of destruction.

To clarify the very complex interplay between destruction, negation, and subtraction, I propose to read with you a fragment of a magnificent poem by Pier Paolo Pasolini.

Pasolini is well known as a filmmaker; in particular, during the sixties and the seventies, he directed profound contemporary visual readings of the two great Western intellectual traditions: the ancient Greeks, with movies like *Medea* and *Oedipus*, and Judeo-Christianity with *The Gospel according to Matthew* and a very complex script about the life of Saint Paul. All of that constitutes a difficult enterprise of thinking about the relationship among history, myths, and religion. Pasolini was simultaneously a revolutionary Marxist and a man forever influenced by his religious childhood. So his question was: do the revolutionary becoming of history and political negativity represent a destruction of the tragic beauty of the Greek myths and of the peaceful promise of Christianity? Or do we have to speak of a subtraction where an affirmative reconciliation of beauty and peace becomes possible in a new egalitarian world?

Pasolini is also well known for the relationship between his private life and his public convictions. Not only he was gay, but this was a part of his political vision, many years before the beginning of the gay and lesbian movement. He perfectly knew that desire — and in his own case, desire for young poor workers of the suburbs of Rom — is not independent of our ideological choices. Once more, the question is one of inscribing sexual desire in political negativity not as a purely subversive and destructive feature, but as a creative displacement of the line that separates the individual subjectivity from the collective one.

Pasolini was murdered in November 1975. He was fifty-three years old. The circumstances of this horrible murder are still obscure today. But certainly they are located exactly at the point where political determinations are linked with sexual situations. It is this point which was for Pasolini a constant source of new truths, but also an existential tragedy.

Marvellous movies, political commitments, critical essays, great novels, a new existential style... beyond all that, Pasolini is the greatest poet of his generation. His work can be mapped out as belonging to three different stylistic eras. We can distinguish three major political collections.

1. The poems written when Pasolini was twenty years old, in a specific Italian dialect, Friulan. Here we have the attempt to subtract poetry from the authority of official Italian language and to use a popular language

against the State language. It is a characteristic example of what Deleuze names 'minoritarian politics' in poetry.

2. The significant collection published in 1957, the heart of which is the magnificent poem, 'The Ashes of Gramsci', a complex meditation concerning history, Marxist ideology, the Italian landscape and personal feelings... The title is in itself a metaphor of melancholic negation. It is as though Gramsci, the Master, the Father of Italian Marxism, were here dissipated in History's dust.

3. The two collections of the beginning of the sixties: *The Religion of My Time* (1961) and *Poetry in the Form of a Rose* (1964). We have here the context of the fragment I shall explain today. Fundamentally, it is the bitter disappointment of Pasolini concerning the practices of the Italian Left and, more precisely, two very serious failures of the Communist Party.

First, its infidelity to the armed struggle of thousands of young men against fascism and Nazism during the war. Second, its inability to organize the revolt of thousands of young workers in the suburbs of Italian towns.

So we have here a double negation of the young people. In the past, where their fighting was forgotten; in the present, where their revolt is despised.

But Pasolini has two very important reasons for being passionately interested in the existence and the struggles of young people. First, his younger brother, Guido, was killed during the war while fighting as a partisan, a resistance fighter. And the terrible problem is that he was killed not by fascists, but by communists from another country, Yugoslav communists, because of the rivalry between Italians and Yugoslavs concerning control of some border regions. Second, as a gay man, Pasolini always had a real and constant relationship with very poor young workers, or with the unemployed of the suburbs. That is why many poems by Pasolini speak of the contradiction between history, politics, and the concrete existence of proletarian youth.

We shall first listen to one of these poems. It is a fragment of a very long poem, '*Vittoria*' ['Victory']. Let us hear the original Italian version.

> 'Ogni politica è una realpolitica', anima
> guerriera, con la tua delicata rabbia! | Non riconosci un'altra anima, eh? Questa | dove c'è tutta la prosa dell'uomo abile,
> del rivoluzionario attaccato all'onestà | media dell'uomo (anche la complicità | con gli assassinii degli Anni Amari s'innesta
> nel classicismo protettore, che fa | il comunista perbene): non riconosci il cuore | che diventa schiavo del suo nemico, e va

dove il nemico va, condotto dalla storia | ch'è storia di tutti due, e li fa, nel profondo, | stranamente fratelli; non riconosci i timori
d'una coscienza che, lottando col mondo, | ne condivide le norme della lotta nei secoli, | come per un pessimismo in cui affondano,
per farsi più virili, le speranze. Lieto | d'una lietezza che non sa retroscena | è questo esercito — cieco nel cieco
sole — di giovani morti, che viene | ed aspetta. Se il suo padre, il suo capo, | lo lascia solo nei bianchi monti, nelle serene
pianure — assorbito in un misterioso dibattito | con il Potere, legato alla sua dialettica | che la storia rinnova senza pace —
piano piano dentro i barbarici petti | dei figli, l'odio si fa amore per l'odio, | ardendo solo in essi, i pochi, i benedetti.
Ah, Disperazione che non conosci codici! | Ah, Anarchia, libero amore | di Santità, con i tuoi canti prodi![2]

To have an overview of this fragment we can say something like the following: Everybody is saying that politics must be realistic, that all ideological illusions have been proved dangerous and bloody.

But what is the real for politics? The real is History. The real is the concrete becoming of struggle and negation. But how is it possible to understand or know History? We can do that if we know the rules of History, the great laws of becoming. This is the lesson of Marxism.

But are the laws of History not the same for us and for our enemies? And if that is the case, how can negation be distinguished from approval?

We are in a situation where destruction, having been suppressed — subtraction itself, the opposition, if you want — becomes complicity. As Pasolini writes: we recognize that we are going exactly where the enemy goes, 'led by a History that is the history of both'. And political hope is impossible.

So, if the young dead of the last war could see the present political situation they would not agree with this complicity. Moreover, they could not accept their political fathers, the leaders of the Communist Party. And they would become, by necessity, barbarian and nihilistic people, exactly like the young unemployed of the suburbs.

The poem is a manifesto for true negation. If subtraction is separated from destruction, we have as a result Hate and Despair. The symbol of this result is the fusion of the dead heroes of the last war with the despised workers of our suburbs in a sort of terrorist figure.

---

[2] Pier Paolo Pasolini, 'Vittoria', in *Tutte le Poesie*, ed. by Walter Siti, 2 vols (Milan: Mondadori, 2003), I, p. 1265–66.

But if destruction is separated from subtraction, we have as result the impossibility of politics, because young people are absorbed in a sort of nihilistic collective suicide, which is without thinking and destination.

In the first case, fathers, who are responsible for the emancipatory political orientation, abandon their sons in the name of the real. In the second case, sons, who are the collective strength of a possible revolt, abandon their fathers in the name of Despair.

But emancipatory politics is possible only when some fathers and mothers and some sons and daughters are allied in an effective negation of the world as it is.

With all that in mind, we can now read the poem in English:

> 'All politics is Realpolitik', warring
> soul, with your delicate anger! | You do not recognize a soul other than this one | which has all the prose of the clever man,
> of the revolutionary devoted to the honest | common man (even the complicity | with the assassins of the Bitter Years grafted
> onto protector classicism, which makes | the communist respectable): you do not recognize the heart | that becomes slave to its enemy, and goes
> where the enemy goes, led by a history | that is the history of both, and makes them, deep down, | perversely, brothers; you do not recognize the fears
> of a consciousness that, by struggling with the world, | shares the rules of the struggle over the centuries, | as through a pessimism into which hopes
> drown to become more virile. Joyous | with a joy that knows no hidden agenda, | this army — blind in the blind
> sunlight — of dead young men comes | and waits. If their father, their leader, absorbed | in a mysterious debate with Power and bound
> by its dialectics, which history renews ceaselessly — | if he abandons them, | in the white mountains, on the serene plains,
> little by little in the barbaric breasts | of the sons, hate becomes love of hate, | burning only in them, the few, the chosen.
> Ah, Desperation that knows no laws! | Ah, Anarchy, free love | of Holiness, with your valiant songs![3]

Some remarks:

1. The whole beginning: with the idea of *Realpolitik* we have something like a negation without destruction. I define this 'opposition', in the ordinary democratic sense. Like the Democrats against Bush. We find two excellent definitions of this sort of negation: 'the prose of the clever man'

---

[3] Pier Paolo Pasolini, 'Victory', trans. by Norman MacAfee with Luciano Martinengo (2005) <http://direland.typepad.com/direland/2005/10/a_hitherto_unpu.html> [accessed 14 December 2021].

and 'protector classicism'. You will note that, in both cases, the comparison is with a conservative artistic style.

2. The 'bitter years' are the years of the war, which, in Italy, was also largely a civil war.

3. The heart of 'opposition' is to substitute some rules for the violence of the real. In my jargon, I can say: to substitute rules of history, or rules of economy, for the rupture of the Event. And when you do that, you 'share the rules of the struggle' with your enemy. And finally you become a 'slave of your enemy', a 'brother' of your enemy. So opposition is in fact the death of negation. And it is the death of political hope.

4. In this context, Pasolini has a sort of magnificent and melancholic vision. The army of dead young men of the last war — and among them certainly his younger brother Guido — are coming to see their father, their leader. That is, in fact, the revolutionary leadership of today. This army, 'blind in the blind sunlight', comes and waits 'in the white mountains, on the serene plains'. And they see their father, their leader, absorbed in the very weak form of negation, the dialectical negation. This negation is not separate from power. This negation is only an obscure relationship to power itself. It is 'a mysterious debate with Power'. So the father is in fact without freedom; he is 'bounded' by the dialectics of power.

5. The conclusion is that this father 'abandons them'. You see the problem, which is clearly a problem of today. The army of dead young men was on the side of destruction, of hate. They existed on the hard side of negation. But they wait for an orientation, for a negation which, under some paternal law, would reconcile destruction and subtraction.

But contemporary leaders abandon them. So they have only the destructive part of negation. They have only 'desperation that knows no laws'!

6. And the description of their subjectivity is quite an expressive one. Yes, they were on the side of hate, of destruction. They were 'angry young men'. But now — it is a very striking formula — 'hate becomes love of hate'. This love of hate is negation as purely destructive. Without access to subtraction, without fathers or leaders, we have to face the nudity of 'the barbaric breasts of the sons'.

7. Great poetry is always an anticipation, a vision, of the collective future. We can see here that Pasolini describes the terrorist subjectivity. He indicates with an astonishing precision that the possibility of this subjectivity among young men or women is the lack of any rational hope of changing the world. That is why he creates a poetical equivalence between Desperation (the nihilistic consequence of false negation), Anarchy (the

purely destructive political version), and 'free love of Holiness', which is the religious context of terrorism, with the figure of the martyr. This equivalence is certainly clearer today than it was forty years ago, when Pasolini wrote 'Victory'.

We can now conclude: the political problems of the contemporary world can be solved neither in the weak context of democratic opposition, which in fact abandons millions of people to a nihilistic destiny, nor in the mystical context of destructive negation, which is another form of power, the power of death. Neither subtraction without destruction, nor destruction without subtraction.

This is, in fact, the problem of violence today. Violence is not, as was said during the previous century, the creative and revolutionary part of negation. The way of freedom is a subtractive one. But to protect the subtraction itself, to defend the new kingdom of emancipatory politics, we cannot radically exclude all forms of violence. The future is not on the side of the savage young men and women of working-class suburbs; we cannot abandon them to themselves. But the future is not on the side of the democratic wisdom of mothers' and fathers' law. We have to learn something from nihilistic subjectivity.

The world is made not of law and order, but of law and desire. Let us learn from Pasolini not to be 'absorbed in a mysterious debate with power', not to abandon millions of young men and women either 'in the white mountains' or 'on the serene plains'.

Roberto Esposito
COMMUNISM, CAPITALISM, FASCISM[1]

1. Speaking about Pasolini's work, without referring to the three terms communism, capitalism, and fascism, is impossible. Yet none of those words, nor their relation, can completely capture his oeuvre. Albeit fundamental, they stand on a different plane regarding the content of his writings; although, in other ways, they interact with his biography. How can one understand this peculiar relationship of exclusion and inclusion? To envision an answer, it is necessary to extrapolate those terms from an immediate political meaning and assign them with one that is both metapolitical and biopolitical. Pasolini does not relate to communism, capitalism, and fascism in a strictly political sense, but through a broader and deeper anthropological horizon. Moreover, he always deals with them in relation with the sphere of corporeality and sex. More than ideologically oriented by them, his work is vitally marked in a direction that has never been fully explored.

Let us start with communism. Since the beginning, Pasolini relates to it with a nuance that is not political, nor truly historical, according to that dystonia between 'passion' and 'ideology' standing as a distinctive feature of his biographical and intellectual story. A dystonia that is destined to become an overt contradiction, as we read in *Gramsci's Ashes* where he speaks of 'the scandal of self-contradiction — of being | with you and against you; with you in my heart, | in the light, against you in the dark of my gut'.[2] What Pasolini was approaching then, emotionally more than intellectually, is not the working class (which the Communist Party addresses), but the peasant and urban sub-proletariat, placed by him in a natural dimension — or, more properly, in a biological one. As we stated earlier, regarding communism the writer places himself in a liminal space vis-à-vis the

---

1 Translated from the Italian for this volume by Valeria Dani.
2 Pier Paolo Pasolini, 'Gramsci's Ashes', in *The Selected Poetry of Pier Paolo Pasolini*, ed. by James Ivory and Stephen Sartarelli, A Bilingual Edition (Chicago: The University of Chicago Press, 2014), p. 175.

ideological orbit of the leftist culture of the Gramscian matrix. What moves Pasolini is not the adhesion to the Communist Party and its struggles, but the need for a communism irreducible to the political debate of those years. A communism that is rather recognizable in a vital and corporeal layer not coinciding with political activity: 'this life is nothing but a shudder; | a bodily, collective presence; | [...] as if they | were a race of animals [...]'.[3] Since then, and more so in the ensuing years, the gap between ideology and passion tends to broaden in both spatial and temporal terms. This does not mean that the sentimental need for communism – the tendency to side with the weak and the oppressed – falters. It will, in fact, characterize Pasolini's entire biography. Rather, instead of translating into participation in the workers' struggles, it leads towards a broader, and mainly more distant, perspective. As Michael Hardt rightly states, using a Foucauldian expression, Pasolini's is a communism of the 'outside',[4] placed in a space and time that differs from the ones he lives in. When in *Poem in the Shape of a Rose* he sharply juxtaposes life to history — 'The disappointment of history! | It leads us to death | without having lived | and, because of that, we stay in life | contemplating it, as a piece of junk | a stupendous possession we do not possess'[5] — he clarifies most explicitly the biopolitical nature of his own existential experience. Communism, much more than a political organization or a system of economic production, is a form of material life clinging to the bodies and faces of those who recognize themselves in it. The films of the so-called *Life Trilogy*, set in the Middle Ages or in the East, represent that movement towards the 'outside' in which the need for communism becomes flesh: it does not identify with ideologies, but with the living bodies of the characters. From Friulian peasants to the Roman sub-proletarians of *Ragazzi di Vita* and *A Violent Life*, from those living in the Third World to Neapolitan street children, Pasolini's figure of communism is not established in the heart of capitalist society, but in a space and time that could still preserve those bodies in a natural state (so to speak), snatching them from the anthropological transformation with which all the advanced industrial societies were by then experimenting. If the Italian 'workerists', starting with Mario Tronti, place the construction of communism 'inside' and 'against' capitalism, Pasolini puts it 'outside of' or 'before' it.

---

3   Ibid., pp. 183–85.
4   Michael Hardt, 'Pasolini Discovers Love Outside', *Diacritics*, 39, 4 (2009), p. 113.
5   Pier Paolo Pasolini, 'Poesia in forma di rosa', in *Le Poesie* (Milan: Garzanti, 1975), p. 378. [*Translation mine — Trans.*]

2. Capitalism is not characterized by Pasolini in historical-political terms, or simply economic ones: rather, it is interpreted through an anthropological and biopolitical lens. If communism is the space and time of the 'outside', capitalism is what consumes the dimension of exteriority, erasing it. Capitalism is pure 'inside'. It incorporates everything, every experience and language, functionalizing them to its own goals. It also encompasses every social class. This does not mean that classes, including the working class (still recognizable in the Seventies), had disappeared. However, they are homologated to the point of becoming indistinguishable in the lexicon, in the way of reasoning, and above all in their exteriority. The faces, bodies, and clothes of the young bourgeois, the workers, or the sub-proletarians, cannot be distinguished from one another. Capital's strategy spreads out everywhere, without leaving anything (or almost anything) in its exterior. This is true both for the Friulian peasant world and the Roman sub-proletariat. And ultimately, even for those living in the Third World: their tastes, desires, and aspirations are gradually more superimposable to those of the First and Second Worlds. Observing that 'currently, neo-capitalism seems to follow the route that coincides with the aspirations of the "masses"',[6] Pasolini grasps the common denominator of all regimes: the performance principle. It corresponds with, on the one hand, the extinction of desire; on the other, with the compulsion for enjoying consumer goods and human bodies (primarily considered as sexual objects). Pasolini's analysis thus resembles Michel Foucault's (which was, more or less, contemporary to it) regarding the passage of sexuality from repression to continued stimulation. Or, perhaps even better, to repression obtained through the expansion of its own opposite: a generalized hedonism. What is striking about the current neo-capitalist structure is the capacity of covering each of its own features under the guise of its opposite, so that today 'true intolerance is the one carried out by consumer society, the permissiveness granted and desired from above. This is the truest, worst, most deceitful, coldest and cruelest form of intolerance: it is intolerance in the guise of tolerance'.[7]

What the neo-capitalist regime implements is therefore a politics, but a politics that mainly acts upon bodies, thwarting their subversive potential. Bodies, to a certain degree, constitute a locus of resistance against power:

---

6   Pier Paolo Pasolini, 'Il sogno del Centauro', in *Saggi Sulla Politica e Sulla Società*, ed. by Walter Siti and Silvia De Laude (Milan: A. Mondadori, 1999), p. 1448. [*Translation mine — Trans.*]

7   Pier Paolo Pasolini, *Il Fascismo Degli Antifascisti* (Milan: Garzanti, 2018), pp. 78–79. [*Translation mine — Trans.*]

a sort of resistance, or protest, that is not necessarily expressed in terms of explicit opposition, but determined by their own being, by their erotic power, by the difference that characterizes them. But these differential characters are now disappearing, almost dematerialized by the homologation processes that traverse Western society and beyond, to the point of encompassing the social body as a whole. Compared to the biologization of politics theorized by Foucault, the dynamics pieced together by Pasolini present a similar hue: the sequence of events, from one decade to the other, is surely much lesser than the one outlined by the French philosopher, but with just as evident performative effects, etched in the bodies of individuals. While a few years before 'the last bulwark of reality seemed to be "innocent" bodies with the archaic, dark, vital violence of their sexual organs', now it has been 'violated, manipulated, enslaved by consumerist power — indeed such violence to human bodies has become the most macroscopic fact of the new human epoch'.[8] The young generation, once carrying out the hope for transformation, represents the place where the anthropological turn has been engraved most precisely. Their regression to a stage that is not premodern nor postmodern, as a product of the general homologation, is unrepresentable: this is because it is essentially inexpressive, imprinted in the gestures, the words, and the behaviour of young people who are now indistinguishable from each other. This is a physical decline that wholly corresponds to the psychological one; one that seems to block any escape towards that 'outside' where, until a few years prior, Pasolini had placed the project of a form of communism yet to be fulfilled.

3. Its outcome — the extreme outcome of the said closure of any external space outside of capitalism — is what Pasolini meant with 'new fascism'. It is different from the one historically experimented during Italy's fascist era, but somehow worse. While historical fascism carried within itself the contradiction from which it was born (the forced overthrowing of mass society in an oppressive regime that would plunge the country into war), neo-capitalist fascism is free from contrasts, internally one with a homologation that does not allow any alterity. Young people during the fascist era, when taking their fascist uniforms off, could go back to their places of origin or their fields not looking very different from Italians from the previous century: even if fascism subjugated them, it did not drastically change their way of being. On the other hand, 'this new fascism, this consumer society,

---

8   Pier Paolo Pasolini, 'Trilogy of Life Rejected', in *Lutheran Letters* (Manchester: Carcanet New Press, 1983), pp. 49–50.

has instead transformed the young generations: it has touched them at their core, giving them other feelings, other ways of thinking and of living, other cultural models'.[9] A funereal authoritarian scenography is not at stake, as in historical fascism, but a regimentation capable of stealing one's soul. It is namely this passage that robs contemporary antifascism not of its *raison d'être* (which is still valid), but of its own efficacy, neutralized by sharing the same anthropological trait with fascists. In this manner, similarly to communism and capitalism, even fascism does not obtain a historical-political framework from Pasolini: rather, a metapolitical and biopolitical characterization that renders the political fronts interchangeable, although they seem to stand in opposition with one another. They correspond to each other from a cultural, physical, and psychological point-of-view in a way that neutralizes any distinction. What differentiates those fascists who detonated bombs in public squares during the Seventies from the vast majority of their peers is only an abstract element, pertinent to ideology: in the past, you could recognize them at a glance. Pasolini bears witness to the formation of a socio-cultural blend (neither popular nor bourgeois) in Italy, similar to the hybrid mass that had emerged in Germany just prior to the onset of Nazism (a mass that will later represent its anthropological glue). In this sense, the new power that dominates the neo-capitalist block presents truly 'total' characteristics, born from the superimposition between apparent tolerance and real ferocity. As Pasolini writes regarding *Accattone*, 'Between 1961 and 1975 something essential changed: a genocide took place. A whole population was culturally destroyed. And it is a question precisely of one of those cultural genocides which preceded the physical genocides of Hitler'.[10] New fascism, much more than the previous, also literally recalls the *fascio*[11] between very different elements that generate, as a whole, a front bound together by its apparent heterogeneity. A sort of functional anarchy, like the one that Franz Neumann saw materializing between the powers of the Nazi regime, which were simultaneously adversarial and convergent.

4. The theme of anarchy is famously evoked by Pasolini regarding his final film *Salò*, which he considered the last and extreme representation of fascism. We are well aware that a complete interpretation of the movie, of which no one knows what the finale would have been had Pasolini

---

9 Pasolini, *Il Fascismo Degli Antifascisti*, p. 73. [*Translation mine — Trans.*]
10 Pier Paolo Pasolini, 'My "Accattone" on TV after the Genocide', in *Lutheran Letters*, pp. 101–02.
11 [The fascist emblem; a bundle.— *Trans.*]

survived, is truly problematic. Aside from the judgment of its artistic performance (the opinions on this matter differ), the intent of the author was to evoke the spectre of fascism without representing it directly or allegorically. For that matter, Dante's reference, which is beyond and inside Sade's, invites an interpretation that is not allegorical, but rather figural.[12] In fact, Pasolini aims at rendering representation impossible through the construction of an Unrepresentable. Far from addressing the audience and the critics, the author chooses to break all relationships with them by rendering impossible not only the interpretation, but even the vision of the film. Only a few managed to watch it in its entirety, namely because its most extreme scenes are hard to bear.[13] Pasolini does not limit himself to this — to the interruption of the relationship with the cultural industry, willingly sabotaging the understanding of the film. His operation is even more radical, and it goes back to the question of fascism — once again not invoked through a historical-political lens, but biopolitical (or, in this instance, thanatopolitical). According to the director's intentions, *Salò* should remain incomprehensible. To this extent, Pasolini replied to those who asked whether he was worried of not being understood, 'No, because mine is a mystery; it is what is called *mystery*, the medieval mystery: a sacred play, hence very enigmatic. It should not be understood'.[14] However, in his interview with Gian Luigi Rondi, he identifies the three paradigmatic nuclei around which the movie revolves: 'the anarchy of power, the inexistence of the story, the circularity between perpetrators and victims (which is neither psychological, nor psychoanalytical)'.[15] Let's start from the non-existence of the story. Pasolini refers to the 'story' of the film as being non-existent because it does not have any internal development, compulsorily repeating the same sadistic ritual of torment by the four libertines onto their victims. But this inexistence can also refer to history as a process, in the sense that a staged representation of the Unrepresentable does not possess a historical character, but actually a paradigmatic one: it does not pertain to fascism as

---

12 See Barnaba Maj, 'Vecchio e nuovo fascismo e la questione del sadismo in *Salò*', in *Corpus XXX: Pasolini: Petrolio-Salò*, (Bologna: CLUEB, 2012), pp. 49–64.
13 Roberto Esposito, 'Passage IV: The Unbearable', in *Living Thought: The Origins and Actuality of Italian Philosophy*, trans. by Zakiya Hanafi (Stanford, CA: Stanford University Press, 2012), pp. 201–16.
14 Pier Paolo Pasolini, 'De Sade e l'universo dei consumi', in *Per il cinema*, ed. by Walter Siti and Franco Zabagli, 2 vols. (Milan: Mondadori, 2001), II, p. 3020. [*Translation mine — Trans.*]
15 Pier Paolo Pasolini, 'Nulla è più anarchico del potere': Interview with Gian Luigi Rondi, in Gian Luigi Rondi, *Il cinema dei maestri: 58 grandi registi e un'attrice si raccontano* (Rusconi, 1980). Now in *Communitas*, 49 (2010), p. 239.

it has been historically, and neither to Salò, but rather to 'eternal fascism' and, in other words, a transhistorical one. This is because it is in some way present in each one of us, beginning with Pasolini himself. He declared that he was both fascinated and horrified by what he was filming; however, as much as it is hard to admit, this is also true for those who have watched the movie. In this sense, the question posed by Pasolini goes well beyond the worn-out dichotomy of fascism/antifascism, and it pertains to the fascism of antifascists: not only other people's fascism, but also the dormant one within us, 'our' fascism. This leads to the other two paradigmatic axes of anarchy and power; and of the circularity between perpetrators and victims. Firstly, it is important to say that the anarchic character does not only concern the power represented in the film but, at least in some ways, any power. We mentioned Nazi anarchy, but something similar could also be said about Stalinism in the paroxysmal phase of purges and trials in the Soviet Union. In that terribly chaotic situation (not dissimilar to the Nazi high command) each moved on their own account, only aiming to ingratiate themselves with the commander-in-chief in order to increase their power or, at the very least, to get a better chance at saving their own lives. In the same interview with Rondi, the writer recalls that it is Sade himself that states that 'nothing is more anarchic than power'.[16] Now, the anarchy of power — that excludes its own concentration in the hands of few and recognizes it in every corner of the scene — implies, as a necessary consequence, that it is somehow shared even with those that endure it on their own bodies and souls. We then come to the third paradigm indicated by Pasolini: the circularity, or reversibility, between perpetrators and victims (somehow superimposable to the one between the director and his audience). There is no dividing line between the two categories, meaning that even the victims in *Salò* participate in the sadistic game performed by the perpetrators, collaborating repeatedly with them: they accuse one another and take active part in the erotic games to which they are subjected, enjoying their own torment. It is namely this — not the torment, nor the elaborate scatological rituals into which the young deportees are forced, which is the unbearable element of the movie — that renders watching the film so difficult. The victims themselves are perpetrators: against one another, and against themselves. Similarly, given the inevitable implication between sadism and masochism, the perpetrators 'play' the role of victims, asking to be sodomized and mortified by them: the tormentor Blangis observes that 'the sophistication of libertinage lies in being both a perpetrator and

---

16 Ibid.

a victim'. Already in *Orgia*, after all, Pasolini had written 'I as victim, you as perpetrator. You are a victim who wants to kill, I am a perpetrator who wants to die'.[17] The climax of this contamination is the one in which victims and perpetrators sing the same hymn in tune, in an insoluble blend of suffering and pleasure. A pleasure that, pushed beyond any limit, not only stops the establishment of desire, but even of orgasm as it appears in the finale — where the gaze from afar (through binoculars) prevents sexual intercourse, with whiplashes in the air by the Monsignor and a macabre dance around corpses. If we had to define fascism, this extreme fascism beyond any historical character as described by Pasolini, we could identify it as absolute power — one that, yet, is unable to govern because it is fundamentally anarchic and in the midst of an unlimited enjoyment that prevents not only desire, but an *effective* enjoyment — discovering once again, beyond the pleasure principle, a drive to death.

---

17 Pier Paolo Pasolini, 'Orgia', in *Porcile; Orgia; Bestia da stile* (Milan: Garzanti, 1979), p. 143. [*Translation mine — Trans.*]

Harun Farocki

ON PASOLINI'S NOTES TOWARDS AN AFRICAN ORESTES[1]

He came to shoot notes for a film — not a film. How often has someone called an inferior text 'notes' or an inferior painting a 'sketch'... These notes truly are notes, someone trying out images for an upcoming project.

Let's think up a crime movie in which a person in a tough situation is searching the floor with their eyes for an important object. The camera films something through this gaze, panning or tracking over the floor. Cracks between the floor tiles, unevenness in the asphalt, a flaw in the varnish on the floorboards, moisture on the mudbrick: the gaze scans them, searching for something specific, maybe a cartridge case. But the things that are not concerned here do not remain unspecified. By not being searched for, but still possibly present, they prove their being-for-itself, come into focus and gain presentness. In our memory, they can acquire the same rank as the thing that was sought or replace it.

The images in Pasolini's film are drafts and the gaze cuts through them to something else. In doing so, they must prove themselves. There are many films about the making of a film, but hardly any that deals with the gaze with which someone processes a landscape, house, or person before he can shoot a film.

The lover's gaze — it takes something from the beloved's face and embellishes it. Is it also beautiful without this gaze? This is a question about the truth of love that should not be asked. It should be investigated! In an investigation, one always fears that the subject under investigation could be damaged. In reality, it is the question that is in danger. In the past few years, biologists have asked what life is. Thereby, the question has become unimportant. (It turns out that life is nothing special.)

---

1   Translated by Ted Fendt; originally published in German as 'Einleitung zu Pier Paolo Pasolinis Film "Appunti per un Orestiade africana"', *Filmkritik*, 311 (November 1982), 530–32. The original text is untitled. We have used the title that appears in the table of contents.

The words in the text to Pasolini's film are directly related to the images. The words designate what is in the images and what is going on with them. An actor or shooting location is looked at, although it is sometimes only a matter of a person's gesture and one location is cut together from images of multiple places. The text comments on this. Later, there are stagings (staging rehearsals) and images that the text says could metaphorically reproduce something out of the *Oresteia*.

When Pasolini shows documentary footage of the Nigerian Civil War (1967–70), he interrupts himself. He jumps from Africa to a Roman (?) studio and has a passage from the *Oresteia* sung. In this scene, the camera is conspicuous, wandering around in the short clip and gambling with the music that it will be in the right place at the right time; a gamble it always wins too. In other moments, the camera is not permitted to raise its voice. Simple images, if such a thing exists.

It means a lot when, among people looking into the camera, a man sits there and sleeps, or when a pan swings from a meadow with Warholesque blooming white flowers up to the horizon. Men with sewing machines in the open air or plants twisting on the clay ground of the market square, bottles and funnels, which are everyday commodities for the inhabitants of huts on Lake Victoria: this all means a lot, but what?

The *Oresteia* is a foreign, perhaps unknown language ("You all know the drama of Aeschylus' *Oresteia*...") and Africa is a foreign, perhaps unknown language. Pasolini translates from a language we do not understand into another. We watch this work (the search for specific words, trying out specific expressions) and understand more than we can understand.

The images are recorded with a silent 16mm camera. African sounds are not heard. Shortly before the end, when the film shows a dance that, it is said, could be a metaphor for the Furies' transformation into Eumenides, the music alongside the dancers' movements is not propulsive, it is a commentary. Before this, Pasolini shows trees and bushes moving in the wind and briefly tries out a wind sound from a sound library, but there is hardly a sound that sounds so unbelievable as the blowing of the wind. So, he replaces the wind with a jazz crescendo. The storm of the music is bigger than that of the leaves moving in the wind, and this has the fortunate effect of liberating the music from being a sound. Aside from jazz, there are also Russian choirs, *political music* that also resounds at the film's end when the words *future*, *longing*, and *patience* are brought together.

Twice in the film, we see African students, who are studying in Italy, and to whom Pasolini has projected some images, images from the *Notes Towards an African Orestes*. Pasolini is holding a microphone and it is not entirely clear if his lips are saying what we hear. At one point, one of the Africans says something and the camera looks for but does not find the speaker. A mistake that is not smoothed out in the editing, which probably means that nothing else in this sequence has been cheated. Adeptly clumsy, it probably does not only mean the opposite, but should also indicate: I am making Africans speak.

GIOVANBATTISTA TUSA

THE PASOLINIAN CENTURY

> *I am fully aware of the special kind of irrationalism which the word 'to act' always carries with itself, inevitably, in philosophy.*
> Pier Paolo Pasolini, 'The Written Language of Reality'

> *Tra i due mondi la tregua, in cui non siamo* [Between the two worlds, a truce not our own].
> Pier Paolo Pasolini, 'The Ashes of Gramsci'

'What are a hundred years, a thousand years, when a single instant effaces them?'[1] — asks Alain Badiou in the first of his lectures held at the *Collège international de Philosophie* at the end of the 20th century. A century is not a chronological unit, it begins in the instant that effaces the past century. And the 20th century has been caught up in the vertigo of this unique, ferocious instant. It has been obsessed with the need to destroy the old, to create the new[2]. As a consequence of this ferocious obsession, Badiou concludes, in the 20th century an 'entirely new configuration of the relation between end and beginning'[3] is born.

Thinking our own time philosophically is not easy, and it is not reassuring. Philosophy is a contested, seismic place. It is a place of contamination, since philosophy is not a discipline of which it is possible to define the object or trace a linear and progressive history.[4] Philosophy is always in search of

---

1 Alain Badiou, *The Century*, trans. by Alberto Toscano (Cambridge: Polity Press, 2007), p. 2.
2 See Giovanbattista Tusa, 'Infinity of Truths: A Very Short Essay on the End of the Ends', in Alain Badiou and Giovanbattista Tusa, *The End*, trans. by Robin Mackay (Cambridge: Polity Press), pp. 105–31.
3 Badiou, *The Century*, p. 17.
4 Philosophy, as Žižek argues, is by definition excessive, since it exists only 'through the excessive connection to external conditions, which are of either an amorous, political, scientific or artistic nature'. Slavoj Žižek, 'Philosophy is not a

the origins of 'its own time apprehended in thoughts' — as Hegel famously stated in the *Outlines of the Philosophy of Right*. It constantly contaminates actuality and ancestrality, to produce the difference of the new within the old. In a certain sense, philosophy is the process of returning to the art of giving birth. It is indeed the *praxis* of becoming present, contemporary to what escapes any identity of time with itself. Therefore, we could argue with Rancière that philosophy is anachronistic, if anachrony is 'a word, an event, or a signifying sequence that has left "its" time, and in this way is given the capacity to define completely original points of orientation'.[5]

In his famous lecture on the 'contemporary', Agamben insists on the relationship between the contemporary and the untimely, and defines the 'contemporary' as an anachronism, a non-coincidence that does not let us adhere completely to our own time; or, rather, contemporary is who lives her time only by transforming it and putting it in relation with other times. Contemporary is therefore the one who 'has broken the vertebrae' of her time, but then who also 'makes of this fracture a meeting place, or an encounter between times and generations'.[6] The contemporary is a temporal, generative mixture that conflagrates heterogenous elements. The substantive *tempus* was allegedly born as an 'abstract derivation of terms such as *tempestus, tempestas, temperare* and, therefore, *temperatura, temperatio*, etc.',[7] and in this case it would be comparable to the Greek *Kairós* — the due, appropriate time — rather than to *Chronos* — the time devourer of the moments that he himself had generated. *Tempus* would then be the stratified combination of different entangled elements, an interface 'from which the reality of evolution derives'.[8]

Pier Paolo Pasolini's work is philosophical in the sense that it is an endless quest for this heterogeneous encounter, which carries with it a difference that is qualitative and not merely chronological. Pasolini's critical confrontation with the past beyond all interpretations from the

---

Dialogue', in Alain Badiou and Slavoj Žižek, *Philosophy in the Present*, ed. by Peter Engelmann, trans. by Peter Thomas and Alberto Toscano (Cambridge: Polity Press, 2009), p. 69.

5   Jacques Rancière, 'The Concept of Anachronism and the Historian's Truth', *InPrint*, 3, 1 (2015) <https://arrow.tudublin.ie/inp/vol3/iss1/3> [accessed 6 October 2021].

6   Giorgio Agamben, 'What Is the Contemporary', in *What Is an Apparatus? and Other Essays*, trans. by David Kishik and Stefan Pedatella (Stanford: Stanford University Press, 2009), p. 52.

7   Giacomo Marramao, *Kairós: Towards an Ontology of 'Due Time'*, trans. by Philip Larrey and Silvia Cattaneo, (Aurora: Davies Group, 2007), p. 70.

8   Ibid.

tradition takes the form of a history of insurgence. It accounts for historical discontinuities that radiate 'the most exalted sensation' in the most common moment we live, 'in that oblivion of the infant, of the beastly or innocent lecher [...] in that common human act consummated in a morning dream'.[9]

In *Heretical Empiricism* Pasolini writes that 'that reality is, in the final analysis, nothing more than cinema in nature'.[10] In order to perceive this reality we need a sentient thought that enable us to imagine a world that is simultaneously real and allegorical, living and dead — so as to give images a specific gravity, liberated from the burdens of European and Western history. We need a living thought that is written with the fragments of the real itself: inaugural, archaic, and yet at the same time new.

This contradiction is embodied in the concrete universality of Paul of Tarsus, on which Pasolini wanted to make a film[11] to present the irremediable conflict between 'the world of history, which tends, in its excess of presence and urgency, to escape into mystery, into abstraction, into unalloyed interrogatives — and the world of the divine, which, in its religious abstractness, on the contrary, descends among men, becoming concrete and effective'.[12] Paul's words remain untimely, contradictory, even if, as Pasolini clearly writes, 'it is our society that he addresses; it is our society for which he weeps and that he loves, threatens and forgives, assaults and tenderly embraces'.[13] For Pasolini, with the power of his religious message, Paul revolutionarily subverts a society 'founded on the violence of class, imperialism, and above all slavery'.[14] The 'temporal violence' of his life requires 'a long series of transpositions',[15] as Paul's

---

9 Pier Paolo Pasolini, 'The Lament of the Excavator' [1957], *Poetry*, 155, 1/2 (1989), p. 49.
10 Pier Paolo Pasolini, 'The Written Language of Reality', in *Heretical Empiricism*, trans. by Ben Lawton and Louise K. Barnett (Indianapolis: Indiana University Press, 1988), p. 198.
11 Pasolini wrote a first version of his St. Paul in 1968: the 'Draft of a Screenplay for a Film of St. Paul (In the Form of Notes to a Producer)'. The 'Project for a Film of St. Paul', which precedes the *Draft* in the original Italian edition, was written during the same period. Pasolini could not make the film at that particular time. Later, in 1974, a renewed attempt was made with different producers. However, the subject was deemed too risky and too expensive.
12 Pier Paolo Pasolini, *Saint Paul: A Screenplay*, trans. by Elisabeth A. Castelli (London and New York: Verso, 2014), p. 5.
13 Ibid., p. 3.
14 Ibid., p. 4.
15 Ibid., p. 3. As Pasolini writes in his 'Plan for a film about Saint Paul', the world in which Paul lives and works needs to be displaced: 'the centre of the modern world — the capital of colonialism and of modern imperialism — the seat of modern

life itself is a perseverance in the moment of caesura with the current state of things. 'Do not be conformed to the present century but be transformed by the renewal of your thought (voῧς)' (*Rom. 12.2*), writes Paul of Tarsus; and Pasolini's unfinished film was meant to be precisely a journey into this event of rupture with the present, the journey of an experience of saintliness into actuality.[16]

This living, embodied contradiction suspends our time and re-enchants it; Pasolini's cinema translates reality into a paradoxical time, an age of historical revolt and, simultaneously, the end of all history. Pasolini, as Michael Hardt notes, is fascinated by the shameless exposure of Christ's body on the cross, whose wounds are open, 'burning under the gazes of the crowd and the elements', whose entire body is 'an open piece of flesh, abandoned, exposed'.[17]

Pasolini offers himself unreservedly to the century. He incessantly exposes himself to the reading of others while maintaining the constitutive illegibility of his works. From a certain point of his life onwards, it is as if Pasolini's incompleteness, his methodical instability became the very characteristic of his works. His works, composed as monstrous hybrids out of materials taken from the daily news and from episodes of Italian society in transformation,[18] have no literary or artistic autonomy that would protect them from life, they are 'inseparable from his rejection of poetry as an immunitary body — both protected from and protective of the violent life by which he, instead, was relentlessly interpellated, seduced, and violated'.[19] This is why the Pasolinian century is unfinished. Pasolini's

---

      power over the rest of the earth — is not any longer, today, Rome. [...] The theatre of Saint Paul's travels is, therefore, no longer the Mediterranean basin but the Atlantic'; ibid., p. 4.

16 This is the idea expressed by Alain Badiou in his *Saint Paul*. For Badiou 'no one has better illuminated the uninterrupted contemporaneousness of Paul's prose than one of the greatest poets of our time, Pier Paolo Pasolini [...], for whom the question of Christianity intersected with that of communism, or alternatively, the question of saintliness intersected with that of the militant'. Alain Badiou, *Saint Paul: The Foundation of Universalism*, trans. by Ray Brassier (Stanford: Stanford University Press, 2003), p. 36.

17 Michael Hardt, 'Exposure: Pasolini in the flesh', in this volume.

18 Perhaps the most remarkable example is the unfinished novel on which Pasolini was working when he was killed, published posthumously under the title *Petrolio*, which consists of a collection of handwritten and typed documents, only partially numbered, and often conflicting with one another.

19 Roberto Esposito, *Living Thought: The Origins and Actuality of Italian Philosophy*, trans. by Zakiya Hanafi (Stanford: Stanford University Press, 2012), pp. 206–07.

violent death has not closed it, has not put an end to its incompleteness, but rather it has left it exposed to the times to come.

In a series of interviews with Jean Duflot, Pasolini claimed to love more and more the word 'barbarism' [*barbarie*] because, as he explains with a reference to his film *Teorema* (1968), the industrial, bourgeois society was born in conflict with every society that preceded it. This society is capable of perpetrating only conscious, calculated, terrorist crimes, as opposed to the barbarian, who still possesses 'the mercy of tears [*la grazia delle lacrime*]'.[20] According to Pasolini, this difference is not only epistemological, but ontological, for it is an abysmal division[21] that involves not only sexuality or knowledge, but more generally the mode of being in the world. The bourgeoisie is condemned to its embarrassing silences or to the vacuous conversations in the mansions and palaces of urban civilization; contrasting with it, barbarously, is the wild anarchy of suburban meadows, the mythical deserts of Yemen, or the remote volcanic rocks of Sicily. In these desolate and abandoned spaces, Pasolini's bodies appear in transition between humanity and animality, or perhaps divinity. They are supernatural yet material bodies that announce the end of this world, messengers of another time: one that decolonizes the present from its empire — from its claim to be a unique time, which has dared to englobe all other past and future temporalities.

The apocalypse is not in the future, rather we could say with Jean-Luc Nancy that 'the fact that the world is destroying itself [...] is in a sense the fact from which any reflection on the world follows'.[22] In the era of planetary globalization, in which the world of Capital extends over all other possible worlds, Pasolini considered himself to be a man without a

---

20 Pier Paolo Pasolini, *Il sogno del centauro: Incontri con Jean Duflot* [1969–1975] (Rome: Editori Riuniti, 1983), p. 88.
21 As Boaventura de Sousa Santos explains, modernity is marked by an abyssal line that social sciences and critical theories have never recognized. According to Sousa Santos we fail to recognize that Western modernity does not exist without the emergence of a corresponding subhumanity. Capitalism (and colonialism which is the central, structural form of relationship with the world) is for Sousa Santos inherently incapable of renouncing this subhumanity, since it is an integral part of its idea of humanity as a totality built on the project of universal human rights. See Boaventura de Sousa Santos, *The End of the Cognitive Empire: The Coming of Age of Epistemologies of the South* (Durham and London: Duke University Press, 2018).
22 Jean-Luc Nancy, *The Creation of the World, or Globalization*, trans. François Raffoul and David Pettigrew (Albany: State University of New York Press, 2007), p. 35.

world, sharing perhaps what the anthropologist Ernesto De Martino wrote in the pages published posthumously under the title *La fine del mondo* [*The End of the World*], namely that in our age apocalypses are no longer exceptional events, but ordinary administrative operations of capitalism's hellishly mechanistic vitality,[23] daily apocalypses without *eschaton*.[24] To Pasolini, this age appears caught in the suspended intemporality of a latent apocalypse in which conflict is abolished, but a relentless devastation is at work everywhere.

'Be careful. Hell is rising up toward you',[25] he declared in the last interview of his life, published with the title 'We're All in Danger'. For Pasolini, the attempted self-annihilation that occurred between 1933 and 1945 is followed by an epoch that is shapeless, in which both acting and suffering seem to be afflicted by an impotence that does not coincides with deprivation, but with an unrestrained excess of disposable faculties, lacking modes of life that could channel their potential towards actualization.[26] An epoch that Roberto Calasso designated as the 'Unnamable Present', in which what prevails is a deadly, overpowerful insubstantiality. It is the elusive epoch of a shattered world that has no style of its own and therefore uses every style.[27]

But a shattered world is not a bad stepping stone for thinking beyond a totalitarian, unique, and globalized present. We live in a synchronized world where all information — writes Walter Benjamin in his short essay on the 'Storyteller' — is consummated in the instant of its novelty, and it 'lives only at that moment; it has to surrender to it completely and explain itself to it without losing any time'.[28] But then, as Benjamin suggests, there

---

23 Marcello Tarì, *Non esiste la rivoluzione infelice: Il comunismo della destituzione* (Rome: DeriveApprodi, 2017), p. 71.
24 Ernesto De Martino, *La fine del mondo: Contributo all'analisi delle apocalissi culturali* (Turin: Einaudi, 2002).
25 Pier Paolo Pasolini, 'We're All in Danger' [1975], in *In Danger: A Pasolini Anthology*, ed. and trans. by Jack Hirschman (San Francisco: City Lights, 2010), p. 240. This interview with Italian journalist Furio Colombo took place on Saturday, November 1, 1975, a few hours before Pasolini was murdered. The next day, Sunday, the lifeless body of Pier Paolo Pasolini was at the police morgue in Rome.
26 See Paolo Virno, *Dell'impotenza: La vita nell'epoca della sua paralisi frenetica* (Turin: Bollati Boringhieri, 2021).
27 See in particular chapter 1, 'Tourists and Terrorists', in Roberto Calasso, *The Unnamable Present*, trans. by Richard Dixon (New York: Farrar, Straus and Giroux, 2019).
28 Walter Benjamin, 'The Storyteller: Observations on the Works of Nicolai Leskov', trans. by Harry Zohn, in *Selected Writings*, ed. by Michael Jennings, 4 vols.

are stories with a different destiny, because they preserve their power of flourishing over time. A story maintains an indestructible posthumous germinative force when storytelling preserves it from explanation. This is why a story on ancient Egypt told by Herodotus in antiquity is still capable of provoking astonishment, as if the 'seeds of grain that have lain for centuries in the airtight chambers of the pyramids have retained their germinative power to this day'.[29]

Every narration, interrupted, continues another, unfinished story. Every story, in this present reduced to the timeless dimension of a unique progress, can reactivate other emergent temporalities. And in this way storytelling has the power to generate new forms of inhabiting the world. The poverty of experience, the incompleteness of our exhausted interpretations of the global situation, may actually be necessary conditions for mobilizing a time whose creations take upon themselves precisely this fragility and this intermittence because, as Merleau-Ponty concluded at the end of his *Eye and Mind*, 'if creations are not acquisitions, it is not just that, like all things, they pass away; it is also that they have almost their entire lives before them'.[30]

Pasolini's cinema, his poetry, his writings, his political interventions, are a militant assault on the fictitious assemblages of the state of affairs, on the violence of the present, inscribed in its images. They are positions of a subjectivity that will remain as close as possible to the point of impossibility of the current organization of the state of things, as they counter point by point the criminal narrative that legitimizes it. This subjectivity will no longer accept being immersed in the repetitive sterility of *divertissement*. It will not continue to survive in these uncertain times by abandoning the 'desperate passion for being in the world'[31] — because it is precisely from dispersed and damaged materials of this world that the vanished body of our passion unexpectedly emerges.

    (Cambridge: Belknap Press of Harvard University Press, 2002), III, p. 148.
29   Ibid.
30   Maurice Merleau-Ponty, 'Eye and Mind', in *The Merleau-Ponty Reader*, ed. by Ted Toadvine and Leonard Lawlor (Evanston: Northwestern University Press, 2007), p. 378.
31   Pier Paolo Pasolini, *Gramsci's Ashes* [1957], in *The Selected Poetry of Pier Paolo Pasolini: A Bilingual Edition*, ed. and trans. by Stephen Sartarelli, with a Foreword by James Ivory (Chicago and London: The University of Chicago Press, 2014), p. 183.

MIMESIS GROUP
www.mimesis-group.com

MIMESIS INTERNATIONAL
www.mimesisinternational.com
info@mimesisinternational.com

MIMESIS EDIZIONI
www.mimesisedizioni.it
mimesis@mimesisedizioni.it

ÉDITIONS MIMÉSIS
www.editionsmimesis.fr
info@editionsmimesis.fr

MIMESIS COMMUNICATION
www.mim-c.net

MIMESIS EU
www.mim-eu.com

Printed by
Rotomail Italia S.p.A.
April 2022

www.ingramcontent.com/pod-product-compliance
Lightning Source LLC
Chambersburg PA
CBHW031900220426
43663CB00006B/708